FIFTH EDITION

Music Fundamentals, Methods, and Materials for the Elementary Classroom Teacher

René Boyer
Professor Emerita, College Conservatory of Music, University of Cincinnati

Michon Rozmajzl

PEARSON

Boston   Columbus   Indianapolis   New York   San Francisco
Upper Saddle River   Amsterdam   Cape Town   Dubai   London   Madrid   Milan
Munich   Paris   Montreal   Toronto   Delhi   Mexico City   Sao Paulo   Sydney
Hong Kong   Seoul   Singapore   Taipei   Tokyo

Dedication

To Caleb James Goldner and all the children of tomorrow.

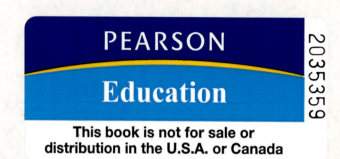

Editor: Kelly Villella Canton
Editorial Assistant: Annalea Manalili
Marketing Manager: Darcy Betts
Production Editor: Janet Domingo
Editorial Production Service: Nesbitt Graphics, Inc.
Manufacturing Buyer: Megan Cochran
Electronic Composition: Nesbitt Graphics, Inc.
Interior Design: Nesbitt Graphics, Inc.
Photo Researcher: Annie Pickert
Cover Designer: Linda Knowles

Credits and acknowledgments borrowed from other sources and reproduced, with permission, in this textbook appear on page 392. Unless specified otherwise, photos of musical instruments are ©Shutterstock.

Library of Congress Cataloging-in-Publication Data
Boyer-Alexander, René.
   Music fundamentals, methods, and materials for the elementary classroom teacher /
René Boyer.—5th ed.
   p. cm.
Includes index.
ISBN 978-0-13-256359-8
   1. School music—Instruction and study—United States. I. Title.

MT1.R85 2012
372.87'044—dc22

2011009870

10 9 8 7 6 5 4 3 2 1   15 14 13 12 11

www.pearsonhighered.com

ISBN-10: 0-13-256359-2
ISBN-13: 978-0-13-256359-8

ABOUT THE AUTHOR

René Boyer is a Professor Emerita of Music Education at the University of Cincinnati's College Conservatory of Music. She is known nationally and internationally for her work in multicultural and urban music education. Her publications include: *Share the Music* and *Spotlight on Music* published by Macmillan McGraw-Hill; *Expressions of Freedom: An Anthology of African American Spirituals* in three volumes; *Walking in the Light of Freedom*, also in three volumes; and *Songs and Rhythms of a Nation: A Journey of American Heritage*, all published by Hal Leonard.

"The Ballad of the Underground Railroad," and "United We Stand," also published by Hal Leonard, are two popular choral works composed by René.

Her *Music Fundamentals, Methods, and Materials for the Elementary Classroom Teacher* published by Pearson is one of our nation's best selling music textbooks used by classroom teachers as well as music specialists.

René received her B.M. and M.M. from Southern Illinois University in Edwardsville, Illinois, and her Doctorate from Washington University in St. Louis, Missouri. She possesses all Levels of Orff Certification as well as Kodaly Certification from Hungary.

Contents

8   Teaching Harmony to Children   205

SECTION 2   Developing Musical Skills   231

9   The Singing Voice   231

10   Playing Musical Instruments   256

Preface

Welcome to the fifth edition of *Music Fundamentals, Methods, and Materials for the Elementary Classroom Teacher*. For those of you who are using this text for the first time, you should know that this book was originally designed and written by authors who together possessed more than seventy-five years of experience working with and teaching music to children. It continues to be used widely by elementary teachers as well as by elementary general music students who are searching for a resource to help them better understand how to present the basic elements of music to children in a well-sequenced and creative manner.

In addition, *Music Fundamentals* includes beginning lessons in developing skills such as playing a piano or keyboard, developing beginning guitar skills, playing unpitched percussion in a drum circle, and playing the soprano recorder and Orff instruments. You will also learn about the importance of a child's most unique instrument—the singing voice.

WHAT'S NEW IN THE FIFTH EDITION?

In addition to providing a well-sequenced instructional approach to teaching music to children, the fifth edition of *Music Fundamentals, Methods, and Materials* will include:

- **Expanded ideas on integrating music across the curriculum to enhance a child's knowledge of language arts, social studies, math, and science.** This will be demonstrated through creatively designed cross-curricular ideas found in Section I of this book.

  Icons representing these curricular areas make it easier for users of this text to know when these cross-curricular ideas are being emphasized:

 Bright Ideas!

 Math Connections

 Language Arts Connections

 Social Studies Connections

 Science Connections

- **CD includes inspirational accompaniment tracks** for selected songs found throughout the text.
- More attention to the **National Content Standards** and how they can assist prospective teachers in focusing on their own creativity, participation, self-evaluation, and critical thinking.
- More **multicultural, patriotic** folk songs and rhymes.
- More easy-to-follow **listening maps** to enhance an appreciation of a variety of musical styles.
- More tools and suggestions for the **assessment of concepts** learned.

ORGANIZATION OF THE TEXT

This text is divided into four sections. **Section 1 "Teaching the Elements of Music to Children"** introduces prospective teachers of music to the same step-by-step process that they would present to children to help them understand the fundamentals of music. Each of the musical components is introduced and reinforced through musical experiences that are comprehensive, yet easily understood by non-musicians.

Each section contains chapters that are designed to address important information that deals with the section topic. For example, Chapters 2 through 8 address each of the basic musical elements. Each chapter has been designed to give the user a consistent step-by-step journey through the materials presented within the chapter.

A **Focus** box introduces each new component for easy identification and retrieval. Following each **Focus**, one or more **Learning** statements specify the aspect of the Focus that is presented. **Strategies** for teaching each new music component follow the Learning statements. For added clarity in this edition, the National Standard that is being focused on is reinforced alongside the strategy in a user-friendly way. The purpose of the **step-by-step teaching procedures** that then follow is twofold: First, they provide a methodology that prospective teachers can use later, when teaching music in their own classrooms. Second, they provide the means whereby prospective teachers with limited or no musical background will come to understand the material being taught by increasing their knowledge of the structural components of each music element.

Visuals that help clarify **Strategies** are included throughout the various chapters. These visuals will not only help the users of this text understand the material being presented, but also give direction for the future preparation of charts, PowerPoint presentations, flash cards, and handouts that will one day be used in their own elementary classrooms.

Music selections included in each chapter have been chosen for their appeal to children and their potential for clearly demonstrating each **Learning** statement. We have chosen songs that provide a wide representation of our culturally diverse population and that illustrate a variety of tonal centers and time signatures. A complete list of songs—with their origins, tonal centers, and time sequences—appears in the back of the text.

Sequencing charts are included at the end of many chapters, serving the practical purpose of suggesting at what grade level each musical component might be introduced.

Section 2, "Developing Musical Skills," focuses on the learning of minimum musical skills required of teachers who plan to incorporate a music program into their classroom curriculum. The skills of playing musical instruments, singing, listening, and moving are essential to the better understanding and reinforcement of musical elements and their structural components presented in Section 1. The incorporation of these skills also reinforces a multisensory approach so desperately needed when presenting materials into today's classroom.

Section 3, "Organizing Musical Experiences," presents students with the mechanics of preparing, sequencing, and evaluating the music activities contained in each music lesson. Attention is given to ways in which the formulation of goals and objectives can assist a teacher in the lesson planning process.

Section 4, "Teaching Music in Specialized Areas" addresses the integration of music with other subjects. Background information and teaching strategies are included in this section.

An alphabetized **song list**, a **glossary**, and an **index** are included at the end of the text.

Technical music terminology has been italicized where it is defined in the text. These terms are included in the **Glossary** for easy reference.

HOW TO USE THIS TEXT

For ultimate effectiveness, the user of this text should be prepared to refer to other sections of the text as needed. In short, each of the sections in this book is specifically designed to support the others. There will indeed be times when the user of the text will want to flip forward in the book to receive a more extended or supportive view of materials they are currently using. For example, Chapter 2 is specifically designed to teach students how to read melody. A step-by-step sequenced approach has been outlined to do this. Carefully selected examples of songs and song fragments have been chosen to accomplish specific goals regarding how to read melody.

However, users of the text may feel that they need further information on how to better sing these songs, while they are learning to read pitches. If this is the case, users have several other choices. They can flip to Chapter 4, which focuses on timbre and addresses the voice as an instrument. This chapter will help the user of the text understand his or her voice and its relation to the quality of sound that it produces. In this new edition, vocal health will also be addressed. Many examples will be provided for different voice types and musical preferences. Finally, Chapter 9 will provide the user with even more information about the singing voice and how to use it. This chapter clearly analyzes the vocal mechanism and its ranges. It is also here that users will discover creative methods and ways of actually teaching children to sing.

Finally, the most important approach used in this book comes from the author's basic philosophy: What is taught in a music lesson should flow from the musical experience in which the children are engaged. Whenever possible, the elements of music and their structured components should not be taught in isolation from the music or rhyme in which they occur. Rather, children should experience the music first. Afterwards, a structural component such as triplet or a phrase can be isolated for conscious learning.

The fifth edition of *Music Fundamentals, Methods, and Materials for the Elementary Classroom Teacher* is designed for success! No matter how you arrange the materials in this book, you will find that your goal to enhance the musical knowledge of children, as well as yourself, will be successful.

ACKNOWLEDGMENTS

I would like to thank Andrew Perry, President of Peripole-Bergerault for his assistance in providing many instrumental photographs for this textbook. Without his support, it would have been a daunting task to collect photographs of so many unique and quality instruments.

I would also like to thank the following reviewers of the fifth edition of *Music Fundamentals, Methods, and Materials for the Elementary Classroom Teacher*, who took time to offer suggestions as to how this book would continue to serve their students: Susan Dill Bruenger, University of Texas at San Antonio; Catherine Christensen Dunafin, North Central College; June Grice, Morehead State University; Nan L. McDonald, San Diego State University; Kris Tiner, Bakersfield College; and Erin Wehr-Flowers, The University of Missouri. I want them to know that I read every suggestion and did my best to incorporate their requests. I am most appreciative of their comments.

Lastly, I would like to thank the editors of this text. You are the best! I am humbled by your abilities to guide a publication such as this one that will serve to help educate our children.

CHAPTER  **Music and the Child**

WHY MUSIC?

For years, there have been ongoing debates regarding the importance of music and fine arts in the curriculum. Consequently, whenever educational budgets need to be cut, it is generally fine arts, especially music, that is targeted for elimination.

The No Child Left Behind Act provided a breath of encouragement when it named music as a core subject. At the same time, however, it stated that children must be grade-level proficient in their math and language skills by the year 2014. Sadly, this focus on proficiencies in math and language not only caused mass confusion, but also once again made music an expendable subject area in many school districts nationwide.

Fortunately, with the ongoing surge of research-based studies that continue to prove the value of the arts in the overall education of the child, fewer programs are choosing to deny our nation's children access to this most important aspect of their educational training.

Donald A. Hodges, Covington Distinguished Professor of Music Education and Director of the Music Research Institute at the University of North Carolina at Greensboro states, "Nothing activates as many areas of the brain as music." His research, along with that of countless others, has begun to provide a legitimate rationale for the value of the arts in the curriculum.

- A set of research results entitled the *Mozart Effect* indicated that listening to Mozart's music would induce a short-term improvement on the performance of certain kinds of mental tasks known as "spatial-temporal reasoning."
- A Neurological Research Study completed by Texas State University in 1999 showed correlations between young children studying piano and their improvement in math, science, and language.
- In 2004, a large-scale research study at the University of Toronto proved that music helps to train the brain to work more efficiently in processing language. It was also proven to have a positive effect on the development of phonetic skills.
- Concurrently, at Stanford University's Psychology Department and Lucas Center for Magnetic Resonance, research proved that music helps children differentiate rapid syllable changes and combinations of pitches. The 2005 Stanford Report concluded that music helps with reading and language skills and facilitates remembering spoken words.
- A McGill University Study showed that music boosts a child's self-esteem and improves pattern recognition.

As schools continue in their efforts to realign approaches to learning so that no child will be left behind, it becomes increasingly evident to many educators and administrators that arts programs must be included as a visible and viable part of the curriculum if the teaching-learning process is to be effective.

More and more researchers point to the important role of the arts in improving students' achievement and preparing them for a life that demands creative solutions to challenging problems. Several studies confirm the numerous benefits of music in children's development.

- **Music motivates curiosity and creativity in students. It increases students' engagement in learning as well as their social development.** Many of today's employers seek individuals who have skills in creative thinking and collaboration. Consider what students do when challenged to create their own musical composition, dance, or opera. After deciding on a theme, they do research and collect necessary materials. They continue this creative process by judging their work against their own standards for what is "good." They take risks, make changes, evaluate the results and decide when the work is finished. Finally, they have an end product that can be communicated to others through a performance or sharing. Clearly, experiences like these are likely to be remembered and valued.

- **Music directly enhances learning through increased spatial development.** Both math and reading are improved by learning rhythms and decoding notes and symbols. Older students have opportunities to grasp mathematical concepts such as ratio and proportion through musical training in rhythm and notation.

- **Music improves cognitive skills involved in reading, language development, and mathematics; it also develops problem-solving and critical and creative thinking skills.** Through movement, young students may recognize shapes of letters, or add drama to a story or poem to better understand its meaning. Texts of songs are simply poetry in motion. It must be noted that every song or composition is tied to a specific person and/or place in time.

- **Music helps in the development of a student's self-esteem and self-confidence.** Music provides endless opportunities for both personal and group success. The process and eventual rewards of learning to play an instrument, dance a country reel with a group of friends, or learn to sing "Take Me Out to the Ball Game" or the "Star Spangled Banner" help to build confidence in any individual.

- **Music reaches and increases communication and performance of students who often struggle to succeed in school, including disadvantaged students, English language learners, and students with disabilities.** The ability to develop fluency in a language is greatly enhanced through singing lyrics. Melody and rhythm together represent a foundation upon which speech is added to form song.

- **Music provides new challenges for those students who already excel in their academic performance.** The ability to carefully analyze what is taking place in a song or other musical composition demands high-level cognitive skills. The ability to read notation, count time, provide proper fingering on an instrument, add expression, and play in ensemble or as a soloist significantly challenges the best of students.

- **Activity in music programs motivates students to increase their attendance in school.** Although this may not be a significant reason to have music programs in schools, it is important. It is very difficult to not give your best to a group if you have personally committed to your peers.

Research regarding the importance of music in our lives continues to prove particularly useful as it strives to include music's importance in helping the development of the "whole" person. For example, in the December 2010 issue of *Discover: Science, Technology, and the Future*, Carl Zimmer states

> Last year Sylvain Moreno of York University in Toronto and his colleagues showed that giving third graders nine months of music classes improved their ability to read…. Finnish psychologists had stroke patients spend two months listening to music. Six months later, the patients had better verbal memory than stroke victims who had not had music therapy.

LEARNING THEORY

Learning theory has paved the way for many of the innovative and effective teaching approaches used in classrooms today. Knowledge of learning theory not only gives teachers a better understanding of the children they teach, but also provides them with a framework upon which their curricula and lessons may be developed.

Howard Gardner

In his book *Frames of Mind*, Howard Gardner formulated the following list of intelligences that continues to influence educators in their development of multisensory educational programs.

1. **Linguistic intelligence** is sensitivity to spoken and written language. This intelligence includes the ability to effectively use language to express oneself rhetorically or poetically and language as a means to remember information. In the music classroom this intelligence is realized in the performance, analysis, memorization, and creation of lyrics to songs.

2. **Logical-mathematical intelligence** consists of the capacity to analyze problems logically, carry out mathematical operations, and investigate issues scientifically. A thorough understanding and analysis of all the basic elements of music—rhythm, melody, form, harmony, texture, dynamics, tempo, and timbre—are dependent on one's ability to use this intelligence.

3. **Musical intelligence** involves skill in performance, composition, and appreciation of musical patterns. It encompasses the capacity to recognize and compose musical pitches, tones, and rhythms. *Music Fundamentals, Methods and Materials* is devoted to the development of this musical intelligence.

4. **Bodily-kinesthetic intelligence** entails the potential for using one's whole body or parts of the body to solve problems. It is the capacity to use mental abilities to coordinate bodily movements. Although many activities throughout this book assist in developing intelligence, Chapter 12 "Movement and Children," is devoted entirely to the importance of bodily-kinesthetic skills.

5. **Spatial intelligence** involves the potential to recognize and use patterns of wide space and more confined areas. In this book, movement activities have been designed to reinforce this intelligence in the chapter on "Movement," as well as in several of the suggested Cooperative Learning Activities found at the end of each chapter in Section I.

6. **Interpersonal intelligence** is concerned with the capacity to understand the intentions, motivations, and desires of other people. It allows us to work effectively with others. The Cooperative Learning Activities found at the end of selected chapters will help students and prospective teachers enhance this intelligence.

7. **Intrapersonal intelligence** entails the capacity to understand oneself and to appreciate one's feelings, fears, and motivations.

8. **Naturalistic intelligence,** exemplified by archeologists and botanists, concerns the ability to distinguish, classify, and use features of the environment. The musical instruments that we use in the classroom every day are integrally connected to this intelligence. How the instruments are made, where they originated, how tone is produced on them, and how they are ultimately categorized according to winds, percussive, or bowed or plucked is important here.

Jean Piaget

Jean Piaget, a Swiss psychologist, described four levels of cognitive growth and development in children and emphasized that young children learn through imitation and active participation. As children grow older, they are able to reason and think more abstractly. Piaget's stages of cognitive growth are as follows:

- **Sensorimotor stage**—from birth to age 2. Children experience the world through movement and senses.
- **Preoperational stage**—from 2 to 7 (creative thinking predominates). Children acquire motor skills; egocentrism begins strongly and then weakens; children cannot use logical thinking.
- **Concrete operational stage**—from 7 to 12 (children begin to think logically, but are very concrete in their thinking). Children can now conserve and think logically, but only with practical aids. They are no longer egocentric.
- **Formal operational stage**—from age 12 onwards (development of abstract reasoning). Children develop abstract thought and can easily conserve and think logically.

Jerome Bruner

Educational psychologist Jerome Bruner believed that any subject can be taught effectively in some intellectually honest form if the material is presented at the child's readiness level. This hypothesis served as the philosophical basis upon which the concept of a "spiral curriculum" would evolve. The spiral curriculum represents a step-by-step development of cognitive growth over time. In a spiral curriculum, material is presented in its simplest form and gradually moves to more complex levels.

In addition to this most valuable philosophy, Bruner presented three modes of representation through which learning or the encoding of one's memory would take place. These modes included the following:

- **Enactive mode** (action-based): The learner manipulates the environment and gains knowledge of it through sensory contact.
- **Iconic mode** (image-based): The learner represents this sensory contact in some form that looks like the experience.
- **Symbolic mode** (language-based): The learner represents the experience in universally understood symbols.

Rather than neatly delineated stages, the modes of representation are integrated and only loosely sequential as they translate into each other.

Each of the elements presented in this textbook is presented using a spiral curriculum approach.

LEARNING THEORY APPLIED TO MUSIC EDUCATION

How children learn at each stage in their development influences what they are capable of doing physically and neurologically. Children grow in their love for music and become increasingly more secure with musical concepts and skills when musical activities are well planned for successful completion. To accomplish these objectives, teachers should be not only aware of the eight intelligences that children possess when they enter into the learning environment, but also well-schooled in how children learn and what they are capable of doing and understanding during each of their growth stages. The following charts are designed to give the reader a quick, yet comprehensive overview of the varying expectations of elementary students based on their assigned grade levels. All of these guidelines are, of course, subject to change based upon the readiness level of the child.

General Characteristics

Nursery School and Kindergarten	First and Second Grade	Third and Fourth Grade	Fifth and Sixth Grade	
Their large muscles are better developed than smaller ones.	Their fine motor skills are improving.	They are more coordinated, and have improved fine motor skills.	Their body growth and body changes cause self-consciousness.	They are completely coordinated.
They are constantly active; they have a short attention span.	They alternate between active and quiet activities.	Their attention span is expanding.	They can be defiant and overly critical of themselves and others.	Some students take on leadership roles.
Their voices are small and the pitch is undeveloped.	Their voices are light and high in pitch.	Their voices are improving in quality and range; most can sing in tune.	Their voices begin to change; boys' voices lower in pitch.	Boys tend to reject singing in their higher registers.
They enjoy repetitious and fun activities.	They enjoy being involved.	They enjoy learning about their world.	They are shy when it comes to using singing voices.	They are very self-conscious in front of audiences.
Their attention spans vary depending on interest.	Their reasoning is developing quickly.	They are sensitive to criticism and seek praise from adults.	Many prefer to be left alone.	They will not participate if they do not like the literature or activity.
They are imitative and talkative.	They learn through imitation activities and rote learning.	Peer groups rise in importance.	Peer group approval and belonging take top priority.	They have more self-discipline and focus.
They learn best by manipulating concrete objects.	They learn through manipulation of concrete materials.	They enjoy guided, active participation in classroom activities.	They can make choices; their cognition, kinesthetic, and aesthetic appreciation is growing.	They possess lots of facts and can reason and make critical decisions.
Much of their learning is non-verbal.	Their verbal development taking place rapidly; they are reading and writing.	Their cognitive skills are developing rapidly.	Their abstract thinking is well developed.	
They are inquisitive, creative, and spontaneous, and they ask many questions.	They are eager to learn: inventive, imaginative, imitative, and curious.	They enjoy role playing, acting out, and drama.	They have a strong desire to master things they are interested in.	They are creatively motivated.
They can group things according to similarities.	They like to construct things out of many odd materials.	They are able to do self-evaluation and tell right from wrong.	They realize the importance of learning.	
They are self-centered, but capable of working in small groups.	They look for positive feedback.	They possess self-confidence and joy and pride in learning new things.	They are open to learning many things; they want to look and sound good.	They cannot tolerate being embarrassed in front of peers or others.
They enjoy organizing sounds that represent a story or accompany a song.	They love to act out simple stories and folk tales.	They can create their own stories, with guidance.	They are interested in popular music, but are open to all styles of music.	They keep up with current trends; they can become fully involved in musicals.
They enjoy action songs and finger plays.	They enjoy singing, playing percussion instruments, and Orff instruments.	They are developing a varied repertoire of songs from a variety of cultures.	They can sing in two or three parts successfully.	They love to drum and create interesting rhythms rather than singing.

(Continued on next page)

Nursery School and Kindergarten	First and Second Grade	Third and Fourth Grade	Fifth and Sixth Grade	
They love silly songs with silly words.	They love to sing all kinds of songs, perform simple dances, and play instruments.	They enjoy folk songs, popular songs, games and dances.	They love popular songs sung by pop artists.	
They love rhymes.	They learn through rhyme.	They love materials from a wide variety of cultures.	They enjoy rap and hip-hop.	They enjoy being successful. Success is never forgotten.

Musical Expectations

Nursery School and Kindergarten	First and Second Grade	Third and Fourth Grade	Fifth and Sixth Grade	
They can match pitch, with practice	They have more accuracy in singing pitches in tune.	Their harmonic sense is developing.	They can sing, but they do not prefer singing at this stage.	Boys respond best when singing and moving together.
They can classify sounds: high, medium, low.	They can sing simple rounds and canons.	They can sing in simple two part harmony.	They can make their own instruments.	They can compose their own rhythms and songs.
They can determine loud and soft.	They can identify dynamic symbols in music.	They can learn the Italian names of symbols.	They are sensitive to dynamic changes in a variety of musical styles.	They can create musical pieces that incorporate dynamic changes.
They can determine fast and slow.	They can identify tempo markings in music.	They can identify and react to the Italian names of tempo markings.	They can use symbols depicting tempo in their own creative pieces.	
They can differentiate between smooth and disconnected.	They can identify legato and staccato and other symbols.	They can put into practice knowledge of symbols related to style.		
They can play simple repeated accompaniments.	They can create and play simple accompaniments on rhythm and melody instruments.	They can play and improvise harmonic accompaniments to songs.	They love drumming, playing the piano, guitar, recorder, and Orff instruments.	They can create their own accompaniment.
They can improvise on simple classroom instruments.	They can differentiate between various kinds of timbres.	They can classify all instruments; they can hear differences in timbres.	They can work with all percussion in an ensemble.	They can improvise on barred instruments, drums, etc.
They can move to the basic beat.	They can distinguish between beat and rhythm.	They are capable of mastering symbolic systems and can classify objects and ideas abstractly.	They are easily able to master symbolic systems.	They can create complex syncopated rhythms and movements.
They can perform simple dances.	They can participate in partner and folk dances.	They can move to more complex folk dances.	They can master many styles of dances.	They can perform complex folk dances and engage in other movement activities, if they are interested.

Nursery School and Kindergarten	First and Second Grade	Third and Fourth Grade	Fifth and Sixth Grade	
They can begin to read with the help of icons.	They can read and write musical notation.	They can read and write music, and can compose music.	They readily respond to reading and writing music.	They are able to participate in band, orchestra, or choral activities.
	They can begin soprano recorder.	They can progress rapidly on soprano recorder and piano.	They enjoy engaging in both choral and instrumental music.	They will often begin private study of an instrument; they love to play in an ensemble.
They can work together in a circle.	They can form circles, lines, and squares for folk dance.	They can enjoy reels and other folk dances.	They are not interested in partnering with same sexes while dancing.	They prefer not being touched.

LEARNERS WHO PRESENT VARIATIONS IN THE MUSIC SETTING

In most classrooms, students' abilities cover a wide range. Some students grasp concepts quickly, and others require a great deal of assistance and much more time. Some students are well behaved, and others need structure and support to achieve acceptable behavior. Some students feel comfortable with their peers, and others struggle to feel at ease. Music has the power to engage and motivate this extremely diverse group of students because it involves personal experience.

In order to accommodate the variations in students' abilities, the Individuals with Disabilities Education Act (IDEA) was passed in 1975. It mandated that all children receive a free, appropriate public education regardless of the level of severity of their disability. It provides funds to assist states in the education of students with disabilities and requires that states make sure that these students receive an individualized education program based on their unique needs in the least restrictive environment possible. IDEA also provides guidance for determining what related services are necessary and outlines a "due process" procedure to make sure these needs are adequately met.

In recent years, the term inclusion has been extensively used to describe a process and philosophy associated with the mainstreaming law, but is not synonymous with the term *mainstreaming*. Mainstreaming is viewed as a benchmark through which students earn their way back into the classroom, but inclusion establishes the students' "right" to be there in the first place. Services and supports are brought to the regular classroom as needed.

The latest legal addition to inclusion, the Individuals with Disabilities Education Act Amendments of 1997, was signed into law by President Clinton on June 4, 1997. A primary implication of the 1997 amendments is the need for all educators to share in the responsibilities for services provided to all students, including those with disabilities. The IDEA Amendments reflect a step beyond compliance in pursuit of quality. The amendments allow educators to plan for at-risk students even though they are not disabled.

The current inclusive movement clearly challenges all teachers to look beyond mainstreaming to find inclusive strategies to meet students' individual needs. In an inclusive setting, it is crucial to invite parents, teachers, community members, and students to join together to be a part of a new culture. Each person should be encouraged to participate to the fullest of his or her capacity—as partners and as members.

Although students with special needs, gifted and talented students, and ethnically diverse students are indistinguishable from their peers in most ways, their learning needs can be quite demanding and, consequently, present a challenge

Which Learners Present Variations?

Title	Characteristics	Challenges
Attention Deficit Hyperactivity Disorder (ADHD)	Rowdy, unruly, disruptive, aggressive	• often fidgets, squirms in seat • has difficulty sitting still • is easily distracted • has difficulty waiting turns • often blurts out answers • has difficulty finishing assignments • has difficulty focusing • doesn't finish tasks • has difficulty playing quietly • often talks excessively • often interrupts others • does not listen • often loses things needed to complete a task • involves self in physically dangerous activities without considering consequences • is usually quite intelligent • usually succeeds in school and other life activities
Academically challenged	Usually falls within the lowest 2–3 percent of students in the same age group	• is delayed in most, if not all academic subjects • has a slower rate of learning • has greater difficulty with reasoning tasks • has difficulty with focusing • has difficulty with tasks involving abstract reasoning • has difficulty with problem solving • is often frustrated because of repeated failures • has poor communication skills
Students with speech and language impairment	Communication problems are primary	• speech is hard to understand • language development may be delayed • may experience language problems such as stuttering or, impaired articulation
Students with sensory deficits	Experience difficulty processing information through any sensory pathway such as vision and hearing	• may be blind or partially sighted • may be deaf or have impaired hearing • may have difficulty in mobility • has difficulty in reading print or other visual materials • has difficulty in oral communication
Students who are challenged by physical and health disabilities	Represent a variety of conditions and diseases: cerebral palsy, paralysis, epilepsy, diabetes, AIDS, etc.	• health and physical problems dominate life • some may need help in areas such as mobility, communication, and basic skills • dependency on others is one of the greatest challenges
Gifted and talented students	Very bright and quick to complete tasks; advanced thought processing, problem solving abilities and critical thinking skills; anxious, bored	• High performance capabilities in areas such as intellectual or creative endeavors • require special attention • formulate concepts quickly
Ethnically diverse students	Racially and culturally different students from diverse backgrounds	• may feel left out • face two sets of expectations • cannot understand because of language differences

to the teacher. The fifth edition of *Music Fundamentals and Methods for the Classroom Teacher* provides guidelines and suggestions for working with the complex and often perplexing diversities that may confront teachers when planning for students who vary in their ways of accessing and experiencing information in their environment. However, unlike past editions, these experiences will be duly noted and incorporated within the normal body of the text and not separated into their own chapter.

INCLUSION IN THE MUSIC CLASSROOM

Developing Sensitivity

Music adds an important dimension to the emotional and aesthetic growth of all children, regardless of physical or mental limitations. This makes the music program a prime area in which inclusion can take place successfully. However, successful inclusion in the music classroom depends on a combination of variables that must be addressed before proper learning can take place. First and foremost, the teacher must be sensitive to and understanding of students who present variations in their learning styles. To help develop sensitivity in themselves and in their students, teachers should:

1. Be open and honest with students from the beginning. Don't avoid answering questions. Hold class discussions that will allow students to ask questions and explore feelings.
2. Discuss with the class the importance of positive attitudes, and instill a sense of responsibility within all children in the classroom setting.
3. Use different types of media, such as smart boards, DVDs, and projectors with Internet access to display examples of children learning and playing music in diverse settings. Discuss the examples with the class.
4. Emphasize similarities rather than differences.
5. Be honest with yourself. Find help if you need assistance or advice.

Music Fundamentals, Methods, and Materials for the Elementary Classroom Teacher provides an abundance of musical materials and experiences that will help motivate prospective teachers and students to appreciate music as an integral part of all of our lives. Gardner's theory of multiple intelligences has met with a strong positive response from many educators because it provides teachers with a conceptual framework for organizing and reflecting on pedagogical practices and assessment. In turn, this reflection has led educators to develop creative approaches that might better meet the needs of the range of learners that many teachers encounter in today's classrooms.

One of the direct influences of the identification of these intelligences was realized in the development of the National Content Standards for Music Education. Each standard clearly reflects Gardner's attempt to assist educators to realize the importance of a multisensory approach to learning, as well as Piaget's and Bruner's contributions to developmental learning theories.

NATIONAL CONTENT STANDARDS FOR MUSIC EDUCATION

Each of these standards will be acknowledged throughout this book as the major concepts and their prospective experiences are addressed. They involve the following competencies:

1. **Singing alone and with others, a varied repertoire of music.** Students will be expected to achieve the following:
   a. sing independently, on pitch and in rhythm with appropriate timbre, diction, and posture.
   b. sing expressively with appropriate dynamics, phrasing, and interpretation.
   c. sing and perform from memory a varied repertoire of song and rhythmic pieces from diverse cultures.
   d. sing ostinatos, partner songs, rounds, and canons.
   e. sing in groups, blending vocal timbres, expressing appropriate dynamic levels, and responding to the directions of the conductor.
2. **Performing on instruments, alone and with others, a varied repertoire of music.** Students will be expected to achieve the following:
   a. Perform on pitch and in rhythm, with appropriate dynamics and timbre, and maintain a tempo.
   b. Perform easy rhythmic, melodic, and chordal patterns accurately and independently.
   c. Perform diverse pieces of literature expressively.
   d. Echo short rhythmic and melodic patterns.
   e. Perform in groups and blend instrumental and vocal timbres, matching dynamic levels and following the cues of a conductor.
   f. Perform instrumental parts to accompany singing and other contrasting parts.
3. **Improvising melodies, variations, and accompaniments.** Students will be expected to achieve the following:
   a. Improvise questions and answers vocally and instrumentally.
   b. Improvise simple rhythmic and melodic ostinato accompaniments.
   c. Improvise rhythmic variations and simple melodic embellishments.
   d. Improvise short songs and instrumental pieces, using a variety of sounds.
4. **Composing and arranging music with specified guidelines.** Students will be expected to achieve the following:
   a. Create and arrange music to accompany poetry, short stories, and other creative writings.
   b. Create and arrange short songs and instrumental pieces.
   c. Use a variety of found sounds, musical sounds, and electronically produced sounds while composing.
5. **Reading and notating music.** Students will be expected to achieve the following:
   a. Read whole, half, dotted half, quarter, eighth, and sixteenth note patterns and rests simple and compound meters.
   b. Use a system of reading notation, similar to Kodaly, to read notation in the treble clef.
   c. Identify traditional symbols relating to dynamic and tempo markings and perform these appropriately when in concert.
6. **Listening to, analyzing, and describing music.** Students will be expected to achieve the following:
   a. Identify simple forms when presented aurally and visually.
   b. Demonstrate perceptual skills by moving or responding dramatically to pieces of music from ethnically diverse backgrounds.

c. Use appropriate terminology in explaining music, notation, and instruments from different cultures, as well as different voice categories (soprano, alto, tenor, and bass).

d. Respond to purposeful movement ideas while listening to music from a variety of cultures.

7. **Evaluating music and music performances.** Students will be expected to achieve the following:

a. Devise criteria for evaluating performances and compositions.

b. Explain, using appropriate music terminology, their opinions of composers' works and as well as their own creative projects.

8. **Understanding relationships between music, the other arts, and disciplines outside the arts.** Students will be expected to achieve the following:

a. Analyze, create, and perform a musical work that captures the interdisciplinary workings of the arts.

b. Explain, using appropriate terminology, how composers, visual artists, and dancers use related themes and techniques in their artistic expressions.

9. **Understanding music in relation to history and culture.** Students will be expected to achieve the following:

a. Identify, practice, and perform songs and instrumental works from a variety of periods throughout history.

b. Use an appropriate historical timeline or base to analyze the circumstances and conditions under which selections of music were created.

c. Aurally recognize, based upon specific practices at a given time and/or lyrics, where a piece originates.

REFERENCES

Bruner, J. (1960). *The Process of Education*. Cambridge, MA.: Harvard University Press.

Campbell, Don (1997). *The Mozart Effect: Tapping the Power of Music to Heal the Body, Strengthen the Mind, and Unlock the Creative Spirit*. New York: Harper Collins.

East Texas State University. (1999, March 15). *Neurological Research Study*.

Gardner, Howard. (1993). *Multiple Intelligences: The Theory and Practice*. New York: Basic.

Gardner, Howard. (2000). *Intelligence Reframed: Multiple Intelligences for the 21st Century*. New York: Basic.

Hodges, D. (2008). A Layman's Guide to the Musical Brain. *Opus Magazine*, 6:2. 8–13.

Piaget, Jean. (1995). *A Child's Conception of the World*. Lanham, MD: Littlefield Adams.

CHAPTER 2

Teaching Rhythm to Children

INTRODUCTION

Rhythm is the most important of all musical elements. It is found in nature, in art and architecture, in speech, in movement, and in everyday life. The recurrence of day and night, the change of seasons, the rotation of our planet on its axis, the progression from life to death, and the flow of the tides are symbolic of the powerful presence that rhythm has in our environment.

There is rhythm in physiology in the beat of your pulse and in regular breathing. In athletics, rhythm is evident in the consistent strokes used to swim, operate a rowboat or canoe, and in the strides of a runner or hurdler. Children consistently engage in rhythmic activities when jumping rope, swinging, tossing a ball, and even playing video games. The introduction of electronic games similar to the *Wii* and others clearly makes necessary an understanding of the importance of rhythmic consistency in everyday life.

Rhythm in music suggests a similar flow of motion with intervening points of relaxation. In this more restricted sense, *rhythm can be defined as the varied lengths of sounds and silences over a basic beat.*

> *The whole of man's life stands*
> *in need of a right rhythm.*
> *—Plato*

FOCUS

Beat/Pulse

Learning In our environment and in our own bodies, we experience the repetition of sounds and movements.

Strategies **NS 6** (Listening to, analyzing and describing sounds in the environment.)

Listen to sounds in the classroom that repeat—a clock ticking, feet walking, the ringing of a bell, an emergency siren.

VISUAL R1

clock ticking   feet walking   bell ringing   emergency siren

Recall repeated movements and sounds in the environment outside the classroom—the ringing of a cellular telephone, the hammering of a nail, a boy rowing in a kayak, a leaky faucet, the ticking of a grandfather clock, a toddler stirring his first cupcakes.

VISUAL R2

Place your hand on your chest and feel the consistency of your own heartbeat. Pay attention to the regular inhalation and exhalation process within your own body. Both are dependent on the regularity of what is called *beat* or *pulse* and reflect the existence of life itself.

 Tell students that with the help of a stethoscope, doctors are able to listen to the regularity or irregularity of your heartbeat or your breathing to determine your physical condition.

Listen to the sounds of your footsteps as you walk.

Learning Beat is the underlying, unchanging, repeating pulse found in most music.

Strategies **NS 2** (Performing and creating sound, using body percussion to reinforce beat.)

While performing "Going On A Bear Hunt," tell students to pat the beat by alternating their hands on their laps (called *patsching*).

Bear Hunt

I'm goin' on a bear hunt.	(Alternate hands on lap)
I'm not afraid.	
I've got my trusty camera,	
And my film by my side.	
All right?	
O.K.?	
Let's go!	
I see a wheat field.	
Can't go over it.	
Can't go around it.	
I'll have to go through it.	Swish hands together 16 times.
I see a bridge.	Softly thump chest 16 times.
I see a mud hole.	Grab at the air with a clawed hand.
I see a stream.	Swim, using strokes for 16 times.
I see a tree.	Do an upward climbing motion by placing one fist on top of another.
I see a cave.	Slow down as students enter imaginary cave IMAGINE IN DARKNESS, what the bear would look like.
What is this?	
IT'S A BEAR!!!!	SCREAM!!!!

(Reverse direction, repeat all movements in double time until safely back at home. Slam the gate!)

 Let children suggest and then act out other kinds of hunts: a lion hunt, a search for a pot of gold, a veggie hunt, a pumpkin hunt, a cookie hunt.

 Direct children's attention to the words that give direction in the "Bear Hunt": *over, under, through, around*. These words are called *prepositions. Invite students to think of other prepositions.*

When teaching students to identify the basic beat or pulse, use colorful charts, similar to the ones provided here, that contain symbols or icons representing pulse and rhythm, rather than the musical notation itself. Students at all levels enjoy this activity. Have students look at the pictures and say the words in rhythm.

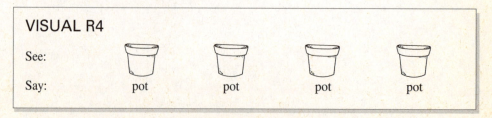

VISUAL R4

See:

Say: pot   pot   pot   pot

VISUAL R5

See:				
Say:	eye	eye	eye	eye

Have students suggest other icons that might represent beat: a nail, a pin, a tack, an ink pen, a pencil, a stake, and a stick. Make cards or charts using these icons. Include these icons in a PowerPoint presentation for the rest of the class.

While reciting the words of a familiar rhythm, have students tap their thighs (called *patsching*) to the underlying pulse, as in **Visual R6.**

VISUAL R6

Say:	Two	Four	Six	Eight
Tap:	X	X	X	X
Say:	Meet me	at the	gar - den	gate.
Tap:	X	X	X	X
Say:	If I'm	late,	Don't	wait,
Tap:	X	X	X	X
Say:	Two	Four	Six	Eight
Tap:	X	X	X	X

1 + 2 = 3 Draw students' attention to the fact that this popular rhyme contains an introduction to skip counting. Ask students to try skip counting starting on other numbers.

Reinforce the awareness of beat by tapping while saying many rhymes or while singing a familiar game song, such as "Icka Backa Boo!" Notice that once the beat is established, it continues to be felt even if no words are sung or spoken.

VISUAL R7

Sing or Say:	Ic- ka	bac- ka	so- da	crac- ker,
Tap:	X	X	X	X
Sing or Say:	Ic- ka	bac- ka	boo!	
Tap:	X	X	X	X
Sing or Say:	Ic- ka	bac- ka	so- da	crac-ker,
Tap:	X	X	X	X
Sing or Say:	Out	goes	you!	
Tap:	X	X	X	X

Have students choose partners and create a hand-clapping game to accompany "Icka Backa Boo." Suggest they use pats, claps, stamps, and snaps to create a pattern. Share results with others in classroom.

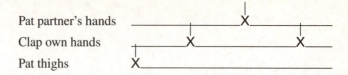

Pat partner's hands

Clap own hands

Pat thighs

Listen to short musical selections that have a strong, steady beat. Have students walk in a variety of ways or play rhythm sticks or a drum to the beat of these selections.

FOCUS

Rhythm

| **Learning** | Rhythm in music is the length of sound and silence in relation to the underlying beat. |

Strategies **NS 5, 6** (Reading and notating music.)

Have students chant a familiar rhyme. First, say the rhyme while tapping the beat. Then, repeat the rhyme while tapping the rhythm of each sound; that is, tap each syllable that is spoken. Write the words of the rhyme so that children can see it. Have a student mark each beat where it occurs in the rhyme. Then, decide which sounds are long and which are short. Long and short sounds can be designated in a variety of ways, such as _____ for a long sound and __ __ for short sounds. Children enjoy using icons to designate long and short durations. Place the long and short duration symbols above the words as students decide where they belong. See **Visual R8**.

VISUAL R8

Duration:	___	___	___	___
Say:	Fudge	Fudge	Call the	judge!
Tap:	X	X	X	X

Duration:	__ __	__ __	__ __	___
Say:	Ma- ma's	got a	ba-	by!
Tap:	X	X	X	X

Duration:	__ __	___	__ __	___
Say:	Not a	boy,	Not a	girl,
Tap:	X	X	X	X

Duration:	__ __	__ __	___	___
Say:	Just a	plain old	ba-	by!
Tap:	X	X	X	X

Have students practice pointing their fingers along the long and short lines as they say the rhyme. (This may be done in the air.) Students should repeat these kinds of activities many times, using a variety of rhymes and songs.

With repeated experiences, students will be able to grow in their ability to distinguish between the even, steady nature of beat in contrast to the uneven, short and long combinations found in the rhythms of the sounds they are experiencing. To reinforce both beat and rhythm when singing a song, have one group tap the beat and the other group tap the rhythm. Alternate parts.

FOCUS

Rhythm Symbols (Quarter and Eighth Notes)

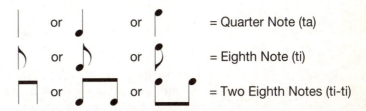

Learning   Beats or long tones performed in rhyme, rap, and song can be identified as *quarter notes*; shorter sounds can be called *eighth notes*.

Two evenly performed short sounds (eighth notes) equal one long sound or quarter note.

Eighth notes are often performed in pairs.

Rhythm syllables (ta, ti—pronounced *tah* and *tee*) are sometimes used as tools to facilitate the verbalizing of rhythm syllables in the early stages of a child's rhythmic development.

Strategies **NS 5, 6** (Reading and notating music.)

Using a "shorthand" notation called *stick notation* (| and ⊓), show students how the symbols used for long and short sounds (— and — —) can be replaced with musical symbols, called *notes*. The musical symbol for a long sound (——) is the quarter note, or tah; two short notes (— —) become eighth notes (⊓) and are often called tee-tee. See **Visual R9.**

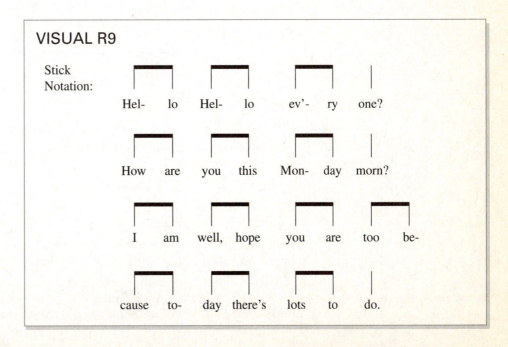

VISUAL R9

Stick notation is a convenient shorthand method for designating notes and can be used at all grade levels. However, students should be able to recognize and reproduce *standard notation*, identifying each of its parts:

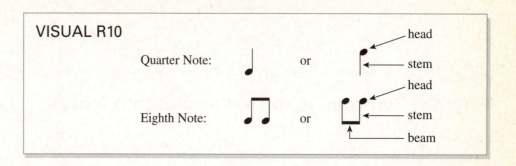

Although pairs of eighth notes are easier to read, students should know that eighth notes can stand alone with head, stem, and flag. Flags are always placed to the right of the note:

$$♪ ← flag \qquad ♪ ← flag$$

Students will find the replacing of stick notation with standard notation a simple process, as in **Visual R11.**

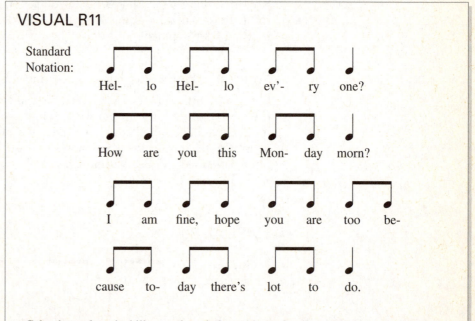

Calendar and math skills may be reinforced here. Students should be encouraged to substitute the appropriate day of the week as well as locate month and day on a yearly calendar.

Because it is harder and slower to use standard notation, stick notation is generally used when notating rhythm activities. Standard notation becomes essential when students begin reading and placing notes on a staff.

Students should have many opportunities to move in a variety of ways to quarter- and eighth-note rhythms. Examples of rhymes like "One, Two, Tie My Shoe" in **Visual R12** are plentiful and may be used to provide practice for students.

VISUAL R12

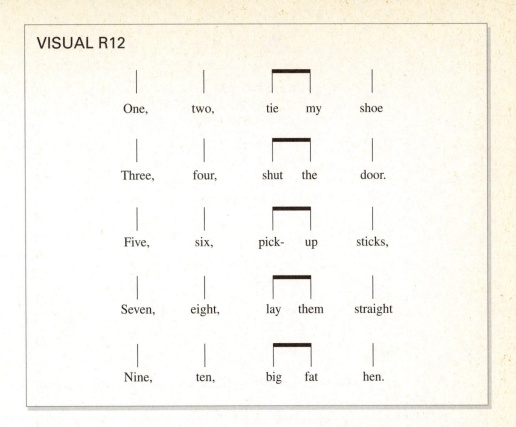

One,	two,	tie	my	shoe
Three,	four,	shut	the	door.
Five,	six,	pick-	up	sticks,
Seven,	eight,	lay	them	straight
Nine,	ten,	big	fat	hen.

1 + 2 = 3 Understanding and recognizing "how many" in a set-up of objects up to ten can be reinforced here. Have students listen as the teacher taps a hand drum. Students should tell how many beats the teacher plays. It could be 2 beats, 9 beats, 3 beats, 10 beats, etc. Try using different languages.

Place a circle containing the symbol of either two eighth notes or a quarter around each student's neck.

VISUAL R13

Art: (Rhythm Tags)

As the teacher plays quarter notes on a drum, students wearing the quarter note symbols should step to that rhythm. When the drum sounds eighth notes, students wearing the eighth note symbols should respond. Later, the drum can be replaced by a melody instrument and can combine both quarter and eighth notes.

 Students who are not ready to process moving to stick or standard notation should be introduced to icons that represent these rhythms. See **Visual R14.**

VISUAL R14

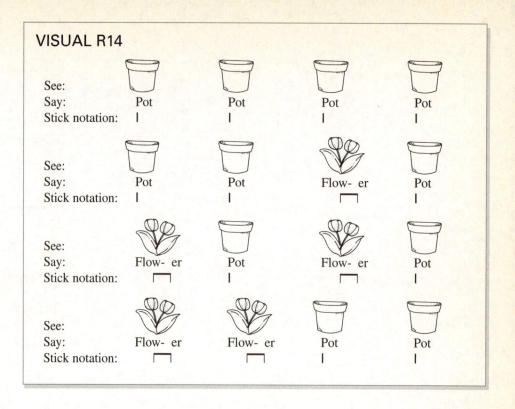

Encourage small groups of students to create icons that represent an equal division of the beat or two eighth notes as well as a quarter note and quarter rest. Icons should share something in common if possible. Suggestions might include: nail/staple, eye/eye glasses, tree/two stemmed cherries/worm.

VISUAL R15

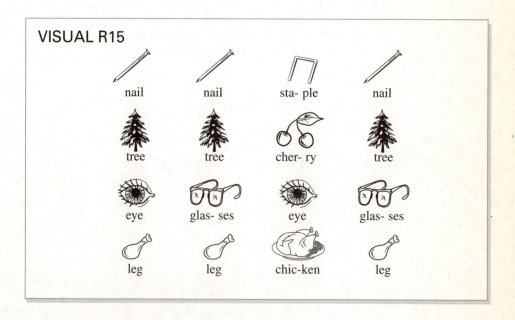

Choose a rhyme or song that the students know well. Work out its rhythms, deciding where there is one sound to the beat and where there are two sounds. Assign the quarter note the nickname "ta" and the eighth notes, "ti" (pronounced tēē). Have students verbalize the rhythms using nicknames, as in **Visual R16.** When completed, try assigning traditional quarter and eighth note names to the rhyme.

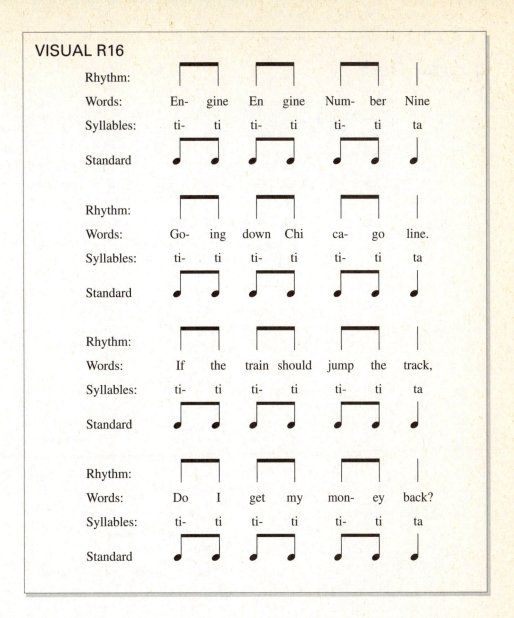

VISUAL R16

Rhythm:							
Words:	En-	gine	En	gine	Num-	ber	Nine
Syllables:	ti-	ti	ti-	ti	ti-	ti	ta
Standard							

Rhythm:							
Words:	Go-	ing	down	Chi	ca-	go	line.
Syllables:	ti-	ti	ti-	ti	ti-	ti	ta
Standard							

Rhythm:							
Words:	If	the	train	should	jump	the	track,
Syllables:	ti-	ti	ti-	ti	ti-	ti	ta
Standard							

Rhythm:							
Words:	Do	I	get	my	mon-	ey	back?
Syllables:	ti-	ti	ti-	ti	ti-	ti	ta
Standard							

Invite students to share their experiences with trains. What kinds of trains have they seen? Have they ridden on a train? Where? What sounds do trains make? Ask them to use their arms to show the motion of the wheels. How would they define the movement in musical terms? (the steady beat) Read, *The Little Engine That Could* by Watty Piper.

FOCUS

Quarter Rest

Learning Music contains both sounds and silence. Silence is represented by musical symbols called *rests*.

The quarter note (♩) has a corresponding rest of equal duration called the quarter rest: 𝄽.

Strategies **NS 1, 5** (Singing with others. Reading and writing music.)

Have students say the lyrics to "Bell Horses." Provide a chart showing the words, the basic beat, and the rhythm, as in **Visual R17**.

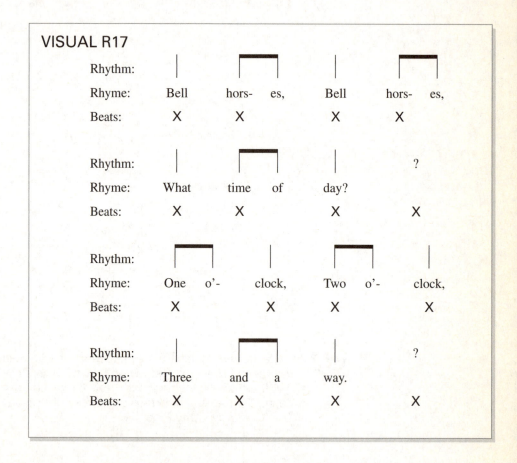

VISUAL R17

Rhythm:				
Rhyme:	Bell hors- es,	Bell hors- es,
Beats:	X X	X X

Rhythm:		
Rhyme:	What time of day?
Beats:	X X X X

Rhythm:		
Rhyme:	One o'- clock,	Two o'- clock,
Beats:	X X	X X

Rhythm:		
Rhyme:	Three and a way.
Beats:	X X X X

`1 + 2 = 3` This rhyme is excellent for launching students' awareness of telling time.

Ask students what is happening on beat 4 in lines 2 and 4 (no sound). Show students the musical symbol—quarter rest—that is to indicate one beat of silence, as in **Visual R18**. Verbalize the rhythms using rhythm syllables. Tap or clap for each note, open the hands for each rest. Initially, the teacher may want the students to verbalize softly the word *rest* when it appears. Once the concept is understood, however, the rest should be represented by total silence.

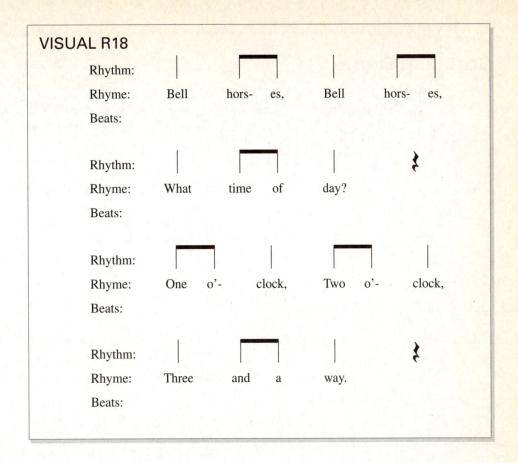

VISUAL R18

Rhythm:
Rhyme: Bell   hors-   es,   Bell   hors-   es,
Beats:

Rhythm:
Rhyme: What   time   of   day?
Beats:

Rhythm:
Rhyme: One   o'-   clock,   Two   o'-   clock,
Beats:

Rhythm:
Rhyme: Three   and   a   way.
Beats:

 Create a rhythmic *ostinato* to accompany *Bell Horses*. An ostinato is a short repeated rhythmic pattern that can be used to accompany different rhymes and melodies. An ostinato pattern can be spoken, played on a rhythm instrument; students also can move to it. After creating the ostinato, practice it by having half the class speak and clap the ostinato while the other group speaks and says the rhyme. Select a rhythmic instrument that can be substituted for the hand-clapping.

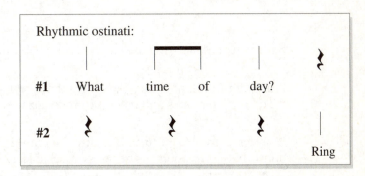

Rhythmic ostinati:

#1   What   time   of   day?

#2

          Ring

Grouping Beats

Learning   A series of basic beats can be organized into groups by the placing of accents: An accent (>) is a symbol placed above or below a note head to emphasize the sound of that note.

Strategies: **NS 5** (Notating music using stick notation.)

The natural inflections of speech are a primary source for studying the accent of sound. Write on the board names containing two and three syllables, whose normal accent is on the first syllable of each name. See **Visual R19.**

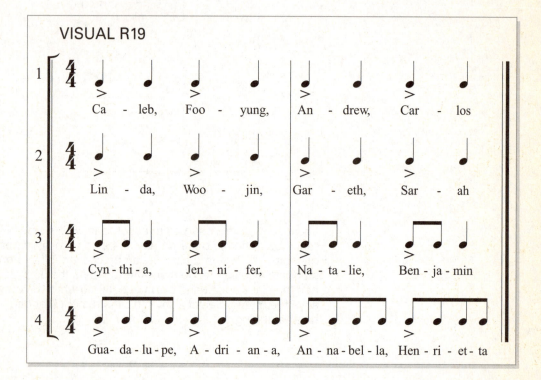

VISUAL R19

1 Ca - leb, Foo - yung, An - drew, Car - los

2 Lin - da, Woo - jin, Gar - eth, Sar - ah

3 Cyn - thi - a, Jen - ni - fer, Na - ta - lie, Ben - ja - min

4 Gua - da - lu - pe, A - dri - an - a, An - na - bel - la, Hen - ri - et - ta

Say the names, marking the emphasized syllables by circling them.

 Work with a partner to compile other names whose accents fall on the first syllable. Say the names and mark the emphasized syllable by circling it.

Transfer each syllable into a quarter note, placing an accent (>) under those notes that correspond to the stressed syllables. Note that the placement of the accents organizes the notes into groups of 2s and 3s.

Group of 2's

Hen-ry,   Mar-la,   Ca-leb

Group of 3's

Jon-a-than,   Cyn-thi-a,   Jen-ni-fer

While saying the various names, tell students to clap the accented syllables and tap their shoulders for the unaccented syllables. Students can also walk while gently stressing the accented syllables in their steps.

Perform the Mexican Game, "Bate Bate." Have students form a circle and pretend to stir a pot of chocolate sauce. Students should immediately feel where the stressed or accented syllables occur.

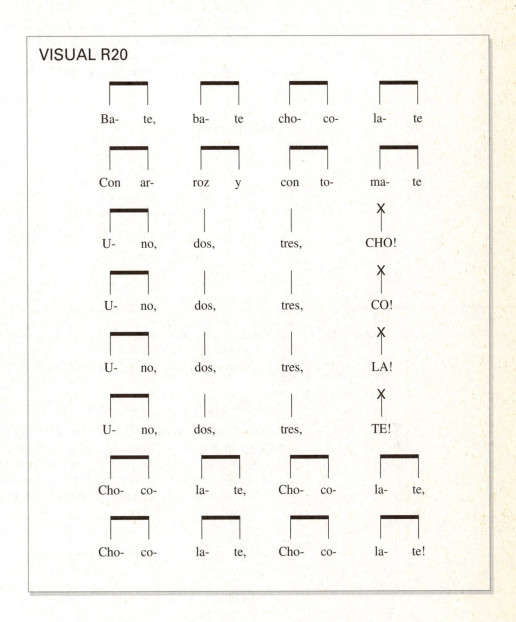

VISUAL R20

Ba- te, ba- te cho- co- la- te

Con ar- roz y con to- ma- te

U- no, dos, tres, CHO!

U- no, dos, tres, CO!

U- no, dos, tres, LA!

U- no, dos, tres, TE!

Cho- co- la- te, Cho- co- la- te,

Cho- co- la- te, Cho- co- la- te!

Pronunciation:
bä-tā, chō-cō-lä-tā, cōn är-rōy ē cōn tō-mä-tā, ü-ño dōs, trēs
Translation: Stir the chocolate, with rice, with tomato.
One, two, three, CHO, One, two, three, CO;
One, two, three, LA, One, two, three, TE.
Chocolate, chocolate, chocolate, chocolate.

Have students discuss what words are being emphasized in "Bate Bate." Circle those words.

Social Science: In Mexico, mole sauce is often served over rice. It consists of tomato, onion, garlic, chili peppers, and chocolate. Have students do further on-line research about the origin of this sauce and then prepare to make it.

 Create a rhythmic ostinato that can accompany "Bate Bate." [See p. 23.]

Recite or sing the words to "Bounce High, Bounce Low." Have students form a circle with the teacher in the center. Bounce the ball to each child in turn; the child bounces it back to the teacher in the center. The ball should always bounce on the accented beat. See **Visual R21.**

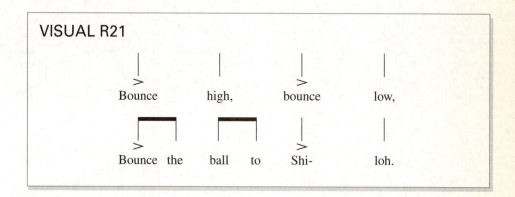

VISUAL R21

>		>	
Bounce	high,	bounce	low,
>			
Bounce the	ball to	Shi-	loh.

Learning   Accented groups may be separated by the placement of a bar line. The area between bar lines is called a *measure*. A double bar line designates the end of either a musical section or the complete work.

Strategies **NS 1, 5** (Reading and notating music.)

Chant or sing "Bounce High, Bounce Low" while clapping the beat. Repeat, clapping the rhythms. Now sing and clap the rhythm one line at a time. Have students decide which beat has one sound (quarter note) and which have two sounds (eighth notes). Notate the rhythms on the board. Have students discover where the accents should be placed. See **Visual R22.**

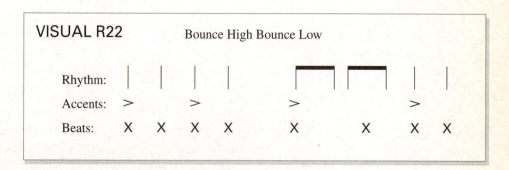

VISUAL R22   Bounce High Bounce Low

Rhythm:								
Accents:	>		>		>		>	
Beats:	X	X	X	X	X	X	X	X

Show students that a bar line can be placed in front of each accented note to separate one group from another, as in **Visual R23.** Two bar lines (*double bar*) are used to show the end of the song or rhyme. The space between two bar lines is called a *measure*.

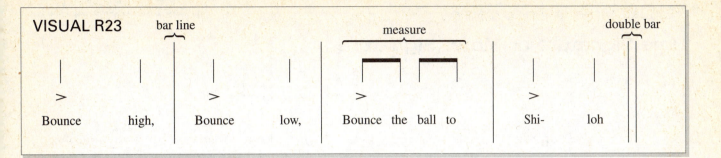

VISUAL R23 · bar line · measure · double bar

| | | | | | | | | | |
> · > · > · >
Bounce high, · Bounce low, · Bounce the ball to · Shi- loh

Give students many opportunities to place accents, bar lines, and double bars where they belong. **Visual R24** can be made into charts or handouts for this purpose. Once students become proficient in forming groups of two beats each, they can be challenged to work with groups of three and four beats each.

Students will discover that the rhythms contained in many jump-rope and hand-clapping games are strongly accented. Encourage students to share some of these games with the class and together explore where the accents are falling.

Have students listen to examples of marches. Have them explore questions such as "where do accents occur in this kind of music and why?"

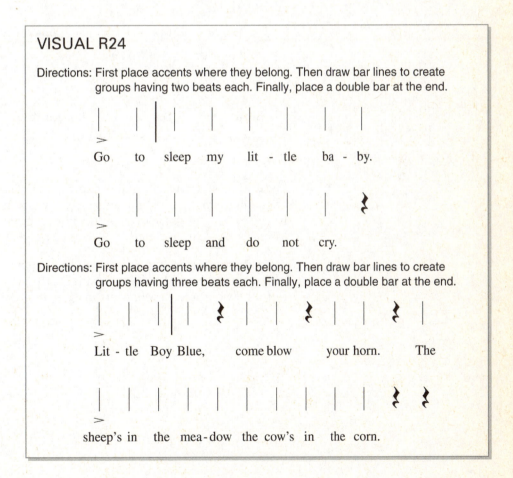

VISUAL R24

Directions: First place accents where they belong. Then draw bar lines to create groups having two beats each. Finally, place a double bar at the end.

>
Go   to   sleep   my   lit - tle   ba - by.

>
Go   to   sleep   and   do   not   cry.

Directions: First place accents where they belong. Then draw bar lines to create groups having three beats each. Finally, place a double bar at the end.

>
Lit - tle Boy Blue,   come blow   your horn.   The

>
sheep's in   the mea-dow the cow's in   the corn.

Time Signature or Meter Signature

$\frac{2}{\bullet}$ or $\frac{2}{4}$　　　$\frac{3}{\bullet}$ or $\frac{3}{4}$　　　$\frac{4}{\bullet}$ or $\frac{4}{4}$

Learning　A *time signature* or *meter signature*, found at the beginning of a musical work, is a symbol containing two numbers, one above the other. The lower number dictates which rhythm symbol will be used to establish the basic pulse in the music. The top number designates the number of beats allowed per measure.

Strategies **NS 1, 5** (Singing a folk song. Reading and notating music.)

Say the words to the song "Bounce High, Bounce Low." Place the rhythms on the board and mark the beats. Place the accents and then separate the rhythms into groups of two, as was done previously. Ask the students how many beats are in each measure. Number them. Show the students that a symbol can be used to indicate that every measure has two beats: 2. Place 2 to the left of the rhythms. See **Visual R25.**

VISUAL R25

X	X	X	X	X	X	X	X
1	2	1	2	1	2	1	2
Bounce	high,	bounce	low.	Bounce the	ball to	Shi -	loh.

Students should have repeated experiences numbering the beats of different songs and rhymes and then placing the appropriate time signatures to the left of the notes. In later grades, songs and rhymes grouped in 3s and 4s can be added. When the students are ready, 2 3 4 can be replaced with 2/4, 3/4, and 4/4.

Create worksheets to reinforce an understanding of time signatures. **Visual R26** contains three examples. By numbering each beat, the student proves that there really are two, three, or four beats in every measure.

Directions: Number the beats in each measure. Then decide what the time signature should be and place it to the left of the rhythms.

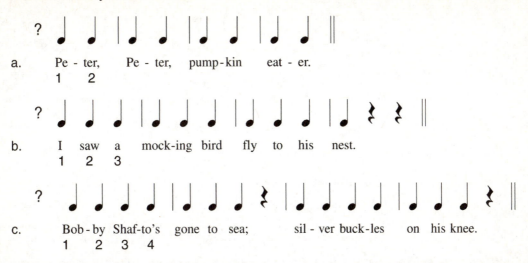

The analysis of beats in a measure is directly linked to addition and grouping. Students should be encouraged to discuss the relationship between these two areas.

1 + 2 = 3

Learning   Time signatures can be translated into hand and arm movements called *conducting patterns*. Each movement tells us where each beat within the time signature occurs.

Strategies **NS 1, 5** (Reading and writing music using 2/4, 3/4, and 4/4 time signatures.)

Students should conduct a variety of music having 2/4, 3/4, and 4/4 time signatures. Use the conducting patterns shown in **Visual R27.** In each conducting pattern, the first beat is always the *downbeat*; the last beat is always the *upbeat*.

Demonstrate the 2/4 conducting pattern as shown in Visual R27. Identify the first beat (usually the accented beat) as the downbeat and the last beat as the upbeat. Apply the 2/4 conducting pattern to "Bounce High, Bounce Low." Sing "America" (p. 104) while conducting in 3/4. Then try conducting in 4/4 while singing the refrain of "Battle Hymn of the Republic" which can be found on page 105 of this book. Find other familiar songs in this book that are written in 2/4, 3/4, and 4/4 meters and practice conducting them while singing the songs.

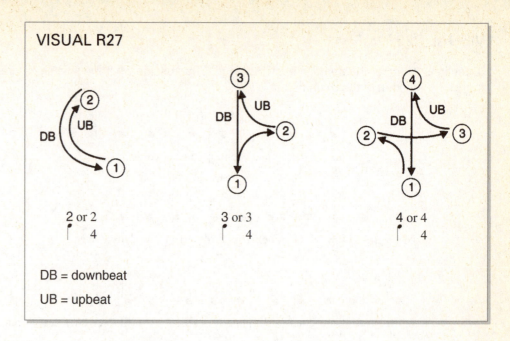

VISUAL R27

DB = downbeat

UB = upbeat

FOCUS

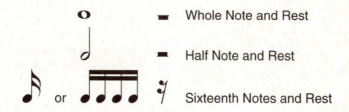

- Whole Note and Rest
- Half Note and Rest
- Sixteenth Notes and Rest

Learning A whole note contains four quarter notes.
A half note contains two quarter notes.
A quarter note contains four sixteenth notes.
The same equivalents are present in the corresponding rests.

Strategies **NS 5** (Transferring process of learning to read and write unknown rhythms.)

To teach additional note values and their corresponding rests, use the same procedures as those that were applied to the teaching of the quarter note and rest and the eighth note. Those procedures are summarized here:

1. Choose a familiar rhyme/song that contains a good example of the rhythm structure being taught.
2. Provide students with the words of the rhyme/song.
3. Say/sing the words and clap the beat while the teacher or a student marks the beats under the appropriate syllables.
4. Clap the rhythms and say/sing the words while the teacher or a student points to the beats.
5. Work out how many sounds or silences occur on each beat of the known rhythms in the rhyme/song, and place the appropriate notation above each syllable.
6. Present the new rhythm structure and write it on the board.
7. Give the new rhythm both its real name and its rhythm syllable, if it has one.
8. Have students clap the rhythm of the rhyme/song while saying/singing the rhythm syllables.
9. Reinforce the new learning with a variety of activities throughout the school year.

These procedures will take more than one day to complete, so don't try to do everything in one short lesson.

To reinforce the strategies listed in the nine procedures above, let's apply them to a new rhythm learning, sixteenth notes: ♪♪♪♪.

1. Choose a song that has a good example of ♪♪♪♪. "Love Somebody" is a good choice. The words should be placed on the board:

   Love somebody, yes I do.
   Love somebody, yes I do.
   Love somebody, yes I do.
   Love somebody, but I won't tell who.

2. Once students learn the rhyme/song well, they should say/sing it while the teacher or a student marks each beat as it occurs, as in **Visual R28.**

VISUAL R28

Love	some-bod-y,	yes	I do,
X	X	X	X
Love	some-bod-y,	yes	I do.
X	X	X	X
Love	some-bod-y,	yes	I do,
X	X	X	X
Love	some-bod-y, but I	won't	tell who.
X	X	X	X

---

3. Repeat the rhyme/song and clap its rhythms while the teacher or a student points to each beat.
4. Work out how many sounds or silences are voiced on each beat for all the known rhythms. Place the appropriate rhythm symbols on the board, as in **Visual R29.**

VISUAL R29

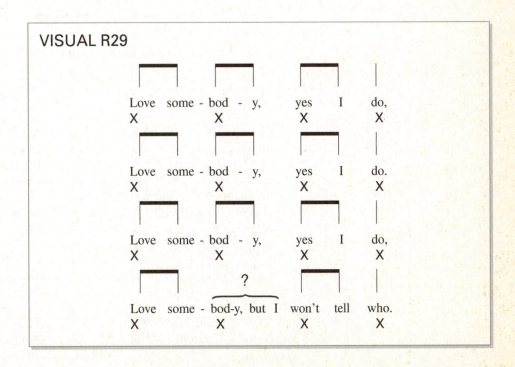

---

5. Ask students how many sounds are in "bod-y, but I." (There are four sounds to this beat.) Show how these sounds should be written: 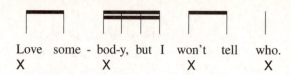. Rewrite the last line of the rhyme/song, inserting the four sixteenth notes:

Love some - bod-y, but I won't tell who.
X   X   X   X

6. Tell students that these are sixteenth notes. They often come in fours, but not always. If the note stands alone, it has two flags = ♬. This should be compared to a single eighth note with one flag = ♪. The rhythm syllables for the four-sixteenth-note group are: ti-ri-ti-ri.

7. Students should clap the rhythms of the rhyme/song while saying/singing the rhythm syllables, as in **Visual R30.**

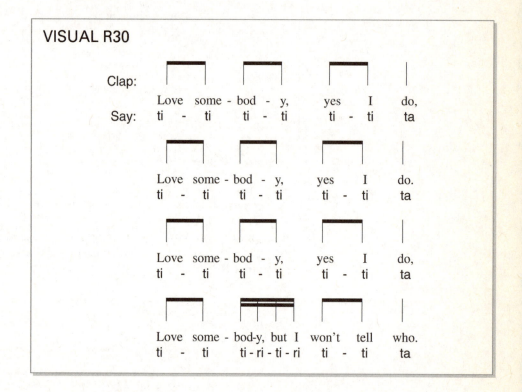

VISUAL R30

Clap:

Say: Love some - bod - y, yes I do,
ti - ti   ti - ti   ti - ti   ta

Love some - bod - y, yes I do.
ti - ti   ti - ti   ti - ti   ta

Love some - bod - y, yes I do,
ti - ti   ti - ti   ti - ti   ta

Love some - bod-y, but I won't tell who.
ti - ti   ti-ri-ti-ri   ti - ti   ta

8. Reinforce the new learning by discovering ♬ in other rhymes and songs included within this book. After examining the song, try tapping out the new rhythm using rhythm syllables (ti-ri-ti-ri). Try adding the words to the rhythm. Next, create simple accompaniments that can be played on rhythm instruments that use this rhythm. Add the accompaniment to another song of your own choosing. Songs using ♬ include:

Paw Paw Patch
When That I Was a Little Tiny Boy
Riding in the Buggy
Old Brass Wagon
A-Hunting We Will Go

Use similar procedures to teach the remaining rhythm symbols found in **Visual R31.**

Appropriate portions of Visual R31 can be displayed for each grade level in the classroom.

VISUAL R31

Whole note: **o**
Whole rest: ▬

Duration Syllables:	ta	-	a	-	a	-	a
Counting:	1		2		3		4

Half note: 𝅗𝅥   𝅗𝅥
Half rest: ▬   ▬

Duration Syllables:	ta	-	a	ta	-	a
Counting:	1		2	3		4

Quarter note: ♩   ♩   ♩   ♩
Quarter rest: 𝄽   𝄽   𝄽   𝄽

Duration Syllables:	ta	ta	ta	ta
Counting:	1	2	3	4

Eighth note: ♫ ♫ ♫ ♫
Eighth rest: 𝄾 𝄾 𝄾 𝄾 𝄾 𝄾 𝄾 𝄾

Duration Syllables:	ti	-	ti	ti	-	ti	ti	-	ti	ti	-	ti
Counting:	1		&	2		&	3		&	4		&

Sixteenth note: ♬♬ ♬♬ ♬♬ ♬♬
Sixteenth rest:

Duration Syllables:	ti - ri - ti - ri	ti - ri - ti - ri	ti - ri - ti - ri	ti - ri - ti - ri
Counting:	1 ee & a	2 ee & a	3 ee & a	4 ee & a

Note: Stick notation can be used for all the above note values except for the half note (♩) and the whole note (o).

[1 + 2 = 3] An analysis of how many quarter notes are in a half or whole note, how many eighth notes are in a quarter, half, or whole note can assist children in understanding "capacity" or volume in math.

Students should use speech to reinforce their understanding of rhythm values. Exercises similar to **Visual R32** may be helpful. Students should be encouraged to find additional words, relating to the categories specified, that will match the rhythms given.

		$\frac{2}{4}$					
Categories		𝅗𝅥	♫ ♫	♫ ♩	♩	♩	♩ ♫
FRUITS		Plum	Wa- ter- me- lon	Tan- ger- ine	Grape-	fruit	Straw- ber- ry
VEGETABLES		Bean	A- vo- ca- do	Broc- co- li	Car-	rot	Green pep- per
NAMES		John	Is- a- bel- la	A- bi- gail	Em-	ma	Rose- ma- ry
FLOWERS		Rose	Ca- la li- ly	Daf- fo- dil	Dai-	sy	Snap- dra- gon
DOG TYPES		Pug	Ger-man Shep-herd	Pe- kin- gese Gre- tan hound	Grey-	hound	French Poodle
TREES		Yew	Weep-ing wil- low	Rub- ber tree	Ma-	ple	Horse chest- nut
TOYS		Drum	Ac- tion fig- ures	Ted- dy bears	Doll	house	Tri- cy- cle

Students should be given metered experiences that reinforce their understanding of notational equivalences, such as those in **Visual R33.** To learn the rhythms, students should say the rhythm syllables and count each measure aloud (refer to Visual R31). To reinforce their understanding, students should perform these activities using percussion instruments and body rhythms. Later, divide the class into five groups, each group performing a different line of rhythm.

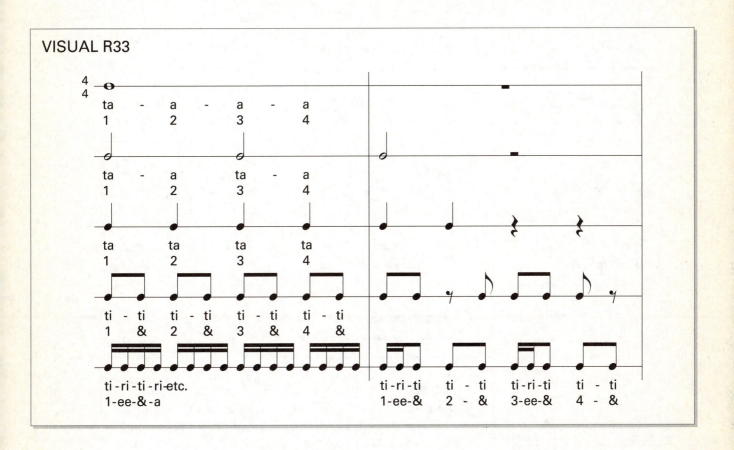

Flash cards, such as those in **Visual R34,** can be reproduced on larger cards for drill, to reinforce the use of rhythmic patterns in 4/4. Similar cards can be constructed to reinforce rhythms in 2/4 and 3/4. These patterns can also be used as ostinati to accompany songs or rhythmic activities.

FOCUS

Tie

Learning A curved line joining two rhythm symbols sung or played on the same pitch results in a *tie*. When two notes are tied, the first note is held for its duration as well as the duration of the note to which it is tied: ♩ ♩.

Strategies **NS 1, 5** (Singing a song with others. Reading and notating ties.)

Have students sing "Are You Sleeping" as the teacher points to the beats.

> Are you sleeping, are you sleeping,
> Brother John, Brother John.
> Morning bells are ringing. Morning bells are ringing.
> Ding, ding, dong. Ding, ding, dong.

Sing the song again while clapping the word rhythms. Now work out the rhythms for the first two lines of the song, as in **Visual R35.**

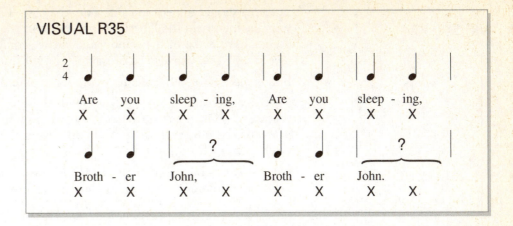

VISUAL R35

Ask students how many beats are felt while singing the word "John" in measures 6 and 8. Show how to extend a sound through the use of a tie ⌣. Rewrite measures 6 and 8, using the tie. Explain how to verbalize this pattern = ta-a. See **Visual R36.**

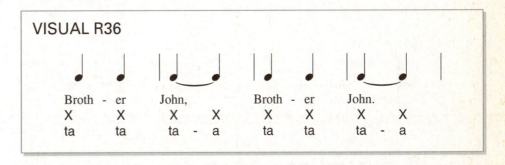

VISUAL R36

Place the last two lines of the song on the board. Work out the rhythms for these lines. Are there any more ties in these lines? Give each note its rhythm syllable, as in **Visual R37.** Sing "Are You Sleeping" again, using the rhythm syllables rather than the words. Clap the rhythms while singing the rhythm syllables.

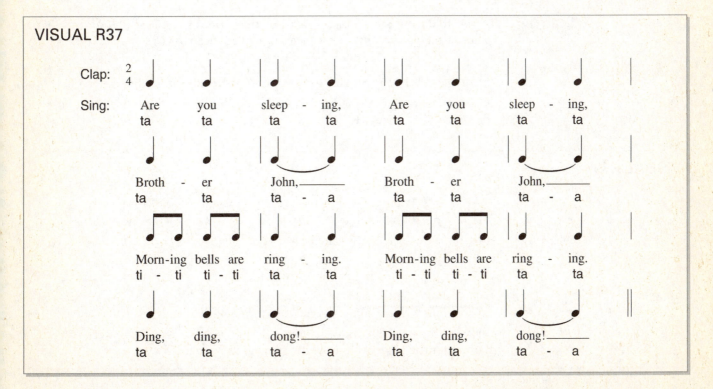

VISUAL R37

Students should understand that only the first note of the tie is "attacked." The sound is then held the length of both notes in the pattern. Both notes of the tie do not have to be of the same value. Other combinations are possible, such as ♩♪ or ♩♩. Notes can also be tied across the bar line: ♩♩.

Sing songs having other examples of the tie to reinforce this learning.

Many teachers use the tie to teach both the half and the whole note. ♩♩ easily becomes ♩ (half note); ♩♩ becomes ○ (whole note). This is a particularly good procedure because it leads students from what they know (tie) to the unknown (half note or whole note).

Once students have experienced the tie in the context of several songs, display visuals to reinforce the learning, using such patterns as those in **Visual R38.**

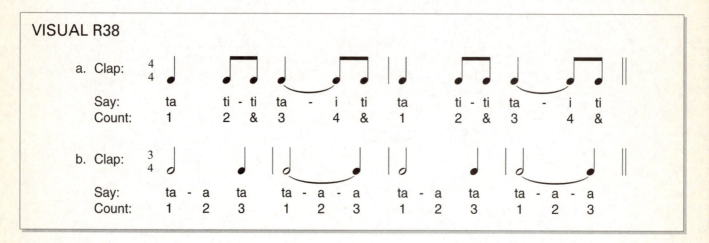

VISUAL R38

FOCUS

Dotted Notes

| Dotted Half Note | Dotted Quarter and Eighth Note | Dotted Eighth and Sixteenth Note |

Learning A dot following a note or rest adds to that note or rest one half of its value. These symbols are called *dotted notes* (♩.) and *dotted rests* (𝄽.).

Strategies **NS 1, 5** (Singing a patriotic song. Reading dotted rhythms.)

Have students sing "America." Place on the board the rhythms for the first six measures, as in **Visual R39.**

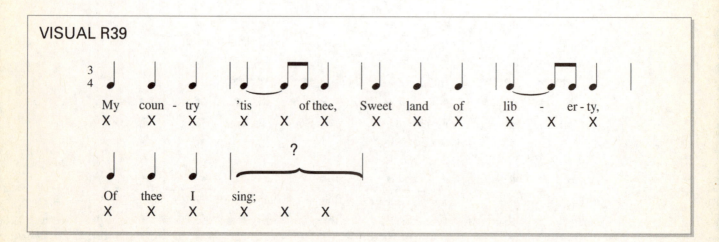

VISUAL R39

Students should sing the song again while the teacher points to the beats. Now have the students clap the rhythms as they sing the words. Ask the students how many beats should be given to "sing" in measure 6. When they respond "three," ask them how we could notate this. Some students may suggest a half note tied to a quarter note = ♩. Place this rhythm in measure 6. Now work out the rhythm syllables for the first six measures, and sing them while clapping the rhythm. See **Visual R40.**

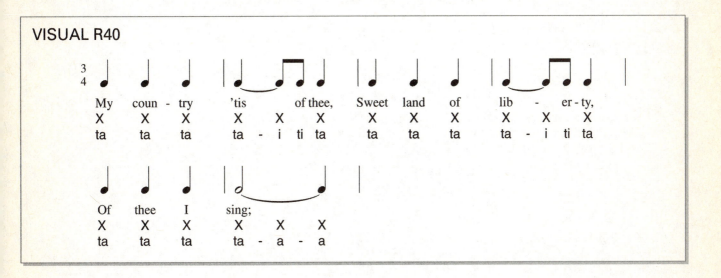

VISUAL R40

In the next lesson, show students that another way to write ♩ in measure 6 is to change the quarter note into a dot. The result is a dotted half note ♩. verbalized ta-a-a. Explain that a dot to the right of any note is always equal to the next smaller value of the note it is with. Replace the pattern ♩ in measure 6 with the new pattern ♩. See **Visual R41.** Sing the rhythm syllables once more while clapping the rhythms.

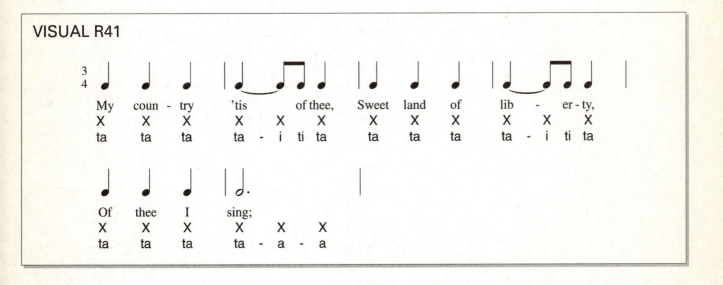

VISUAL R41

"America" can also be used to teach the dotted quarter note, ♩. Show **Visual R41** on the board once more and ask the students for another way to write the tied notes in measures 2 and 4. Because the quarter note is tied to a note having the next smaller value (an eighth note), that eighth note can become a dot beside the quarter note. Rewrite the measures, as in **Visual R42,** and place the rhythm syllables under the notes. Sing the syllables while clapping the rhythms.

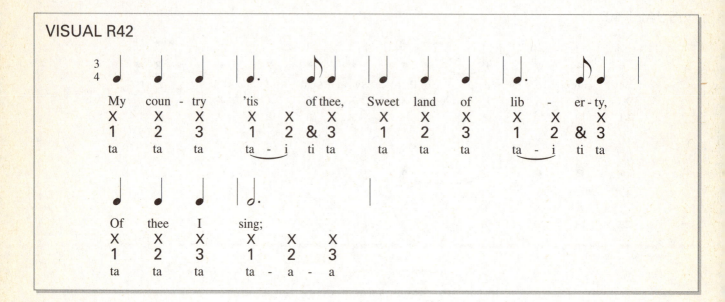

VISUAL R42

	My	coun -	try	'tis		of thee,	Sweet	land	of	lib	-	er - ty,
	X	X	X	X	X	X	X	X	X	X	X	X
	1	2	3	1	2	& 3	1	2	3	1	2	& 3
	ta	ta	ta	ta – i		ti ta	ta	ta	ta	ta – i		ti ta

Of	thee	I	sing;		
X	X	X	X	X	X
1	2	3	1	2	3
ta	ta	ta	ta – a – a		

 Play the National Anthem from England, "God Save the Queen."

 Ask students to compare "America" with "God Save the Queen." What is the same, and what is different?

Charts showing dotted note equivalents can be used to reinforce this learning. Three different charts are given in **Visual R43.** Each example should be used at the appropriate grade level, when the students are ready for it.

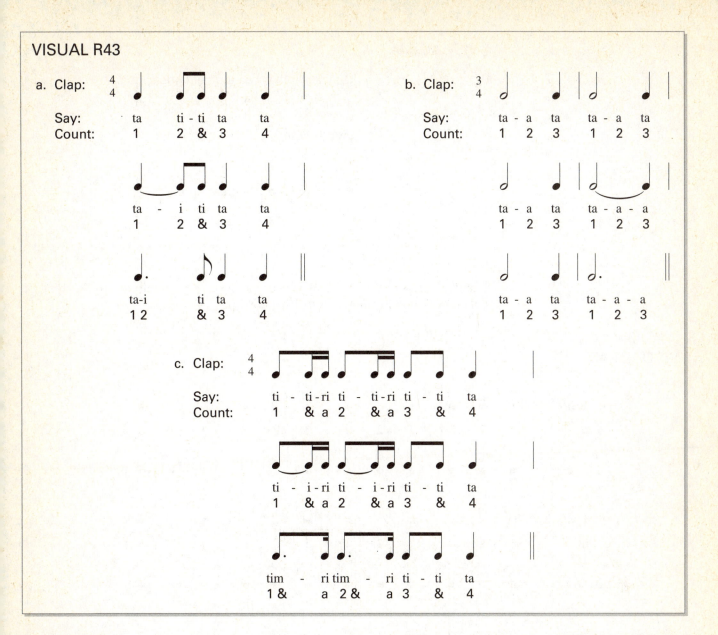

VISUAL R43

a. Clap: 4/4

Say: ta ti - ti ta ta
Count: 1 2 & 3 4

ta - i ti ta ta
1 2 & 3 4

ta-i ti ta ta
1 2 & 3 4

b. Clap: 3/4

Say: ta - a ta ta - a ta
Count: 1 2 3 1 2 3

ta - a ta ta - a - a
1 2 3 1 2 3

ta - a ta ta - a - a
1 2 3 1 2 3

c. Clap: 4/4

Say: ti - ti - ri ti - ti - ri ti - ti ta
Count: 1 & a 2 & a 3 & 4

ti - i - ri ti - i - ri ti - ti ta
1 & a 2 & a 3 & 4

tim - ri tim - ri ti - ti ta
1 & a 2 & a 3 & 4

FOCUS

Simple Meter

When the upper number of the time signature or meter signature is a 2, 3, or 4, the musical composition is in *simple meter*.

Strategies **NS 6** (Analyze simple meter and explain the function of upper and lower numbers.)

The quarter note is not the only note that serves as the *beat note;* that is, as the note that receives one full beat within a measure. Both eighth and half notes are also commonly used as beat notes in music. Students should have repeated experiences with music written in meters where either the eighth or the half note receives one full beat. The most commonly used of these meters are 3/8 and 2/2.

Note that 4/4 is often referred to as *common time*, expressed by the symbol c. 2/2 is commonly referred to as *alla breve* or *cut time*, and may be notated ¢.

Meter in 2s is often referred to as *duple meter;* in 3s, as *triple meter;* and in 4s, as *quadruple meter.* **Visual R44** summarizes these learnings.

Quarter note (♩) as the beat note:

$\frac{2}{4}$ $\frac{3}{4}$ $\frac{4}{4}$ or C

Eighth note (♪) as the beat note:

$\frac{2}{8}$ $\frac{3}{8}$ $\frac{4}{8}$

Half note (♩) as the beat note:

$\frac{2}{2}$ or ¢ $\frac{3}{2}$ $\frac{4}{2}$

Practice charts and flash cards can be produced that reinforce the learning of beat notes in simple meter, as in **Visual R45.**

VISUAL R45

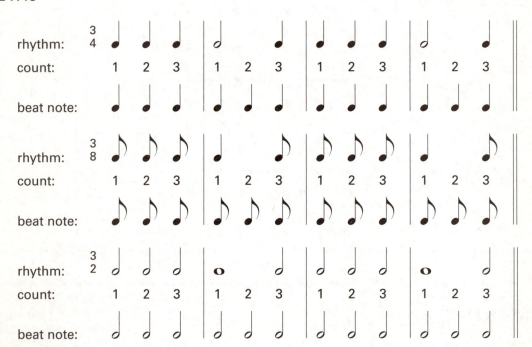

Note: In 3/4 time, there must be the equivalent of three quarter notes $\left(\frac{3}{♩}\right)$ in each measure.

In 3/8 time, there must be the equivalent of three eighth notes $\left(\frac{3}{♪}\right)$ in each measure.

In 3/2 time, there must be the equivalent of three half notes $\left(\frac{3}{♩}\right)$ in each measure.

Marking the beat notes highlights these learnings.

1 + 2 = 3   Children should be encouraged to orally express why 3/4, 3/8, & 3/2 are different.

FOCUS

Compound Meter

When the upper number of the time or meter signature is a multiple of three, the musical composition is in *compound meter*.

Strategies **NS 1, 5** (Sing a folk song with others. Reading time signatures.)

Choose a rhyme or song that the students know well, such as "Hickory Dickory Dock." Write the words of the rhyme on the board, with both beats and rhythms indicated, as in **Visual R46.**

VISUAL R46

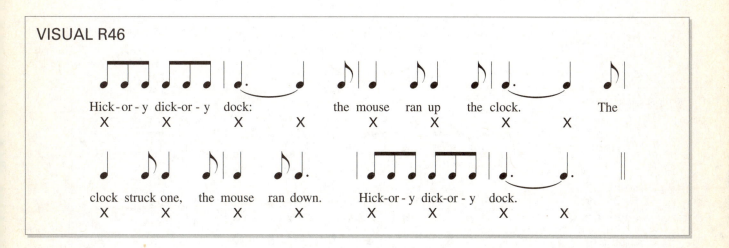

Hick-or-y dick-or-y dock: the mouse ran up the clock. The
clock struck one, the mouse ran down. Hick-or-y dick-or-y dock.

$1 + 2 = 3$ Introduce the topic of "clock". The pendulum reflects beat, pulse.

Have students say the rhyme or sing while the teacher points to the beats. Now, point to the beats again while students clap the rhythm of the words. Ask the students what kind of note will get the beat in this rhythm. If they say "eighth note," mention that this response might be possible, but the beat (X) has not been marked to designate the eighth note as receiving one full beat. The correct response, of course, is the dotted quarter note (♩.), because ♫♪ is equivalent to ♩. in total counts. Because there is no number to represent ♩. in a time signature, we commonly use 6/8 to show this meter.

Have students sing familiar songs in 6/8 found in the text. Clapping the beat and/or rhythm while singing will help to reinforce this new time signature.

After students have had other experiences with songs in 6/8 meter, explain that music having the dotted quarter note (♩.) as the beat note is said to be in *compound meter*. A visual summarizing this information can be exhibited, such as that in **Visual R47.**

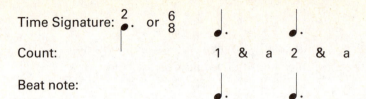

Time Signature: 2. or 6/8

Count: 1   &   a   2   &   a

Beat note:

Note: Other common time signatures in compound meter are 9/8 and 12/8.

Students should know that in compound meter, the eighth note does function as the beat note when the music is performed very slowly. This can be emphasized by showing students a visual, similar to **Visual R48.**

VISUAL R48

When students understand the difference between a slow and a fast 6/8, or any other compound meter, they should conduct "Hickory Dickory Dock" using both a fast and a slow 6/8 conducting pattern, as shown in **Visual R49.**

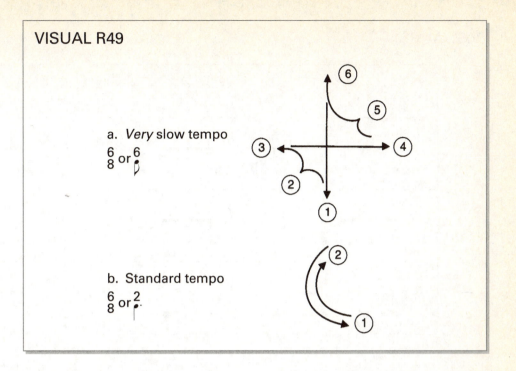

VISUAL R49

a. *Very* slow tempo
   6 or 6
   8   ♪

b. Standard tempo
   6 or 2
   8   ♩.

Students should have practice in conducting music written in common compound meters. The conducting patterns shown in **Visual R27** are used for both simple and compound meters. Because compound meters in 6 (6/8) are grouped in 2s (two beat notes per measure), 6/8 meter is conducted with two arm movements. A very slow tempo, however, would necessitate conducting each eighth note, rather than the dotted quarter note.

Note that other compound meters are possible, such as 6/4, 9/4, 12/4, 6/2, 9/2, and 12/2, but these meters are seldom used by most composers.

Patterns such as those in **Visual R50** can be used to reinforce reading music in a common compound meter. Clapping and other body movements can be used when practicing these patterns.

VISUAL R50

 Work with a partner to create lyrics to the above rhythm. Share with the class.

Flash cards, such as those in **Visual R51** can be reproduced for drill to reinforce the use of rhythmic patterns in 6/8. Similar cards, or a computer program designed to display rhythms in other compound meters, can also be presented, if desired.

FOCUS

Other Rhythms: Triplet and Syncopation

Learning — A note (not a dotted note) divided into three equal parts becomes a *triplet*, chanted tri-o-la.

Strategies **NS 5** (Reading triplets.)

Have students say a well-known rhyme or song such as "Jack Be Nimble." Post a copy of the rhyme with the beats marked. Point to the beats as the students clap them and say the rhyme. Repeat while students clap the rhythms of the words. Work out the rhythms, as in **Visual R52.**

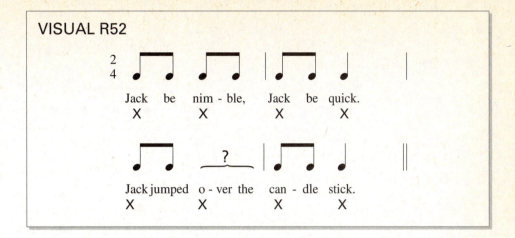

VISUAL R52

Have students say the rhyme once more, concentrating on how many sounds are heard on the second beat of measure 3. Show how these three sounds should look: ⊔. Identify the symbol as a *triplet*, whose nickname is *triola*.

Notice that a triplet is identified by the presence of the number "3" and usually by a curved line. Rewritten, measure 3 would look like this:

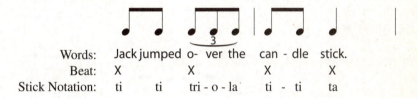

Words: Jack jumped o- ver the   can - dle stick.
Beat: X   X   X   X
Stick Notation: ti   ti   tri - o - la   ti - ti   ta

Students should understand that a triplet is not always equal to one full beat. The three notes in a triplet are equal to two notes of the same value:

a.

b.

c.

Have students create rhymes using the triplet figure, as in **Visual R53.**

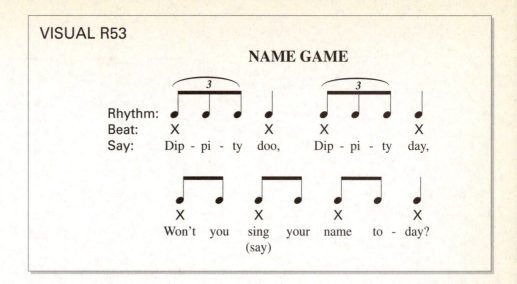

Students should perform, by singing, saying, clapping, or patsching, a variety of rhythmic patterns incorporating the triplet figure, as in **Visual R54.** Remember to say the rhythm syllables when performing the patterns.

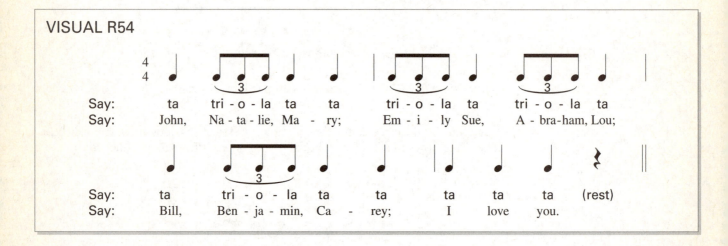

| **Learning** | *Syncopation* (♪♩♪), pronounced "ti ta ti" or "syn-CO-pa," occurs when the accent of a rhythm pattern does not coincide with the normal metrical accent. |

Strategies **NS 5** (Reading syncopated rhythms.)

Choose a rhyme or song containing a good example of syncopation, such as "Old Mother Twitchett." See **Visual R55.**

Old Moth - er Twit - chett had but one eye,_____
X   X   X   X   X   X   X   X

And a long tail which she let fly;_____
X   X   X   X   X   X   X   X

And ev - ery time she went through a gap,
X   X   X   X   X   X   X

A bit of her tail she left in a trap._____
X X   X   X   X   X   X X   X

Display only the words and beat symbol (X) on a visual. Point to the beats while the students clap them and say the rhyme. Repeat this activity, but now ask the students to clap the word rhythms. Place above the words the rhythms for the first two measures of the rhyme, as in **Visual R56.**

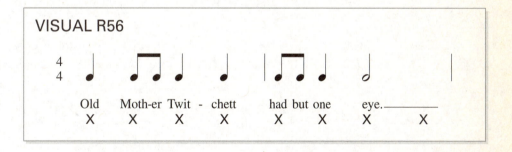

Old Moth-er Twit - chett had but one eye._____
X   X   X   X   X   X   X   X

Say these words again while pointing to each beat. Ask students if they can discover which rhythms are incorrect. Repeat several more times if necessary. Once they've discovered that measure 1 is not correct, have them verbalize why this is so. Ask them how to change measure 1 so that it looks right. Someone will probably suggest

ti ti - i ti ta   ta
Old Moth - er Twit - chett

which is correct. Replace the incorrect measure 1 with the new measure containing the tie. Then perform the measures using both the words of the rhyme and the rhythm syllables. Ask students if they know another way to write ♩‿. They will probably suggest using a quarter note.

Now rewrite measure 1 using the syncopated pattern:

ti ta   ti ta   ta
Old Moth - er Twit - chett

Say the words in measures 1 and 2, using the correct syncopated pattern. Clap the rhythms while saying the rhythm syllables.

In a subsequent lesson, students can discover other syncopated patterns in this rhyme.

 Ask students "Who is Old Mother Twitchett?" (She is a needle.)

Begin with the rhythm pattern. ♪♩♪ is the most common syncopated pattern, but other patterns can also occur in music, such as those found in **Visual R57.** Notice the "short-long-short" nature of syncopation, as highlighted in this visual. Give students many opportunities to say and sing rhymes and songs containing syncopated patterns.

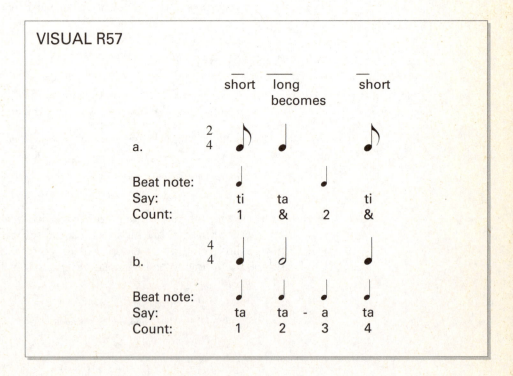

VISUAL R57

Flash cards, such as those in **Visual R58,** can be reproduced on larger cards for drill, to reinforce the use of rhythmic patterns containing ties, triplets, syncopation, and dotted notes.

Students should be encouraged to discover the syncopated patterns in the flash card examples in Visuals R34 and R51. Then, try performing "The Syncopated Rondo" found in **Visual R59.**

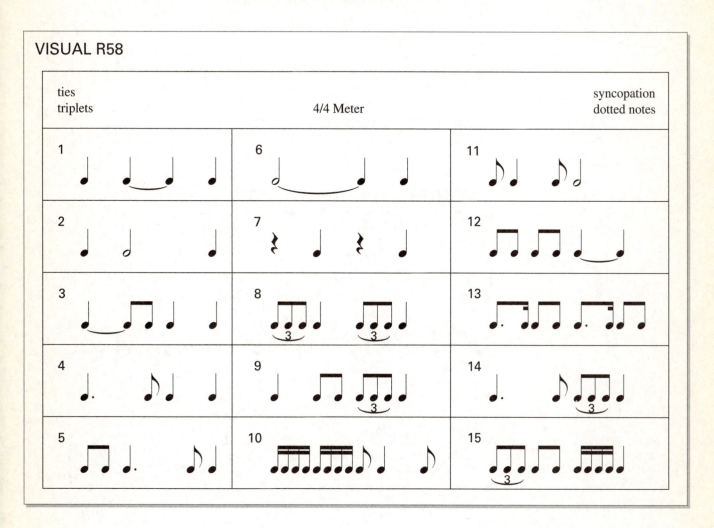

VISUAL R58

FOCUS

Anacrusis (Pick-up)

Learning When musical compositions begin with an incomplete measure of one or more notes, these notes are called an *anacrusis* or *pick-up*. A composition beginning with an anacrusis has an incomplete final measure; the combination of the final measure and the anacrusis equals a complete measure.

Strategies **NS 5** (Identify incomplete measures of notes at the end and beginning of a musical composition.)

Place on the board the rhythm for "The Old Woman Under the Hill," found in **Visual R60.** Perform the rhyme several times, with half the class clapping the dotted-quarter-note beat (♩.) and the other half clapping the rhythms. Ask students how many eighth notes are in the last measure. When they respond "5," ask them how many there should be. Following their response, ask where the sixth beat is. Someone will note the lone eighth note at the very beginning of the piece. Identify this note as the pick-up or anacrusis. Mark the counting for both the anacrusis and the last measure, as in **Visual R60,** noting that the anacrusis, added to the last measure, will form one complete measure.

VISUAL R60

There was an old wo-man lived un-der a hill;

And if she's not gone, she lives there still.

Visual **R61** contains a rhythmic composition beginning with an anacrusis. Have students learn the rhythms well. Then perform the work as a two-, three-, or four-part rhythmic canon, adding body percussion or rhythm instruments. A *rhythmic canon* is a composition in which the same rhythm is performed by different people or groups, each beginning at a different time, as indicated by the numbers 1, 2, 3, and 4.

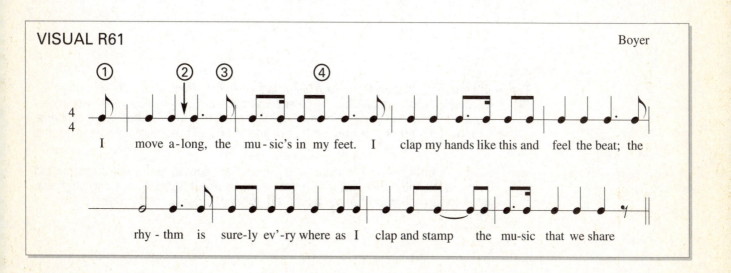

VISUAL R61   Boyer

I move a-long, the mu-sic's in my feet. I clap my hands like this and feel the beat; the

rhy-thm is sure-ly ev'-ry where as I clap and stamp the mu-sic that we share

The following activities can be used for review of rhythmic structures or as motivators for student creativity. Ask students to indicate where there is an anacrusis and to circle the syncopated rhythms in the examples.

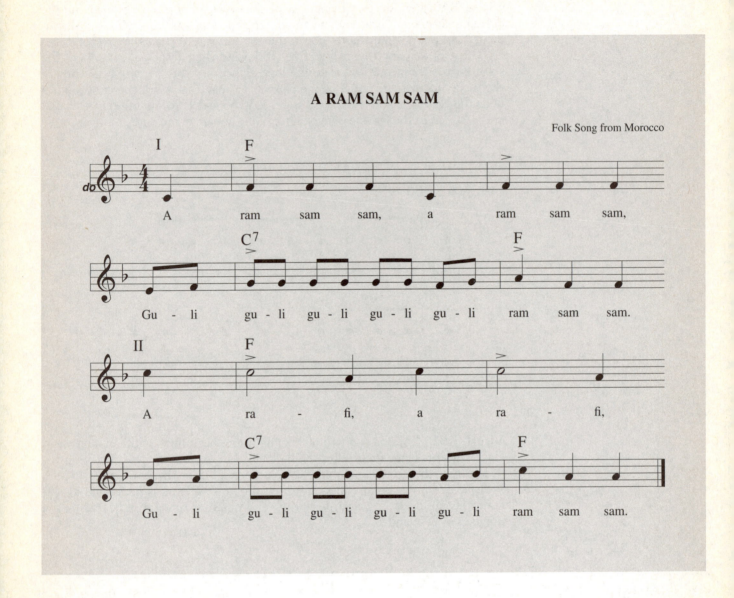

A RAM SAM SAM

Folk Song from Morocco

 Tell students that "A Ram Sam Sam" is a folk song from Morocco, a country located in Northwest Africa. It is a special place because it has a long coastline along the Atlantic Ocean that reaches past the Strait of Gibraltar. Have students find this country on the map and go online to find out more information about it.

Have students analyze "A Ram Sam Sam." They should recognize the accented quarter and half notes that fall on the first beat of each measure. Have students listen to the song and pat the accented notes as they occur throughout the song.

FEBRUARY CELEBRATIONS

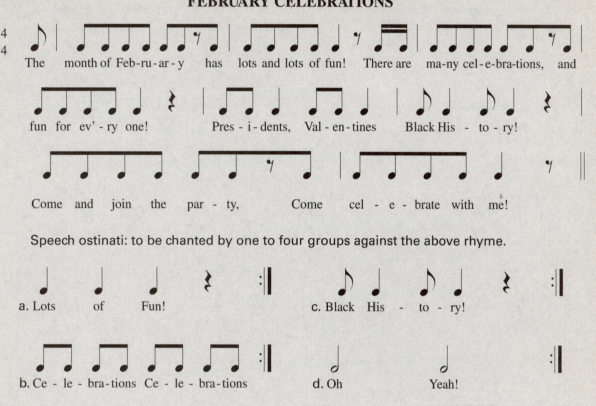

Speech ostinati: to be chanted by one to four groups against the above rhyme.

Styles like hip-hop, disco, rhythm and blues, and jazz contain many syncopated rhythms. The following raps have been widely accepted by upper elementary school students in an all-inclusive setting. Have students analyze the pieces before performing them. Tell them to point to the anacrusis. Challenge them to circle the many examples of syncopation found in these two pieces.

JUST GIMME THE BEAT

Boyer

WE'VE GOT TO CHANGE

Rene Boyer

We've got to change, Yeah! We've got to change! Yo! We've got to

change our way of do-ing things it helps us grow! We've got to change! Yeah! We've got to

change Yo! We've got to change our way of do-ing things This we know!

Rhy-thm is a good thing. It helps us move and sway! But it's the syn-co-pa-tion that

helps to make our day! Syn-co-pa-ta-ta. Syn-co-pa ti-ti ta.

Syn-co-pa ti-ri-ti-ri ta. Ta, ta, ta! Our gran-nies sang it one way, so

ma-ny years a-go. But now it's time for us to change this Do Re Mi Fa So! Some-

times we sing up high! Some times we sing down low. There's noth-ing wrong with eith-er way.

WE'VE GOT TO CHANGE

So Fa Mi Re Do, We've got to change, Yeah! We've got to change! Yo! We've got to

change our way of do-ing things it helps us grow! We've got to change! Yeah! We've got to

change Yo! We've got to change our way of do-ing things, it helps us grow!

We just love our four four time, it keeps us on the beat! But some-times ev'-ry now and then six

eight is might-y sweet! One two three four five six! One two and three four five six!

One two three four five six! Just watch us sway! One two three four five six!

One two and three four five six! One two three four five six! Change is O-Kay!

 Have students create their own syncopated ostinato patterns to accompany, "We've Got to Change."

ADDITIONAL RHYMES FOR RHYTHM ACTIVITIES

One little flower, one little bee.
One little blue bird, high in the tree.
One little brown bear smiling at me.
One is the number I like, you see.

Five little monkeys jumping on the bed.
One fell off and bumped his head.
Mama called the doctor and the doctor said,
"No more monkeys jumping on the bed!"

Red and yellow, blue and green,
Which of these have I not seen?
Purple, orange, black and white,
I must choose the one that's right.

Buenos dias, como estas? Good
day and how are you?
Estoy bien, gracias
I'm fine-------y tu?

Cobbler Cobbler mend my shoe
Give it one stitch, give it two.
Give it three stitch, give it four,
If it needs it, give it more.

Lanterns, lanterns, shining bright.
Lighting paths throughout the night
Stars of bamboo, moon-cakes too.
A special time for me and you.

Mary had a little lamb
Little lamb, little lamb
Mary had a little lamb its
Fleece was white as snow.

Jack and Jill went up the hill
To fetch a pail of water.
Jack fell down and broke his crown
And Jill came tumbling after.

Dale, dale, dale
No pierdas el tino;
Mide la distancia
Que hay en al campo.

Diddle Diddle Dumpling, My son John
Went to bed with his stockings on
One shoe off and one shoe on.
Diddle Diddle Dumpling, My son John.

Fudge, Fudge call the judge
Mama's got a baby
Not a boy, not a girl,
Just a plain old baby.

INTRODUCING THE STRUCTURAL COMPONENTS OF RHYTHM

Suggested Sequencing by Grade Level

Kindergarten

1. sound and silence
2. steady beat
3. short and long sounds

Grade One

1. ♩ ♫ ♩
2. accent
3. 2/4 meter
4. bar line, measure, double bar
5. ostinato

Grade Two

1. tied notes
2. ♩ -
3. 4/4 meter

Grade Three

1. ♬♬
2. ♫♫ and ♫
3. 3/4 meter
4. ○ -
5. ♩
6. ♪♩♪ = syncopation

Grade Four

1. ♩♪ and ♪♩
2. anacrusis (pick-up)
3. 6/8 meter
4. ♪
5. ♩♩♩ and ♪♩♪ = more difficult syncopation

Grade Five

1. ♫♫ and ♫
2. ♪

Grade Six

1. triplet
2. ¢ meter

WRITTEN AND PERFORMANCE-RELATED ASSESSMENTS THROUGH COOPERATIVE LEARNING ACTIVITIES: RHYTHM NS 2, 4, 5, 7

1. Give each group a different rhyme. Students read through the rhyme to discover on which syllables the beat initially falls; the beat symbol (X) is placed under those syllables. Students then work out the rhythms of the words and place them above each syllable. After the teacher checks their solutions, students practice together the rhythms of the rhyme on instruments of their choice. It may be helpful if they chant the rhythm syllables while performing the rhythms. **NS 5, 7**
2. Give each group a worksheet with a series of four-beat rhythm patterns on the left side of the page and a list of first lines of familiar songs or rhymes on the right. Students must match each rhythm pattern to the words having the same pattern. When finished, each student in the group should clap the rhythms correctly and say the rhythm syllables for each rhythm pattern. **NS 5, 7**
3. Give students a list of rhythm patterns. They must discover what familiar rhyme or song uses each pattern in its opening phrase. **NS 5, 7**

4. Give each group a different rhyme in 2/4, 3/4, or 4/4 meter. Students must
   a. mark the accents in each phrase and decide what time signature to place at the beginning of the rhyme.
   b. place the bar lines.
   c. number each beat of the rhyme.
   d. clap the rhythms while counting aloud each beat. **NS 5, 7**
5. Give each group Visual R32. The group must find at least one additional word to place under each rhythm pattern in every category. **NS 5, 7**
6. Give each group a set of flash cards containing different combinations of known rhythms. Each card contains a four-beat pattern. Every student must be able to clap the rhythms on each card while saying the rhythm syllables. **NS 5, 7**
7. Distribute six blank flash cards, a felt marker, a worksheet, and a pencil to each group. Group members are to create six flash cards, each containing four beats. Every card should contain one dotted note: ♩·, ♪·, or ♩· ♪, plus whatever other notes/rests are chosen to complete the four beats (ex.: ♩· ♪ ♫ ♩ ♩). Patterns should be written on the worksheet first and checked by the teacher before members draw them on the cards. When the cards are completed, each group member should correctly clap the rhythm pattern on each card while saying the rhythm syllables. (This activity can be used with other rhythm combinations such as ♬♬, ♫♫, and ♫♫, or ♬♬, ♩· ♪, and ♫·.) On another day, after cards are completed, each group's cards can be exchanged with those of another group to use in clapping and verbalizing. **NS 5, 7**
8. Each group must create four measures of rhythms within changing meters. 2/4 and 3/4, 3/4 and 4/4, or 2/4 and 4/4 are assigned to each group. When finished, the group should be able to perform the rhythm on rhythm instruments while saying the rhythm syllables or words set to the rhythms. **NS 2, 4, 5, 7**
9. Assign several rhythm patterns in Visual R54 to each group. Group members must place the numbers 1 through 4 on the beats where they occur. Members should decide how to perform together each pattern by stamping, patching, clapping, and/or snapping. After practicing its routines, the group performs its rhythms for the class while counting aloud the beat numbers. **NS 5, 7**

CHAPTER 3

Teaching Melody to Children

INTRODUCTION

A *melody* consists of a linear succession of sounds and silences ordered in time. By its very nature, melody cannot be separated from rhythm. Each musical sound in a melody has two fundamental qualities: pitch and duration. When used in succession, pitch-plus-duration values form melodies.

When pitches change in a melody, they give the melody direction, sometimes moving upward, sometimes moving downward, and other times staying the same. The upward and downward motion of a melody, the ease or tension that results when a melody changes direction, and the rate of change in a melody's direction contribute to the expressiveness of the melodic line.

The concept of the nature of a melody has changed over the centuries to encompass a variety of characteristics. Although early composers of Western music wrote melodies that were unaccompanied and rhythmically free, without bar lines and measures, composers today are much more diversified in their approach to the melodic line. Some melodies may be smooth and connected, whereas others tend to be irregular and unpredictable. For most of us, however, melody will always be the most memorable element in the music we love— the "tune."

> —*It is the melody which is the charm of the music,*
> *and it is that which is most difficult to produce.*
> *The invention of a fine melody is a work of genius.*
> —*Joseph Haydn*

FOCUS

Pitch: High/Low

Learning	Pitch is the relative highness or lowness of a musical sound. Sounds in our environment are high, medium, low, or the same in relation to one another.

Strategies **NS 6** (Listening to, analyzing, and describing environmental sounds.)

Identify environmental sounds that are high.

Bird chirping	Garbage truck backing up	Whistling kettle	Hooting owl

Identify sounds in the environment that are low.

Growling lion	Quacking duck	Croaking frog	Girl blowing a tuba
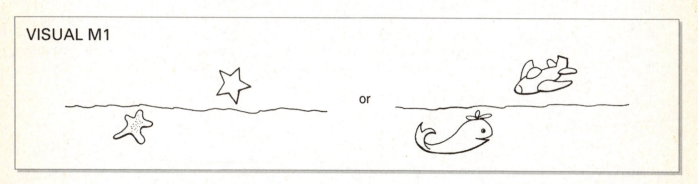			

Have students explore and identify extreme highs and lows of melodic instruments, such as the piano, resonator bells, or xylophone.

Draw a wavy line on the board to represent the ocean. When students hear a high sound, they can place a star in the sky; when they hear a low sound, they can put a starfish in the ocean, as in **Visual M1**. Other visuals, such as a plane or whale, could be used. This activity can also be reversed. When a student places a star in the sky, another student can play a high sound on a melody instrument.

VISUAL M1

or

Children can express their awareness of high and low sounds through body movements such as standing on tiptoe or reaching upward when they hear high sounds and crouching down low when they hear low sounds.

Once students can identify the highs and lows of a single instrument, such as the piano, expand their listening abilities by playing different instruments that are either high or low, for example, the flute versus the tuba, or the soprano glockenspiel versus the bass xylophone.

 Creative dramas can be developed to help students identify and manipulate high, medium, and low sounds. Select stories like *The Three Little Pigs, The Three Billy Goats Gruff*, and *The Three Bears* for the children to either read and/ or act out.

Assign a high, medium, or low voice to each of the characters in the story. Then, tell students to use their voices accordingly. For example, students can choose to use a low voice for Papa Bear, a medium voice for Mama Bear, and a high voice for Baby Bear in *The Three Bears*.

FOCUS

Staff

Learning   Pitches are usually represented by symbols called *notes*, which are placed on a staff. A *staff* consists of five parallel lines and four spaces.

Strategies **NS 5** (Reading and notating music on a staff.)

Draw a staff on the chalkboard and number the lines and spaces from bottom to top as in **Visual M2**. The first line is always the bottom line, representing the lowest pitch on the staff.

VISUAL M2

5th line	
	4th space
4th line	
	3rd space
3rd line	
	2nd space
2nd line	
	1st space
1st line	

Provide multiple experiences for students to become familiar with the staff by having them place notes on designated lines and spaces. The teacher may also reverse this procedure by having students identify notes already placed on the staff, as in **Visual M3.** Be sure that students are aware that, when recording a series of notes, the notes move from left to right on the staff, just as their printing or writing moves from left to right on the page.

VISUAL M3

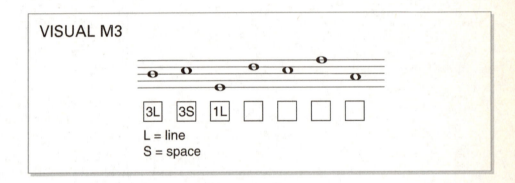

3L 3S 1L ☐ ☐ ☐ ☐

L = line
S = space

 Students should be made aware that reading music is similar to reading words on a page. Musical notation, like words, is read from left to right.

Learning Because a staff has only five lines and four spaces where a pitch can be placed, extra lines are often added above and below the staff to accommodate additional pitches. These lines are called *ledger lines.*

Strategies **NS 5** (Reading and notating ledger lines.)

Ledger lines are taught to children only as they are needed. The manner in which they ascend and descend is presented in **Visual M4** as a source of needed information for the adult learner at this point. Note that a ledger line is slightly wider than the width of a note head. Remember that the lowest pitch is always on the lowest ledger line.

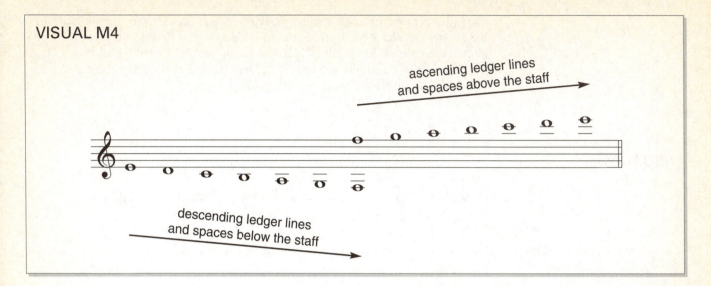

ascending ledger lines
and spaces above the staff

descending ledger lines
and spaces below the staff

Ledger lines that extend far beyond the staff can be notated more simply by using 8va, the common abbreviation for 8 *ottava*, rather than multiple ledger lines. 8va means that the notes should be played eight tones (an *octave*) higher or lower than written. See **Visual M5.**

VISUAL M5

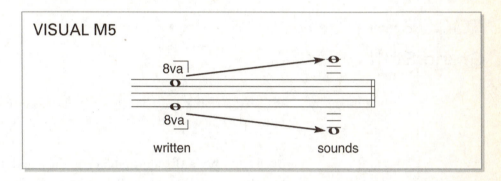

8va

8va

written   sounds

FOCUS

Clef Signs

Learning The placement of a *clef sign* on the far left side of a staff indicates the relative highness or lowness of pitches. A *treble clef sign* usually denotes pitches that are considered high in contrast to the *bass clef sign*, which usually denotes lower pitches.

Strategies **NS 5** (Reading and notating music using treble and bass clef signs.)

Show the students a treble or a bass clef sign, depending on which is being taught. Identify the clef sign, as in **Visual M6.**

VISUAL M6

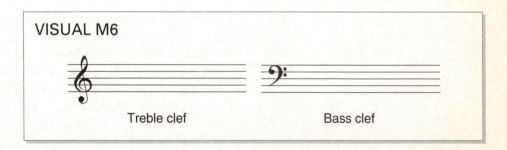

Treble clef   Bass clef

Carefully demonstrate for students a step-by-step procedure for drawing the treble or the bass clef sign, as in **Visual M7.** Because the final scroll movement encircles the second line (called "G"), the treble clef is often referred to as G *clef.* The bass clef is often referred to as F *clef* because the two dots to the right of the bass clef sign are placed on either side of the F line.

VISUAL M7

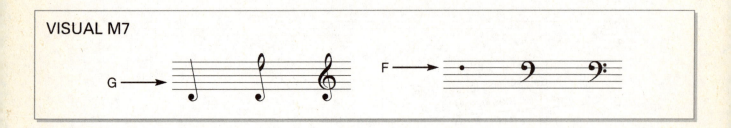

Students should practice drawing treble and bass clef signs.

The treble and the bass clefs are presented here together. It should be noted, however, that the bass clef is usually not presented to children until the upper grades.

FOCUS

Grand Staff

Learning	When the treble and bass clefs are placed on two staves joined by a vertical line and a brace at the left, the *grand staff* is formed.

Strategies **NS 5** (Reading pitches on the grand staff.)

Because the bass clef is usually taught to children in the upper grades, the grand staff, as seen in **Visual M8,** would also be presented to older children.

VISUAL M8

The grand staff is used for the notation of keyboard music and is useful for other purposes, because it is capable of representing a great range of pitches. The treble clef sign, however, is the most commonly used clef sign in children's song literature. Therefore it is emphasized in the strategies that follow.

The note placed on the first ledger line above the bass staff represents the same pitch as the note placed on the first ledger line below the treble staff. This note is called *Middle* C. Middle C derives its name from its location approximately in the middle of the grand staff.

FOCUS

Musical Alphabet

Learning
With the addition of the treble clef sign to the staff, pitches can now be assigned specific names. Their names will change, however, if a clef sign other than the treble clef is used.

Pitches take their name from the first seven letters of the alphabet: A, B, C, D, E, F, G. These seven letters are known as the *musical alphabet*.

Strategies **NS 1, 5** (Sing a folk song. Read pitches on treble clef. Analyzing & describing the musical alphabet.)

Draw a staff. Explain to the students that each line and space has its own name, taken from the first seven letters of the alphabet. Show these letters, as in **Visual M9.** Now place the treble clef on the staff and remind students that this clef always tells us where "G" can be located. Sing the song "Hot Cross Buns." Under the staff write the first three words of the song and place the note G above the word "cross." Again, see Visual M9.

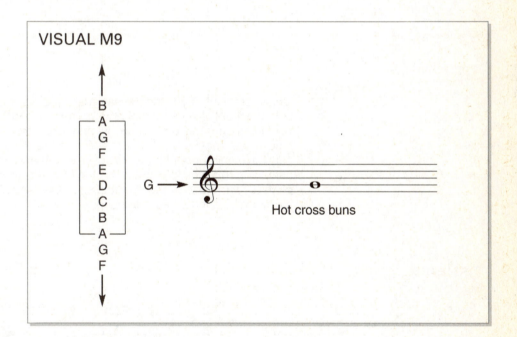

VISUAL M9

Hot cross buns

Have students check out the history of "Hot Cross Buns." The bun refers to the spiced English bun associated with Good Friday.

If the word "cross" is sung on G, then there are only two more pitches to learn. Sing the three pitches for "hot cross buns" and ask students if the pitch for "buns" is higher or lower than the pitch for "cross." Because it is just a little lower, its name will be the alphabet letter that comes just before G; that is, its name is F. This can easily be seen by checking the alphabet ladder to the left of the staff. Place F on the staff. Sing the three pitches for "hot cross buns" one more time. Ask students if the pitch for "hot" is higher or lower than the pitch for "cross." The students will know it is a little bit higher. By checking the alphabet ladder again, the students will be able to identify the pitch for "hot" as "A." Sing just the first three pitches of the song again, but instead of singing the words, have the students sing the alphabet names: A, G, F.

On another day, provide students with the whole song and work out the rest of the pitches, as in **Visual M10.** Then, sing both the song words and the alphabet names of the pitches.

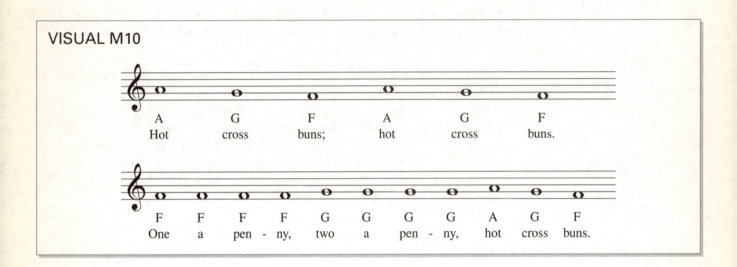

VISUAL M10

A   G   F   A   G   F
Hot   cross   buns;   hot   cross   buns.

F   F   F   F   G   G   G   G   A   G   F
One   a   pen - ny,   two   a   pen - ny,   hot   cross   buns.

 On subsequent days, use the same song to discover the location of the pitches in the rest of the musical alphabet. See **Visual M11.** Sing "Hot Cross Buns" beginning on B (example b below) and, later, on E (example c below). Because students already know the pitches for "cross" and "buns" in example b, they only have one more pitch to discover—B. In example c, all three pitches must be named. In this example students should notice that lines can be added—for the pitch C—if more than the five staff lines are needed. At this time, the ledger line for middle C should be introduced.

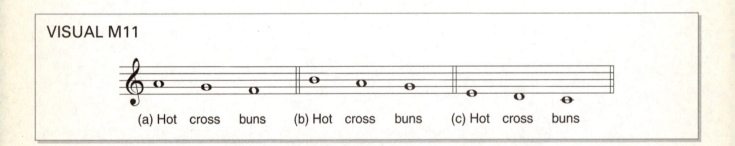

VISUAL M11

(a) Hot cross buns   (b) Hot cross buns   (c) Hot cross buns

Now the musical alphabet is complete. All seven letters have been used.

Students need to sing and play many songs containing the musical alphabet. One of the best ways to learn to read pitches and rhythms from a staff is through the playing of the soprano recorder. At this point, adult students may want to parallel their learning of melodic concepts by turning to Chapter 10 on "Playing Musical Instruments" and learning to play the recorder by proceeding through the sequence provided.

Once students have learned the musical alphabet—often referred to as *absolute pitch names*—a chart similar to that in **Visual M12** can be posted. This chart helps students realize that once the seven letters of the musical alphabet have been used, they are repeated over and over again.

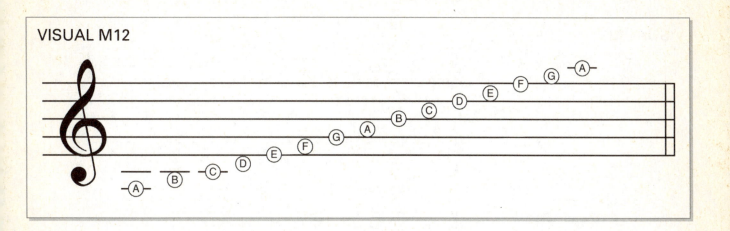

VISUAL M12

Help students become comfortable with the musical alphabet by providing experiences that reinforce it. Learning the musical alphabet in both its forward and backward sequences should be stressed. Asking students questions similar to these may be helpful:

What comes after D?
What comes before F?
What comes after G?
What comes before A?

Some teachers find that learning key words or phrases can help students remember the names of the lines and spaces of the staff. See **Visual M13.**

$1 + 2 = 3$ An understanding of the relative position of objects in the environment is important when it comes to not only musical notation on a staff, but also "geometry." Words and phrases like *up, down, over, under, top, bottom, in front of* and *behind* are relative to both fields: music and math.

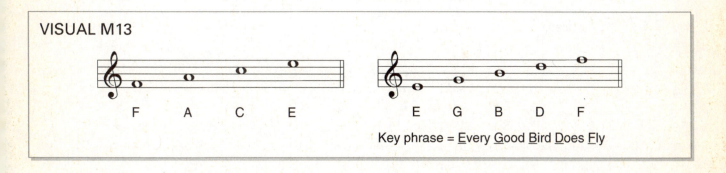

VISUAL M13

F A C E   E G B D F

Key phrase = <u>E</u>very <u>G</u>ood <u>B</u>ird <u>D</u>oes <u>F</u>ly

Have students create other key phrases that can help reinforce the names of lines and spaces.

Provide a number of worksheets containing exercises for naming only spaces and only lines. Worksheets containing a combination of lines and spaces should follow. Once students have facility in naming notes placed on the staff, the naming of ledger lines should be added. Examples are provided in **Visual M14.**

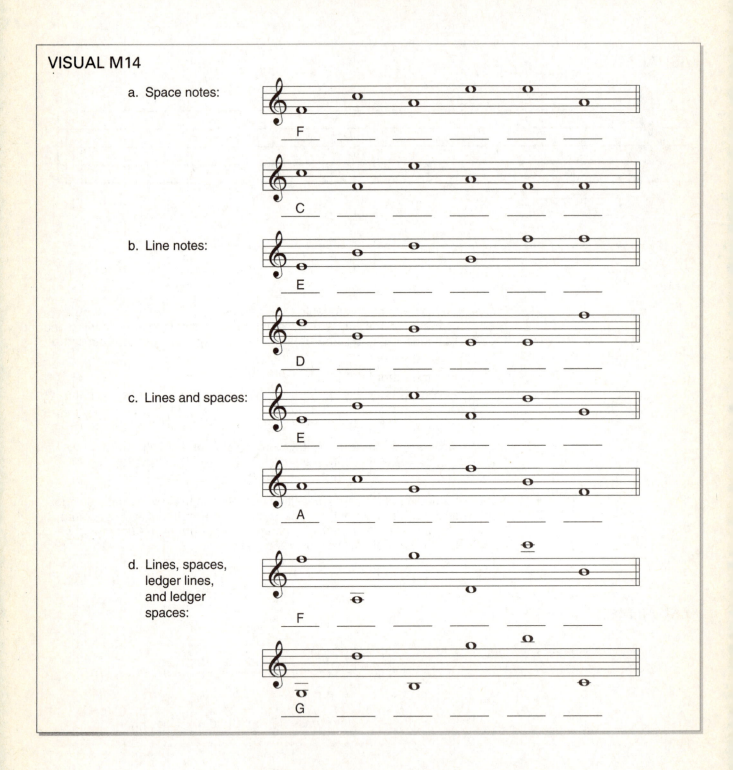

VISUAL M14

a. Space notes:

b. Line notes:

c. Lines and spaces:

d. Lines, spaces, ledger lines, and ledger spaces:

Students often find it helpful to name groups of notes that spell words, such as those in **Visual M15.**

F A C E ☐ ☐ ☐ ☐ ☐ ☐

☐ ☐ ☐ ☐ ☐ ☐ ☐ ☐ ☐ ☐ ☐ ☐ ☐

FOCUS

Note Stems

Learning   When note heads with stems are placed on the staff, special rules must be followed. When the note head is placed on the third line or above, its stem must be placed downward to the left of the note head. When the note head is below the third line, the stem must extend upward to the right of the note head. The direction of all stems, when notes are beamed or connected to one another, is determined by the note farthest from the third line.

Strategies **NS 5** (Reading and writing notation on a staff.)

Provide an example of a staff containing a series of notes whose stems are correctly placed according to the rules stated above. See **Visual M16.**

VISUAL M16

Have students take turns going to the board to place stems on note heads provided by the teacher, as in **Visual M17.**

VISUAL M17

Provide examples of notes that have been beamed, as in **Visual M18.** Provide opportunities for students to create combinations of beamed note groupings.

VISUAL M18

Have students examine the placement of stems on note heads found in simple song literature.

FOCUS

Unorganized and Organized Pitches

Learning　When musical ideas are created by adding rhythms to a linear succession of pitches and rests, a *melody* results.

Strategies **NS 5** (Reading and notating music.)

Show students the difference between unorganized and organized pitches, as in **Visual M19.**

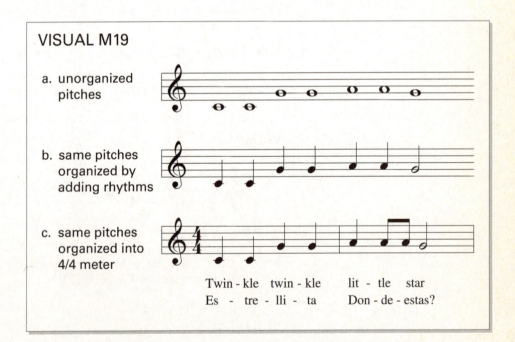

VISUAL M19

a. unorganized pitches

b. same pitches organized by adding rhythms

c. same pitches organized into 4/4 meter

Twin - kle twin - kle　lit - tle star
Es - tre - lli - ta　Don - de - estas?

Provide experiences for students to manipulate pitches to form melodies. Have students study the unorganized linear succession of pitches as presented in **Visual M20.** The teacher may wish to have the entire class sing or play the pitches on a melody instrument until they discover the name of the song (Frère

Jacques). After students realize the name of the song, have them organize the pitches into a melody by changing the open note heads to appropriate rhythm symbols and adding bar lines and a time signature.

VISUAL M20

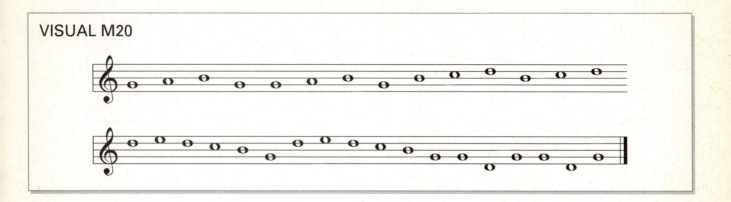

FOCUS

Contour

Learning   *Contour* is the direction or shape of a melody.

Strategies **NS 5** (Reading and notating music.)

Sitting in a circle, students should take turns vocalizing their names in a creative manner. The rest of the class should immediately repeat the name, using the same voice inflections. Simultaneously, the students should trace in the air the contour of the name. When the students are ready, the teacher—and later the students themselves—should reproduce the contours on a visual, as in **Visual M21.**

VISUAL M21

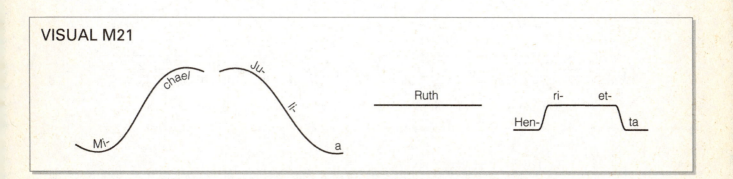

Be sure to emphasize that contours progress upward, downward, or stay the same. Using flash cards containing a variety of contours, have students vocalize the contours using improvised neutral sounds, words, or phrases, as in **Visual M22.** Flash cards can be turned in any direction to create additional contours.

VISUAL M22

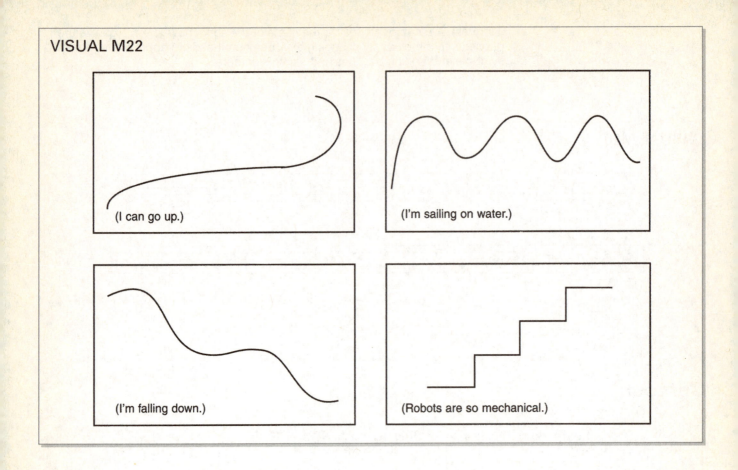

(I can go up.)

(I'm sailing on water.)

(I'm falling down.)

(Robots are so mechanical.)

Have students move their hands to the contours of familiar songs, such as "Go to Sleep," demonstrated in **Visual M23.**

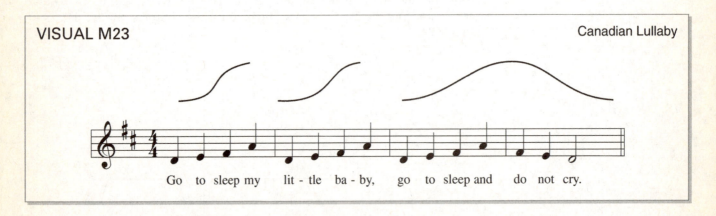

VISUAL M23   Canadian Lullaby

Go to sleep my lit - tle ba - by, go to sleep and do not cry.

Use very short phrases for students to sing and demonstrate contour, such as "Row, Row, Row Your Boat." [*Row Row Row your boat.*] They will notice that the first 3 pitches are exactly the same.

Demonstrate an alternative way of showing contour by lining a melody, reproducing more exactly the direction of the line and the relative length of time each note is held, as in **Visual M24.**

Hot ____   hot ____   __ __ __ __   hot ____

cross _____   cross _____ __ __ __ __   two - a - pen - ny,   cross _____

     buns,   buns,   one - a - pen - ny,   buns.

Have students record or write down a lined pattern to a familiar song while the class sings it. The finished product might resemble that in **Visual M25.**

VISUAL M25

"Mary Had a Little Lamb"

Provide the class with the contour of a "mystery song" that they should be able to identify. Later, have students challenge the class in identifying the contour of a song they write out.

Students should create their own contours for members of the class to reproduce vocally or on a melodic instrument. Students can also do interpretive movement to different contours.

FOCUS

Steps, Skips, Repeated Notes, and Leaps

Learning   Pitches within a melody move by steps, skips, repetition, and leaps. Pitches step when they move from line to adjacent space, or space to adjacent line on the staff; pitches *skip* when they move from line to adjacent line, or space to adjacent space. *Repetition* results when pitches stay on the same line or space of the staff. Anything larger than a skip is called a *leap.*

Strategies   **NS 5** (Reading music.)

Create a visual that shows notes that step, skip, repeat, or leap as in **Visual M26.**

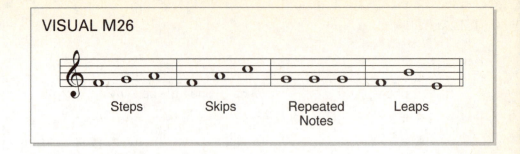

VISUAL M26

Steps   Skips   Repeated Notes   Leaps

Reinforce students' understanding of how melodies move by creating flash cards or PowerPoint presentations containing many examples of steps, skips, repeated notes, and leaps for students to identify, as in **Visual M27.** Students should sing or play the examples on a melodic instrument so that they identify the symbols with the sounds.

VISUAL M27

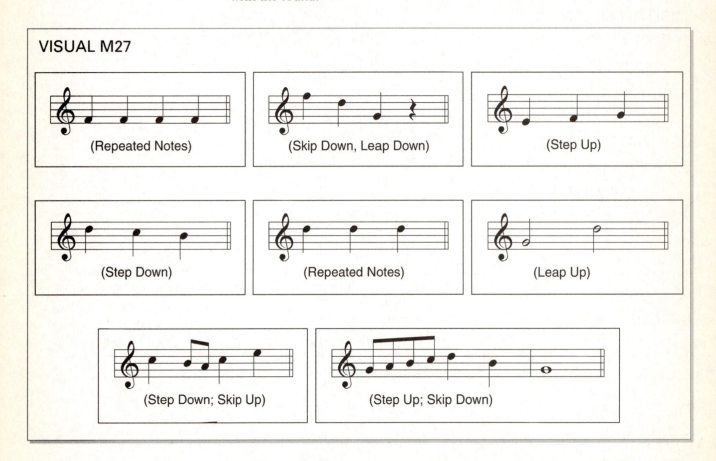

(Repeated Notes)

(Skip Down, Leap Down)

(Step Up)

(Step Down)

(Repeated Notes)

(Leap Up)

(Step Down; Skip Up)

(Step Up; Skip Down)

Students should have many opportunities to identify a mixture of steps, skips, repeated notes and leaps found in their song literature. An approach to reinforcing these skills is provided in **Visual M28.** Students should verbalize how the song moves as shown in the visual.

B = begin   SU = step up   LU = leap up
SD = step down   SkU = skip up   LD = leap down
R = repeat   SkD = skip down

CHURCH BELLS

Boyer

B   R   R   SD   R   R   SD   R   R   SD

Lis - ten,   oh   lis - ten,   now   what   do   you   hear?

SD   R   R   SD   R   R   SD   R   R   SD

Church   bells   are   ring - ing;   they   sound   loud   and   clear.

TOUCH A STAR

Boyer

B   R   R   SU   R   R   SU   R   R   SU

Here   we   go   fly - ing   so   high   in   the   sky;

SU   R   R   SU   R   R   SU   R   R   SU

Up   to   the   stars   we   go,   just   you   and   I.

MOON SHINE

Boyer

B   R   R   R   R   R   R   R   R   R   LU

The   moon   when   it's   shin - ing,   so   round   and   so   high,

R   R   R   R   R   LD   R   R   LU   R   R   LU

Is   a   Ja - pa - nese   lan - tern,   hung   up   in   the   sky.

DANCING LEAVES

Rozmajzl

B   R   SD   R   SD   SkU   LD   R   SD   SU   SkD   SkD   SU   SkD   SU

Fall-ing   leaves   come   twirl-ing   down,   like   bal - le - ri - nas   whirl-ing   'round.

FOCUS

Melodic Intervals

Learning   A *melodic interval* is the distance in pitch between two notes sounded consecutively. Melodies contain a succession of melodic intervals.

Strategies **NS 5** (Reading melodic intervals.)

Show the main intervals used within a melody or display them on a visual, as in **Visual M29.**

VISUAL M29

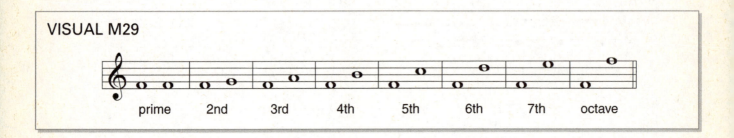

prime   2nd   3rd   4th   5th   6th   7th   octave

Intervals are named by counting the number of lines and spaces involved in the interval. Both the lower and the upper notes are part of the interval and must be included in the count. Call the lower note "1"; then count each line and space, ending with the upper note, as in **Visual M30.**

VISUAL M30

interval of a 6th

Have students study their song literature to identify the intervals each song contains, as in **Visual M31.**

ESTRELLITA
(TWINKLE, TWINKLE LITTLE STAR)

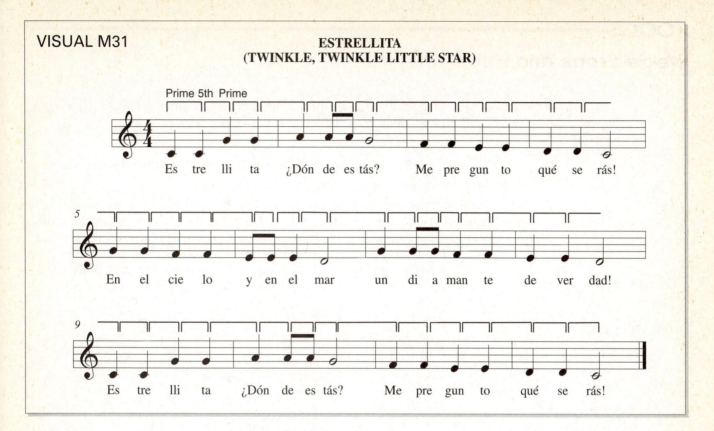

Es tre lli ta ¿Dón de es tás? Me pre gun to qué se rás!

En el cie lo y en el mar un di a man te de ver dad!

Es tre lli ta ¿Dón de es tás? Me pre gun to qué se rás!

Translation:

Little Star, Where are you?
I wonder what you are.
In the sky and in the sea,
One real diamond
Little Star, where are you?

To reinforce the learning of melodic intervals, provide worksheets, as in **Visual M32.** Each measure in this visual can be made into a flash card. Students should be challenged to play these intervals on melodic instruments.

Identify each interval:

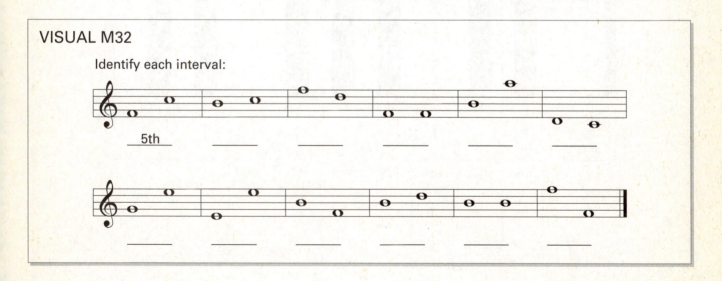

5th

FOCUS

Whole Steps and Half Steps

Learning The *half step* is the smallest interval used in most of the music of Western civilization. Two half steps combine to make a *whole step*.

Strategies **NS 2, 5** (Reading half and whole steps and playing them on an instrument.)

Place on a staff a series of adjacent notes, as in **Visual M33.** Each note appears to be equidistant from the preceding and the following note. In this example, the notes on the staff are deceptive; between the notes E and F, and B and C, there is a half step, whereas between all other adjacent notes there is a whole step. When notes are placed on the staff in alphabetical sequence—either ascending or descending—the succession is said to be stepwise, or *diatonic*. Visual M33 is a *diatonic sequence*.

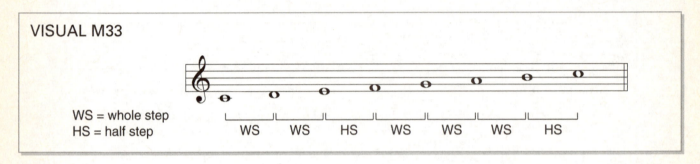

VISUAL M33

WS = whole step
HS = half step

Provide a picture of a section of a piano keyboard. The white keys on the piano are a good example of a diatonic sequence. Show the relationship of the diatonic white keys to the diatonic series on the staff. See **Visual M34.**

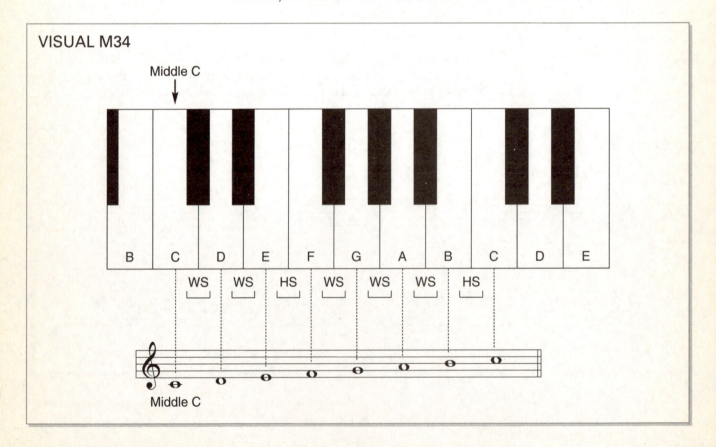

VISUAL M34

Middle C

Students should play on a piano or keyboard instrument each of the half and whole steps in the diatonic series. Middle C is the white key directly to the left of two black keys located in the middle of the piano keyboard.

Play a variety of whole steps and half steps; have students echo each interval vocally after it is played.

Provide students with opportunities to identify half steps and whole steps, as in **Visual M35.** The measures in Visual M35 can also be made into flash cards to provide another means for learning intervals. These melodic intervals should be sung and played on melodic instruments.

VISUAL M35

Identify each progression as half step (HS) or whole step (WS).

WS

| 1 + 2 = 3 | The **measurement** of half steps and whole steps in music is important. Students should be made aware that in math class, they will also have to compare the attributes of objects; which is bigger, lighter, heavier, taller, etc. In music class, on the other hand, half steps and whole steps form intervals. Intervals are measuring devices in music. |

FOCUS

Accidentals

Learning   *Accidentals* are symbols that can be applied to any pitch to alter it in some way. There are three basic accidentals: a *sharp* (♯) raises the pitch of a note a half step; a *flat* (♭) lowers the pitch of a note a half step; a *natural* (♮) cancels a previous sharp or flat.

Strategies **NS 5, 6** (Reading and notating music with accidentals. Analyzing and describing accidentals.)

Have students sing a song they know well, such as "Bounce High, Bounce Low." Provide a visual of the song, as in **Visual M36.**

VISUAL M36

Bounce   high,   bounce   low,   Bounce the ball to   Shi - loh.

Now play the song on a melody instrument, exactly as it appears on the visual. Ask the students if the song sounds correct. Sing and play the song again, so that the problem note F can be identified. Ask students if F should be played higher or lower. After their "high" response, show how a note can be raised one half step higher by placing a sharp sign (♯) to the left of the note, as in **Visual M37.**

VISUAL M37

Traditional

Bounce   high,   bounce   low,   Bounce the   ball   to   Shi - loh.

Choose other songs to demonstrate how to lower a pitch one half step, by placing a flat (♭) to the left of the note; demonstrate how a natural sign (♮) will cancel either a sharp or a flat.

Provide visual experiences that demonstrate the effect that an accidental has when placed to the left of any pitch on a staff. Make accessible a picture of a piano keyboard that has each key name clearly marked. Underneath the picture place a staff containing each note that directly correlates with each key on the piano as in **Visual M38.**

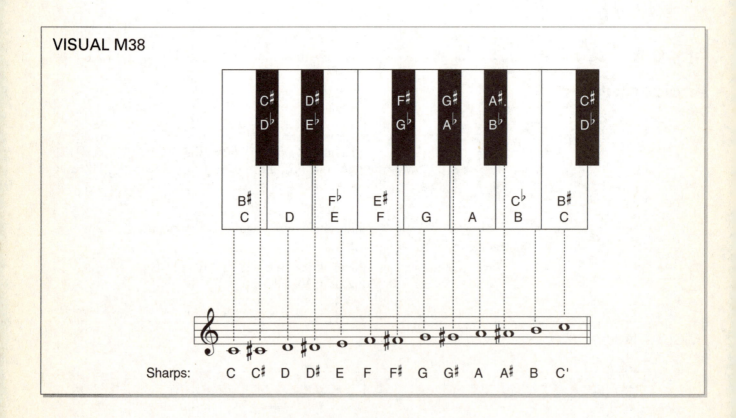

VISUAL M38

Explain that when a series of notes progresses from high to low, flats rather than sharps are used, as in **Visual M39.**

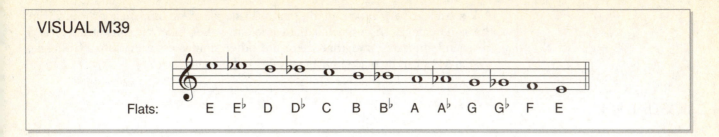

Flats: E E♭ D D♭ C B B♭ A A♭ G G♭ F E

Have students identify notes altered by sharps, flats, and natural signs. See **Visual M40** for a sample worksheet. Note that when identifying an altered note, the accidental is placed to the right of the note name: A♯, B♭, C♮. The measures in Visual M40 may also be reproduced as flash cards.

VISUAL M40

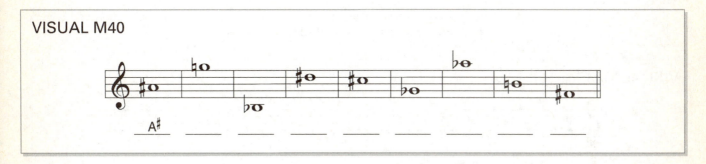

A♯ _____ _____ _____ _____ _____ _____ _____ _____

Provide some measures containing examples of notes that have been altered by accidentals, as in **Visual M41.** Note that accidentals remain in effect throughout the measure in which they occur; they are automatically cancelled (no natural sign needed) by a bar line. The only exception to this rule occurs when an altered note is tied across a bar line. The accidental remains in effect for the length of the tied note.

VISUAL M41

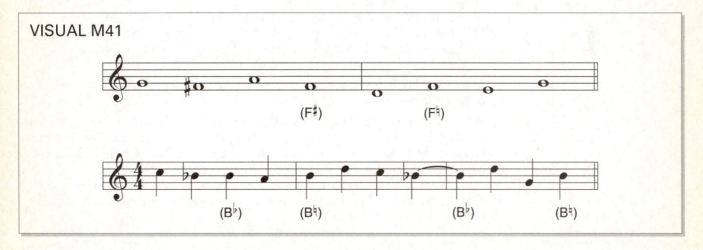

FOCUS

Enharmonic Equivalents

Learning When two pitches have the same sound but are written with different letter names, these pitches are called *enharmonic*.

Strategies **NS 5, 6** (Reading and notating music using enharmonic note spellings. Analyzing and describing music.)

Ask a student to play F♯ on the piano. Have a second student play G♭ within the same octave. Discuss what is heard. Once the students realize that F♯ and G♭ sound the same and that there are other similar combinations of pitches, **Visual M42** can be placed on a chart or on the board.

VISUAL M42

Enharmonic pitches

Have students write the enharmonic equivalents of designated pitches. A worksheet similar to that in **Visual M43** can be used.

VISUAL M43

FOCUS

Major Scales and Key Signatures

Learning A *scale* is an orderly ascending or descending arrangement of pitches within the limits of an octave. A *major scale* is composed of the following whole- and half-step relationships: W W H W W W H. A major scale can be built on any pitch. The starting pitch gives the scale its name and is known as the *key note*.

Strategies **NS 2, 5** (Sing songs, play scales on a keyboard instrument, analyze major scales in music.)

Sing a familiar song using the major scale, such as "Touch a Star," found in Visual M28. Show how this song uses all the tones of a major scale beginning on C. As students say each tone, draw it on a staff, as in **Visual M44**. Analyze and label the half- and whole-step relationships occurring between the notes of the scale. Point out that half steps always occur between the scale degrees of 3 and 4, and 7 and 8 in a major scale. Have students sing the letter names of the scale, both ascending and descending.

VISUAL M44

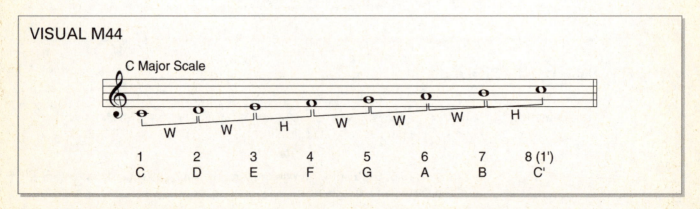

On the keyboard, the white keys from C to C' represent a major scale. Students can "build" a human scale by representing the keys contained in an octave of the keyboard. Each student representing a white key can play a resonator bell whose pitch corresponds to the student's place in the major scale. Play simple melodies like "Estrellita or Twinkle" on the resonator bells in the key of C.

Have students construct additional major scales beginning on any diatonic pitch. Mark each half and whole step, inserting accidentals where needed. See **Visual M45.** Remember, scales always end one octave above or below their beginning pitch.

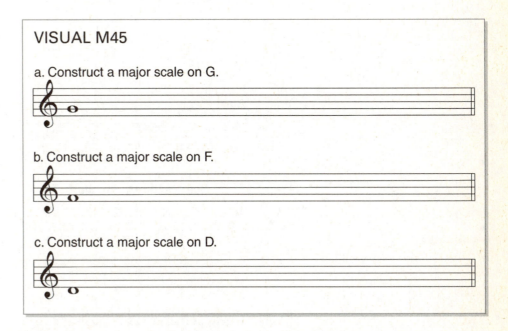

VISUAL M45

a. Construct a major scale on G.

b. Construct a major scale on F.

c. Construct a major scale on D.

Have students sing "C-Saw" to demonstrate a song built on a major scale. Students can play the song on melody instruments. After students learn the song well, they can play it beginning on diatonic pitches other than C.

C-SAW

I climb up the moun-tain, I climb up the hill;

I keep go - ing high - er, like Jack and like Jill.

And now I climb down, it's so ea - sy you see.

I keep go - ing low - er 'til I reach Mid - dle "C".

A *key signature* is a sign, placed at the beginning of a song immediately following the clef sign, that tells the performer the names of the sharps or flats occurring in the music.

Strategies **NS 5** (Learning to read music.)

Build an E-flat major scale, as in **Visual M46.** Note that accidentals have been placed before every E, A, and B. To ease the burden of having to place a flat sign on these three notes every time they occur, composers use a key signature instead. The key signature tells the performer to flat E, A, and B every time they occur in the music, unless the composer indicates otherwise.

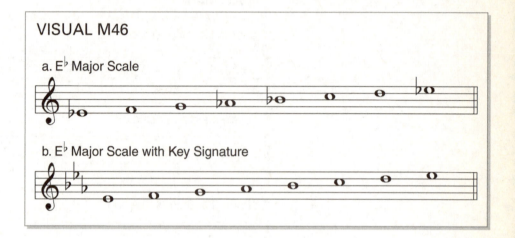

VISUAL M46

a. E♭ Major Scale

b. E♭ Major Scale with Key Signature

Because there are seven different pitches in every major scale, a key signature may have as many as seven sharps or flats. The absence of a key signature indicates that the composition may be in C major.

Provide a chart containing the key signatures for all the major scales, as in **Visual M47.** Notice that accidentals in key signatures always occur in the same order; that is, F♯ is always the first sharp; B♭ is always the first flat. Sharps and flats are always placed from left to right in the key signature. To remember the order in which the sharps and flats are placed on the staff, the following slogans may be useful:

sharps: Fine cut glass dishes are easily broken.

flats: Bill, Ed, and Don go cod fishing.

Have students create other key phrases that can help reinforce the names of sharps and flats in correct order.

Notice that the order of the flats is the reverse of the order of the sharps. Except for the key of F, a flat sign must always accompany the name of a flat key. Each measure in **Visual M47** can be made into a flash card to reinforce students' understanding of key signatures.

VISUAL M47

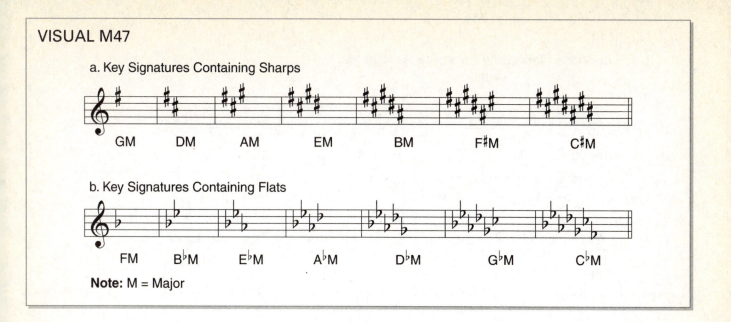

a. Key Signatures Containing Sharps

GM   DM   AM   EM   BM   F♯M   C♯M

b. Key Signatures Containing Flats

FM   B♭M   E♭M   A♭M   D♭M   G♭M   C♭M

Note: M = Major

Have students construct a variety of major scales and assign the proper key signature.

Provide worksheets that reinforce students' understanding of key signatures, as in **Visual M48.**

VISUAL M48

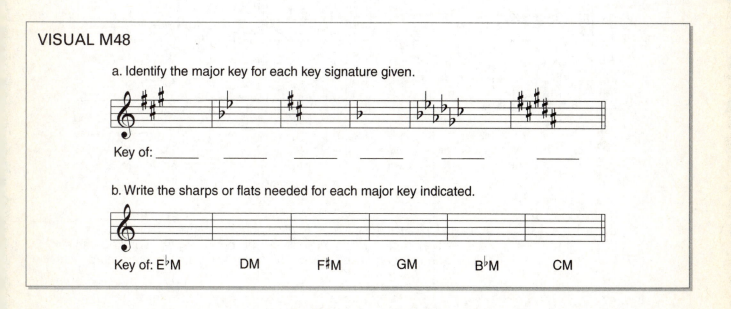

a. Identify the major key for each key signature given.

Key of: ____   ____   ____   ____   ____   ____

b. Write the sharps or flats needed for each major key indicated.

Key of: E♭M   DM   F♯M   GM   B♭M   CM

To complete the exercises in Visual M48, students can use shortcuts. To discover the key of a composition that has sharps in the key signature, refer to the last sharp in the signature. This sharp is the seventh scale degree in every major scale. The key, therefore, is the name of the pitch that is one half step higher. For example, if the last sharp is C♯, the key of the composition will be D major. If the key signature consists of flats, refer to the last flat in the signature. This flat is the fourth scale degree in every major scale. Count down to "1," or the first scale degree, for the name of the key. For example, if the last flat is E♭, then the song is in B♭ major. Notice that for key signatures having more than one flat, the second to the last flat will always be "1" or the name of the key. **Visual M49** diagrams these shortcuts.

VISUAL M49

a. Shortcut for reading key signatures with sharps.

Key of: EM   BM   F♯M

b. Shortcut for reading key signatures with flats.

Key of: E♭M   D♭M   G♭M   FM

Study the following songs and determine the major key in which each song is written. Circle the key note.

LA PIÑATA

Key of _____ major

Mexican Folk Song

Da - le, da - le, da - le, no pier - das el ti - no;
Hit it, hit it, hit it, See that you don't miss it!

mi - de la dis - tan - cia que hay en el ca - mi - no.
Try to find the dis - tance so that you can find it.

 In Mexico, piñatas are believed to have come from the Aztecs, Mayans, and other native peoples. Made originally of clay pots, they were broken with sticks. Candies and other goodies spill out of the broken pots and are shared by all.

WHERE IS THUMBKIN?

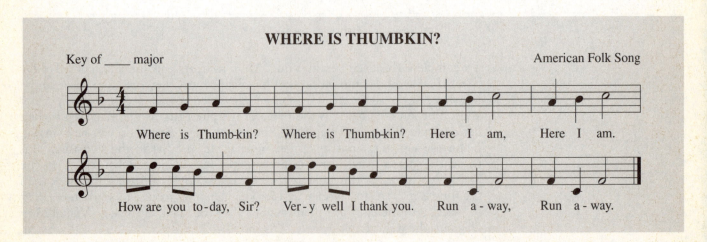

Key of _____ major

American Folk Song

Where is Thumb-kin? Where is Thumb-kin? Here I am, Here I am.

How are you to-day, Sir? Ver - y well I thank you. Run a - way, Run a - way.

BINGO

Key of _____ major

Scotland

There was a farm-er had a dog and Bin-go was his

name - o. B - I - N - G - O! B - I - N - G - O!

B - I - N - G - O and Bin-go was his name - o.

NEW RIVER TRAIN

Key of _____ major

American Folk Song

I'm rid-in' that new riv-er train,_____ I'm rid-in' that

new ri-ver train,_____ That same old train that

brought me here, Gon-na take me back home a-gain._____

PAW PAW PATCH

Key of ____ major

American Singing Game

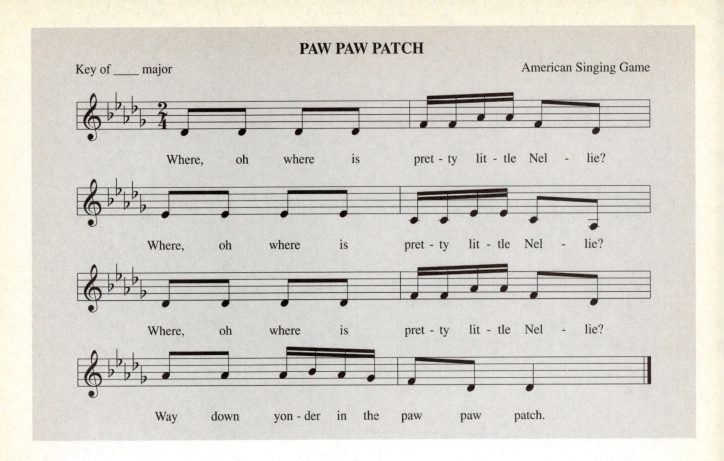

Where, oh where is pret - ty lit - tle Nel - lie?

Where, oh where is pret - ty lit - tle Nel - lie?

Where, oh where is pret - ty lit - tle Nel - lie?

Way down yon - der in the paw paw patch.

 The "Paw, Paw" is a small tree with large leaves and fruit. It is native to North America.

Teachers of young children often add creative movement to the songs they teach. This is because movement and/or other activities tend to keep children engaged. However, when dance steps or other movement activities are added to a song, the original key of the song often changes. Just think about it! While moving and singing with young children, it is essential to move with the children, making it impossible for the teacher to accompany them on an instrument. Therefore, unless a recording to the song is available, many of the songs that are sung with young children are left unaccompanied, making it difficult at times to stay "in tune." Teachers must therefore focus on ending a song in the same key in which it was begun, unless otherwise indicated. Some teachers, who are not comfortable with their own singing voices, can sometimes sing the same song in three or four different keys at the same time. This practice will severely confuse students for years to come.

For practice, it would be helpful to sing through all of the songs in this section in the key indicated. Use an instrument to help start the song, making sure to match all of the pitches, then sing the rest of the song without instrumental help. When finished with the song, check to see if you are in the same key in which you started the song.

PIN PON

Key of _____ major

English Words by Sue Ellen LaBelle

Folk Song from Latin America as Sung by Maria de Leon Arcila

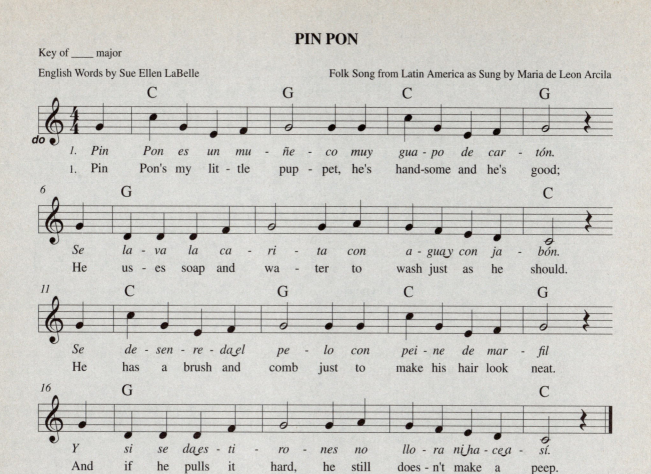

do

1. Pin Pon es un mu - ñe - co muy gua - po de car - tón.
1. Pin Pon's my lit - tle pup - pet, he's hand-some and he's good;

Se la - va la ca - ri - ta con a - gua y con ja - bón.
He us - es soap and wa - ter to wash just as he should.

Se de - sen - re - da el pe - lo con pei - ne de mar - fil
He has a brush and comb just to make his hair look neat.

Y si se da es - ti - ro - nes no llo - ra ni ha - ce a - sí.
And if he pulls it hard, he still does - n't make a peep.

2. Cuando toma la sopa
    no ensucia el delantal,
Pues come con cuidado
    parece un general.
Y cuando las estrellas
    empiezan a brillar,
Pin Pon se va a la cama
    se acuesta a descansar.

2. Pin Pon joins me for dinner;
    he is a welcome guest;
He sips his soup so nicely
    and doesn't make a mess.
When nighttime comes upon us
    and stars are twinkling bright,
Pin Pon gets in his bed
    and I hear him say "Good night."

Source "Pin Pon": English words © 2002 Pearson Education, Inc. GR. 1, p. 146 (TE).

SHENANDOAH

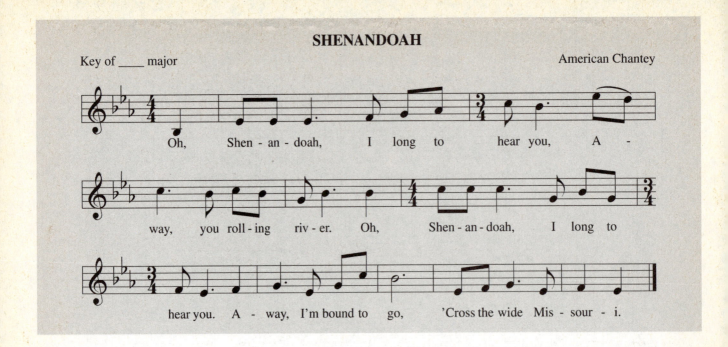

Look at a variety of key signatures in additional song literature written in major keys. Determine the key of each song.

Have students compose their own song in a major key. The length of the song can be limited to 16 measures. Perform the song for the class. Create their own text or lyrics to go with the song.

FOCUS

Minor Scales and Key Signatures

Learning   Every major scale has a corresponding minor scale using the same key signature. The *minor scale* is built on the sixth tone of the major scale, which is its key note. There are three types of minor scales: the natural, the harmonic, and the melodic, each having a slightly different pattern of whole and half steps.

Strategies **NS 5** (Reading music in minor keys.)

Sing a familiar song that uses a major scale, such as "Row Row Row Your Boat." Then, sing the song again, this time in the minor mode. See **Visual M50.** Have students describe the differences in sound between the minor and major modes.

ROW, ROW, ROW YOUR BOAT

Song in D Major

Anonymous

Send a student to the piano to play a diatonic scale beginning on A. Notate the scale for all to see. Identify the whole- and half-step relationships between the notes, as in **Visual M51.** Number each note in the sequence. Students should recognize that the half steps now occur between 2 and 3, and 5 and 6, resulting in the pattern W H W W H W W. This pattern identifies the *natural minor scale.*

Have students sing the letter names of the scale, both ascending and descending.

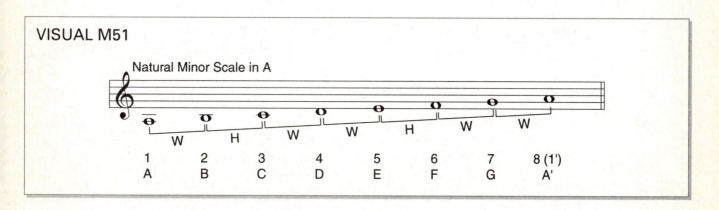

VISUAL M51

Natural Minor Scale in A

Students can build a human scale to represent the natural minor scale. Organize the students to represent the white keys on the keyboard from A to A'. Each student can play a resonator bell whose pitch corresponds to the student's place in the minor scale.

Have students build natural minor scales in a variety of keys, indicating each whole and half step. See **Visual M52.**

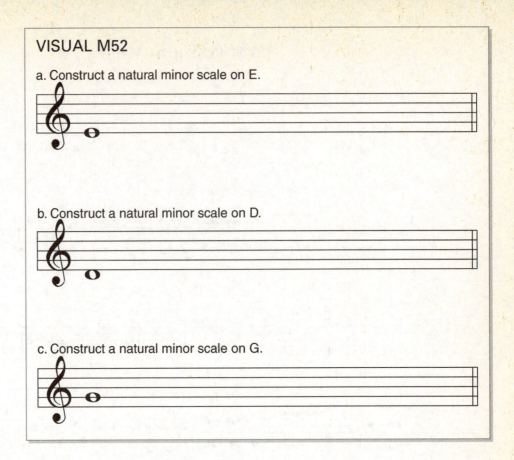

VISUAL M52

a. Construct a natural minor scale on E.

b. Construct a natural minor scale on D.

c. Construct a natural minor scale on G.

Often, there is little time to teach more than the natural minor scale to children. Therefore, the other two minor scales are not presented here.

 Have students compose their own song in a minor key. The length of the song can be limited to 16 measures. Perform the song for the class. Have them create their own lyrics.

Learning When a major and a minor key utilize the same key signature, the two keys are referred to as *relative*. There is a relative minor key for every major key.

Strategies **NS 6** (Listening to, analyzing and describing major and minor melodies.)

Have students play a C major scale and then an A minor scale. Notate these scales on the board. Observe that both scales use the same letter names and therefore possess the same key signature; the key signature of C major and A minor has no sharps or flats. See **Visual M53.**

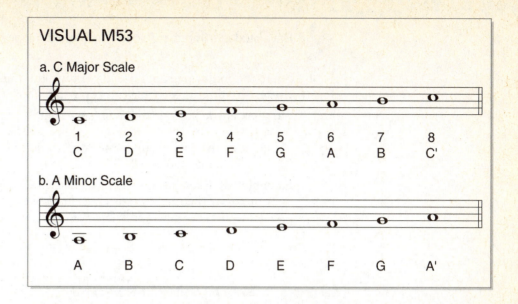

VISUAL M53

a. C Major Scale

b. A Minor Scale

Give students examples of relative major and minor keys sharing the same key signature, as in **Visual M54.** Note that the *key note* (starting note) of the relative minor key is located on the sixth degree of the major scale.

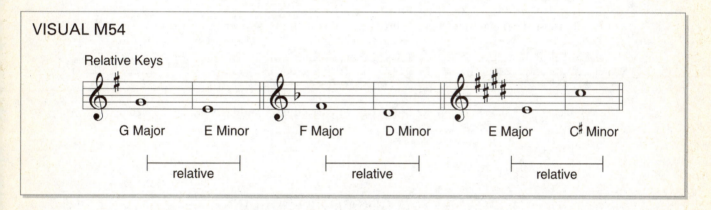

VISUAL M54

Relative Keys

G Major   E Minor   F Major   D Minor   E Major   C# Minor

relative   relative   relative

Provide exercises to reinforce the understanding of relative major and minor keys. See **Visual M55.** These measures can be reproduced as flash cards.

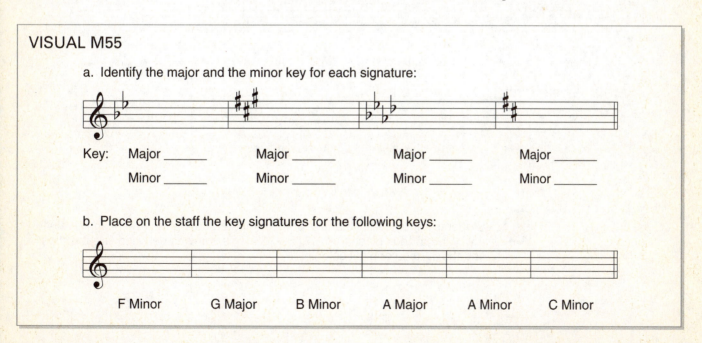

VISUAL M55

a. Identify the major and the minor key for each signature:

Key: Major _____   Major _____   Major _____   Major _____

Minor _____   Minor _____   Minor _____   Minor _____

b. Place on the staff the key signatures for the following keys:

F Minor   G Major   B Minor   A Major   A Minor   C Minor

Have students improvise songs in different minor keys.

Study the following songs and determine the minor key in which each song is written. To do this, students can apply the following guidelines:

a. Look at the key signature. This will tell you both the major and the relative minor keys in which the song could be written.

b. Look at the final note of the song to determine the key. The final note is usually the key note or "1."

Example If a key has no sharps or flats, the song will probably be in C major or A minor. If the final note is C, then the key is probably C major; if the final note is A, then the key is probably A minor. Circle the key note.

WAYFARING STRANGER

Key of ____ minor

Spiritual

I'm just a poor way-far-ing strang-er, A-trav'-ling through this world of woe;

But there's no sick-ness, toil nor dan-ger in that bright world to which I go.

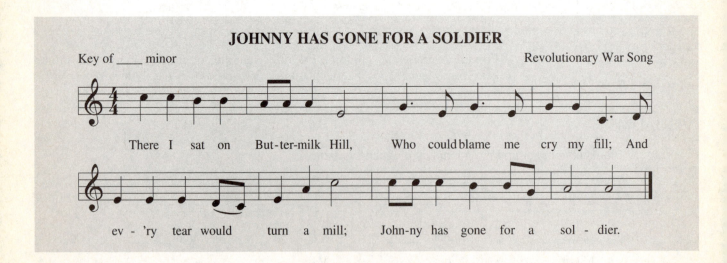

JOHNNY HAS GONE FOR A SOLDIER

Key of ____ minor

Revolutionary War Song

There I sat on But-ter-milk Hill, Who could blame me cry my fill; And

ev-'ry tear would turn a mill; John-ny has gone for a sol-dier.

 Students should know that this song originated during the American Revolutionary War that took place from 1775–1783. This war was between Great Britain and the thirteen original colonies.

WILLUM

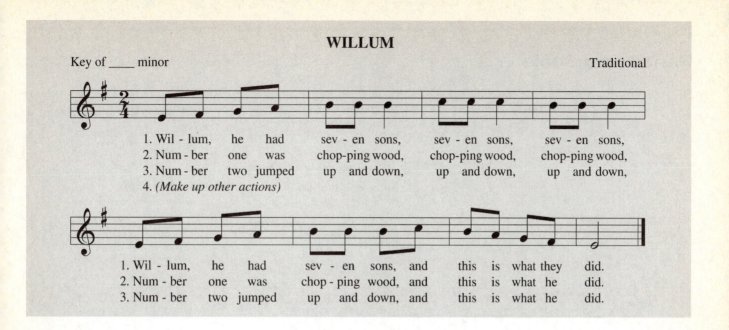

Key of _____ minor   Traditional

1. Wil - lum, he had   sev - en sons,   sev - en sons,   sev - en sons,
2. Num - ber one was   chop-ping wood,   chop-ping wood,   chop-ping wood,
3. Num - ber two jumped   up and down,   up and down,   up and down,
4. *(Make up other actions)*

1. Wil - lum, he had   sev - en sons, and   this is what they did.
2. Num - ber one was   chop-ping wood, and   this is what he did.
3. Num - ber two jumped   up and down, and   this is what he did.

GO DOWN, MOSES

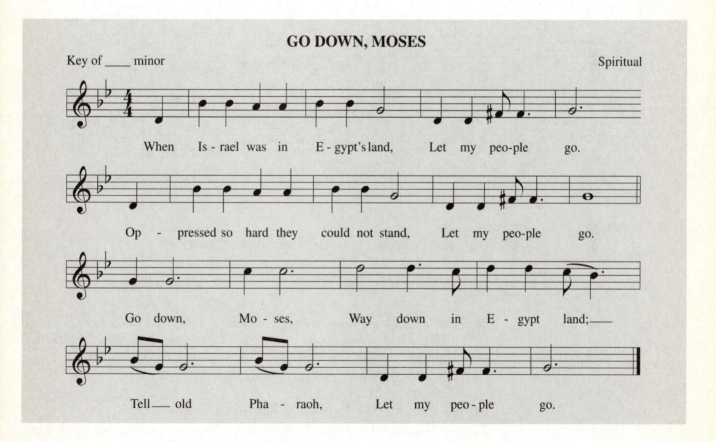

Key of _____ minor   Spiritual

When Is - rael was in E - gypt's land,   Let my peo - ple go.

Op - pressed so hard they could not stand,   Let my peo - ple go.

Go down,   Mo - ses,   Way down in E - gypt land;____

Tell___ old   Pha - raoh,   Let my peo - ple go.

 This song draws its inspiration from the Biblical story of Moses. He was commanded to lead the Hebrew people out of Egyptian bondage. Moses was also the name adopted by Harriet Tubman, who was a famous conductor on the Underground Railroad, the network of people who helped slaves escape to freedom in the Northern States and Canada.

Pentatonic Scale

Learning Any scale that consists of a sequence of five tones within the octave is called a *pentatonic scale*. No half steps are present.

Strategies **NS 5** (Reading pentatonic scales.)

Place a copy of the song " 'Liza Jane" on a projector or the board.

'LIZA JANE

American Folk Song

You got a gal and I got none, Lit-tle 'Li - za Jane,

Come my love and be my one, Lit-tle 'Li - za Jane.

Oh, E - li-za! Lit-tle 'Li - za Jane. Oh, E - li-za! Lit-tle 'Li - za Jane.

 Have students create a dance to accompany " 'Liza Jane."

1 + 2 = 3 Analyze the number of phrases in this song; then create a dance.

Sing through the song with students. Analyze the piece and locate the key note (C). Construct a scale using only the tones of this song, as in **Visual M56.** Discuss the makeup of this scale. The following questions may be helpful:

a. How many different tones are in this scale? (5)
b. What are they? (C D E G A)
c. Are there any half-step relationships in this song? (No)

Teacher identifies this song as being built on a pentatonic scale that has five different tones and no half-step relationships.

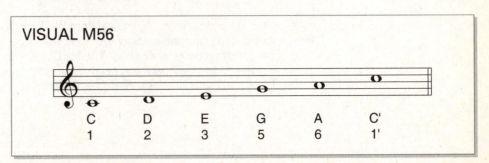

VISUAL M56

C	D	E	G	A	C'
1	2	3	5	6	1'

Examine the following songs and determine the pentatonic scale used. Write the scale on the staff beneath the song. Have students note that the 4th and 7th tones of the major and minor scales are missing from the pentatonic.

BLUEBIRD

Game Song

Here comes a blue - bird in through my win - dow,

Hey, did - dle - dum a day, day, day.

Take a lit - tle part - ner, hop in the gar - den,

Hey, did - dle - dum a day, day, day.

BUTTON YOU MUST WANDER

Children's Game Song

But - ton you must wan - der, wan - der, wan - der.

But - ton, you must wan - der ev - 'ry - where.

Bright eyes will find you. Sharp eyes will find you.

But - ton, you must wan - der ev - 'ry - where.

This singing game and others throughout this book strongly enhance a young student's understanding of what it means to work in a group. In "Button You Must Wander" it is necessary for students to not only give their attention to a button that is passed secretly from student to student, but to those participating in the circle. At the end of the song, one child must determine where the button might be. The social interaction found in this game clearly supports Benchmark Standards that focus on children and their ultimate development as citizens. Have students sing this song and play the game.

Directions:

Children should sit in a circle with their legs crossed in front. Hands should be placed behind the back. One child should sit in the center. A medium-sized button should be passed around the circle. Children who do not have the button should pretend to have it and pass it as well. At the end of the song, the child in the center is given three chances to guess who in the circle has the button. If the child guesses correctly, he/she might get a special prize. If the child does not guess correctly, the child holding the button takes his/her place in the center of the circle.

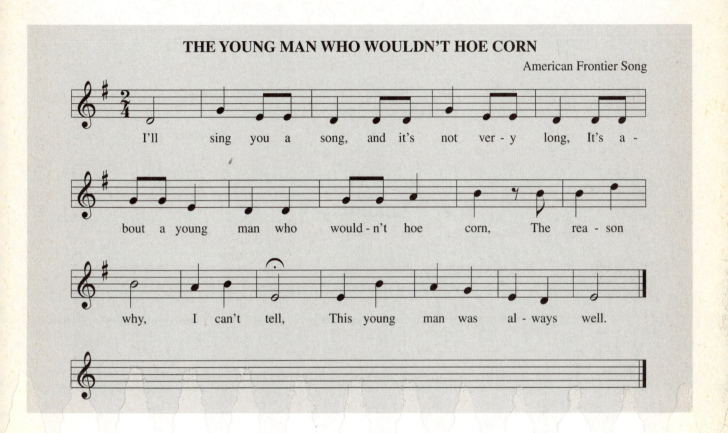

THE YOUNG MAN WHO WOULDN'T HOE CORN

American Frontier Song

I'll sing you a song, and it's not ver-y long, It's a-bout a young man who would-n't hoe corn, The rea-son why, I can't tell, This young man was al-ways well.

Have students improvise their own pentatonic songs on melody instruments. It is recommended that Orff instruments be used so that the half steps can be removed; this will facilitate the construction of the pentatonic scale.

FOCUS

Transposing

Learning *Transposing* is the technique of rewriting a song in a key different from that in which it was originally written. If a song is too high or too low for a child's voice, it can be transposed to a more comfortable key.

Strategies **NS 1** (Singing alone and with others, a varied repertoire of music.)

Have the class sing the song "Pat Works on the Railway" in the key of B minor. Students will immediately discover that the song is too high.

Help them transpose the song to a more comfortable key. To do this, number each tone of the song according to its place in the B minor scale, as in **Visual M57.**

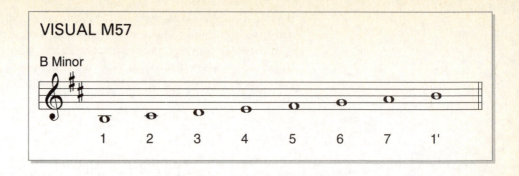

VISUAL M57

B Minor

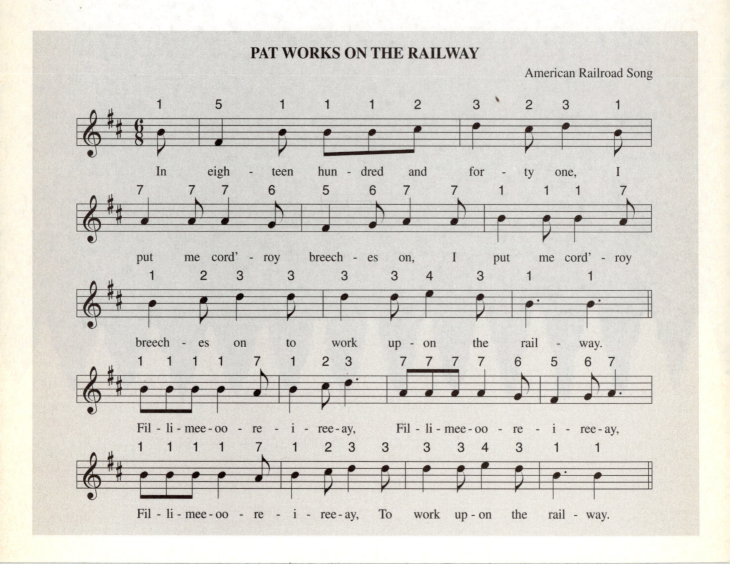

PAT WORKS ON THE RAILWAY

American Railroad Song

In eigh-teen hun-dred and for-ty one, I put me cord'-roy breech-es on, I put me cord'-roy breech-es on to work up-on the rail-way. Fil-li-mee-oo-re-i-ree-ay, Fil-li-mee-oo-re-i-ree-ay, Fil-li-mee-oo-re-i-ree-ay, To work up-on the rail-way.

A more comfortable key might be E minor. To transpose to E minor or any other key, observe that notes in the new key must be used that correspond to the same scale degrees as in the original key; that is, if the song began on the first degree of the scale in B minor, then it must also begin on the first degree in E minor. See **Visual M58.**

VISUAL M58

E Minor

1   2   3   4   5   6   7   1'

"Pat Works on the Railway" transposed to E minor

1   5   1   1   1   2   3   2   3   1   7   7   7   6

5   6   7   7   1   1   1   7   1   2   3   3   3   3   4   3   1   1

Be sure that students understand that a song in a minor key can be transposed only to another minor key and that a song in a major key can be transposed only to another major key.

Have students aurally transpose other short songs to different keys. Listen to or sing the song in its original key. Determine whether the key is too high or too low. Then, have each student try putting the song in a key that is perfect for his/her voice. Follow up by having each student tell in what key he/she is singing.

The following patriotic, Halloween, Thanksgiving, Christmas, and Hanukkah songs will provide a great starting point for this activity since these songs remain popular throughout our country.

AMERICA THE BEAUTIFUL

Katherine Lee Bates

Samuel A. Ward

 Katherine Lee Bates wrote the lyrics to this patriotic song as she looked out over Pike's Peak. She originally wrote the words as a poem.

AMERICA

Samuel Francis Smith

Henry Carey

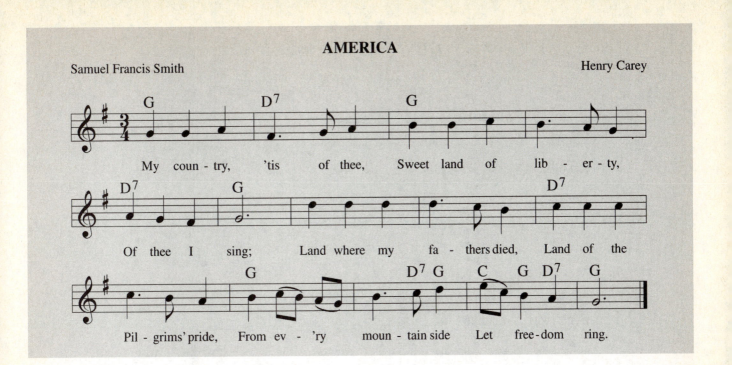

My coun - try, 'tis of thee, Sweet land of lib - er - ty,

Of thee I sing; Land where my fa - thers died, Land of the

Pil - grims' pride, From ev - 'ry moun - tain side Let free - dom ring.

 The lyrics of this song were written in 1832 by the Reverand Samuel F. Smith. The melody is that of the British national anthem, "God Save the Queen."

BATTLE HYMN OF THE REPUBLIC

Julia Ward Howe

William Steffe

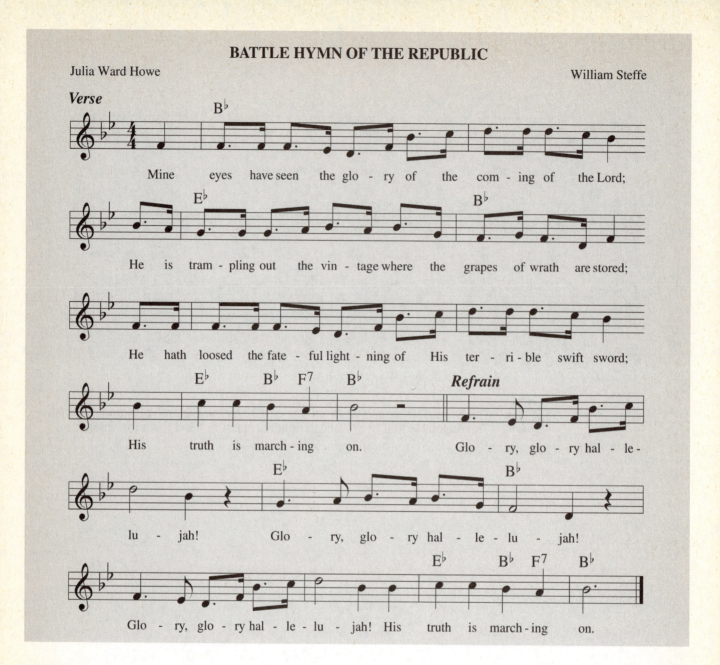

Verse

Mine eyes have seen the glo-ry of the com-ing of the Lord;

He is tram-pling out the vin-tage where the grapes of wrath are stored;

He hath loosed the fate-ful light-ning of His ter-ri-ble swift sword;

His truth is march-ing on. *Refrain* Glo-ry, glo-ry hal-le-

lu-jah! Glo-ry, glo-ry hal-le-lu-jah!

Glo-ry, glo-ry hal-le-lu-jah! His truth is march-ing on.

 In 1861, Julia Ward Howe wrote a poem that later came to be called "The Battle Hymn of the Republic." She was inspired by a visit to the Union Army Camp. It was first published in 1862 in *The Atlantic Monthly*.

THE STAR-SPANGLED BANNER

Francis Scott Key

John Stafford Smith

Oh,— say can you see, by the dawn's ear - ly light,

What so proud - ly we hailed at the twi - light's last gleam - ing,

Whose broad stripes and bright stars, through the per - il - ous fight,

O'er the ram - parts we watched were so gal - lant - ly stream - ing?

And the rock - ets' red glare, The bombs burst - ing in air,

Gave proof through the night that our flag was still there.

Oh, say does that— Star - Span - gled Ban - ner— yet wave—

O'er the land— of the free and the home of the brave?

Students should be encouraged to research the history of this song. The words were written by Francis Scott Key, who during the war of 1812, sailed to the British fleet to obtain the release of a captured American. He was detained by

the British and was forced to witness, from his ship, the bombing of Fort McHenry near Baltimore in 1814. The fort withstood the attack and Key was inspired to write the lyrics to this song. Originally the tune was a British drinking song.

LIFT EV'RY VOICE AND SING

J. Rosamond Johnson

Lift ev'-ry voice and sing 'til earth and Heav-en ring; ring with the har-mo-

nies of lib - er-ty. Let our re-joic-ing rise, high as the lis-t'ning—

skies; let it re-sound loud as the roll-ing sea. Sing a song full of the

faith that the dark past has taught us; sing a song full of the hope that the pre-sent has

brought us. Fac-ing the ris-ing sun of our new day be-

gun; let us march on 'til vic-to-ry——— is won.———

 Often called the African-American national anthem, this song was written as a poem by James Weldon Johnson and then set to music by his brother John Rosamond Johnson in 1900. It addresses the topic of freedom for all men, women, boys, and girls.

YANKEE DOODLE
FATHER AND I WENT DOWN TO CAMP

Traditional

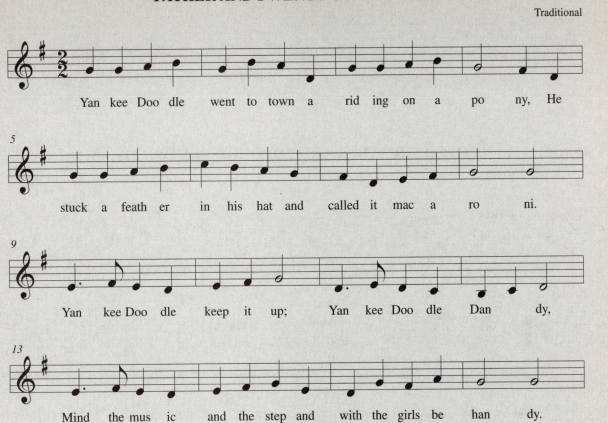

Yan kee Doo dle went to town a rid ing on a po ny, He
stuck a feath er in his hat and called it mac a ro ni.
Yan kee Doo dle keep it up; Yan kee Doo dle Dan dy,
Mind the mus ic and the step and with the girls be han dy.

A "doodle" is a fool or simpleton. "Macaroni" is a high-fashion wig that was worn in the 1770s.

SKIN AND BONES

Southern Folk Song

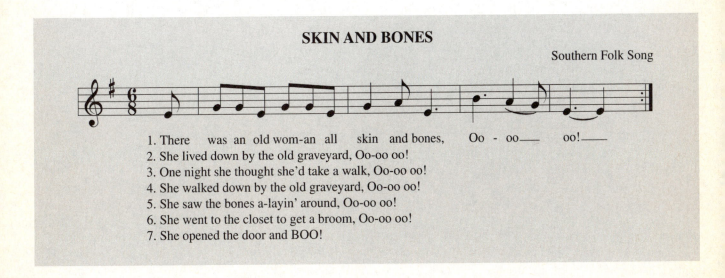

1. There was an old wom-an all skin and bones, Oo - oo—— oo!——
2. She lived down by the old graveyard, Oo-oo oo!
3. One night she thought she'd take a walk, Oo-oo oo!
4. She walked down by the old graveyard, Oo-oo oo!
5. She saw the bones a-layin' around, Oo-oo oo!
6. She went to the closet to get a broom, Oo-oo oo!
7. She opened the door and BOO!

FOR HEALTH AND STRENGTH

Old English Round

OVER THE RIVER AND THROUGH THE WOOD

Lydia Maria Childs

Traditional

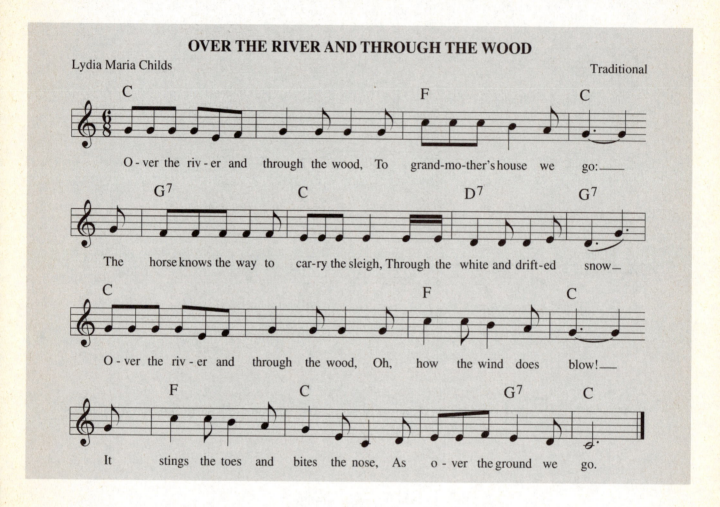

DONA NOBIS PACEM

Traditional. Attributed to Joseph Haydn.

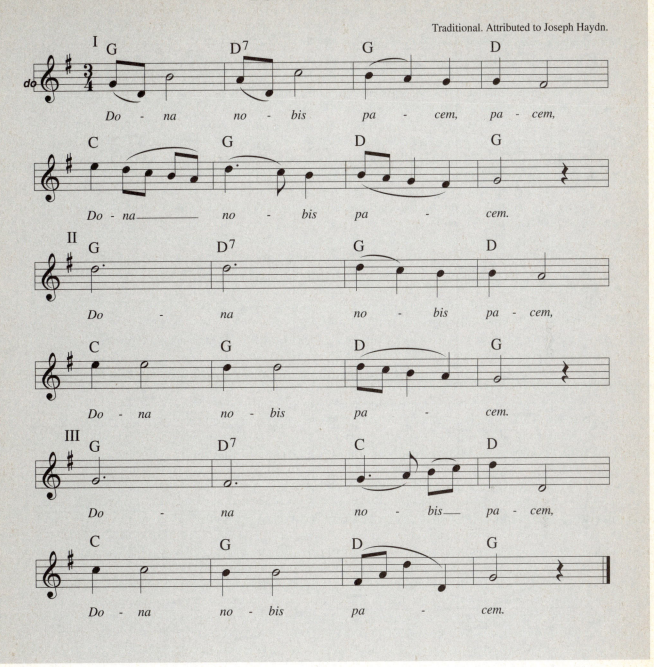

The lyrics in this song are in Latin, a language originally spoken in ancient Rome. It means "Give Us Peace." Physicians write prescriptions using this language.

THE TWELVE DAYS OF CHRISTMAS

English Traditional

1. On the first day of Christ-mas my true love sent to me A par-tridge in a pear tree.

2. On the sec-ond
3. On the third day of Christ-mas my true love sent to me
4. On the fourth

Two tur-de-doves.
Three French hens, And a par-tridge in a pear tree.
Four call-ing birds

5. On the fifth day of Christ-mas my true love sent to me.

Five gold-en rings; Four call-ing birds, three French hens,

Two tur-tle-doves and a par-tridge in a pear tree.

6. On the sixth day of Christ-mas my true love sent to me
7. On the seventh...
8. On the eighth...
9. On the ninth...
10. On the tenth...
11. On the eleventh...
12. On the twelfth...

6. Six   geese a - lay - ing;
7. Seven   swans a - swim - ming...
8. Eight   maids a - milk - ing...
9. Nine   la - dies danc - ing...
10. Ten   lords a - leap - ing...
11. Eleven pip - ers pip - ing...
12. Twelve drum - mers drum-ming...

O HANUKKAH

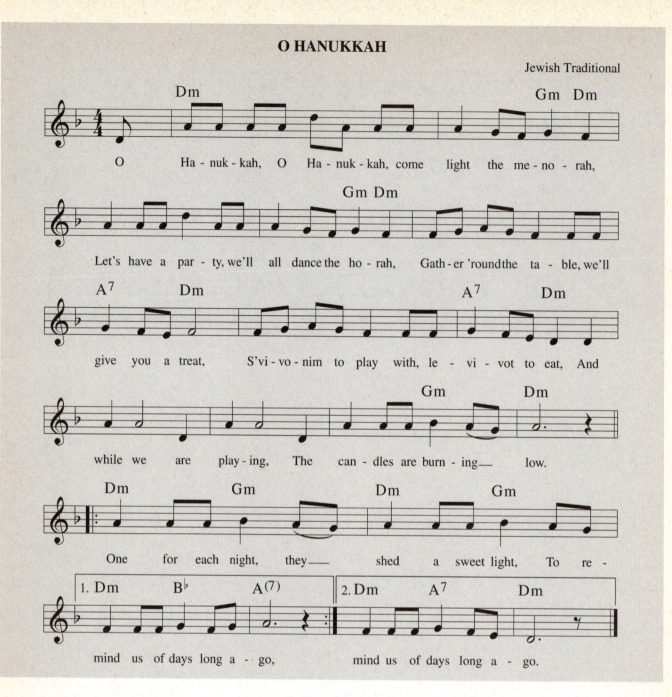

Jewish Traditional

This song is often included in the eight-day Hanukkah celebration. Hanukkah commemorates the victory and success of the Maccabees against the tyranny of Antiochus IV Epiphanes, and the subsequent miraculous burning of candles of the "Menorah" for eight days in a temple in Jerusalem.

ROCK OF AGES

M. Jastrow/G. Gottlieb

Jewish Traditional

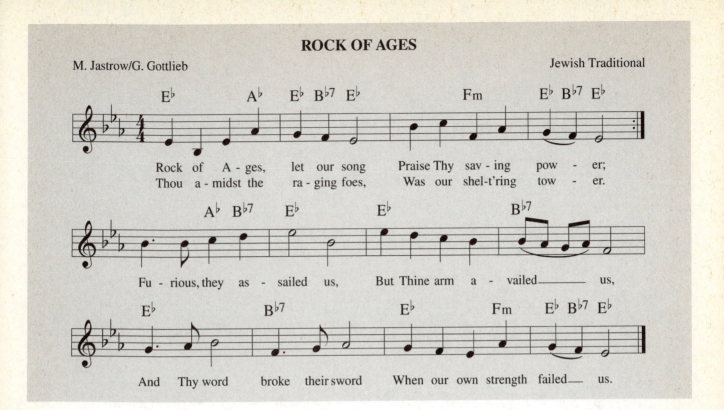

Rock of A - ges, let our song
Praise Thy sav - ing pow - er;
Thou a - midst the ra - ging foes, Was our shel-t'ring tow - er.

Fu - rious, they as - sailed us, But Thine arm a - vailed____ us,

And Thy word broke their sword When our own strength failed____ us.

The lyrics to this song were written about a thousand years ago in Europe. The Hebrew name for this song is "Maoz Tzur." It is traditionally sung after reciting Hanukkah blessings and lighting the menorah.

Maoz is an acrostic poem with five stanzas. The first letter of each stanza spells the poet's name, Mordechal, in Hebrew.

LOOK AT ME

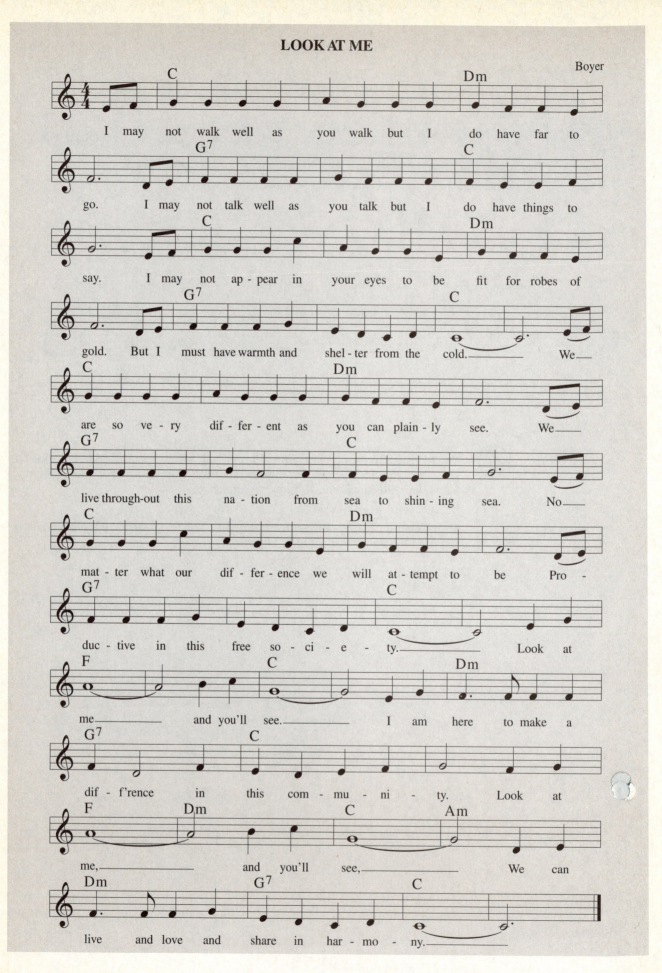

FREE AT LAST

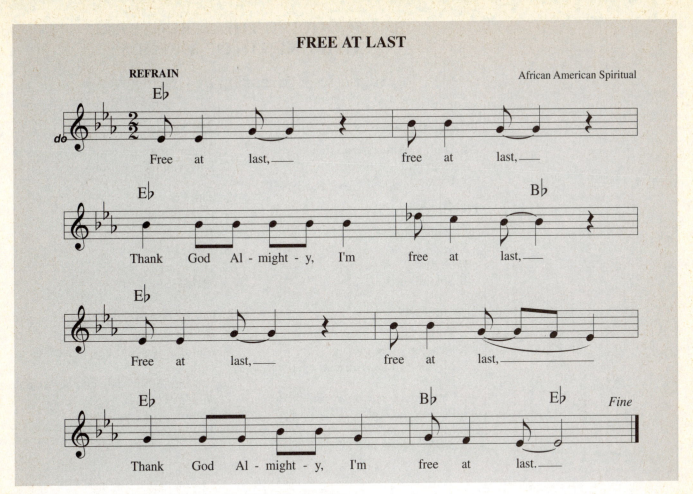

Source: Arrangement © 1995 Silver Burdett Ginn GR. 2, p. 396.

INTRODUCING THE STRUCTURAL COMPONENTS OF MELODY

Suggested Sequencing by Grade Level

Kindergarten

1. High, medium, low ranges
2. High and low pitches
3. Upward, downward, stay the same

Grade One

1. Higher, lower
2. Staff
3. Notes
4. Sol, mi, la

Grade Two

1. Treble clef
2. Absolute note names
3. Middle C ledger line and D ledger space
4. Organized versus unorganized pitches
5. Pentatonic scale
6. Melodies move by step, skip, repeated notes, and leaps

Grade Three

1. Sharps, flats, naturals
2. Direction of note stems

Grade Four

1. Ledger lines
2. 8va
3. Bass clef
4. Grand staff
5. Melodic intervals

Grades Five and Six

1. Whole steps and half steps
2. Major scales and key signatures in C, F, G
3. Natural minor scale and key signatures in A, D, E
4. Enharmonic equivalents
5. Transposing

WRITTEN AND PERFORMANCE-RELATED ASSESSMENTS THROUGH COOPERATIVE LEARNING ACTIVITIES: MELODY NS 1, 2, 3, 4, 5, 7

1. Give each group a "note on a stick" (♩) and a staff containing a treble clef sign. Students take turns placing the note on different lines and spaces, while the group identifies that line or space by letter name. When the group feels ready, each student should be given a copy of Visual M14 to complete. Teacher checks responses. **NS 5, 7**

2. Distribute to each group a sheet with several staffs on it, each staff containing a treble clef sign. Students place notes on the staff so that each measure spells a word, as in Visual M15. When finished, groups exchange papers and name the notes to discover the words they spell. **NS 5, 7**

3. Give each group a staff containing note heads, similar to Visual M20. Students must first discover the name of the song. To do this, they may need to play the pitches on a barred instrument. Next, they should change the open note heads to the rhythms appropriate for the song, add bar lines, and finally, place the time signature. Teacher checks the finished product. **NS 2, 5, 7**

4. Give each group a paper containing a familiar melody lined out, as in Visual M25. When the group guesses the song, a member whispers its name to the teacher. If correct, the group exchanges papers with another group that has successfully guessed its assigned song. So that some groups are not sitting around waiting for others to finish, let groups who have finished guessing all songs try their hand at lining out the melodies of familiar songs of their choice. These can be used as "mystery songs" later, in follow-up activities. **NS 5, 7**

5. Give each group three songs, each song in a different major key. The songs should be on separate sheets, with a blank staff at the bottom of the page. Group members must determine the key of the song, place the key signature on the score, and draw the corresponding major scale on the blank staff. Each student in the group must be able to play one of the three songs on a barred instrument. This activity can be repeated using songs in natural minor keys. **NS 2, 7**

6. Have students compose their own songs. Give each group some staff paper. On the top staff, the teacher places the pentatonic scale to be used in the composition. If the teacher wants to limit the rhythms or the time signature that can be used, those should also be indicated. The staff is divided into the number of measures that the song should contain. When the group members have finished their song, they should test it on melody bells to see if they want to make any changes. Group members should then create a poem whose words can be set to the song. The group should be able to sing and play its song for the class. **NS 1, 2, 4**

   This activity can be repeated using major or minor scales, or different rhythms and time signatures.

7. Have students improvise pentatonic melodies on melody bells, Orff instruments, or other keyboard instruments. **NS 2, 3**

Teaching Timbre to Children

INTRODUCTION

There are sounds all around us. In our external environment, we hear sound when we listen to the ticking of a clock, chimes ringing in the clock tower, or the starting of an engine in a car or boat.

Even if our external environment were silent, we would still be surrounded by the sounds our own bodies make: breathing, sneezing, coughing. Each of these sounds has distinctive qualities that distinguish it from the others. These qualities are referred to as *timbre* (tam-bur) or *tone color*.

Children instinctively recognize differences in tone color. The response that many infants and toddlers display when hearing the sound of their mother's voice in comparison to the voice of a stranger is evidence of their abilities to discriminate between sounds. As children grow and are guided in exploring sound, they begin to identify and ultimately place the origins of these sounds into different categories. They learn quickly, for example, to recognize the sounds of various animals, the sounds of nature, the sounds of people, and the sounds produced by different musical instruments. Guidance by the classroom teacher will help them discover and realize more subtle differences that exist between the various sounds in their environment. As their skill in recognizing tone color develops, their ability to discriminate, understand, and appreciate not only music but also the host of sounds offered to them in their everyday environment will take on added meaning.

> I sing!
> I shout!
> Just listen as I move about.
> I stop … No sound.
> Now listen …
> Silence.
> —René Boyer

FOCUS

Environmental and Body Sounds

Learning | Sounds in our environment have their own characteristic qualities by which the sound and its source may be identified.

Strategies **NS 6** (Listen to and analyze sounds in your environment.)

Ask students to close their eyes and listen carefully, noticing any sounds they hear. For thirty seconds, let them listen to the natural sounds in the environment; then add a few sounds by doing such things as taking a step, rustling paper, pounding a desk, whistling, or sighing. At the end of the thirty seconds, signal children to open their eyes. List all the sounds they heard.

Discuss how sounds can be placed into categories according to their similarities and differences. **Visual TM1** provides an example of categories that may result from the discussion.

VISUAL TM1

Mechanical Sounds	People Sounds	Sounds of Nature
automobile engines	breathing	thunder
boat engines	whistling	rain falling
blender	talking	wind
mixer	crying	trees rustling
airplane	laughing	insect sounds
furnace	moaning	waterfall
lawn mower	yawning	river flowing

At-Home Sounds	Music Sounds	Animal Sounds
telephone	piano	purring of a cat
door bell	singing	barking of a dog
clock ticking	violin	hissing of a snake
television	trumpet	chirping of a bird
radio	guitar	mooing of a cow

 Have students discover how many ways sounds can be produced using their own bodies. Each sound can be assigned a symbol and included in a body-sound composition similar to the ones provided here.

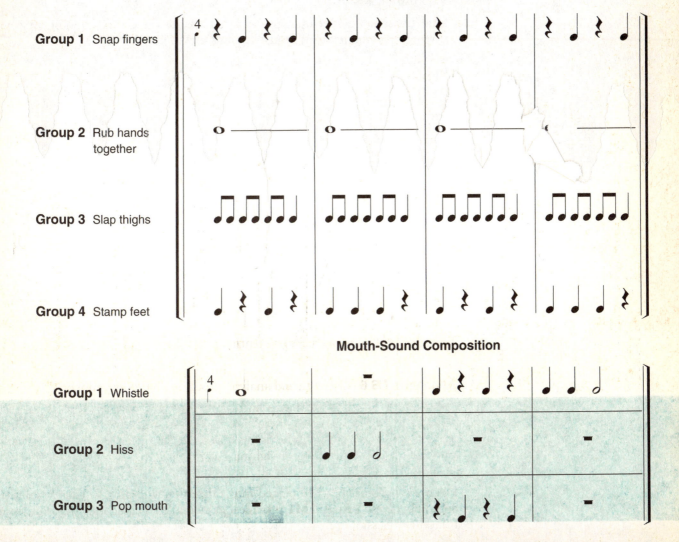

Body-Sound Composition
(Can be performed in canon)

Group 1 Snap fingers

Group 2 Rub hands together

Group 3 Slap thighs

Group 4 Stamp feet

Mouth-Sound Composition

Group 1 Whistle

Group 2 Hiss

Group 3 Pop mouth

Tone Color of Rhythm Instruments

Learning Rhythm instruments provide an excellent source for the exploration and understanding of timbre or tone color.

Strategies **NS 2, 6** (Perform on rhythmic instruments. Analyze and describe their sounds.)

Make available a variety of rhythm instruments that students can explore. Have students pay attention to the many ways sound can be produced on each instrument. (See Chapter 10 for a listing of frequently used rhythm instruments.) After this hands-on experience, identify each instrument by name and demonstrate how each is commonly used by musicians.

Have students group those rhythm instruments whose tone is produced in a similar manner. For example, students may choose to classify the rhythm instruments in the following way:

Rhythm Instrument Classification Chart

I. Instruments that are hit or struck: triangle, drum, wood block, claves, cymbals
II. Instruments that are shaken: maracas, jingle bells, tambourine
III. Instruments that are scraped: guiro, grooved tone block, grooved sticks
IV. Instruments that are rubbed: sand blocks, drum head

Students can also develop categories that address the composition of the various rhythm instruments being used, as demonstrated below.

Skins

hand drum	congas	bongos	tambora
			© istockphoto

Rattles

maracas	shakaree	bells	cabasa
	Peripole-Bergerault, Inc.		

Metals

cowbell	bell tree	gong	triangle
	Peripole-Bergerault, Inc.		

Woods

claves	woodblock	guiro	sticks

Peripole-Bergerault, Inc.   Peripole-Bergerault, Inc.

1 + 2 = 3

Some rhythm instruments have distinctive geometric shapes that students encounter when studying math. For example, students learn that a **triangle** is a three-sided shape. Every triangle has three sides and three angles, some of which may be the same. Have students identify which is the triangle among the non-pitched percussion instruments.

Woodblocks are usually made up of six **rectangles.** Have students find and then describe the woodblock. They should know that a woodblock has six faces. A **rectangle** has two sides of equal length opposite each other, and two other sides of equal length opposite each other, and four corners, all right angles (90 degree angles). Have students measure the woodblock and then tell its area and its perimeter.

Most **drumheads** are in the shape of a circle. A **circle** is a special kind of ellipsis with one center point instead of two focal points.

Every circle or drum head has a **radius,** a **diameter,** a **circumference** and an **area,** all of which are important when learning to make sound on a drum.

Claves are in a cylindrical shape. A **cylinder** is a solid object with two identical flat circular ends.

Our world is filled with different shapes, and most of them can be found in the music classroom among the non-pitched instruments.

Learning   Some stories, nursery rhymes, and poems are enhanced by the addition of sound effects or sound imagery.

Strategies **NS 6** (Listen to a poem or story and add appropriate sound effects using unpitched percussion.)

Provide students with examples of poems and stories similar to the one outlined next. After students have read the poem or story thoroughly, the teacher can assign appropriate sound effects.

MONICA AND JOEY

Monica and Joey went for a walk. (*wood block*)
They came to a bridge and marched over it. (*drum*)
They came to a stream and swam across it. (*tambourine*)
They came to a field and brushed through it. (*sand blocks or cabasa*)
They came to a grassy hillside and walked down it. (*descending minor scale on bass xylophone*)
They came to a rocky hillside and walked up it. (*ascending major scale on piano or soprano xylophone*)
They came to a cave and looked in. (*triangle*)
A bear looked out…and growled at them! (*cymbals, vibra-slap, and guiro*)
Well, the bear did not have to growl twice. Monica and Joey turned and ran.

Down the rocky hillside,
Up the grassy hillside,
Through the field,   *(repeat sounds in reverse)*
Across the stream,
Over the bridge,
Into their house and slammed the door. *(slap stick)*
Whew!
Going for a walk is great,...but staying at home is even better!

Have students experiment with a variety of instruments that can be used to interpret each line in a poem; then evaluate their appropriateness to the poem. The poem that follows can be used for this experience.

SEVEN DAYS INDOORS

One day a little dog decided to stay indoors because he refused to get his feet wet
     and...
That was the day it rained...
And the fog rolled in...
And the snow melted...
And there was a tornado...
And a hurricane...
And a breeze...
And a shower...
Then the sun came out, and all the flowers came up because it was spring.
Because the sun was shining, the little dog decided to take a walk.
As he walked, the bright light of the sun began to dim.
And the stars came out...
And the moon came out...
And it was night...
And the wind began to blow gently through the trees.

Have students add to the enjoyment of other stories such as "The Three Bears," "The Three Billy Goats Gruff," and "The Three Little Pigs" by adding appropriate instruments and sound effects.

 Have groups of students select a poem, story, or nursery rhyme. Select a narrator, choose instruments to enhance the story, make scenery, create simple costumes, and then perform for the class or another audience.

After they have explored the variety of rhythm instruments used in the classroom, students should refine their aural ability to distinguish various timbres by identifying rhythm instruments by sound alone. A number of approaches may be taken to help reinforce this skill. For example, all eyes might be closed while one student performs a short rhythmic pattern on a rhythm instrument. At the completion of the pattern, students guess which instrument was played. A screen might be provided to separate player from listeners. A correct response might provide an opportunity for an aurally perceptive listener to become the next player.

FOCUS

Vocal Sounds

Learning   The categorization and development of an individual's singing voice are determined not only by the range of the voice but also by the quality of sound that it produces.

Strategies **NS 6** (Listen to and analyze the singing voice.)

Record the voices of two students singing the same song. Compare the two voices, describing their quality of tone. Urge students to provide adjectives to adequately describe what is heard. Their ability to verbalize will be helpful in better understanding the concept of timbre.

Have students compare the vocal sounds of adults and children. Describe similarities and differences in these voices.

Provide recordings of both male and female voices. Students should begin to recognize, identify aurally, and verbalize the differences in timbre that exist between these two groups of voices.

As students listen to music of other countries, they should discover that the timbre of the singing voice varies from culture to culture. Exposure to different cultural styles helps students become more musically sensitive to and appreciative of the great diversity of music characteristics of other countries.

Students should recognize that the adult voice may be classified according to similar and contrasting differences in range as well as differences in quality of sound, as seen in the following diagram:

Vocal Ranges

Female	Soprano	High
	Mezzo-soprano	Medium
	Alto	Low
Male	Tenor	High
	Baritone	Medium
	Bass	Low

Have students listen to examples of vocal performances that highlight each male and female vocal range. Some examples might include:

a. Soprano: "Depuis le jour," from *Louise* by Carpentier
b. Mezzo-soprano: "Habanera," from *Carmen* by Bizet
c. Alto: "Dido's Lament," from *Dido and Aeneas* by Purcell
d. Tenor: "Celeste Aïda," from *Aïda* by Verdi
e. Baritone: "Evening Star," from *Tannhäuser* by Wagner
f. Bass: "Mephisto's Serenade," from *Faust* by Gounod

Have students analyze their own voices and then analyze the voice of one of their classmates. Share this information with the class.

Learning   Because students come from a variety of social and cultural backgrounds, many will have musical preferences based on the styles of music they have heard at home and in their community.

Strategies **NS 1, 6** (Sing and listen to songs from a variety of music styles.)

Give students an opportunity to talk about some of their favorite singers. Write the singers' names on the board. Then, ask students to determine which vocal category their favorite singer falls into—soprano, alto, tenor, or bass. Discuss their reasons for this determination.

Compliment their choices and proceed to tell them that the singers they have chosen are well known for the style or kind of music they sing. Each singer has his or her own musical preference. Many of these preferences are shaped during the singer's early years at home, in school, or in their community.

Tell students that if they go online to buy music, they will notice that there are different classifications of music based on style or genre. Poll students to see if they can make a list of these categories.

Classical	Pop
Rhythm and Blues (R&B)	Folk
Soul	Patriotic
Opera	Jazz and Blues
Gospel	Country, Bluegrass, Western
Multicultural	Hip-Hop
Show-Tunes/Musicals	Bluegrass
World Music	Electronic Music
Dance (Lady Gaga)	Rock
Swing	Rap

Provide a list of musical styles, and give students an opportunity to assign their favorite singers to a style.

Emphasize that singing is a great way to reinforce who you are. Whether you want to be a professional singer or sing only at home, in church, or at school, you should discover your true style of singing to maximize your performance.

Work with students to formulate a description of some of the above singing styles. The following chart provides an example.

Classical	Gospel	Pop/Rock	Country/Western	Jazz/Blues/R&B	Rap/Hip-Hop
This field of singing focuses on opera, art songs, and ballads. Singers are expected to give recitals. Much vocal preparation, reading music, theory, and learning languages is needed in this kind of singing	Beginning with simple hymns, a gospel singer needs inspiration and the ability to effectively convince others. A strong voice that projects and is passionate is essential.	This style is usually fast and energetic. You need a unique singing voice that can project. You must "turn on" the young at heart. Playing guitar and knowledge of recording devices are basic musts in this field of singing.	If you have a strong whining voice, you might consider country/western music. It entails a wide variety of songs, from fast to slow, from brawling to soothing. Usually these singers have special guitar, banjo, or harmonica skills as well.	Jazz encompasses a wide variety of songs and keys. It requires a good "ear" and the ability to improvise. Blues and R&B is similar to jazz, but both tell a personal story. There are classic jazz songs that are expected of all jazz singers.	Rhythmic accuracy, the ability to tell a story through rhyme and understand phrase length, are required. An understanding of syncopation is important, as is the ability to dance.

Once students have reviewed the various styles, assign them a familiar song such as, "Twinkle, Twinkle Little Star" to perform in a style of their choice. Students should be given the opportunity to work in groups on this task, if they wish. They can perform their song for the class.

FOCUS

Vocal Health

Learning Vocal health is important for everybody, especially for teachers who use their voices constantly. Classroom and music teachers are extremely susceptible to developing vocal damage while on the job. In fact, there are many known factors that cause vocal fatigue and damage that can be prevented if teachers are aware of them.

Strategies **NS 1** (Singing on pitch in an appropriate range for children while using good vocal technique.)

Review and then discuss the following behaviors that may lead to vocal health problems. Teachers, and students who are training to be teachers, tend to exhibit these behaviors in front of their classes and during peer teaching activities. After the discussion, do a quick self-analysis to see if there is anything you can do to insure your own vocal health.

A. Potential Problem

Many teachers tend to raise their voices to "talk over" the children. They are literally in competition with twenty or more voices in the classroom.

What Can You Do?

1. Never try to talk over the children. Not only will this damage you vocally but it will establish a lack of respect on the part of the children toward you.
2. Be aware of and sensitive to how you are using your voice. How loudly and how much are you talking/singing?
3. Pace yourself.
4. Have rest breaks, if possible, between periods of use.
5. Insist on lowering the level and amount of unnecessary "chatter" that is taking place in the classroom. Learn to use your eyes and facial expressions rather than your voice to do the talking.

B. Potential Problem

Some teachers tend to scream or yell while supervising on the playground, in the school cafeteria, in the classroom, or while doing bus duty.

What Can You Do?

1. If possible, use a whistle.
2. Create a colorful, two-sided sign that reads, "STOP TALKING" or "STOP RUNNING" that you can hold up. Design it in the octagon shape of a stop sign.
3. Positive reinforcement is extremely effective. Set up a token, gold star system or some kind of reward system in which children will be rewarded for good behavior.
4. In case positive reinforcement fails, develop a disciplinary system in the classroom in which you simply walk over and write an unruly child's name on the board. Consequences should follow after a name has been recorded three times. You need not say a word.

C. Potential Problem

The voices of children tend to be in a higher register than those of many adults. Therefore, in order to best accommodate the children, teachers should be able to sing in their higher register.

What Can You Do?

1. Be honest with your students. Let them know that although you cannot sing high, they should try to do so.
2. Use recordings with children's voices as much as possible, or find a child who matches pitch well and let him or her serve as a vocal model.

D. Potential Problem

Coughing and clearing the throat causes the vocal bands or folds to be abrasively rubbed together, ultimately causing long-term damage to the folds. Many teachers tend to develop this behavior in order to get students' attention in the classroom.

What Can You Do?

1. Refrain from clearing your throat.
2. Use your "teacher" facial expressions to get students' attention, or physically move closer to where the unruly child is sitting or standing.

E. Potential Problem

Talking when stressed will lead to emotional and/or physical tension, which in turn leads to vocal fatigue.

What Can You Do?

1. Chill out! Try to relax! Close your eyes, take in a deep, long breath through your nose and breathe out slowly through your mouth.
2. Maintain good posture while sitting and standing. Balanced posture is very helpful in reducing stress of the body and promoting optimum vocal tone.

F. Potential Problem

Sometimes the voice can be too high, too soft, too nasal, or hoarse, or can even cause pain to the classroom and music teacher. Symptoms of vocal damage include breathiness, huskiness, hoarseness, loss of voice, monotone, sore or tense throat, pitch breaks, and easy vocal fatigue.

What Can You Do?

1. Take a couple of voice lessons from a professional. A trained vocal specialist will be able to immediately analyze your problem and set you on the right track within two or three lessons. A nearby college or university is a good place to find these professionals.
2. If you are experiencing pain, you should see your doctor.
3. Drink lots of water, especially when talking and singing.
4. Avoid being in a room that does not have good air circulation.

5. After work, rest your voice as much as possible. Try to stay relaxed and your voice will, too.
6. Whispering will work for you, if done correctly. However, if you feel that your throat is not relaxed while whispering, you should stop. Excessive whispering can cause vocal fatigue.
7. If you can, avoid things that will dry out your throat. During the winter months, home heating can dry out the air in your house or apartment. Drinking plenty of water will help. Also, a humidifier can work to keep the air in your home at an optimal level to prevent dryness.

FOCUS

Orchestral Sounds

Learning

A *symphony orchestra* consists of four major families of instruments: strings, brass, woodwinds, and percussion. The instruments in each family are grouped together because they share physical characteristics and have similarities in the way they produce tones.

Strategies **NS 6** (Describing and analyzing woodwind instruments and listening to some of their most famous works.)

Make available many opportunities to view and hear orchestral instruments. Students need to hold and feel the instruments, as well as hear them played. The study of orchestral instruments should be presented over a period of time, not all at once.

These hands-on experiences should be followed by presentations of visuals and recordings of the instruments. The Internet is one of the greatest sources for accessing actual performances on these instruments.

Students should identify the physical characteristics of each instrument so that they can eventually draw conclusions as to why the instrument belongs to a particular family.

The Young Person's Guide to the Orchestra, by Benjamin Britten, is a composition featuring each orchestral instrument in turn. This recording, which can be purchased online, can be used with older students as an introduction to or review of instrumental sounds.

Learning

The *string family* includes four basic instruments: violin, viola, cello, and double bass, also known as string bass or bass viol. Tone is produced on these instruments when the strings vibrate. Strings are set in motion by plucking them, called *pizzicato*, or by drawing a bow across them with one hand, called *arco*. The other hand produces definite pitches by pressing one or more strings against the fingerboard. This action produces varying lengths of the string, which in turn causes the pitch to ascend or descend. The harp also belongs to the string family.

The shorter and thinner the string on any stringed instrument, the higher the pitch or sound. Likewise, the longer and thicker the string, the lower the pitch or sound. The same principle can be applied to the size of all instruments; the smaller the instrument, the higher its pitch.

The **violin** is the soprano of the string family. Because of its small size, it produces the highest pitches. The tone color of the violin closely resembles the human voice and is capable of much versatility. The violin is held firmly underneath the chin.

The **viola** corresponds to the alto voice. It is slightly larger than the violin and has thicker strings. It also is held under the chin.

The **cello** is much larger than the violin or viola. Consequently, it has to rest comfortably between the thighs while the player is in a seated position. A peg at the base of the cello allows the instrument to stand upright on the floor. The tone of the cello is often described as mellow.

The **double bass** is the largest of the four stringed instruments. Because of its enormous size, a person who plays it often needs a van to transport it from one place to another. Players either stand or sit on a high stool to play the stringed bass. The thickness and length of the strings on the bass make it one of the lowest sounding instruments in the orchestra.

The **harp** does not look like the other stringed instruments. It is about six feet tall, is shaped liked the number 7, and has 47 strings of varying lengths. There are usually one or two harps in the orchestra. Harp players sit down with their legs on either side of the instrument, with the neck of the harp leaning against the right shoulder. Each harp string sounds a different pitch and comes in different colors to help the player distinguish between the different intervals. Harp strings are usually plucked with the fingertips and the thumb. There are seven pedals on the harp, which when pressed down, shift the strings. This shifting allows the harp to play chromatics or sharps and flats.

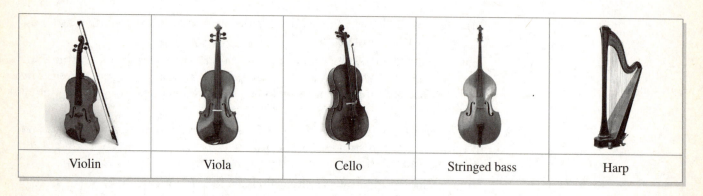

| Violin | Viola | Cello | Stringed bass | Harp |

Strategies **NS 6** (Listening to, describing, and analyzing string instruments and some of their most famous works.)

Provide students with opportunities to explore stringed instruments. Examine and discuss their general makeup. Examine the bow; explain that a substance called rosin is used on the bow to produce tension between the bow and the string. The tension causes the string to vibrate and sound results.

Invite students from the school orchestra to demonstrate the playing of a stringed instrument. If available, invite a professional to perform for the students.

Have students listen to a variety of artists perform on their stringed instrument. Both teachers and students should be aware that many of the most famous string "classics" are accessible online. Online listening and viewing is extremely rewarding because it affords all the opportunity to hear and see some of the world's most famous artists performing these pieces.

   a. **Violin**
      (1) *Violin Concerto in E Minor* (Rondo) by Mendelssohn
      (2) *Flight of the Bumblebee* by Rimski-Korsakov

   Look online for violinists like Joshua Bell, Gareth Johnson, Itzhak Perlman, and Sarah Chang.

   b. **Viola**
      (1) *Concerto for Viola and Orchestra* by Bartok
      (2) *Concerto for Viola and String Orchestra* by Telemann.

   Look online for violists like Paul Hindemith, Lillian Fuchs, and Lionel Tertis.

c. Cello
   (1) "The Swan" from *Carnival of the Animals* by Saint-Saëns
   (2) *Sonata No 1 for Cello and Piano, Op 45* by Mendelssohn

   Look online for artists like Yo-Yo Ma, Christopher Bunting, Anna Bylsma, Joan Jeanrenaud, and Chao Yu.

d. Double Bass, also called the string bass, upright bass or contra-bass
   (1) "Jimbo's Lullaby" by Debussy
   (2) "Elephant" from *Carnival of the Animals* by Saint-Saëns

   Look online for artists like Oscar Zimmerman and Gary Karr.

e. Harp
   (1) "Musique Gaelique" by Alan Stivell
   (2) *The Nutcracker Suite* by Tchaikovsky

   Look online for famous harpists like Marcel Grandjany, Alfonse Hasselmans, Carlos Salzedo, and Harpo Marx.

The teacher can now bridge students' understanding of the string family and how the process of making and playing strings reinforces their knowledge of science, specifically acoustics and physics.

The teacher should emphasize that a vibrating string produces a motion that is rich in harmonics (different frequencies of vibrations). Bowing the string not only allows a range of expressive techniques but also supplies energy continuously and maintains the harmonic richness. However, a string on its own makes little sound.

If you put your finger gently on a loudspeaker, you will feel the sound vibrations. If you observe the fingers on the left hand of a string player, you will see that they are assisting the string to vibrate by means of a gentle, yet controlled shaking motion.

The pitch of a vibrating string depends on three things:

1. The **thickness** of the string affects the vibration. The larger the string, the more slowly it vibrates.
2. The **frequency** (the number of vibrations that pass a fixed point per time unit) can be adjusted by changing the tension in the strings using the tuning pegs. The tighter the string, the higher the pitch.
3. The **length of the string** affects the frequency.
4. The **mode of vibration**. When you play a stringed instrument, sound can be produced by plucking it and/or playing it with the bow. More than one string can also be sounded at the same time to produce harmony. This technique is called performing a "double or triple stop" on the instrument and is very difficult to do in tune. All of these methods will affect the instrument's vibrations and ultimately its sound in some way.

Do an experiment to find out about string length and its effect on sound production. Make a stringed instrument.

You will need:

- a wire clothes hanger
- a length of nylon fishing string

Directions: Tie two ends of the string across the bottom part of the hanger. Tighten it until the bottom wire bends up out of the way and tie it off so that it stays tight with your hand. Now you are ready to play it by plucking it.

You can also use a sturdy branch from a tree. It does not matter how long it is. If you try different sizes, you will discover that you will have different pitches, based upon the length of the string.

Match the pitch that you have created to a key on the piano and record your results.

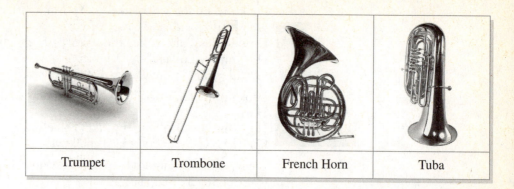

| Trumpet | Trombone | French Horn | Tuba |

Learning

The *brass family* consists of four major instruments: the trumpet, French horn, trombone, and tuba. Unlike the string family, brass instruments produce tone as a result of lips vibrating into either a cone-shaped or cup-shaped mouthpiece, causing the air being blown into the instrument to vibrate. Pitch is changed by pressing valves and tightening or loosening the lips; both will change the length of the air column being blown into the instrument. This process is consistent in the brass family except for the trombone. In place of valves, the trombone slide is pushed out or pulled in to shorten or lengthen the column of air.

The bright and brilliant tone color of the **trumpet** makes it one of the most popular instruments in the brass family. The trumpet has three valves that, singly or in combination, lower the natural pitch of the instrument. Because of its brilliance in tone, mutes made of metal, wood, and synthetic materials are inserted into its bell to change its tone quality.

The **French horn** is a brass instrument with a distinctive circular body. It has the reputation of requiring the most difficult technique of all the orchestral instruments. The French horn has a wide bell and a narrow, cone-shaped mouthpiece. Both its tone quality and pitch are influenced by a technique called "stopping," which involves the insertion of the hand into the bell. The mellowness of tone that results affords the French horn opportunities to blend easily with other families of the orchestra as well as its own.

Both the size of the instrument and the cup-shaped mouthpiece of the **trombone** are larger than those of the trumpet, causing its tone to be lower and perhaps more dignified and solemn. The trombone's sliding mechanism allows a player to glide quickly up and down, from one tone to another, through all degrees of pitches. This sliding technique is called *portamento*. There are four sizes of trombones; the tenor and the bass are the most popular.

The **tuba** is the lowest pitched instrument in the brass family. It exists in many shapes and sizes and may have as many as five valves. Because of its large size and weight, the tuba lacks versatility and is therefore often limited to providing supportive tones for the rest of the orchestra; however, the tuba is capable of playing a legato, melodic line. Its tone color is deep and warm.

Strategies **NS 6** (Analyze and describe the sounds of brass instruments.)

Students should examine as many members of the brass family as possible. They should observe that cone- and cup-shaped mouthpieces are used. They should also note that the trombone's slide shortens or lengthens the air column. Valves perform this same function for the other brass instruments.

If possible, invite students from band or orchestra to demonstrate some of the instruments for the class.

Student should eventually be able to identify the brass instruments by sight and sound.

The following recordings can be used to help students identify the sound of each brass instrument. All of these pieces may be accessed via the Internet.

a. Trumpet
(1) "Finale" from *William Tell Overture* by Rossini
(2) *Pictures at an Exhibition* by Mussorgsky

Check online to see performances and hear recordings of some of the most famous trumpet players, including:

Louis Armstrong	Arturo Sandoval
Miles Davis	Al Hirt
Dizzie Gillespie	Kenny Hubbard
Clifford Brown	Roy Eldridge
Wynton Marsalis	Ruby Braff
Maynard Ferguson	Kenny Dorham
Roy Hargrove	Clark Terry

b. French horn
(1) *Peter and the Wolf* (hunter's theme) by Prokofiev
(2) *Symphony No. 5* (2nd movement) by Tchaikovsky

Check out famous French horn players online. Names to look for are: Dennis Brain, Phillip Farkas, Barry Tuckwell, and Dale Clevenger.

c. Trombone
(1) *Stars and Stripes Forever* by Sousa
(2) *Equali for Four Trombones* by Beethoven

Check the following trombone players online. Look at some of their performances.

Classical Trombonists	Jazz/Big Band Trombonists
Joseph Alessi	Glenn Miller
Frank Rosolino	Tommy Dorsey
Arthur Pryor	Paul William Rutherford
Don Lusher	J.J. Johnson
Nick Hudson	Slide Hampton

d. Tuba
(1) "Bydlo" from *Pictures at an Exhibition* by Mussorgsky
(2) *Finlandia* by Sibelius

Check out the following tuba players online.

Classical	Jazz
Tommy Johnson (Played the "Jaws Theme"	Walter Page
Roger Bobo	Red Callendar
Harvey Phillips	Joe Murphy
William Bell	Howard Johnson
	Anthony Lacen (Tuba Fats)

Teachers should reinforce that brass players blow air into a tube. The lips act as a **vibrating valve**. Once the air in the instrument is vibrating, some of the energy is radiated as sound out of the bell. Again, through the study of instruments and how they produce their sounds, we learn about physics.

Tell students that brass players can make musical sounds with just their lips. This is one of the first things a brass player learns to do. Have students practice closing their mouths, pulling their lips back into a tight smile and then blowing. Ask students to describe the result.

Perform an Experiment

Materials Needed: garden hose about three feet long and a funnel.

Try adding a mouthpiece to one end of a garden hose and a funnel at the other end. (You can cut the garden hose into different lengths.) Blow through the mouthpiece by buzzing the lips.

Record the pitches that resulted from applying the funnel and mouthpiece to different lengths of hoses. Answer the question, "Did the theory hold that the longer the tube was the lower the pitch would be?"

Students should realize that the technique is exactly the same for producing sound on any brass instrument.

Learning

The *woodwind family* is one of the most diversified of the four instrumental groups because it contains seven major members: piccolo, flute, clarinet, oboe, English horn, bassoon, and contrabassoon. Different sounds are produced by the player closing holes, which lengthens the vibrating column of air, or opening holes, which shortens the vibrating column of air. The woodwind family is divided into single-reed, double-reed, and no-reed members.

The **clarinet** is a single-reed member. When the clarinet is played, the reed vibrates, creating a vibrating column of air that produces sound. The bass clarinet is a member of the clarinet family. It possesses a characteristically deep, mellow sound and is often found in the orchestra.

There are several sizes of clarinets, ranging from soprano to bass. The B-flat clarinet, however, continues to be one of the most popular among beginning players.

The **saxophone**, although not a traditional member of the orchestra, is often scored in contemporary orchestral music. It is traditionally used to play popular styles of music, such as blues, jazz, and rock. The saxophone is a single-reed instrument, but instead of being made of wood, is made of metal.

On the oboe, English horn, bassoon and contrabassoon, two reeds vibrate. The **oboe** is similar in structure to the clarinet except for its double reed. Its quality of tone is often described as being nasal yet plaintive. The double-reed mouthpiece requires a different embouchure or mouth placement from its single-reed counterpart.

The **English horn** is actually an alto oboe. It is longer than the oboe and contains a pear-shaped bell. It has a lower range of pitches and a somewhat melancholy tone quality.

The **bassoon** and **contrabassoon** possess large amounts of tubing that allow them to produce very low tones. The contrabassoon is the lowest sounding instrument in the orchestra. It is pitched one octave lower than the bassoon. Both the bassoon and the contrabassoon are double-reed instruments. Their tone quality is both nasal and plaintive, like the oboe.

Other double-reed instruments include bagpipes, an instrument common to Scotland; and the piri, a Korean double-reed instrument, used in both folk and classical music of Korea.

The tone on the **flute** and **piccolo** is produced by blowing a column of air over an open hole. The **flute** and the **piccolo** are transverse instruments, meaning that they are held at a right angle to the body.

The **piccolo** is the smallest of the woodwind family and thus produces the highest pitches. Its tone, unlike the mellow and lyric quality of the flute, is almost piercing. Both instruments were originally made of wood and therefore were classified as woodwinds. Today, the piccolo and the flute are usually made of silver.

Have students use the Internet to research other double- and single-reed instruments from other countries. Compare these woodwinds to those played in the United States.

Single Reeds

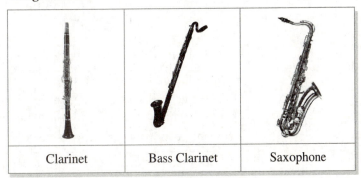

| Clarinet | Bass Clarinet | Saxophone |

Double Reeds

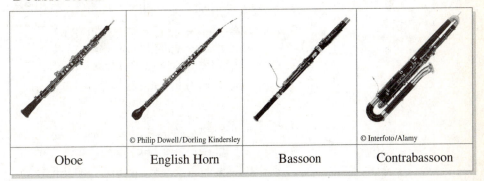

© Philip Dowell/Dorling Kindersley

© Interfoto/Alamy

| Oboe | English Horn | Bassoon | Contrabassoon |

No Reeds

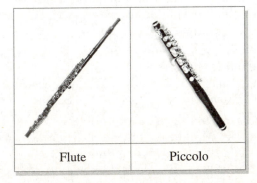

| Flute | Piccolo |

Strategies **NS 6** (Describe and analyze woodwind instruments. Listen to music featuring woodwind instruments.)

Students should examine instruments of the woodwind family, giving special attention to the mouthpieces.

Have students from band and orchestra demonstrate their instruments. Reinforce this activity by inviting professional musicians to play for the class.

Students should compare the flute to its predecessor, the recorder. (See Chapter 10.) Discuss similarities and differences between the instruments.

Students should be given opportunities to recognize woodwind instruments on recordings.

The following list provides some of the most beloved highlights of woodwind instruments in the symphony orchestra. The examples are brief and engaging and have been listened to by children around the world for many years.

a. **Flute**
   (1) *Afternoon of a Faun* by Debussy
   (2) "Dance of the Toy Flutes" from the *Nutcracker Suite* by Tchaikovsky

   Search online for music and performances by James Galway, one of the world's most famous flute players.

b. **Piccolo**
   (1) *Stars and Stripes Forever* by Sousa
   (2) "Chinese Dance" from the *Nutcracker Suite* by Tchaikovsky

c. **Clarinet**
   (1) *Peter and the Wolf* (the cat) by Prokofiev
   (2) "Cuckoo in the Deep Woods" from *Carnival of the Animals* by Saint-Saëns

   Check online for performances of some of the greatest clarinet players, such as:

Benny Goodman (jazz)	Darren Costen (classical)
Artie Shaw (jazz)	Larry Combs (classical)
Woody Herman (jazz)	Stanley Drucker (classical)
Don Byron (classical)	Bernard Izen (classical)

   Bass Clarinet
   (1) *Daphnis and Chloe* by Ravel
   (2) Most of Puccini's operas

   Check online for performances by Eric Dolphy, one of the world's most prominent Bass clarinetists.

d. **Saxophone**
   (1) "My Favorite Things" from *The Sound of Music* by John Coltrane
   (2) "Now is the Time" by Charlie Parker

   Check online for musical performances by John Coltrane, Charlie Parker, and Stan Getz.

e. **Oboe**
   (1) *Peter and the Wolf* (the duck) by Prokofiev
   (2) "Bacchanale" from *Samson and Delilah* by Saint-Saëns

   Check online for performances by these great oboe players: John Mack, Hansjorg Schellenburger, John De Lancie, and Marcel Tabuteau.

f. **English Horn**
   (1) "Largo" from the *New World Symphony* by Dvorak
   (2) *Roman Carnival Overture* by Berlioz

   Check out the following online:
   • Paul McCartney on the cover of *Sgt. Pepper's Lonely Hearts Club Band*. (He is holding an English horn.)
   • *Schindler's List* (film score) by John Williams
   • *Harry Potter and the Sorcerer's Stone* (film score) by John Williams
   • *Tristan und Isolde* (Act 3, Scene 1) by Wagner

g. **Bassoon**
   (1) "In the Hall of the Mountain King" from *Peer Gynt Suite No. 1* by Grieg
   (2) *Rondo for Bassoon and Orchestra No. 35* (Andante and Rondo) by von Weber
   (3) "The Grandfather's Theme," from *Peter and the Wolf* by Prokofiev
   (4) *The Sorcerer's Apprentice*, widely known because of its use in the movie *Fantasia*; the main melody is first heard in a high bassoon solo.

Check out these famous bassoon players online:

Judith LeClair	Simon Kovar
Eitenne Ozi	Leonard Sharrow
Julius Weissenborn	Archie Camden
Walter Richie	Sol Schoenbach
Carl Almenrader	Maurice Allard

h. Contrabassoon

(1) "Conversations of Beauty and the Beast" from *Mother Goose Suite* by Rave

(2) *Scheherazade* (second movement) by Rimsky-Korsakov

Two great contrabassoon players whose performances can be found online are Adam Siminiceanu and Susan Nigro.

Learning

The percussion family consists of innumerable members, because, by rule, any surface that is struck is considered percussive. Percussion instruments can be categorized as having definite pitch or indefinite pitch. Instruments having definite pitch are tuned to specific pitches, such as the piano, the timpani, and the chimes. Instruments that are indefinite in pitch are not tuned. These include the woodblock, the triangle and the tambourine.

Strategies **NS 6** (Describe and analyze a variety of percussion instruments and listen to some of them as they are used in orchestras.)

SOME PERCUSSION INSTRUMENTS FOUND IN THE ORCHESTRA

Timpani (definite pitch)	Bass Drum (indefinite pitch)	Chimes or Tubular Bells (definite pitch)
		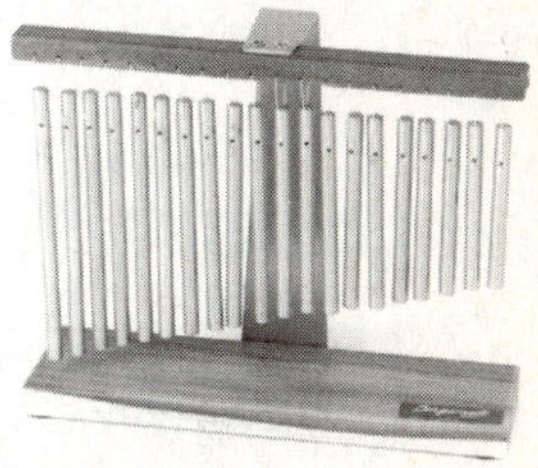 Peripole-Bergerault, Inc.
Snare Drum (indefinite pitch)	Xylophone (definite pitch)	Tambourine (indefinite pitch)

Triangle (indefinite pitch)	Gong (indefinite pitch)	Cymbals (indefinite pitch)
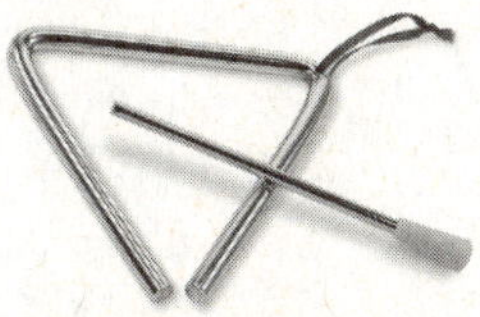		

Direct students' attention to the classroom rhythm instruments that they have used, and indicate which ones are also members of the orchestral percussion family. (The answer is: They all are members.)

Play creative games that allow students to recognize aurally the sounds generated by the instruments. See Chapter 10 for concrete examples.

The following list of recordings can be used to acquaint students with the sounds of different instruments in the percussion family:

THE FOLLOWING PERCUSSION INSTRUMENTS ARE EASILY RECOGNIZED BECAUSE COMPOSERS WROTE SPECIAL PIECES THAT FEATURED THEM

Instrument	Picture of Instrument	Composers/Works
Piano (definite pitch)		Works by Listz, Schumann, Bach; *Nocturnes*, *Preludes*, *Etudes*, and *Waltzes* by Chopin
Harpsichord (definite pitch)		*Brandenburg Concerto No. 5* (1st movement) by Bach
Castanets (indefinite pitch)		*Capriccio Espanol* by Rimsky-Korsakov
Orchestra Bells Also called glockenspiel (definite pitch)		"Witches Sabbath" from *Symphony Fantastic* by Berlioz

Instrument	Picture of Instrument	Composers/Works
Celesta (definite pitch)	© Dorling Kindersley	"Dance of the Sugar Plum Fairies" from the *Nutcracker Suite* by Tchaikovsky
Organ (definite pitch)		*Toccata and Fugue in D minor* by Bach

In addition to the selections mentioned above, the following pieces of orchestral music are also recommended.

Timpani	*Symphony No.1* (3rd movement)	Tchaikovsky
Tambourine	"Tarantella" from *Fantastic Toy Shop*	Rossini
Snare Drum	Check online to hear Evelyn Glennie playing the snare drum. Evelyn is an internationally renowned percussionist who happens to be deaf.	

There is a plethora of dynamic and leading percussionists who have made names for themselves playing styles other than classical. Some of the leading jazz percussionists, for example, are Elvin Jones, Max Roach, Art Blakely, Buddy Rich, and Connie Kay, just to name a few.

Students should be given the opportunity to listen attentively to the "rhythm section" that backs up their favorite singer or that is part of their favorite band.

Be encouraged to attend a live concert or watch your favorite video and see how many of the unpitched and pitched percussion instruments you can recognize on stage.

 Materials needed to make a percussions instrument are all around you. You need only to use your imagination.

A. Make a simple coffee can into a drum. Remove both ends of the coffee can with a can opener. Cover one end with a piece of rubber, cloth, or plastic. Tie the head onto the drum with a strong string or place a strong rubber band around the head to keep it firmly in place. Tautness of the head is very important. Get a stick and hit it.

B. Many detergent bottles have grooved sides. Take a stick or thin dowel rod and scrape it. (guiro)

C. Obtain a box from the grocery store and use it as a drum. You will discover that different size boxes make different sounds. Use wooden spoons, mallets, or sticks to hit your box.

D. Put a few beans or rice into a soda can. Cover the opening with a plastic lid or tape it shut. Shake it. (maracas/shaker)

E. Collect any old keys from around the house. Get some nylon fish line. Tie the strings onto a clothes hanger. (wind chimes)

In addition, the chart in **Visual TM2** shows the seating chart of an orchestra. A larger version of this chart should be displayed in the classroom.

It is often helpful to summarize the information about orchestral instruments by providing students with a chart similar to that shown in **Visual TM3**.

VISUAL TM2

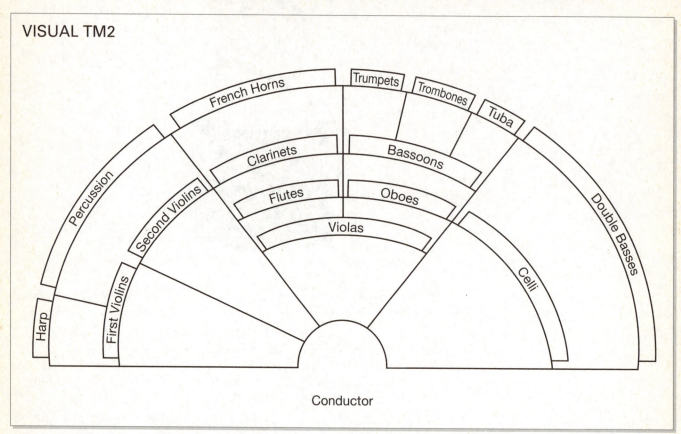

Conductor

VISUAL TM3

Families of the Orchestra

String Family		*Brass Family*	
Violin	Soprano	Trumpet	Soprano
Viola	Alto	French horn	Alto
Cello	Tenor	Trombone	Tenor
Double bass	Bass	Tuba	Bass

Woodwind Family		*Percussion Family*	
No Reed		*Definite Pitch*	
Piccolo	Soprano	Xylophone	Piano
Flute	Soprano	Marimba	Organ
		Celesta	Harpsichord
Single Reed		Timpani	Glockenspiel
Clarinet Family	Soprano, Bass		
Saxophone Family	Soprano, Alto,	*Indefinite Pitch*	
	Tenor, Baritone	Wood block	Triangle
		Maracas	Tambourine
Double Reed		Cymbals	Snare drum
Oboe	Soprano	Gong	Bass drum
English horn	Alto		Castanets
Bassoon	Bass		
Contrabassoon	Bass		

INTRODUCING THE STRUCTURAL COMPONENTS OF TIMBRE

Suggested Sequencing by Grade Level

Primary: K, 1, 2, 3
1. Environment and body sounds
2. Tone color of rhythm instruments

Intermediate: 4, 5, 6
1. Vocal sounds
2. Orchestral sounds

WRITTEN AND PERFORMANCE-RELATED ASSESSMENTS THROUGH COOPERATIVE LEARNING ACTIVITIES: TIMBRE NS 2, 4, 5, 6, 7, 8

1. Have each group create a composition using body sounds. Decide whether the composition will include hand, foot, or mouth sounds or a combination of these three. Score the composition using the examples under Visual TM1 for a guideline. Perform the work for the class. **NS 4, 5, 7**
2. Ask each group to create a poem or make up a story that lends itself to instrumental sound effects. Decide which instruments will best enhance the literary work, and prepare a performance of the poem or the story for the class. **NS 2, 4, 8**
3. Give each group a cassette tape and player. Each tape should be the same and contain excerpts of songs sung by different singers. Ask each group to list adjectives that characterize the timbre of each of the taped voices. Groups should try to identify each vocal range—soprano, tenor, and so forth. Return students to the large group and discuss the characteristics identified in the small groups. **NS 6**
   This activity can be repeated using tapes containing the sounds of different musical instruments.
4. Provide each group with a set of cards, each card containing the picture of a different orchestral instrument. Students should be able to identify each instrument by name, family, and range.
5. Distribute to each group a short, taped instrumental composition; each tape is different. Students should listen to the tape and identify as many musical instruments as possible. Finally, students should list everything they know about the instruments they heard. **NS 6**
   On another day, tapes can be exchanged and the activity repeated.
6. Assign children to teams and have each team prepare for a listening identification competition. Some of the standard classical literature that might be used in the competition are: **NS 6**

LISTENING SELECTIONS

1. *Peter and the Wolf* by Prokofiev
2. *Carnival of the Animals* by Saint-Saëns
3. *Flight of the Bumblebee/Tale of Tsar Saltan Suite* by Rimsky-Korsakov
4. "March" from *The Comedians* by Dimitri Kabalevsky
5. "Spring" from *The Four Seasons* by Vivaldi
6. *Tubby the Tuba* by George Kleinsinger
7. "Children's Chorus" from *Carmen* by Bizet
8. *Children's Symphony* (3rd movement) by McDonald
9. *The Nutcracker* by Tchaikovsky
10. "In the Hall of the Mountain King" from *Peer Gynt Suite No. 1* by Grieg
11. Minuet and Trio from *Eine kliene Nachtmusik* by Mozart
12. "Viennese Musical Clock" from *Háry János Suite* by Kodály
13. "Puisque tout passe" from *Six Chansons* by Hindemith
14. *Clair de lune* by Debussy
15. *Symphony No. 94* by Joseph Haydn
16. *Appalachian Spring* by A. Copland
17. *Fanfare for the Common Man* by A. Copland
18. "Erlkönig" by F. Schubert
19. "Hoedown" from *Rodeo* by A. Copland
20. *"La Raspa"* (Mexican Folk Music)
21. *Pictures at an Exhibition* by Mussorgsky
22. "On the Trail" from *Grand Canyon Suite* by Grofé
23. "Variations on Simple Gifts" from *Appalachian Spring* by A. Copland
24. *Bolero* by Ravel
25. *Concerto for Harp, Op. 25 (3rd movement)* by A. Ginastera

CHAPTER 5

Teaching Expressive Elements to Children

INTRODUCTION

Teachers of music are faced with many challenges as they progress through day-to-day lessons in music reading, performance, and appreciation. Thus far, this text has been concerned with the basic structural components of rhythm, melody, and timbre. However, reading and singing songs well includes more than a working knowledge of duration symbols and pitch identification. At some point children must become aware of the expressive potential each song possesses. To perform a song well, children must solve the puzzles it contains: Should this song be sung a little faster? A little slower? Would this song sound better if it were softer? Louder? Could we improve this song by gradually getting louder or softer at some specific point? Should this song be sung smoothly or in a more detached manner? What instruments would best accompany this song? Such questions can help lead children to a more sensitive performance of music, whether sung or played on melodic or rhythmic instruments.

Music expresses that which cannot be said,
And which cannot be suppressed.
—Victor Hugo

FOCUS

Tempo

Learning	The speed of the basic, underlying beat of a composition, ranging from very slow to very fast, is called *tempo*.

Strategies **NS 1, 7** (Singing and moving to fast and slow music. Deciding which is the optimum speed.)

Have students read the lyrics to "All Through the Night." Ask them to decide whether they think this song should be sung fast or slow, and have them explain why.

ALL THROUGH THE NIGHT

Welsh Folk Song

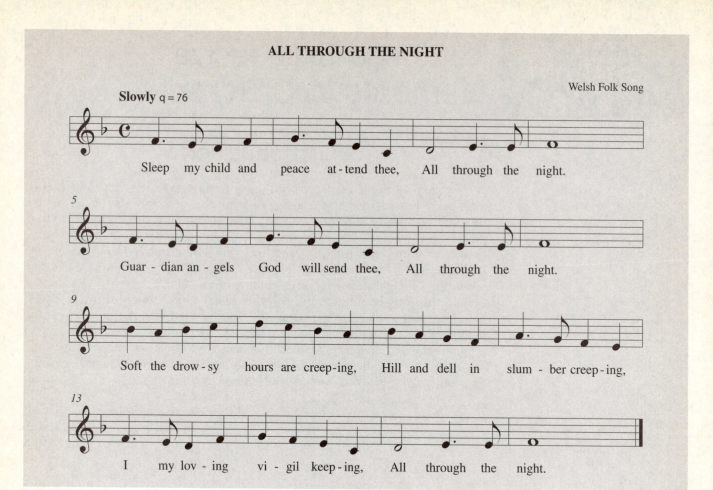

Slowly ♩ = 76

Sleep my child and peace at-tend thee, All through the night.

Guar-dian an-gels God will send thee, All through the night.

Soft the drow-sy hours are creep-ing, Hill and dell in slum-ber creep-ing,

I my lov-ing vi-gil keep-ing, All through the night.

Sing songs containing words that suggest a slow tempo for performance, such as "All Through the Night." Have students explain why they think the song should be sung slowly.

Sing songs containing words that suggest a fast tempo for performance, such as "Down the River." In discussing why this song would be sung more quickly than "All Through the Night," students may discover such words as "river is wide," "channel is deep," "jolly good time," and "sailing along." Also, note the repetition of "down the river."

DOWN THE RIVER

American River Chantey

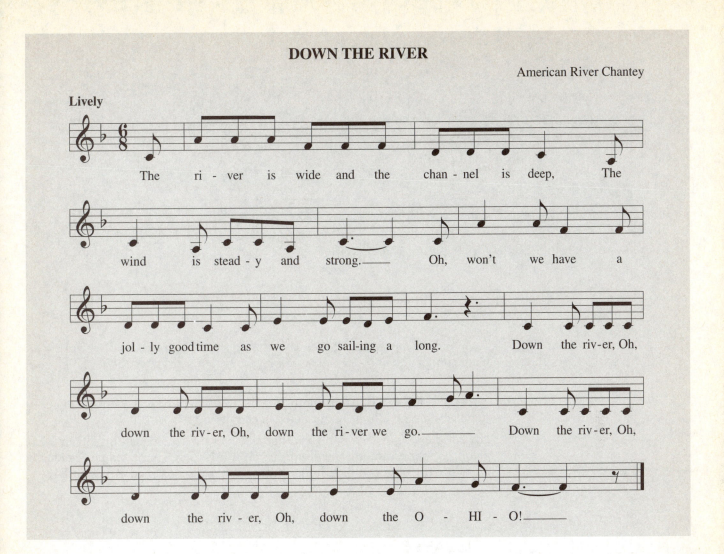

Lively

The ri-ver is wide and the chan-nel is deep, The wind is stead-y and strong.___ Oh, won't we have a jol-ly good time as we go sail-ing a long. Down the riv-er, Oh, down the riv-er, Oh, down the ri-ver we go.___ Down the riv-er, Oh, down the riv-er, Oh, down the O - HI - O!___

Students should know that the Ohio River provided many opportunities for those who lived along its banks. In Cincinnati, Ohio, steamboats were manufactured and repaired in the city. Farmers sent crops down the Ohio and Mississippi Rivers to New Orleans. The Ohio River was one of the physical markers of the Mason Dixon Line, a geographical line that slaves crossed as they escaped to freedom in the North. The Ohio River begins in Pittsburgh and flows south to Cairo, Illinois, where it then flows into the Mississippi River.

Learning Some songs with measures containing notes of shorter duration, such as quarter or eighth notes, seem to move more quickly than others with measures having half notes, even though the tempo of the basic beat does not change.

Strategies **NS 1, 7** (Discovering rates of speed of songs through an analysis of their words and rhythms.)

Sing "I Got a Letter." Have students discover that measures 1 and 5 seem to be faster than the rest of the song because these measures contain mostly notes of shorter duration.

I GOT A LETTER

South Carolina

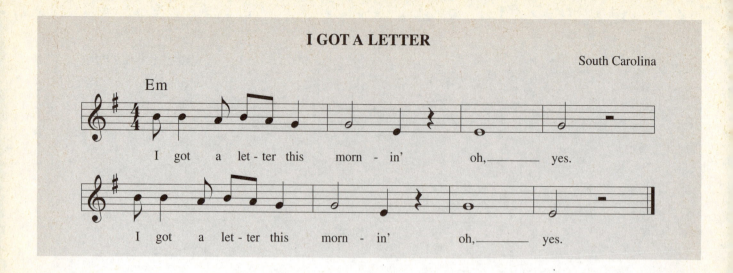

I got a let-ter this morn-in' oh,——— yes.

I got a let-ter this morn-in' oh,——— yes.

Learning Sometimes composers designate how a song should be performed by writing a tempo indication at the top of a song on the far left side above the staff.

Strategies **NS 6, 9** (Understanding tempo. Refer to historical events to understand why a song is to be performed in a certain way.)

Look at the song "Down the River" and discover the tempo marking "lively." Explain that often composers will use Italian words to designate tempo. Gradually introduce the most common Italian tempo markings contained in **Visual E1.**

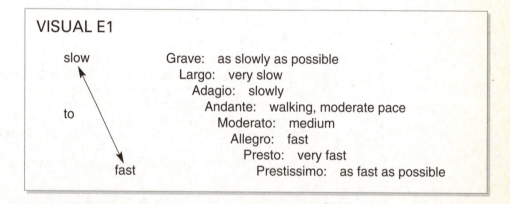

VISUAL E1

slow

to

fast

Grave: as slowly as possible
Largo: very slow
Adagio: slowly
Andante: walking, moderate pace
Moderato: medium
Allegro: fast
Presto: very fast
Prestissimo: as fast as possible

Have students examine the songs in their song books. Discover which songs have tempo markings. If the markings are in Italian, give their English meanings.

Learning Sometimes a piece becomes more expressive if a gradual change of speed occurs. The Italian word *ritardando* (abbreviated *rit.* or *ritard.*) designates a gradual slowing down; *accelerando* (abbreviated *accel.*) indicates a gradual increase in speed.

Strategies **NS 6, 7** (Listening and then analyzing how to move to a recorded piece of music.)

Have students move to melodies that gradually change tempo.

Listen to "Little Train of the Caipira" from *Bachianas Brasileiras* No. 2 by Villa-Lobos. Have students tap the beat to the opening measures of this composition to discover the accelerando. Similarly, tap the last measures of the piece, which incorporate a ritardando. A call chart for this work can be found in Chapter 11.

Choose other recordings having gradual accelerandi or ritardandi (plural forms) and discover the tempo changes.

 Villa-Lobos is a Brazilian composer who wrote this famous piece in 1930. It describes the train journey from the country to the inner city. The train carried peasants to work.

Choose songs in which the addition of an accelerando or ritardando can be used to enhance the meaning of the song. Have children analyze the songs to discover which expressive markings can be used. Sing the songs using the accelerando or ritardando. For example, a ritardando could be used during the singing of measure 12 in the lullaby "All Through the Night", the gradual slowing down of this measure would highlight the text "slumber creeping" to suggest the child is falling asleep.

 Beats per minute (bpm) is a unit typically used as either a measure of *tempo* in music, or a measure of one's heart rate. A rate of 60 bpm means that one beat will occur every second. Have students take their pulse and compare it with a metronome going 60 beats per minute. This activity will afford students an opportunity to collect and compare data, count to at least 60, tell time, and measure a minute. To make this activity more challenging, have students find their average heart rate by measuring their pulse several times, adding the results, and dividing that number by the number of times it was taken.

FOCUS

Dynamics

Learning   The degree of volume in a musical composition is known as *dynamics*. Dynamics range from very soft to very loud.

Strategies **NS 1, 6, 7** (Experience loudness and softness while singing, listening, and playing instruments.)

Tell the children that anyone can sing a series of pitches. However, it is their connection to those pitches that can bring a piece of music alive.

 Place the following sentences on the board and call on different children to read a sentence.

"I don't want to sing the song."
"Stop it!"
"Will you be my friend?"
"Hush little baby and go to sleep."

Ask selected children to read each sentence very softly, and then ask other children to read each sentence very loudly. Allow students to analyze the softness/loudness of each sentence that was read. Ask their opinion about which voice, soft or loud, was best for each of the sentences recited and have them explain why they feel this way. Children should understand that the first two sentences might be better performed in a louder voice. The third and fourth sentences should be performed in a softer voice.

Tell students to name sounds in their environment that might be considered soft or loud sounds. The sound of a music box, for example, might be very soft, whereas a siren from an ambulance or police car might be very loud.

Ask students to name songs that they sing loudly. Then have them name others that they usually sing in their soft voices. For example, a lullaby is always sung very softly. "Jingle Bells", on the other hand, is a happy, upbeat, fun song and people usually sing it loudly.

Sing "Jingle Bells." As mentioned earlier, this is a fun song. It should be sung with joy and enthusiasm using louder pitches.

JINGLE BELLS

James Lord Pierpont
1822-1893

Jin - gle bells, jin - gle bells, Jin - gle all the way.

Oh, what fun it is to ride in a one horse o - pen sleigh, ⸺

Jin - gle bells, jin - gle bells, Jin - gle all the way.

Oh, what fun it is to ride in a one-horse o - pen sleigh.

 Let students know that James Lord Pierpont (1822–1893) wrote "Jingle Bells" in 1857 for a Thanksgiving program at a church in Savannah, Georgia. It has been a popular song ever since. Also, it is interesting that on December 16, 1965, astronauts aboard *Gemini 6* performed "Jingle Bells" on a harmonica and sleigh bells, making "Jingle Bells" the first accompanied song ever performed in space. The instruments used to accompany this song are on display in the National Air and Space Museum in Washington, D.C.

Sing the song, "Hush Little Baby". Students should immediately notice that the words suggest soft pitches.

HUSH LITTLE BABY

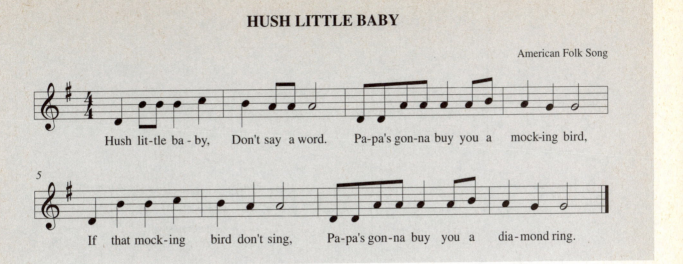

American Folk Song

Hush lit-tle ba - by, Don't say a word. Pa-pa's gon-na buy you a mock-ing bird,

If that mock-ing bird don't sing, Pa-pa's gon-na buy you a dia-mond ring.

And if that diamond ring turns to brass,
Papa's gonna buy you a looking glass.
And if that looking glass gets broke,
Papa's gonna buy you a billy goat.

And if that billy goat won't pull,
Papa's gonna buy you a cart and bull.
And if that cart and bull turn over,
Papa's gonna buy you a dog named Rover.

And if that dog named Rover won't bark,
Papa's gonna buy you a horse and cart.
And if that horse and cart fall down,
You're still the sweetest little baby in town.

 Tell students to do an Internet search to find out what a mockingbird looks like. Also, answer other questions like, "Where can a mockingbird be found?" "What is their natural habitat?" Have them sketch the bird. Ask students to imagine why a father would buy a baby a mockingbird. Write a creative story about this.

Sing other songs whose words imply louder pitches, such as "If You're Happy and You Know It" and "When the Saints." Students should be able to explain why they think these songs should be sung more loudly than "Hush Little Baby."

IF YOU'RE HAPPY AND YOU KNOW IT

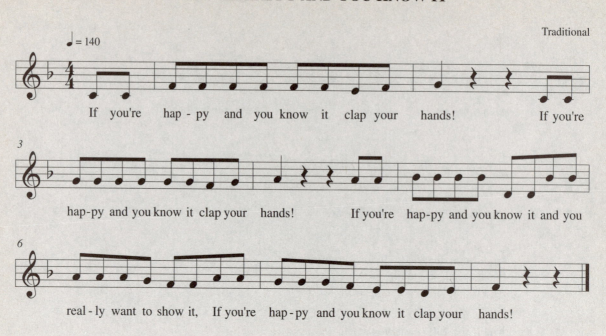

OH, WHEN THE SAINTS

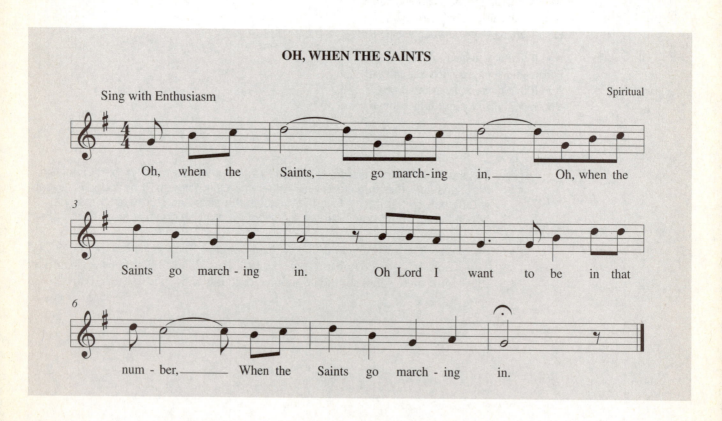

To avoid punishment and sometimes death, many spiritual songwriters used a technique called "mask and symbol." This meant that the text found in many of the spirituals was not as it appeared to be. In this spiritual, the text of "Oh, When the Saints" is masked. The Saints are the slaves. They are marching, not into Heaven, but to Freedom in the North. Marching is one of several symbols used for transportation on the Underground Railroad. The Underground Railroad represents an intricately designed system, made up of people who helped slaves escape to freedom.

Have students choose instruments that could be used to accompany both soft and loud songs. Students should be able to express why they think some instruments would be appropriate for loud songs, but not for songs performed softly.

Learning It is possible to increase the expressiveness of a song by changing the dynamic level at different points within the song.

Strategies **NS 1, 6, 7** (Making decisions as to how to express a song, and then reading musical symbols in the score while singing it.)

Sing "Hoo, Hoo!" Ask students if an echo is loud or soft. Decide how they should sing this song to make it as expressive as possible.

Sing other songs that have words or phrases suggesting a change in dynamic level.

HOO, HOO!

Ethel Crowninshield

There's some-one liv-ing on a big high hill, I won-der who it can be?

There's some-one liv-ing on a big high hill, Who al-ways an-swers me.

Hoo hoo! Hoo hoo! Hoo hoo! Hoo hoo! I won-der who it can be?

Learning Sometimes a song can be more expressive if a gradual change in dynamics occurs. The Italian word *crescendo* (abbreviated *cresc.*) designates a gradual increase in volume, symbolized by $<$. *Decrescendo* (abbreviated *decresc.*) or *diminuendo* (abbreviated *dim.*) implies a gradual decrease in volume and is symbolized $>$.

Strategies **NS 1, 5** (Singing a song while reading with dynamic markings.)

Sing "The Three Rogues." Help students decide where a crescendo and a decrescendo could be placed to increase the song's musical interest.

THE THREE ROGUES

Ohio Folk Song

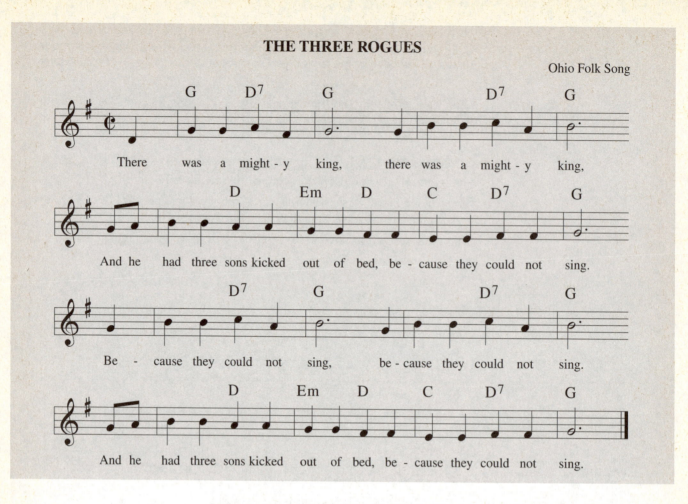

There was a might-y king, there was a might-y king,

And he had three sons kicked out of bed, be-cause they could not sing.

Be-cause they could not sing, be-cause they could not sing.

And he had three sons kicked out of bed, be-cause they could not sing.

Listen to "In the Hall of the Mountain King" from *Peer Gynt Suite No. 1* by Grieg. Students should listen for the gradual crescendo used throughout the piece.

Listen to additional recordings containing gradual crescendos and decrescendos and discover the changes in dynamic level.

Students should know that the music from the *Peer Gynt Suite* is inspired by a five-act play in verse by the Norwegian dramatist Henrik Ibsen. The play was first shown in 1876. It is the story of a life based on procrastination and avoidance. Students should research this play on the Internet and read a synopsis of the story.

Learning   Composers often use dynamic markings to indicate the degree of volume they feel will be most expressive at different points in a composition.

Strategies **NS 1** (Singing at different dynamic levels.)

Gradually introduce the most common dynamic markings contained in **Visual E2.**

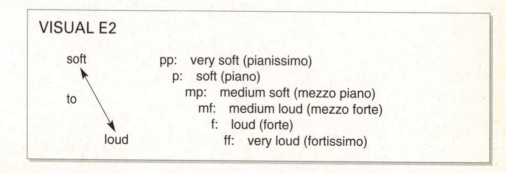

VISUAL E2

soft

to

loud

pp: very soft (pianissimo)
 p: soft (piano)
mp: medium soft (mezzo piano)
mf: medium loud (mezzo forte)
 f: loud (forte)
ff: very loud (fortissimo)

Students should know that by learning the names of the dynamic and tempo markings in music, they are learning how to speak Italian. Most composers use this language to communicate to the performer how they want the music to be expressed.

Have students discover dynamic markings found in the songs in their song books and explain how these markings affect the way the song should be performed. Begin with "Hoo, Hoo!" and discuss the markings found in measures 9–14.

Put "The Three Rogues" on a projector or white board and place dynamic markings on the score to correspond to the way students sang it earlier, with changing dynamic levels. It might look like **Visual E3.**

Sing the song with the dynamics indicated. Ask students if they want to change the dynamics or if they are satisfied with their performance.

VISUAL E3

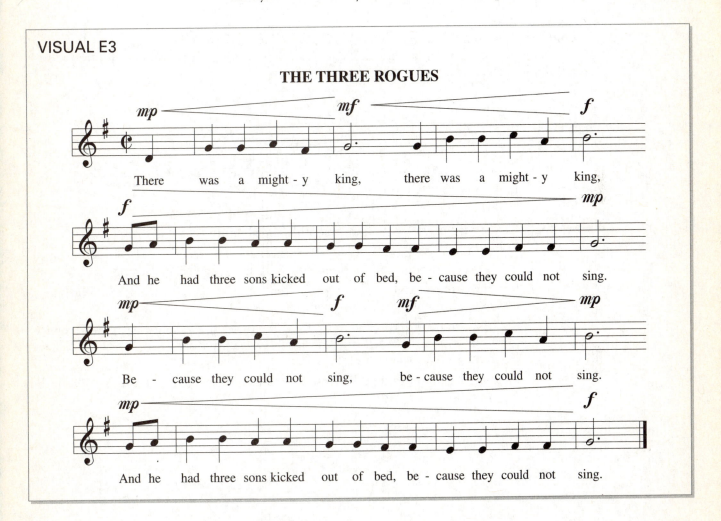

THE THREE ROGUES

In the early years, reading without expression is a common problem. Singing a song with expression can help! In the music classroom it is important that students sing songs expressively and at the appropriate rate of speed.

When children read and then sing the lyrics of a song in their music book, this promotes fluency and expression when they read other texts.

When reading notation while singing, students are urged along by the rhythm and tempo of the words. In the general classroom, many students take time to decipher each word, comprehend what they are reading, and look ahead to know what emotion to put into their voice while reading. Other children simply focus on sounding out the words and comprehending what they are reading, leaving inflection or expression out.

When teaching a child to sing with proper expression, you must first instruct them in the meanings behind the words. For example, few students know the meanings of many words in "The Star Spangled Banner." Once they realize the history of this song, when it was written and under what circumstances, the song takes on an entirely different meaning for students who sing it.

FOCUS

Legato and Staccato

Learning   *Legato* denotes a smooth, connected progression from one note to the next. *Staccato* denotes a quick release of a sound. The staccato note head has a dot placed over or under it.

Strategies **NS 1** (Singing smoothly and abruptly.)

Have students move in a smooth, connected manner, denoting legato performance. Movements could include swimming, ice skating, and ballet dancing.

Have students imitate living things that move smoothly, such as swans on a lake, fish in the water, or birds in flight.

Have students listen and move to recordings that exemplify legato performance, such as "Cradle Song" from *Children's Games* by Bizet or "Ballet of the Sylphs" from *The Damnation of Faust* by Berlioz.

Sing legato songs that demonstrate smooth, connected tones, such as "Kum Ba Yah" and "Cherry Bloom."

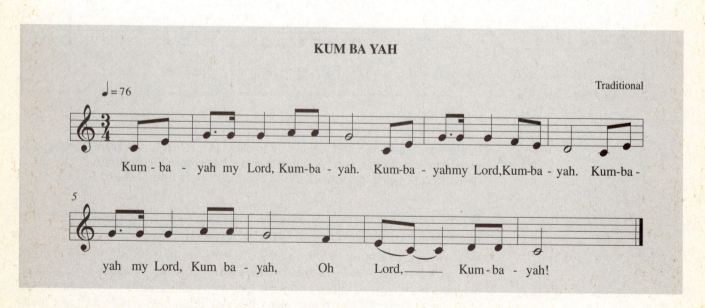

CHERRY BLOOM
(SAKURA)

Japanese Folk Song

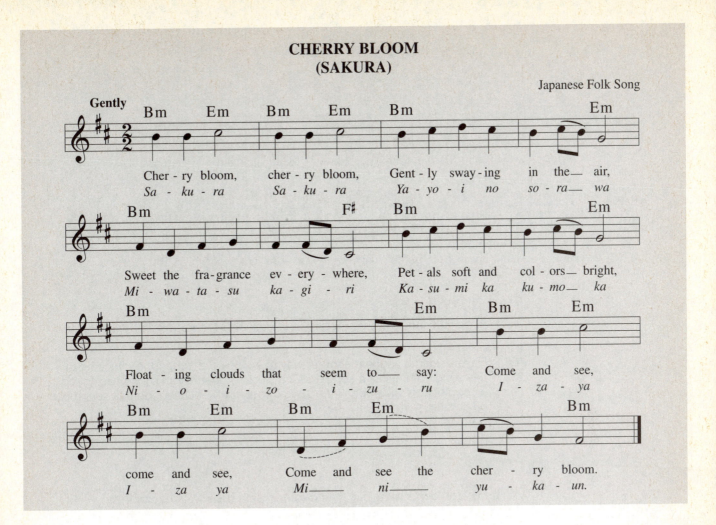

 The teacher should let students know that the cherry blossom is Japan's national flower and has for years appeared in the country's artwork, music and poetry. *Sakura*, which means "cherry blossom or bloom" in the Japanese language, is the national anthem of Japan. From January to June every year, the cherry trees are in full blossom. The melody of this song dates back to medieval times. It remains popular in Japan to this day.

Have students listen and move to recordings that contain examples of staccato performance, such as "Petite Ballerina" and "Pizzicato Polka" from *Ballet Suite No. 1* by Shostakovich.

Sing songs that have some staccato passages, such as "Wind the Bobbin," or contain staccato ostinati, such as "Hickory, Dickory, Dock." Have students explain why the songs or ostinati sound better sung staccato rather than legato.

Have students move in a disconnected, staccato manner, using such movements as hopping, popping balloons, or touching a hot iron.

Students can imitate living things that move in a disconnected manner, such as kangaroos, rabbits, and woodpeckers.

WIND THE BOBBIN

Winding Game

Wind   the bob - bin,   ding dang   gon-na   wind it tight,   ding dang.

Bob - bin a wound up,   Bob - bin a wound up,   Bob - bin a wound up,   Break it!

Have students find the staccato markings in "My Grandfather's Clock."

 Have students suggest another way to include the concept of staccato in this song. (Since it is a song about a clock, students can play a two-toned woodblock to accompany the song throughout. Each woodblock sound can be notated

Have students write out the notation, using the staccato marking.

MY GRANDFATHER'S CLOCK

Henry Clay Work, 1876
Copyright Unknown

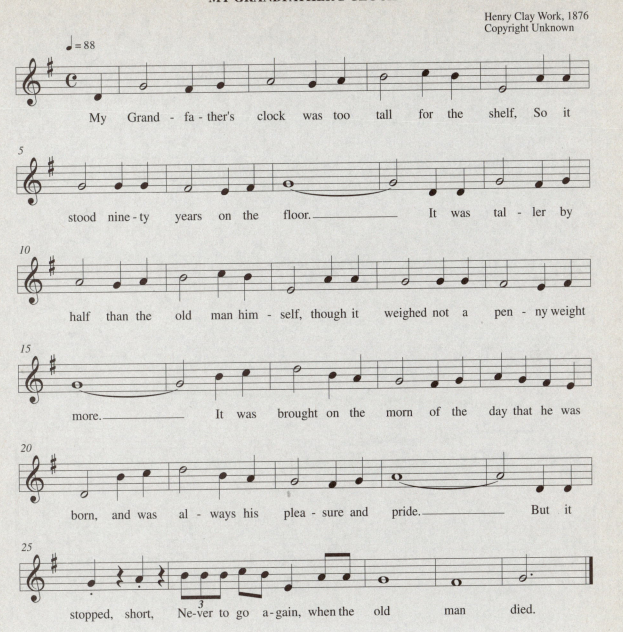

HICKORY DICKORY DOCK

Words from Mother Goose

Melody by: J. W. Elliot
Arr. Rozmajzl

FOCUS

Slur

Learning

A *slur* is a curved line connecting two or more notes on different lines or spaces, as opposed to tied notes, which share the same line or space. This symbol designates that the notes connected by the slur should be sung or played with a single breath. Often, a slur is used to connect two or more notes sharing a single syllable of text.

ba———   by————————

Strategies **NS 1, 5** (While singing songs, identify slur markings.)

Sing a number of songs containing slurs, such as "When That I Was a Little Tiny Boy" and "Mister Rabbit." Find the slur symbols in these songs; discover which slurs connect notes sharing the same, single syllable.

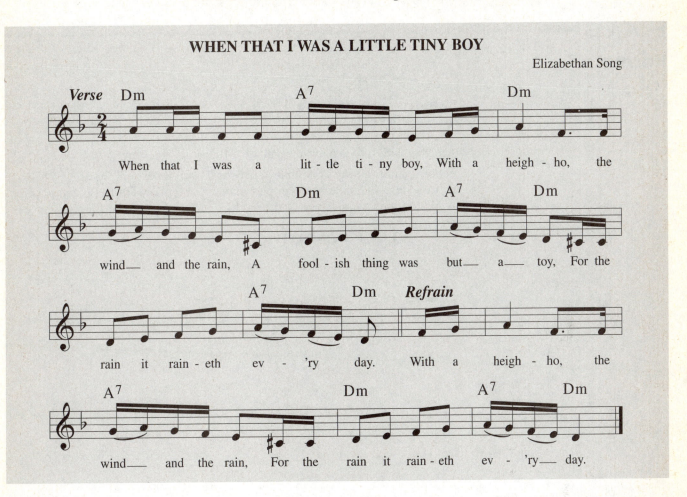

WHEN THAT I WAS A LITTLE TINY BOY

Elizabethan Song

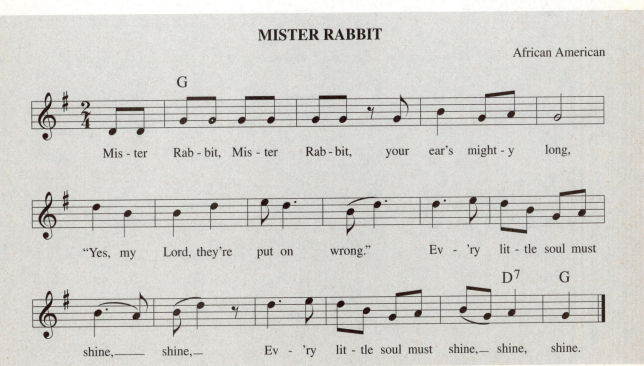

MISTER RABBIT

African American

The term *slur* is not unique to music. It is also used to describe a way of speaking that is not clear. Sometimes people tend to talk fast and slur their words together. Slur is also a remark that is meant to insult someone or damage their reputation.

Study the songs in the students' music book and discover where slurs occur.

FOCUS

Fermata

Learning A *fermata* (⌒) over a note indicates that the note should be held longer than its normal duration. The length of the fermata is determined by the musical director.

Strategies **NS 1, 5** (Analyzing symbols while singing a song.)

Sing songs containing a fermata such as "Loch Lomond" and "Most Done Ling'ring Here." Discuss how the performance of fermatas in these compositions can add to the expressiveness of the work.

LOCH LOMOND

Loch Lomond is in Scotland. It has the largest surface area of fresh water in the United Kingdom. The Loch is 24 miles long and 5 miles wide. Have students find Scotland on a map. Do an Internet search to find out more about Loch Lomond.

Have students find other examples in this text of songs containing a fermata; then, perform the songs.

INTRODUCING EXPRESSIVE ELEMENTS

Suggested Sequencing by Grade Level

Kindergarten

1. Loud/soft
2. Fast/slow

Grade One

1. Loud (f), soft (p)
2. Smooth, disconnected

Grade Two

1. Getting louder, getting softer
2. Getting faster and slower
3. Legato/staccato

Grade Three

1. ff, pp, mf, mp
2. fermata

Grades Four, Five, Six

Italian terminology and abbreviations

WRITTEN AND PERFORMANCE-RELATED ASSESSMENTS THROUGH COOPERATIVE LEARNING ACTIVITIES: EXPRESSIVE ELEMENTS NS 1, 2, 5, 7

1. Give each group a different, familiar song. **NS 1, 2, 5, 7**
   a. Students should sing through the song, determine its tempo using a term from Visual E1, and place the appropriate Italian tempo marking above the song on the left side.
   b. Students should sing through the song again and decide where an accelerando and/or a ritardando could be placed to enhance the song's performance.
   c. They should then practice the song with its expressive markings and perform it for the class.
   d. Students could also play the song on barred instruments.
2. Provide each group with a different, familiar song. **NS 1, 2, 5, 7**
   a. Ask students to sing through their song and to decide what dynamic markings might be placed in the song to enhance the meaning of the words. Refer to Visual E2.
   b. Students should sing the song several times until they are satisfied with their choice of markings.
   c. They should then choose one to three instruments to use in accompanying the song. The instruments and the accompaniment should be appropriate to the song and its dynamic markings.
   d. Finally, students perform the song for the class.
3. Give each group a different, familiar song. Simple instrumental accompaniments should also be included on the manuscript. Students should sing through the song several times to decide what dynamic and tempo markings would enhance the song's performance. These markings should be added to both the vocal and the instrumental parts of the song. When satisfied, students should practice their song until they are able to perform it for the class. **NS 1, 2, 5, 7**

CHAPTER 6 Teaching Form to Children

INTRODUCTION

Form, as a concept, is experienced by children in their earliest years. Nature provides an abundance of objects that have their own distinctive form. The form of a dandelion is different from that of a daisy; the shape of an oak tree is not the same as that of a weeping willow.

Music, too, has many forms that distinguish one composition from another. Music is not a haphazard coming together of various elements; it is an orderly arrangement of many interwoven relationships: Pitches are combined to form melodic and harmonic intervals; duration symbols are combined to form rhythm; and both intervals and rhythm are combined to form phrases. The manner in which musical phrases are arranged within a composition contributes to its form. The *form* of a piece of music refers to its structure or design, to the way its expressive relationships are combined to provide both unity and variety within the music.

The basic, underlying principles of form in music are the concepts of "same" and "different." In a song, some musical parts are exactly the same, some are totally different, and others are only partially different. The repetition and contrast that exist from one part to the next help determine the total effect of the musical work.

In music there is no form without logic, there is no logic without unity.
—Arnold Schoenberg

FOCUS

Phrase

Learning
A *phrase* is a musical line that contains a coherent grouping of pitches, similar to a sentence that contains a coherent grouping of words. Phrases are usually two to eight measures long, but more often four measures in length.

Strategies **NS 1** (Singing a varied repertoire of music.)

Call–Response: Sing "This Little Light of Mine" to students several times. Then sing the Call while students sing the Response. Sing other songs using the Call–Response method of singing.

 Explain that many spirituals are written in a "call and response style." Have students listen to other spirituals to determine if this form is used.

Choose songs that the children know well. Sing each song, adding movements that will show where each new phrase of a song begins. For example, have students form a circle. Move to the right for phrase 1, to the left for phrase 2, and so on. Or pass a pillow or ball to the right on the first phrase; then to the left on the second phrase, as in the song "Oh, Susanna."

THIS LITTLE LIGHT OF MINE

African American Spiritual

Swing

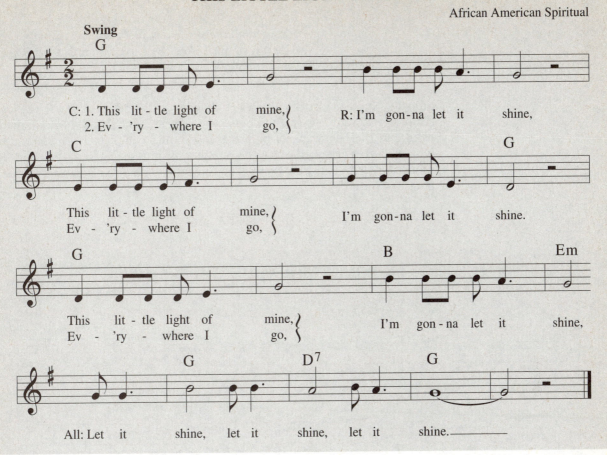

C: 1. This lit-tle light of mine, R: I'm gon-na let it shine,
   2. Ev-'ry - where I go,

This lit-tle light of mine, I'm gon-na let it shine.
Ev-'ry - where I go,

This lit-tle light of mine, I'm gon-na let it shine,
Ev-'ry - where I go,

All: Let it shine, let it shine, let it shine._____

OH, SUSANNA

1. I___ come from Al - a - bam-a with my ban-jo on my knee.
2. It___ rained all night the day I left, the weath-er it was dry;

I'm___ going to Loui - si - an-a my___ true love for to see.
The___ sun so hot I froze to death, Su - san-na don't you cry.

Refrain

Oh, Su - san-na, Oh, don't you cry for me.

I've___ come from Al - a - bam-a with my ban-jo on my knee.

Phrase	Movement	Song
1	Right	I come from Alabama with my banjo on my knee,
2	Left	I'm going to Louisiana my true love for to see.
3	Right	It rained all night the day I left, the weather it was dry;
4	Left	The sun so hot I froze to death, Susanna don't you cry.
5	Right	Oh, Susanna, oh, don't you cry for me,
6	Left	I've come from Alabama with my banjo on my knee.

Students can also identify phrases by drawing in the air an appropriate picture—a sun, a star, a kite—suggested by a song. The student should begin drawing the picture at the beginning of phrase 1 and should complete it by the end of the phrase, so that the picture can be redrawn for phrase 2. Using the song "Rocky Mountain," students can draw a picture of a "mountain" in the air for each phrase of the song.

ROCKY MOUNTAIN

Southern Folk Song

Phrase	Movement (draw "mountains")	Song
1		Rocky Mountain, Rocky Mountain, Rocky Mountain high,
2		When you're on that Rocky Mountain, hang your head and cry.
3		Do, do, do, do, do remember me,
4		Do, do, do, do, do remember me.

Help students understand that musical phrases are similar to sentences in language; therefore we usually breathe between phrases as we would breathe between sentences.

 Tell students that this song represents a folk song whose roots are the Appalachian Mountain region of the United States and is not connected to the Rocky Mountain chain located in the state of Arizona. Students should locate both the Appalachian and Rocky Mountains on a map or a globe. Discuss the characteristics of both mountain ranges, and then create a map legend. Use egg cartons to model the mountain ranges. The well-known song by John Denver, "Rocky Mountain High," is about the Rocky Mountains in the western part of the United States.

Learning   In a musical composition, all phrases may be the same.

Strategies **NS 1, 6** (Sing a song. Analyzing phrases.)

Once students can discover where phrases begin and end, they can begin identifying same and different phrases. Sing a short song containing two phrases that are the same, such as "Marching." Have students discover where the two phrases begin and end.

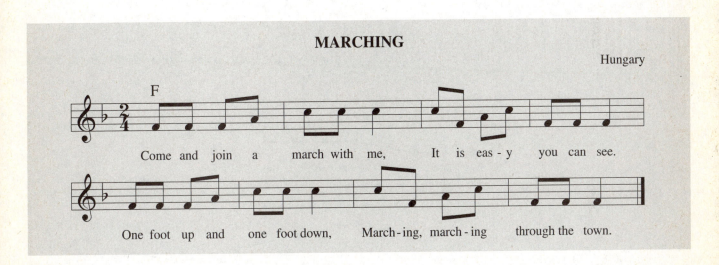

MARCHING

Hungary

Come and join a march with me, It is eas-y you can see.

One foot up and one foot down, March-ing, march-ing through the town.

Draw the melodic contour of each phrase on the board, as in **Visual F1.**

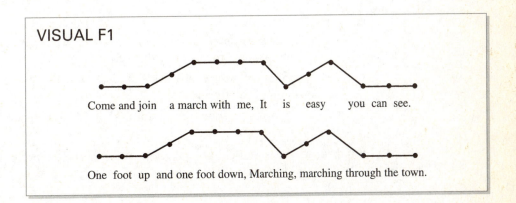

VISUAL F1

Come and join a march with me, It is easy you can see.

One foot up and one foot down, Marching, marching through the town.

Have students study the contour and discover whether the two phrases in Visual F1 are the same or different.

Sing the song again while students move to the contour of each phrase with locomotor movements.

To reinforce the learning, provide students with additional songs containing phrases that are the same.

Learning   In a musical composition, all phrases may be different from each other.

Strategies **NS 1, 5** (Singing a song. Analyzing phrases.)

Sing a song containing two phrases that are different, as in "Bow Wow Wow." Have students discover where each phrase begins and ends.

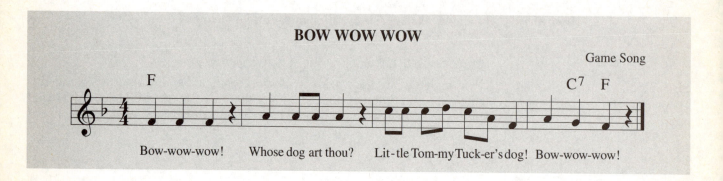

BOW WOW WOW

Game Song

Bow-wow-wow!   Whose dog art thou?   Lit-tle Tom-my Tuck-er's dog!   Bow-wow-wow!

Draw the contour of each phrase on the board, as in **Visual F2.**

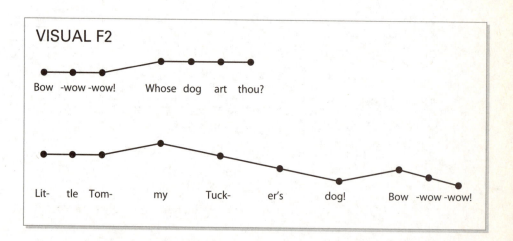

VISUAL F2

Bow -wow -wow!   Whose dog art thou?

Lit-   tle Tom-   my   Tuck-   er's   dog!   Bow -wow -wow!

Have students study the contour of Visual F2 to determine whether the two phrases are the same or different.

Sing the song again while students move to the contour of each phrase with locomotor movements.

Sing other songs with phrases that are different from each other.

Learning   In a musical composition, some phrases may be the same and others may be different.

Strategies **NS 1, 5** (Sing a song. Analyze its structure.)

Sing a song containing both like and unlike phrases, such as "The Jolly Miller." Have students identify each of the four phrases in the song.

THE JOLLY MILLER

New England Song

Draw the contour of each phrase on the board, as in **Visual F3.**

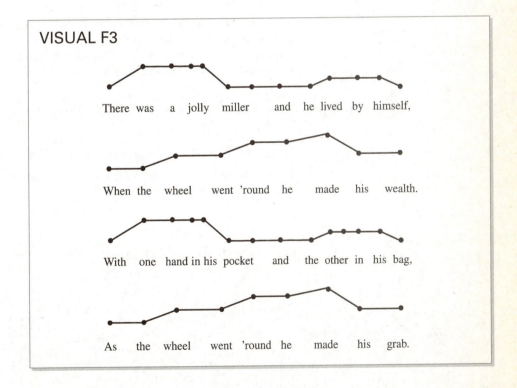

Students should study the contours and identify those that are the same and those that are different.

Sing the song while students use locomotor movements to portray the contour of each phrase in Visual F3.

Discover other songs that combine same and different phrases. Sing them, draw their contours, and move to them.

Have students create their own songs with same or different phrases. When this exercise is first assigned, the teacher will need to give some parameters to help ensure success. The number of phrases and measures to be used, the meter, and the starting and ending pitches might be given. The teacher might also limit students to a few pitches, such as C, D, E, and G, and provide words for the song being created. It may also be helpful to restrict the number of rhythmic symbols used; for example, allow the use of only quarter notes, eighth notes, and quarter rests. **Visual F4** shows how the restrictions can be presented.

Using the format in Visual F4, students can compose two phrases that are the same or two that are different from each other. Have students play their compositions on melody instruments, making changes until they are satisfied. While part of the class performs the composition on instruments, the remainder of the class can sing the song while moving to each phrase in some creative way.

Learning   Some phrases in a musical composition are similar, but not exactly the same.

Strategies **NS 1, 2** (Singing a song and adding an accompaniment.)

Sing a familiar song containing phrases that are similar, but not exactly the same, as in "Poor Little Kitty Cat."

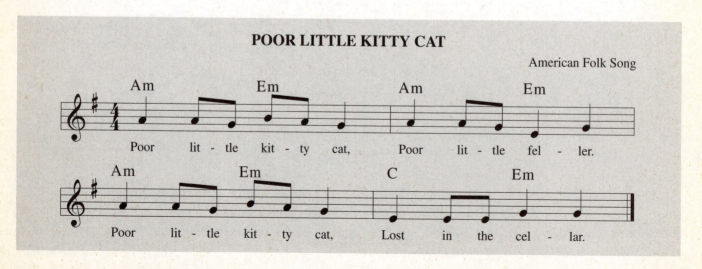

Repeat the song, one phrase at a time, drawing the contour of each phrase on the board, as in **Visual F5.**

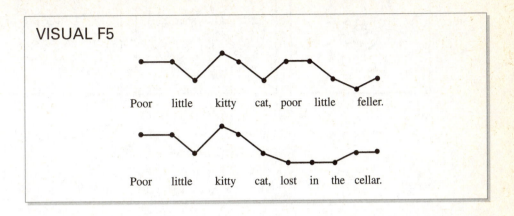

VISUAL F5

Poor   little   kitty   cat, poor   little   feller.

Poor   little   kitty   cat, lost   in   the   cellar.

Help students discover that both phrases begin the same, but end differently. While singing the song again, students can draw the contour of each phrase in the air or move to each phrase with locomotor movements.

Find and compose other songs having similar phrases.

Instruments can be added to reinforce students' awareness of same and different phrases at all stages of the preceding lessons. For example, instruments can be played when singing the song "The Jolly Miller," outlined in Visual F3. Because phrases 1 and 3 are the same, students can play the claves or other appropriate instrument when singing these two phrases. Likewise, phrases 2 and 4 are the same, but are different from phrases 1 and 3. Therefore, a different instrument should be played for phrases 2 and 4, such as a triangle. The chart that follows clarifies this strategy:

Phrase 1	"There was a jolly miller …"	claves
Phrase 2	"When the wheel went 'round …"	guiro
Phrase 3	"With one hand in his pocket …"	claves
Phrase 4	"As the wheel went 'round …"	guiro

Visuals can be used to reinforce an understanding of same and different. Two pictures of the same dog or the same cat can represent two phrases that are the same; a picture of a helicopter and one of a rocket can designate two phrases that are different; two pictures of the same balloon, one colored red and one colored blue, can be used to represent two phrases that are similar, but not exactly the same. Provide a variety of pictures for students to arrange that will match the phrases of any particular song. For example, the teacher could place six pictures in the front of the room: three pictures of a man and three of a wheel. To show the form of the song "The Jolly Miller," students would select appropriate pictures for each phrase, as designated in this example:

Phrase	Words	Picture Card
1	"There was a jolly miller …"	man
2	"When the wheel went 'round …"	wheel
3	"With one hand in his pocket …"	man
4	"As the wheel went 'round …"	wheel

In arranging the picture cards, the following progression would show the form of "The Jolly Miller":

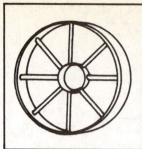

Geometrical shapes, such as □ ○ △, can also be arranged to show *same*: □ □ or *different*: ○ △ or *similar*: □ ■ phrases.

Once students are reading and printing, cards containing lowercase letters can be constructed to designate same, different, and similar phrases:

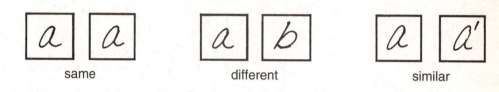

| same | different | similar |

Notice that numbers or other symbols may be used to designate a succession of phrases that are similar, but not exactly the same, such as:

$a\ a^1\ a^2$ or $a\ a'\ a''$

When students are able to use picture cards to show form, as in the example of the song "The Jolly Miller," it is a short step to replace the pictures with cards containing geometrical shapes or letters, as shown here:

| Phrase 1 | Phrase 2 | Phrase 3 | Phrase 4 |

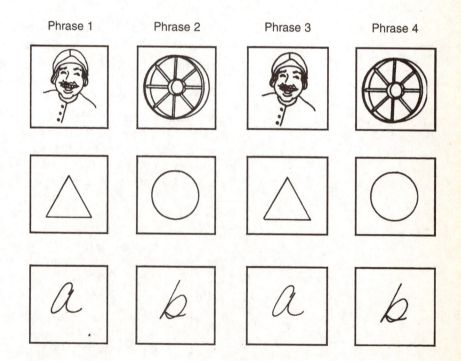

Students can apply the above strategies to recorded music as well. After listening to short examples of recorded music several times, students can draw the contour of each phrase and then arrange, in their proper sequence, cards having lower-case letters, as shown above. Let students decide what locomotor movements to use for each phrase. After performing these movements, students can discuss whether the movements matched what they heard in the music. If not, have them choose a different movement until students are satisfied with their choreographed interpretation of the music on the recording.

 Speaking in phrases leads to fluency in speech. Students who are challenged in their ability to speak fluently should try to sing. Songs are made up of phrases, and singing them in an expressive way will greatly enhance a student's ability to speak fluently.

 Have students expressively recite the lyrics of their favorite song.

FOCUS

Sectional Forms

Learning   Musical phrases can be combined to form larger units called *sections*. Sections can be relatively short or hundreds of measures in length. A *double bar* often separates one section from another. Just as the terms of *same*, *different*, or *similar* characterize phrases, so, too, are sections identified as being *same*, *different*, or *similar*. Common sectional forms are binary (AB), ternary (ABA), strophic (AAA), theme and variations (A A^1 A^2 A^3 A^4 etc.), and rondo (ABACA or ABACABA). Capital letters are generally used to designate each section in a composition.

Strategies   **NS 1, 6** (Sing a song; then analyze its form.)
Sing through the song "Shoo, Fly" until students know it well.

SHOO, FLY

Have students analyze "Shoo, Fly" to discover its three distinct sections, the first and last sections being the same. Notice the double bar dividing each section. Label each section: 1=A; 2= B, 3=A.

Have students examine a musical score of "Jazz Rondo." Have students circle or highlight the "A" section of this rondo. Tell how many times the "A" section repeats; then sketch the form using appropriate sectional lettering.

Have students look through their music textbook to discover other sectional songs.

JAZZ RONDO

Rene Boyer

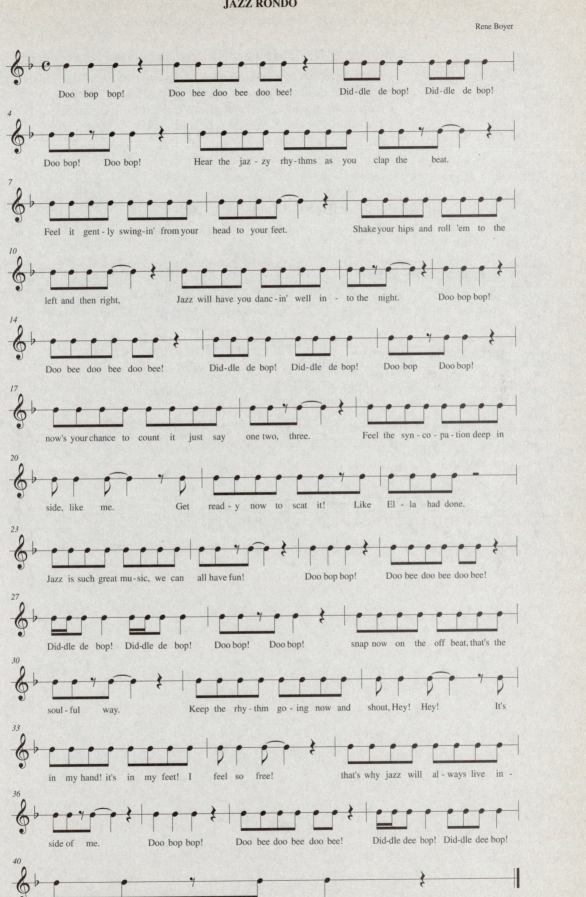

Some compositions are divided into two sections, the second being different from the first. The form of this type of composition is known as *binary* or AB.

Strategies **NS 1, 6** (Sing a folk song. Identify the form of a song.)

Sing a common two-section song, such as "Riding in the Buggy." Have students notice the double bar between the two sections. Because the two sections are different from each other, their design can be indicated as AB. In binary form, either the A or the B may be repeated: AAB, ABB, or AABB.

RIDING IN THE BUGGY

Play-Party Song

Show the design of both the phrases and the sections of a two-part song, such as "Riding in the Buggy" to the class. See **Visual F6**. Sing the song while following its design on a diagram.

VISUAL F6

"Riding in the Buggy"
Binary Form

Design of Phrases	Design of Sections	Song Lyrics/Phrases
a		Riding in the buggy Miss Mary Jane, Miss Mary Jane, Miss Mary Jane,
a'	**A**	Riding in the buggy Miss Mary Jane, I'm a long way from home.
a		Who mourns for me? Who mourns for me?
b	**B**	Who mourns for me, my darling, Who mourns for me?

Note: The lettering of the first phrase in each section begins with "a."

Diagram other familiar, binary form songs.

Have students listen to recordings of music in binary form, such as those listed here. Discover where the "B" section begins, and if either the A or the B section repeats. Write the sectional design on the board.

a. "Copacabana" from *Saudades do Brazil* by Milhaud
    Form: AB interlude AB
b. "Sarabande" from *Suite for Strings* by Corelli-Pinelli
    Form: Introduction AABB Coda
    Note: "Introduction," "Interlude," and "Coda" are discussed in the *Focus* following "strophic form" on page 183.
c. "Gigue" from *French Suite No. 4* in E-flat by Bach
    Form: AABB

Learning | Some compositions are divided into three sections. The second section is different from the first, but the third section is the same as or similar to the first section. Three-part compositions are called *ternary* or ABA.

Strategies **NS 1, 6** (Sing a spiritual. Analyze its form.)

Sing a familiar three-section song such as "Nobody Knows the Trouble I've Seen." Notice the use of *refrain* (same melody, same words) and *verse* (different words, and sometimes a different melody).

NOBODY KNOWS THE TROUBLE I'VE SEEN

Spiritual

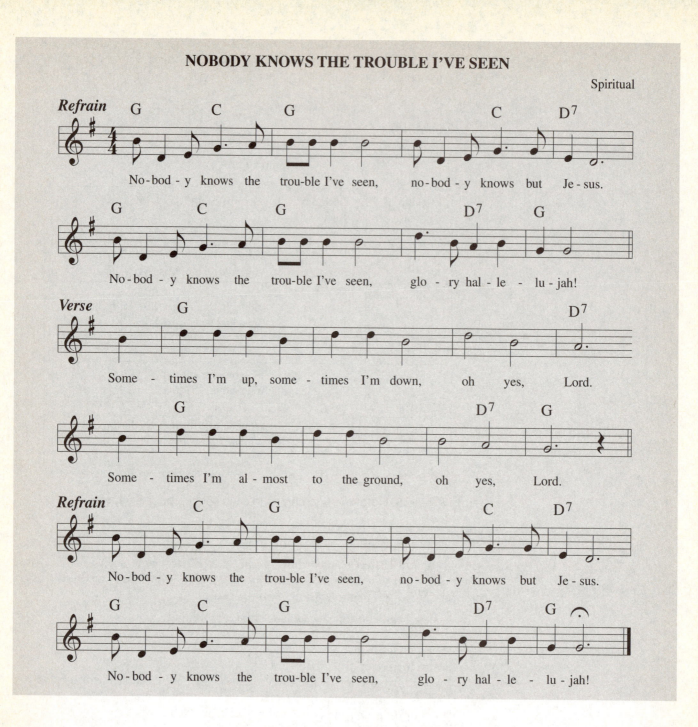

Notice the two sets of double bars that divide the song into three sections of which the first and last are the same. This design can be indicated as ABA, otherwise known as *ternary form*. Although any part in ternary form may be repeated, repetition of the first section is the most common: AABA.

On a projector, show the design of both the phrases and the sections of "Nobody Knows the Trouble I've Seen." See **Visual F7.** Sing the song while following its design on the diagram.

VISUAL F7

"Nobody Knows the Trouble I've Seen"
Ternary Form

Design of Phrases	Design of Sections	Song Lyrics/Phrases
a		Nobody knows the trouble I've seen, nobody knows but Jesus.
a'	A	Nobody knows the trouble I've seen, Glory, hallelujah!
a		Sometimes I'm up, sometimes I'm down, Oh yes, Lord.
a'	B	Sometimes I'm almost to the ground. Oh yes, Lord.
a		Nobody knows the trouble I've seen, nobody knows but Jesus.
a'	A	Nobody knows the trouble I've seen, Glory, hallelujah!

Diagram other familiar, ternary form songs.

Play recordings of music in ternary form, such as the ones listed here. Again, discover where the "B" section begins and whether either the A or the B section repeats. Place the sectional design on the board.

a. *Mazurka No. 24* by Chopin
Form: ABA
b. "Träumerei" from *Scenes from Childhood* by Schumann
Form: AABA[1]
c. "Hoe-Down" from *Rodeo—Ballet Suite* by Copland
Form: Introduction A, Interlude B, Interlude A, Coda

Learning   In some musical compositions the original theme always returns after each digression or contrasting theme. This form is known as *rondo* and is usually symbolized by ABACA or ABACABA.

Strategies **NS 6** (Analyzing music.)

Divide the class into five groups. Let each group know that it is responsible for one section of a five-part composition the group members will be creating. Have each group work on the following assignments:

Group 1: Sing a familiar song.
Group 2: Do an eight-measure rhythmic composition, using only body sounds.

Group 3: Sing again the familiar song with accompaniment on a xylophone or other melody instrument.

Group 4: Perform an eight-measure rhythmic composition using rhythm instruments.

Group 5: Sing the familiar song again.

When they are ready, have the groups present their sections, one after another, without breaks, so that the five sections are perceived as parts of a whole. After students have presented their five-part composition, have them analyze it to discover the overall form of their piece. Their analysis should give the following formal design.

A   Sing a familiar song.

B   Do an eight-measure rhythmic composition, using only body sounds.

A¹ Sing again the familiar song with accompaniment on a xylophone or other melody instrument.

C   Perform an eight-measure rhythmic composition using rhythm instruments.

A   Sing the familiar song again.

Point out that the design ABA¹CA is known as *rondo* form because the theme always returns after a contrasting theme is presented.

Play the opening measures of a composition set in *rondo form,* such as "Waltz" from *Masquerade Suite* by Khachaturian. Being familiar with the beginning of the "A" section, as given in **Visual F8,** will enable students to hear the return of A each time it occurs.

VISUAL F8

Opening Measures of "Waltz"

Theme 1:

After students are familiar with the beginning of the A section, play the recording of "Waltz," having students raise their hands each time A returns.

Place a diagram of "Waltz" on a projector, as in **Visual F9.**

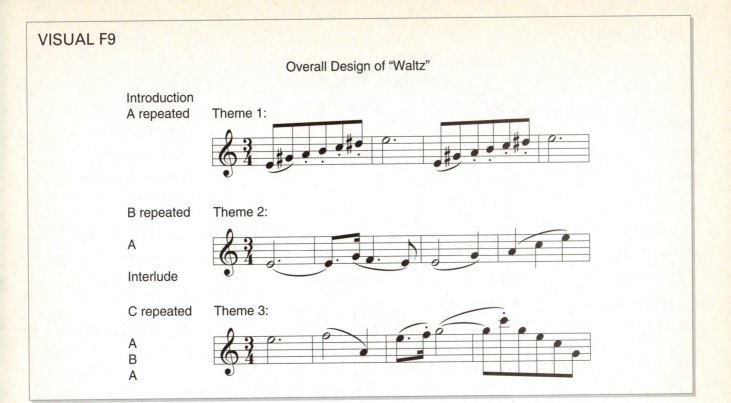

Overall Design of "Waltz"

Introduction
A repeated — Theme 1:

B repeated — Theme 2:

A

Interlude

C repeated — Theme 3:

A

B

A

On a melodic instrument, play the opening measures to sections B and C to familiarize students with these contrasting themes.

Play the recording of "Waltz" again, pointing to each section on the diagram as it occurs in the music.

Provide additional experiences with rondo form. The following recordings may be helpful:

a. "Dance of the Comedians" from *The Bartered Bride* by Smetana
b. *Gypsy Rondo* by Haydn
c. "The March of the Siamese Children" from *The King and I* by Rodgers

Learning   The theme of some compositions is sometimes repeated again and again, but is altered in different ways for each succeeding repetition. The resulting form is known as *theme and variations* or A A^1 A^2 A^3 A^4.

Strategies **NS 5, 6** (Listen to a musical composition. Analyze its form.)

Prepare students to hear music set in theme and variations form by placing on the board the common design used for music having this structure: A A^1 A^2 A^3 A^4 A^5, and so on.

Point out that the original theme is performed again and again, but is altered in some way for each succeeding repetition. Repetition could have changes in tempo, dynamics, key, *mode* (major or minor), instrumentation, accompaniment, harmony, rhythm, or even melody.

Have students notice that although rondo form had contrasting sections based on new themes, the theme and variation form uses only one theme throughout.

Provide a diagram of a composition using theme and variations form, such as *Variations on the Theme "Pop! Goes the Weasel"* by Cailliet. See **Visual F10.**

Variations on the Theme "Pop! Goes the Weasel"
Theme and Variations Form

Sections	Tempo	Dynamics		Other Characteristics
Introduction	fast	loud		fragments of the theme
Theme	fast	loud		full orchestra
Variation I	fast	p	f	different instruments playing different parts of the theme
Variation II	slow	p	mf	dance (minuet) style
Variation III	very slow	very soft		gypsy violin
Variation IV	fast	medium loud		music box (waltz style)
Variation V	very fast	very loud		jazz style
Coda	fast	p	ff	fragments of the theme

Play or sing "Pop! Goes the Weasel." Explain to the students that this is the theme in the new form they are about to study. In theme and variations form, the theme may be original or it may be a tune borrowed from another composer. In either case, it is usually very simple in style, lending itself easily to many variations. The composer, after stating the theme, will present it in different disguises, or variations, one after the other. The overall design for the Cailliet composition should be identified as:

Introduction A A^1 A^2 A^3 A^4 A^5 Coda

Play the recording of *Variations on the Theme "Pop! Goes the Weasel."* Using the diagram in Visual F10, point to each variation as it occurs in the music. After several hearings, the students should be able to recognize each section without the diagram in front of them.

Provide additional listening experiences to reinforce students' understanding of theme and variations form. The following examples may be used:

a. *Ah! Vous Dirai-je Maman* by Mozart
Theme: "Twinkle, Twinkle Little Star," originally a French folk song
b. *Bolero* by Ravel
c. *American Salute* by Gould
Theme: "When Johnny Comes Marching Home"

Have students discover the overall design for each theme and variations recording. Discuss the different techniques the composer uses in each variation to make it different from the theme.

Provide opportunities for students to create their own theme and variations form. The following design could be used:

A Sing a familiar song.
A^1 Sing the same song half as fast.
A^2 Sing the song in its original tempo with rhythmic accompaniment.
A^3 Sing the song in a new key.
A^4 Repeat the song in the new key with autoharp accompaniment.
A^5 Sing the song in its original key with rhythmic and autoharp accompaniment. Add a simple melodic ostinato.

Learning When all the stanzas of a poem are set to the same music, the resulting form is called *strophic* or AAA. Strophic form may have any number of "A's," depending on the number of stanzas in the poem.

Strategies **NS 1, 5, 6** (Sing a song. Analyze its form.)

Sing a strophic-form song, such as "America the Beautiful." Notice that this song has a number of stanzas set to the same music.

AMERICA THE BEAUTIFUL

Katherine Lee Bates

Samuel A. Ward

1. O beau-ti-ful for spa-cious skies, For am-ber waves of grain,
For pur-ple moun-tain maj-es-ties A-bove the fruit-ed plain!
A-mer-i-ca! A-mer-i-ca! God shed His grace on thee,
And crown thy good with broth-er hood From sea to shin-ing sea!

2. O beautiful for Pilgrim feet,
Whose stern impassioned stress
A thoroughfare for freedom beat
Across the wilderness.
America! America! God mend thine every flaw,
Confirm thy soul in self-control,
Thy liberty in law.

3. O beautiful for heroes proved
In liberating strife,
Who more than self their country loved,
And mercy more than life.
America! America! May God thy gold refine
Till all success be nobleness
And every gain divine.

4. O beautiful for patriot dream
That sees beyond the years,
Thine alabaster cities gleam
Undimmed by human tears.
America! America! God shed His grace on thee,
And crown thy good with brotherhood
From sea to shining sea.

To show the repetition of the "A" section, place a diagram of "America the Beautiful" on a projector. See **Visual F11.** Outline both the phrases and the sections of this strophic song. Sing the song while following its design on the diagram.

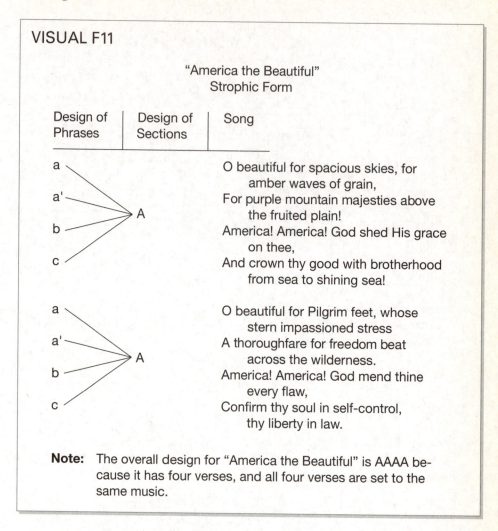

VISUAL F11

"America the Beautiful"
Strophic Form

Design of Phrases	Design of Sections	Song
a		O beautiful for spacious skies, for amber waves of grain,
a'		For purple mountain majesties above the fruited plain!
b	A	America! America! God shed His grace on thee,
c		And crown thy good with brotherhood from sea to shining sea!
a		O beautiful for Pilgrim feet, whose stern impassioned stress
a'		A thoroughfare for freedom beat across the wilderness.
b	A	America! America! God mend thine every flaw,
c		Confirm thy soul in self-control, thy liberty in law.

Note: The overall design for "America the Beautiful" is AAAA because it has four verses, and all four verses are set to the same music.

Diagram other familiar strophic songs. Many of the hymns sung in churches and many folk songs are in strophic design.

Play recordings of songs in strophic form, listening for the repetition of each new stanza. "Who Is Sylvia" and "Heiden Röslein" by Schubert are good examples of songs using strophic form.

FOCUS

Introduction, Interlude, and Coda

Learning

An *introduction* is a passage that occurs before the major sections of a form. Its function is varied, but may be used to set the tempo, the mood, or the key of the musical work, or it may be used to prepare the listener for the first thematic idea.

A *coda* is a passage added to the last major section of a form. A coda's function may also be varied, but it usually serves to bring the music to a more satisfactory close.

An *interlude* is a passage added to the interior of a composition; it connects one section to another more smoothly than would occur if it were absent.

Strategies **NS 1, 4** (Create an introduction and coda to accompany a song. Perform the song.)

Sing a familiar song. Ask students to create a rhythmic introduction and coda for the song. One solution can be found in **Visual F12.** Perform the composition.

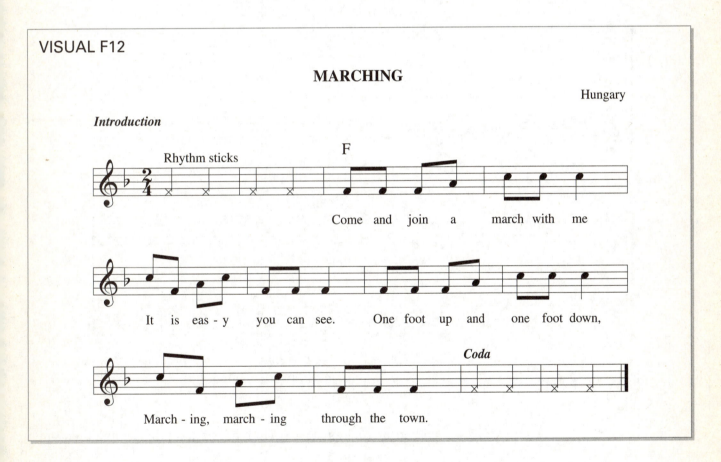

VISUAL F12

MARCHING

Hungary

Introduction

Rhythm sticks

Come and join a march with me

It is eas-y you can see. One foot up and one foot down,

Coda

March-ing, march-ing through the town.

Have students create additional, more difficult rhythmic introductions and codas for "Marching" and other familiar songs.

Create a melodic introduction and coda for a familar song. The introduction can be extended into the song as an ostinato figure, as in **Visual F13.**

SCOTLAND'S BURNING

Traditional
Arr.: Rozmajzl

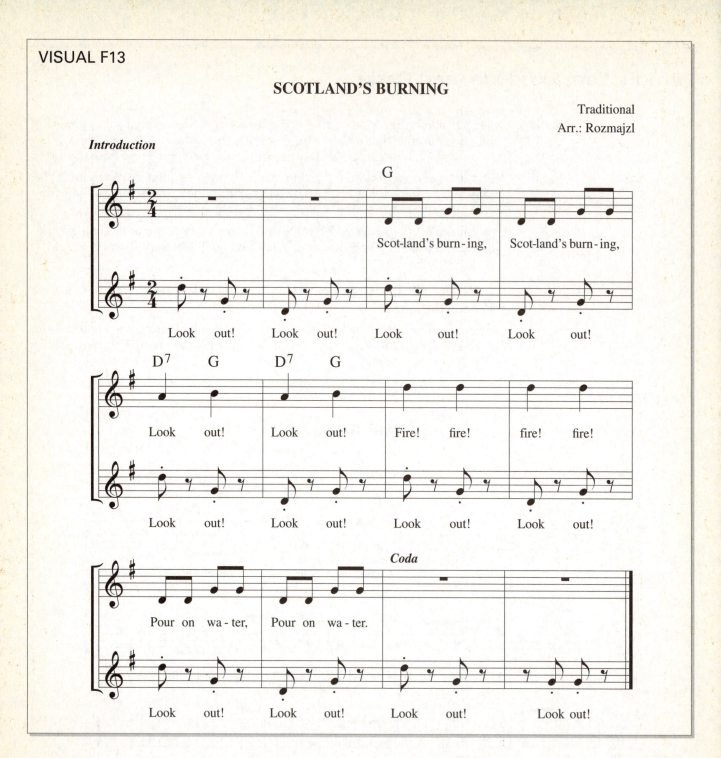

Have students create additional melodic introductions and codas for other familiar songs.

Choose a familiar song with more than one verse. Create an interlude to be sung between verses, as in **Visual F14.**

LONDON BRIDGE

England
Arr.: Rozmajzl

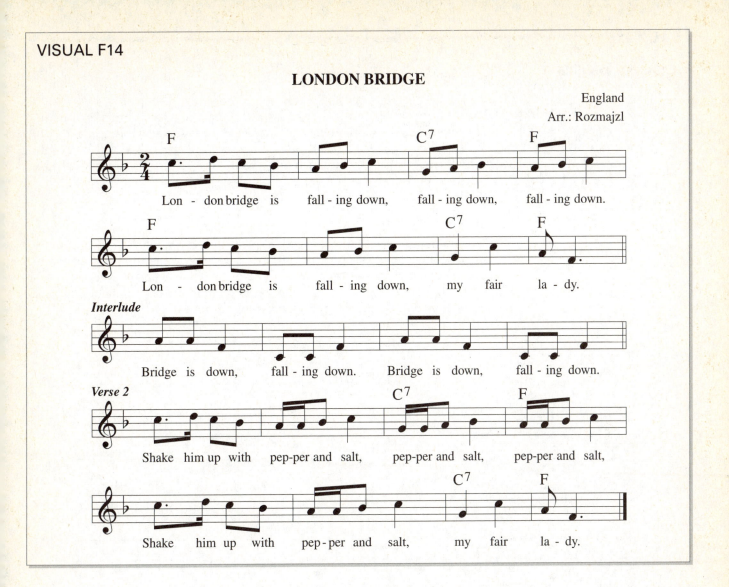

Lon - don bridge is fall-ing down, fall-ing down, fall-ing down.

Lon - don bridge is fall-ing down, my fair la - dy.

Interlude

Bridge is down, fall-ing down. Bridge is down, fall-ing down.

Verse 2

Shake him up with pep-per and salt, pep-per and salt, pep-per and salt,

Shake him up with pep-per and salt, my fair la - dy.

In 1831, London Bridge was built to connect the River Thames with the city of London and Southwark in central London. (Students should find London, England, on a map. They should also find a picture of London Bridge on the Internet.) By 1962, London Bridge was literally falling down. It was bought by Robert McCullough, from Lake Havasu City, Arizona. Amazingly, the bridge was dismantled and reconstructed in Arizona. To reach the bridge from I-40, go south on Arizona Highway 95; then turn left (east) on Mesquite Avenue. Turn right (south) on Lake Havasu Avenue N, and then right onto McCulloch N. to drive over the bridge. (Have students Google the directions to London Bridge.)

Study introductions, interludes, and codas in larger forms. This can be done by replaying appropriate recordings used with the previous lessons on sectional forms. A number of suggested recordings included introductions, interludes, and codas in their overall design.

Repeat Signs

Learning   A variety of symbols are used by composers to denote what material in a musical composition should be repeated. The most common symbols are, ❙❘, ❘❙ , ❘❙, *Da capo al fine*, and *Dal segno al fine*. Composers use repeat signs within a composition to save space on the manuscript and to save the time it would take to write it all out.

Strategies **NS 1, 5**

Place the repeat sign ❘❙ on the board. Explain that this symbol—two dots to the left of double bar lines—is used when the composer wants the performer to repeat the music from the beginning of the piece. Have students find the repeat sign in "Bluebird." Explain that when repeating from the beginning of this piece, the second verse is sung. Sing the song, using the repeat sign.

BLUEBIRD

Game Song

1. Here___ comes a blue - bird in through my win - dow,
2. Take a lit - tle part - ner, hop in the gar - den,

Hey, did - dle - dum a day, day, day.

Bluebird Game

Form a circle and join hands.
Raise arms and hands to make windows.
Choose a leader to weave (fly) in and out the windows.
The leader should then choose a partner and they hop together in the center
   of the ring.
The partner becomes the new leader (bird) that flies in and out the
   windows.

The repeat signs ❘❙ ❘❙ are used when the composer wants only material enclosed by the signs to be repeated. Have students find these signs in the song "Hansel and Gretel Dance." Explain that when repeating lines 3 and 4, the second verse should be sung. Sing the song; repeat lines 3 and 4 as indicated by the repeat signs.

Again, the overall structure of the piece incorporates the material within the repeat signs, resulting in an ABB sectional form.

HANSEL AND GRETEL DANCE

Adelheid Wette
Translated by Constance Bache

E. Humperdinck

Part - ner come and dance with me, Both my hands I give to thee.

Right foot first, Left foot then, Round a-bout and back a-gain.

1. With your foot you tap, tap, tap, With your hands you clap, clap, clap.
2. With your head you nick, nick, nick. With your fin - gers click, click, click.

Right foot first, Left foot then, Round a-bout and back a-gain.

Examine the song "Nobody Knows the Trouble I've Seen." Notice the abbreviation D.C. at the end of the piece. This abbreviation stands for *Da capo al fine*, literally meaning "from the head or beginning to the word *fine* or end." Composers use D.C. al fine or just D.C. when they want performers to repeat a song from the beginning, but not to sing any farther than where *fine* is indicated.

NOBODY KNOWS THE TROUBLE I'VE SEEN

Spiritual

Point out that the song "Nobody Knows the Trouble I've Seen" was used earlier under "Ternary Form," but the first two lines were written out at the end of the verse. To save space and time, the repeat abbreviation D.C. replaces the rewriting of the first two lines. Sing the song, repeating the first two lines until you reach the word *fine*.

"Hop Old Squirrel" provides an example of music containing first and second endings. Place a copy of "Hop Old Squirrel" on a projector. Verbalize how this song should be performed. Have students notice the first and second endings in line 2. Explain that this song is sung to the repeat sign (:||); then repeat the song from the beginning, but skip the first ending and sing the last two measures (second ending) the second time through.

HOP OLD SQUIRREL

African American

FOCUS

Ragtime

Learning | **Ragtime** is a musical form or style that is characterized by a syncopated melody over a regular, march-like bass line. Originally written for piano, ragtime grew out of early period dance music (the cake walk). It was so popular, however, that bands and other instrumental groups quickly adopted it. In fact, ragtime became the craze, one of the most popular performance and dance styles between 1897 and World War I.

Ragtime music requires lots of skill and coordination, but it remains a favorite when it comes to listening and moving to it.

When children listen to this style of music, they will immediately identify a clear form to the music. This clarity in form makes ragtime a wonderful choice for movement and creativity in the elementary classroom.

Strategies **NS 6** (Listen to and analyze the form of ragtime.)

Tell students that this style of music was extremely popular over a hundred years ago. In fact, their great-great-grandparents probably danced to this music, depending on in what country they were born. Just as today many listen and move to hip-hop and rap as popular dance forms, great-grandparents moved to ragtime.

Tell students that one of the most popular composers of ragtime music was Scott Joplin. Joplin was an African American who lived from 1868 to 1917.

| 1 + 2 = 3 | How old was Scott Joplin when he died? (He was 49 years old.)

Tell students that ragtime has a clear identifiable form to it. Direct students to listen to "Maple Leaf Rag" and then "The Entertainer." These are two of the most popular ragtime pieces.

As students are listening to the piece(s) for the first time, the teacher should place colorful letters that represent the form of the "Maple Leaf Rag" on the board. (See **Visual F15**.)

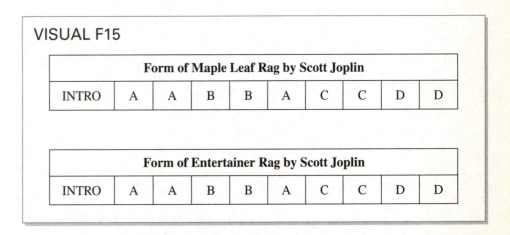

VISUAL F15

Form of Maple Leaf Rag by Scott Joplin									
INTRO	A	A	B	B	A	C	C	D	D

Form of Entertainer Rag by Scott Joplin									
INTRO	A	A	B	B	A	C	C	D	D

Assign students to small groups and have each group create a different movement to characterize a section. They will notice that they will have to perform each of their movement ideas at least twice. Perform for the class.

Students will find that as they listen to other rags they will notice that the form is basically the same.

INTRODUCING THE STRUCTURAL COMPONENTS OF FORM

Suggested Sequencing by Grade Level

Kindergarten

1. Same/different (environmental)
2. Phrase-by-phrase questions and answers (Call–Response)
3. Moving to a phrase

Grade One

1. Same and different phrases using pictures, icons, letters
2. Introduction
3. Repeat sign: ‖

Grade Two

1. Coda
2. First and second endings
3. Sectional forms: AB, ABA, Rondo

Grade Three

1. Sectional form: Theme and Variations
2. Interlude
3. Repeat signs: ‖:   :‖

Grade Four

1. Repeat signs: D.C. and D.S. al fine
2. Sectional form: Strophic

Grades Five and Six

1. Reinforce previous learnings with more difficult examples
2. Ragtime Form

WRITTEN AND PERFORMANCE-RELATED ASSESSMENTS THROUGH COOPERATIVE LEARNING ACTIVITIES: FORM NS 1, 2, 4, 5, 7

1. Give each group a melody instrument. Each group member should be able to improvise two phrases, four to eight measures in length, that are the same (aa) and two phrases that are different (ab). While each student plays his or her phrase, the other students demonstrate each phrase by drawing an arch in the air. When finished, students should perform their phrases for the teacher. **NS 2, 4, 7**

2. Provide each group with staff paper containing the words of a nursery rhyme divided among eight measures, similar to Visual F4. Rhythm, melody, and meter parameters are indicated on the paper. Using the words of the rhyme, students should create a song of two phrases, either the same or different (aa or ab), and notate it on the staff provided. They should be able to play and sing their song for the class. **NS 1, 2, 4, 5, 7**

3. Give each of four groups an opportunity to create one of the sections of a rondo in A B A^1 C A^2 form. Choose a short, familiar song for A. Assign to each of the four groups one of the remaining sections of the rondo: B A^1, C, and A^2. Sections B and C could each be an eight-measure rhythmic composition using mouth sounds, other body sounds, or rhythm instruments. Sections A^1 and A^2 would include the familiar song. Some accompaniment, however, must be added by the group. For example, a rhythmic ostinato, a melodic ostinato, a choreography, or a mime might be added to the song. Set a time limit for the completion of each group's task. Put the sections together and perform the rondo in its entirety. **NS 1, 2, 4, 7**

4. Provide each group with a different short, familiar song; a melodic instrument; and several rhythm instruments. Each group's task is to create an introduction, an interlude, and a coda for its song. When completed, the extended compositions can be performed for the class. **NS 1, 2, 4, 7**

5. Give each group one or two songs, each containing a different type of repeat sign. Each student also has an autoharp, if possible. Chords are marked for each song. Each group must be able to sing and play its song correctly, including the indicated repeat signs. When ready, the group should perform for the teacher. After two groups have completed their tasks, they can exchange songs and try again. **NS 1, 2, 5, 7**

6. Create dance steps to accompany "Hansel and Gretel Dance." The dance steps should be designed to visually show the form of the piece. Create dances or put movement to other pieces already experienced in this book. Again, the movement should show the form of the piece of music. **NS 1, 7**

7. Prepare a set of cards for each student that show the sections of a piece of ragtime. (A, B, C, D). While playing a piece of ragtime, have each student hold up the appropriate card indicating their recognition of form.

INTRODUCTION

Much like the threads that flow through a piece of fabric, the texture of music consists of horizontal and vertical elements that come together to add depth or substance to a musical composition. The texture of a musical work can be determined by how many or how few instruments or voices are being heard or sounded at the same time. It is obvious that when singing an unaccompanied solo, the texture of that solo piece would be described as thin. However, if a choir of sixty-five is singing, accompanied by a one-hundred-piece orchestra, the texture would certainly be described as thick.

As early as 600 A.D., song literature consisted primarily of a single, unaccompanied melodic line known as *chant*. Today, these pieces represent some of the clearest examples of music that emphasize the sounding of a single, unaccompanied melody. By the twelfth century, composers were writing music that combined melody with other similar or contrasting melodies to produce harmony. This style of writing greatly dominated the works of many of the major composers and church musicians through the mid-nineteenth century. Concurrently, musicians began to take the horizontal threads of melody and combine them with the vertical threads of harmony, thus producing texture of an even greater thickness in contrast to the single-line compositions of early centuries. Today, musicians are involved in the exploration of all types of computerized materials that can affect the texture of a composition.

The student's comprehension of texture in music will add a new dimension of understanding and appreciation for the composer's skillful techniques used to create the musical "whole."

> *Counterpoint is just as much subject to constant evolution and flux as are melody and harmony, with which it is indissolubly interwoven.*
> —Ernest Toch

FOCUS

Monophonic Texture

Learning Music that consists of a single, unaccompanied, melodic line is monophonic in texture. The word *monophonic* originates from a Greek word meaning "one voice."

Strategies **NS 6** (Listen to, analyze and describe texture.)

Have students listen to a recording of Gregorian chant. Examples might include:

a. "Alleluia," from *Masterpieces of Music Before 1750*, The Haydn Society, HSE 9038

b. "Lament for the Dead," from *Ethnic Folkways Library, No. 13*, FE 4504D

Play the recording and lead students to discover the basic characteristics of chant. Comments might include:

a. Men's or boys' voices were singing.
b. The chant was unaccompanied.
c. There was a lack of strong accents that marked off groups of beats, thus making the music unmetered.
d. The range of voices was limited.
e. There was no harmony among the voices, only unison singing.
f. There were essentially no extremes in dynamics.

Have students examine "Psalm 22." Point out that this psalm represents a clear example of Gregorian chant, as did the previous examples they heard. Gregorian chant represents one of the earliest musical styles that focuses primarily on the melodic element of music. Because Gregorian chant is a single, unaccompanied line, it is monophonic in texture.

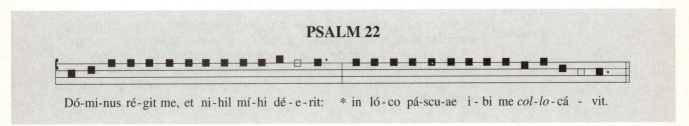

PSALM 22

Dó-mi-nus ré-git me, et ni-hil mí-hi dé-e-rit: * in ló-co pá-scu-ae i-bi me *col-lo*-cá - vit.

Note: The type of notation used in "Psalm 22" is called *neumatic notation*. Each individual note is called a *neume*.

Provide a copy of "Psalm 22" using standard notation. Have students draw the contour of the example, similar to that in **Visual T1.**

PSALM 22

Standard Notation

Do-mi-nus re-git me, et ni-hil mi-hi de-e-rit: in lo-co pa-scu-ae i-bi me col-lo-ca - vit.

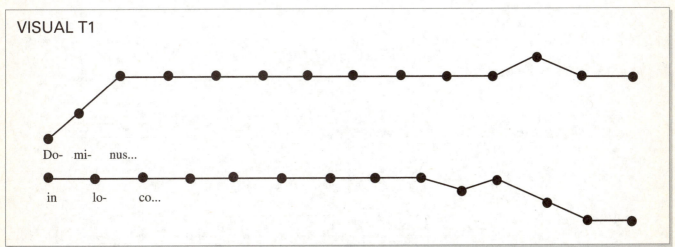

VISUAL T1

Do- mi- nus...

in lo- co...

Folk songs of some cultures are also monophonic in texture. Much of the music of the Asian world, such as China and Japan, and the music of the Arab nations is largely monophonic.

Using examples of songs and other pieces already performed or heard in class, talk about ways to create monophonic texture. Two basic suggestions might include:

1. No accompaniment can be added to the song or piece being sung or performed.
2. Unison singing or playing must take place throughout the composition. This does not mean that more than one instrument or singer cannot perform the same part at the same time.

Have students create, either individually or in small groups, examples of monophonic music.

Provide students with other examples of chant that demonstrate monophonic texture, such as:

a. any "Kyrie Eleison," "Sanctus," or "Agnus Dei"
b. the antiphon "Salve Regina"
c. the canticle of Simeon "Nunc dimittis servum tuum"

 Students can easily guess what the term *monophonic* means by paying attention to its prefix. *Mono-* is a prefix that means "one, only, or single." Thus, In chemistry a *monobasic* is something that contains a single atom. *Monochromatic* means having only one color. Carbon *monoxide* is a carbon attached to a single oxygen atom. A *monotone* is a succession of sounds or words uttered in a single tone or voice.

FOCUS

Polyphonic Texture

Learning   *Polyphonic texture* occurs when two or more independent melodic lines sound simultaneously, causing harmony to result between the horizontal lines. The term *polyphony* means "many voices." The melodic lines may contain the same melody or may be different melodies.

Strategies **NS 1, 6** (Demonstrate ability to sing a song in a round.)

Have students sing a familiar round, such as "Frère Jacques" ("Are You Sleeping") in two parts. Divide the class into two groups; group 2 begins singing when group 1 reaches the third measure in the song.

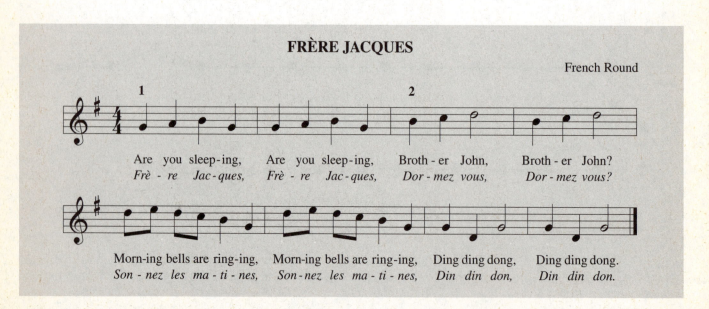

FRÈRE JACQUES

French Round

Are you sleep-ing, Are you sleep-ing, Broth-er John, Broth-er John?
Frè - re Jac-ques, Frè - re Jac-ques, Dor-mez vous, Dor-mez vous?

Morn-ing bells are ring-ing, Morn-ing bells are ring-ing, Ding ding dong, Ding ding dong.
Son - nez les ma - ti - nes, Son-nez les ma - ti - nes, Din din don, Din din don.

Provide a visual, similar to that in **Visual T2,** which demonstrates the interweaving of the two melodic lines in the opening measures of "Are You Sleeping." Identify this texture as polyphonic. Notice that both melodic lines contain the same melody.

VISUAL T2

ARE YOU SLEEPING?

French Round

Explain that polyphonic texture can be created in the classroom through the singing and playing of rounds and canons. A *canon* is a device whereby the melody of one part is strictly imitated from beginning to end in a second voice, or even in a third or fourth voice. The beginning voice in a canon is known as the *leader*; all other voices are *followers*.

A *round* is simply a canon in which each performer returns to the beginning of the song after its conclusion. "Are You Sleeping?" is a round. When singing a round, the performers may repeat it as many times as they wish.

Provide students with other examples of songs and instrumental pieces that are usually performed in canon or in round, such as the examples provided here.

MAKE NEW FRIENDS

Round

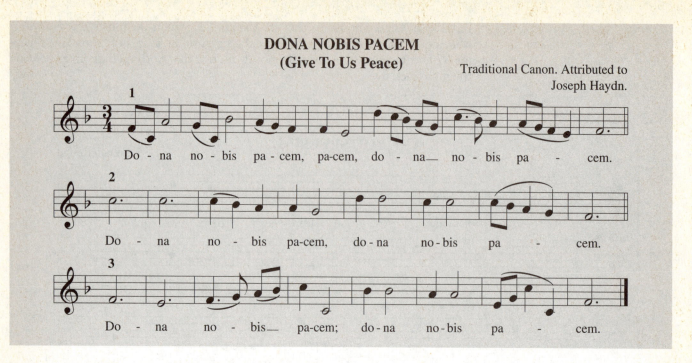

DONA NOBIS PACEM
(Give To Us Peace)

Traditional Canon. Attributed to
Joseph Haydn.

1 Do - na no - bis pa - cem, pa-cem, do - na— no - bis pa - cem.

2 Do - na no - bis pa-cem, do - na no - bis pa - cem.

3 Do - na no - bis pa-cem; do - na no - bis pa - cem.

HEY, HO! NOBODY HOME

English Round

1 Hey, ho! No - bod - y home, **2** Meat nor drink nor mon-ey have I none,

3 Yet will I be mer - ry,— **4** Hey, ho! No - bod - y home.

The following recordings contain other examples that will further reinforce an understanding of polyphonic texture:

a. "Menuetto" from *String Quartet, Op. 76, No. 2* by Haydn. The minuet (not the trio section) is an example of a canon that is in two parts throughout.

b. "Sumer Is Icumen In," composer unknown. This piece is in four-part canon, accompanied by two additional voices.

c. "Little Dance in Canon Form," "Canon at the Fifth," and "Canon at the Octave" from *Mikrokosmos I* by Bartok.

Learning | Although some polyphonic compositions contain only one melody sung by different groups, as in rounds and canons, other polyphonic music may contain two or more *different* songs that share an identical harmonic structure and are performed at the same time. These are known as *partner songs*.

Strategies **NS 1, 6** (Sing a partner song.)

Have half the class sing "Skip to My Lou" while the other half sings "Mulberry Bush." Explain that the simultaneous performance of two or more different, independent melodies also results in polyphonic texture.

SKIP TO MY LOU

American Singing Game

Skip, skip, skip to my Lou! Skip, skip, skip to my Lou!

Skip, skip, skip to my Lou! Skip to my Lou, my dar - ling.

MULBERRY BUSH

English Game Song

Here we go 'round the mul-ber-ry bush, the mul-ber-ry bush, the mul-ber-ry bush.

Here we go 'round the mul-ber-ry bush, so ear-ly in the morn-ing.

Sing additional partner songs as examples of polyphonic texture, such as "This Old Man" and "Skip to My Lou" or "This Old Man" and "Mulberry Bush." Other usable combinations include:

a. "Home on the Range" and "My Home's in Montana"
b. "Frère Jacques" and "Farmer in the Dell"
c. "Go Tell Aunt Rhody" and "London Bridge"

THIS OLD MAN

England

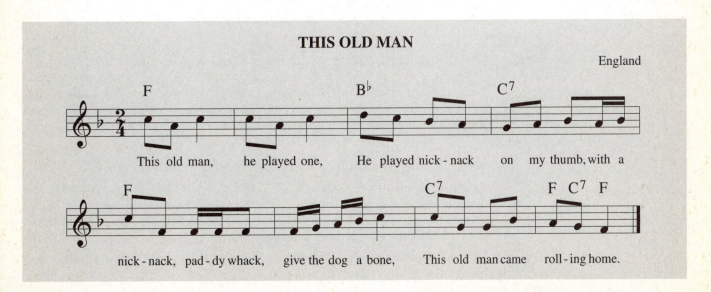

This old man, he played one, He played nick - nack on my thumb, with a

nick - nack, pad - dy whack, give the dog a bone, This old man came roll - ing home.

Learning

A *descant* is a countermelody, or second melody, that is sung higher than the original melody. Songs having descants are polyphonic in texture.

Strategies **NS 1** (Sing a song with a descant.)

Teach "Music Alone Shall Live." After students are comfortable with the song, have them sing it while listening carefully to the upper melody or descant that the teacher will add. Discuss with the students what has taken place. Students may notice that harmony results when both melodies are sung together. Have students transfer the descant to melody instruments. Students can practice both parts until they play and sing them well enough to switch parts.

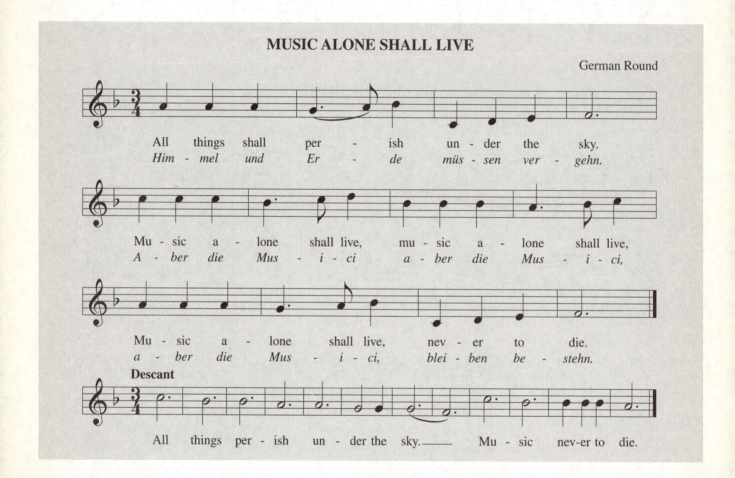

MUSIC ALONE SHALL LIVE

German Round

Learning

One of the most complex examples of polyphonic texture can be found in the fugue. A *fugue* is a polyphonic composition based on a theme, called the *subject*, which is stated at the beginning of the piece and then is taken up imitatively in other voices, called the *answers*, in close succession. The subject and its answers are restated at different points in the composition.

Strategies **NS 6** (Visually and aurally identify the form of a fugue.)

Play an example of a fugue, such as "Little Fugue in G Minor" by Bach. Ask students how this recording is both similar to and different from the recordings of canons heard earlier. Responses will most likely include references to imitation of theme, but not so strictly as in a canon.

Play the opening theme of "Little Fugue in G Minor" on a melodic instrument. See **Visual T3.**

LITTLE FUGUE IN G MINOR

J. S. Bach

Theme 1: Subject

Have students hum along until they are very familiar with the theme. Replay the fugue recording and have students raise their hands each time the subject is repeated.

Explain that fugues contain a *countersubject,* or second theme, that follows the statement of the first theme. When voice 2 enters to sound the main theme, it does so against the countersubject in voice 1. Place a copy of **Visual T4** on a projector so that students can see the interweaving of the melody with the countersubject in this polyphonic example.

VISUAL T4

LITTLE FUGUE IN G MINOR

Theme 2: Countersubject

Theme 1: Answer

Provide opportunities for additional listening to compositions using the fugue form, such as:

a. "The Cat's Fugue" by Scarlatti
b. Any of the fugues in *The Well-Tempered Clavier* by Bach

Students can further their knowledge of word meanings by paying attention to the prefix *poly-*, which means "more than one" or "many". Thus the musical term *polyphonic* means "many voices," In math a *polygon* is a figure with at least three sides. In science, a *polymer* is a large molecule composed of repeating structural units.

FOCUS

Homophonic Texture

Learning   In much accompanied music, the texture consists of a succession of chords that support a melody. This texture is called *chordal* or *homophonic*.

Strategies **NS 1** (Sing a song with a chordal accompaniment.)

Have the class sing "Jolly Old St. Nicholas" while someone plays its accompaniment on the piano. Explain that a single melody with a chordal accompaniment is an example of homophonic texture. Identify the melody and the chordal accompaniment in the song.

JOLLY OLD ST. NICHOLAS

Traditional Carol

Jol - ly old Saint Nich-o - las, Lean your ear this way. Don't you tell a

sin - gle soul. What I'm go'-ing to say. Christ-mas Eve is com-ing soon.

Now you dear old man. Whis-per what you'll bring to me. Tell me if you can.

Compare the vertical harmony of "Jolly Old St. Nicholas" to the horizontal harmony of the rounds sung previously.

Explain that most harmonizations found in songbooks or hymnals are homophonic in texture, as are the harmonies of most popular songs. Provide students with other examples of homophonic music, such as the excerpts that follow. Have students identify the melody and the chordal support found in each example.

BACH CHORALE: "ERMUNTRE DICH, MEIN SCHWACHER GEIST"

J. S. Bach

OH, ROCKA MY SOUL

Arr.: Jester Hairston

Students can continue to make connections between words and their meanings by examining the following words.

In music, as we just learned, homophony means that parts move together rather than independently. A single melodic line with accompaniment is an example of this relationship.

The prefix *homo-* has found similar meaning in other words. *Homology* is the relation of the chemical elements of a periodic family or group. A *homophone* is one of two or more words, such as *knight* and *night*, that are pronounced the same, but differ in meaning, origin, and sometimes spelling. *Homogenized* milk is made by blending unlike elements, especially by reducing one element to particles and dispersing them throughout another substance. Milk that has been made uniform in consistency by emulsifying the fat content is homogenized. A *homogeneous* group contains all of the same or similar people.

Visual T5 provides a succinct summary of the three types of texture found in most musical compositions. Teachers should create a larger prototype of Visual T5 and place it on an erasable whiteboard, chart, or bulletin board. Students can then be asked to add other pictorial examples of different textures as well as names of other musical pieces.

VISUAL T5

Texture Type	Examples	Musical Examples
Monophonic (single, unaccompanied melodic line)	A child whistling	Gregorian Chant
Monophonic	A soldier playing the bugle at sunset	"Taps" or "Reveille"
Polyphonic (two or more melodies being sung or played at the same time)	Most music by Bach; Gregorian chant being performed by a group of monks chanting in unison	Cello Suites by Bach
Polyphonic	Rounds, canons, fugues, inventions	"Are You Sleeping?" "Row, Row, Row Your Boat"; Pachabel's Canon; The final "Amen Chorus" of Handel's *Messiah*
Homophonic (music that has the same rhythms at the same time.)	Choral music in which the parts being sung have the same rhythm; traditional hymns	"Amazing Grace"
Homophonic	A cowboy singing a solo, accompanied by a guitar	

INTRODUCING THE STRUCTURAL COMPONENTS OF TEXTURE

Suggested Sequencing by Grade Level

Kindergarten, Grade One

1. Unaccompanied and accompanied singing
2. Unison singing

Grade Two

1. Monophony: unaccompanied melody
2. Homophony: melody with harmony
3. Polyphony: rounds

Grades Three and Four

1. Polyphony: partner songs and descants

Grades Five and Six

1. Polyphony: fugue
2. Reinforce monophony, homophony, polyphony with a variety of experiences that increase in difficulty

WRITTEN AND PERFORMANCE-RELATED ASSESSMENTS THROUGH COOPERATIVE LEARNING ACTIVITIES: TEXTURE NS 1, 2, 5, 7

1. Invite each group to experiment with changing the texture of a known song through the layering of instruments. Elicit from the students a number of ways to accomplish this task. Their suggestions might include:
   a. begin by singing the song unaccompanied;
   b. add a single rhythmic timbre as accompaniment—play a rhythmic ostinato on the claves or cabasa—while singing the song;
   c. accompany the song with different wood, metal, or skinned instruments; or
   d. mix woods, metals, and skins to accompany the song.
   Students should perform for the teacher when they are ready. **NS 1, 2, 7**
2. Choose a simple, short canon for each group. Ask group members to perform their song on bells to demonstrate monophonic, polyphonic, and homophonic textures. To accomplish their task, groups might:
   a. first play the song unaccompanied (monophony);
   b. play the song in two-part canon (polyphony); or
   c. perform the song with a bordun or melodic ostinato (homophony).
   Group members may choose to sing along with the melody as they perform each of the song's textures. When the task is completed, they should perform for the teacher. **NS 1, 2, 5, 7**
3. Give each group several autoharps and a musical selection. "O Susanna," "Home on the Range," "When the Saints Go Marching In," and "This Land Is Your Land" are good beginning songs. Group members should experiment with chords until they can play the song with a workable chordal (homophonic) accompaniment. Students should sing while playing the chords. Students can perform their accompanied songs for the class. **NS 1, 2, 5, 7**

Teaching Harmony to Children

INTRODUCTION

Most of the music we hear today consists of a melody that is sung or played and supported by other sounds. Whenever this type of simultaneous sounding occurs between the pitches in the melody and the melodic sounds in one or more accompanying voices, *harmony* results. These accompanying sounds may include a few pitches or many tones, as in supportive chords, or could even be one or more melodies, either the same or different from the original melody. The accompanying or supportive sounds, whether produced by voices or instruments, enrich the beauty of the melody.

When harmony is added to a melody, the resulting texture is either homophonic or polyphonic, as studied in Chapter 7. Some of the techniques used to introduce harmonic structures to children have already been studied in relation to these two textures. Even so, these techniques are repeated here, within the new context of harmony, so that a complete overview of the teaching of harmony is presented.

> *In music it is as with chess-playing—*
> *the Queen, melody, possesses supreme*
> *power; but it is the King, harmony,*
> *who ultimately decides.*
> *—Schumann*

FOCUS

Aural Harmonic Awareness

Learning   *Harmony* results when a melody is accompanied with a pitched instrument, such as an Orff instrument, an autoharp, a guitar or dulcimer, or the piano.

Strategies **NS 1, 6** (Singing in parts. Listening to, analyzing and describing music in harmony.)

Students should have many experiences listening to the teacher sing a short melody while playing a simple accompaniment on a pitched instrument. Students should be carefully prepared for these experiences by being invited to sit in a comfortable position with quiet attention. Recordings containing a simple, uncomplicated accompaniment to a melody may also be used for this experience.

FOCUS

Preparation for Harmony

Learning   The simultaneous performance of two different musical activities, one melodic and one rhythmic, or both rhythmic, builds a foundation for some of the skills that will be needed later when playing or singing in harmony.

Strategies **NS 1, 6** (Sing a song while adding appropriate hand and arm movements.)

Have students say rhymes or sing songs while performing accompanying actions. Actions might be suggested by the words of the rhyme or can be newly created, as in **Visual H1.**

VISUAL H1

Teddy Bear

Actions	Rhyme
Turn around	Teddy Bear, teddy bear, turn around.
Touch ground	Teddy Bear, teddy bear, touch the ground.
Show shoe	Teddy Bear, teddy bear, show your shoe.
Shake finger	Teddy Bear, teddy bear, that will do.

DOWN BY THE STATION

Southern Folk Song

Using both hands, draw a circle in the air (sun)

Down by the sta - tion, ear - ly in the morn - ing,

Put right hand above eye and look all around

See the lit - tle puf - fer bel - lies all in a row.

With right hand, pretend to pull a handle

See the en - gine dri - ver pull the lit - tle han - dle,

Move both arms back and forth, like the wheels of a train engine

Chug, chug, toot, toot, off they go.

Have students patsch, clap, or walk to the beat while saying a rhyme or singing a song.

Have students clap the rhythm of a rhyme or song while saying or singing it.

Have students patsch the beat of the first phrase of a song or rhyme, then clap the rhythm of the second phrase. Continue rotating the performance of beat and rhythm to the end of the song or rhyme.

While students say a rhyme or sing a song, such as "Bounce High, Bounce Low," have them perform a rhythmic ostinato. Begin with the two-beat pattern 𝄆 ♩𝄽 𝄇; later, progress to 𝄆 ♫ ♩ 𝄇; and finally, have them perform a four-beat rhythmic ostinato 𝄆 ♩ ♩ ♫ ♩ 𝄇. More difficult patterns should follow over a period of time. See **Visual H2.**

VISUAL H2

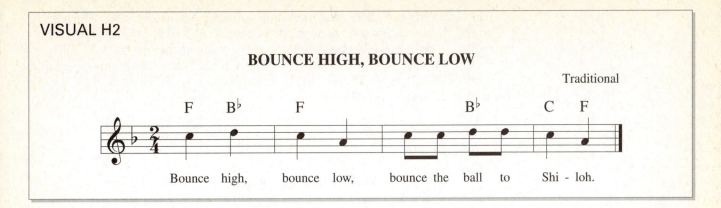

BOUNCE HIGH, BOUNCE LOW

Traditional

Bounce high, bounce low, bounce the ball to Shi - loh.

To challenge the older student, place on the board a series of rhythms from a given song, such as "Arirang," as in **Visual H3.** As students sing the song, point to different rhythms in turn for them to clap as an ostinato to the song.

VISUAL H3

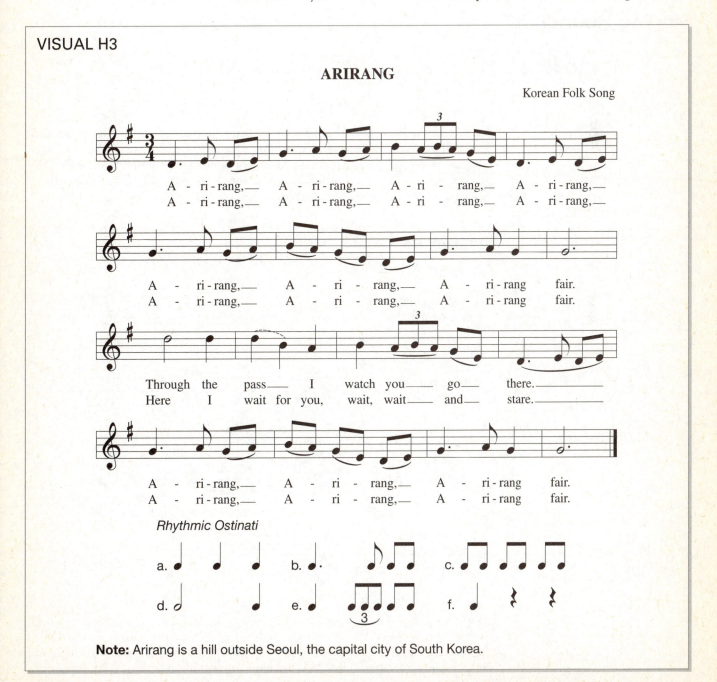

ARIRANG

Korean Folk Song

A - ri - rang,— A - ri - rang,— A - ri - rang,— A - ri - rang,—
A - ri - rang,— A - ri - rang,— A - ri - rang,— A - ri - rang,—

A - ri - rang,— A - ri - rang,— A - ri - rang fair.
A - ri - rang,— A - ri - rang,— A - ri - rang fair.

Through the pass— I watch you— go— there.—
Here I wait for you, wait, wait— and— stare.—

A - ri - rang,— A - ri - rang,— A - ri - rang fair.
A - ri - rang,— A - ri - rang,— A - ri - rang fair.

Rhythmic Ostinati

a.   b.   c.

d.   e.   f.

Note: Arirang is a hill outside Seoul, the capital city of South Korea.

After students can successfully perform a rhyme that has actions, ask them to do the rhyme and actions as a round. Divide the class into two separate circles. Using the rhyme "Teddy Bear," have one group chant the first phrase while performing the appropriate actions. As group 1 begins the second phrase, group 2 starts phrase 1, as in **Visual H4.** Continue through the rhyme and its actions until both groups are finished.

VISUAL H4

Group 1:   Teddy bear. . . turn around.   Teddy bear, etc.

                              Group 2:   Teddy bear. . . around.

FOCUS

Singing Rounds

Learning   Singing in rounds is an effective way to produce harmony.

Strategies **NS 1** (Sing a song in round.)

After students have had a number of experiences performing rhymes in rounds, they will be ready to sing in rounds. Pentatonic songs can usually be sung successfully as rounds. Students should know the song and its actions well before the teacher divides the group into two circles for performing the round. "Bow Wow Wow" is a good starting song for round singing in two parts. See **Visual H5.**

VISUAL H5

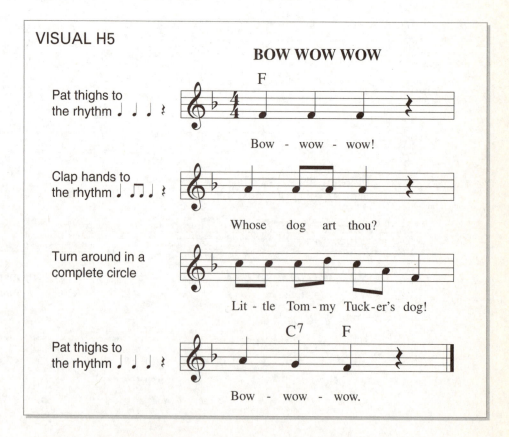

BOW WOW WOW

Pat thighs to the rhythm ♩ ♩ ♩ ♩ ♪   Bow - wow - wow!

Clap hands to the rhythm ♩ ♪♪ ♩ ♪   Whose dog art thou?

Turn around in a complete circle   Lit - tle Tom - my Tuck-er's dog!

Pat thighs to the rhythm ♩ ♩ ♩ ♪   Bow - wow - wow.

As students develop musically, rounds in three and four parts can be added and actions can be omitted. However, students enjoy adding actions to their rounds.

Periodically, have them create their own movements to a round and perform them in groups of two, three, or four, depending on their performance abilities.

FOCUS

Melodic Ostinato

Learning Adding melodic ostinati to a melody is another way to create harmony.

Strategies **NS 1, 5** (Sing a song and add a simple accompaniment to create harmony.)

A single-note *drone* that is played or sung is a good preparatory experience for performing melodic ostinati with well-known songs. Later, students can sing or play two, more interesting beats and then four repeated beats, with the patterns becoming increasingly difficult. See **Visual H6.**

VISUAL H6   **I LOVE THE MOUNTAINS**

Traditional

Learning	Harmony in thirds and sixths can add to the interest of a melody.

Strategies **NS 1, 5** (Singing a song in harmony.)

Add a simple harmony in thirds or sixths at the end of phrases in a song, as in **Visual H7**.

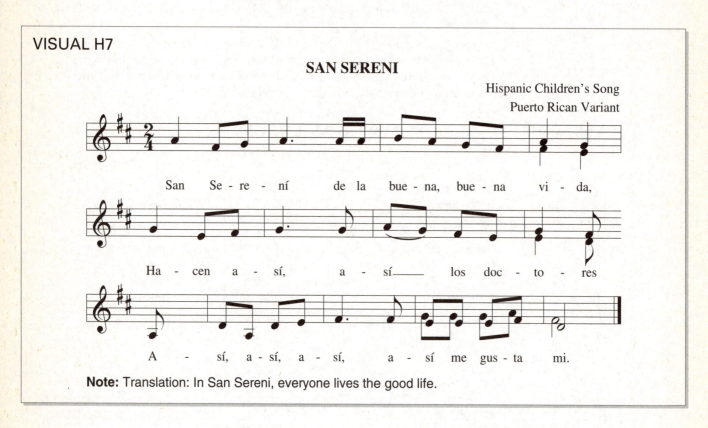

VISUAL H7

SAN SERENI

Hispanic Children's Song
Puerto Rican Variant

San Se - re - ní   de la bue - na, bue - na vi - da,

Ha - cen a - sí,   a - sí___ los doc - to - res

A - sí, a - sí, a - sí,   a - sí me gus - ta mi.

Note: Translation: In San Sereni, everyone lives the good life.

Later, add harmony in thirds and sixths to larger portions of a song, as in **Visual H8**.

SAN SERENI

San Se - re - ní de la bue - na, bue - na vi - da,

Ha - cen a - sí, a - sí___ los doc - to - res

A - sí, a - sí, a - sí, a - sí me gus - ta mi.

FOCUS

Partner Songs and Descants

Learning The simultaneous singing of two or more different melodies that use the same harmonic structure will result in harmony. Different melodies that can be sung together are known as *partner songs*.

Strategies **NS 1** (Sing a song in harmony.)

A number of familiar songs can be sung together as partner songs to create harmony. Be sure each song is well learned before asking students to sing both of them at the same time. "Paw Paw Patch" and "Skip to My Lou" are harmonically satisfying when sung together, as are the following songs:

"Skip to My Lou" and "Mulberry Bush"
"This Old Man" and "Skip to My Lou"
"This Old Man" and "Paw Paw Patch"
"Paw Paw Patch" and "Mulberry Bush"
"Row, Row, Row Your Boat" and "Three Blind Mice"
"The Farmer in the Dell" and "Three Blind Mice"
"Home on the Range" and "My Home's in Montana"

Simple, newly composed melodies can also be played or sung, either above or below a melody, to add harmony to a song, as in **Visual H9.** These simple melodies are known as *descants*.

LAVENDER'S BLUE

England
Arr.: Rozmajzl

Descant

I shall be king; ———— and then

Melody

Lav - en - der's blue, dil - ly, dil - ly, lav - en - der's green.

you shall be queen.

When I am king, dil - ly, dil - ly, you shall be queen.

We'll build a cas - tle

Who told you so, dil - ly, dil - ly, who told you so?

By a flow - ing stream.

'Twas mine own heart, dil - ly, dil - ly, that told me so.

Have students sing, "Oh When the Saints," "Swing Low," and "This Train" by themselves and then together as partner songs.

THIS TRAIN, OH WHEN THE SAINTS, SWING LOW

Spiritual
Arr.: Boyer

To be sung as partner songs

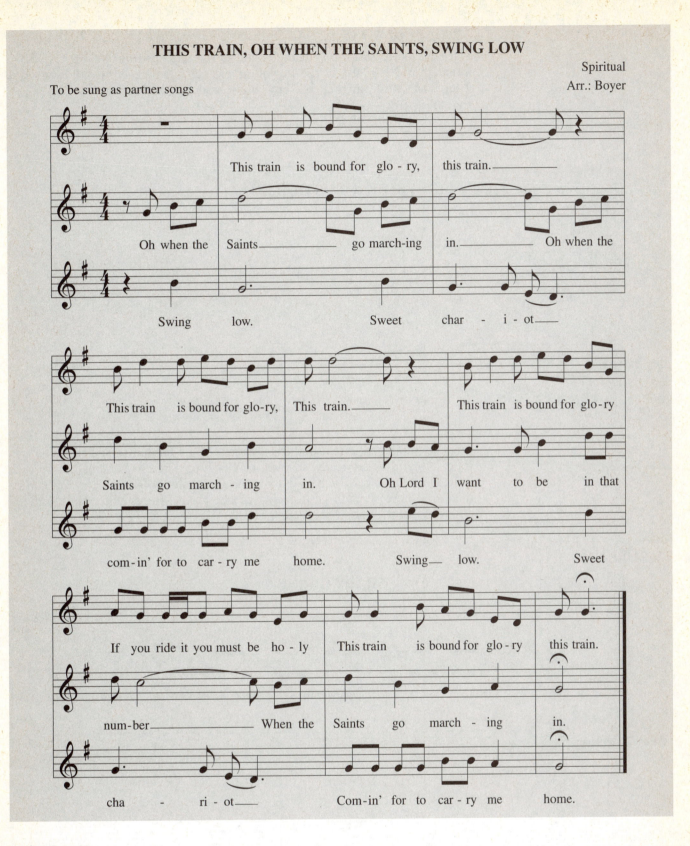

FOCUS

Bordun (pronounced Bor-dōōn)

Learning   A melody can be accompanied by playing one or more *borduns*, which is a repeated pattern, usually consisting of two pitches: the first and fifth tones of the scale.

Strategies **NS 1, 5** (Singing with others. Reading music.)

Place the bordun C to G on the board. Using Orff instruments, have students sound the C bordun on the downbeat of each measure of "Row, Row, Row Your Boat" while singing the song. Show students the bordun as it appears on the staff:

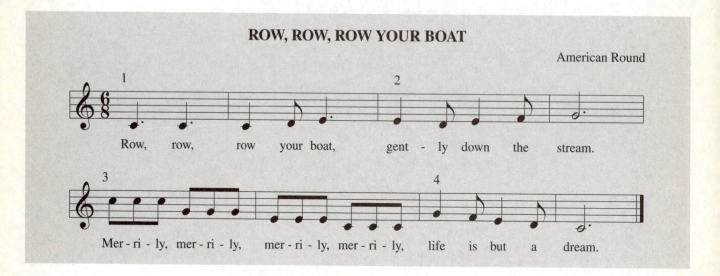

ROW, ROW, ROW YOUR BOAT

American Round

Row, row, row your boat, gent - ly down the stream.

Mer - ri - ly, mer - ri - ly, mer - ri - ly, mer - ri - ly, life is but a dream.

Students should have repeated experiences using a bordun to add harmony to a song. When they are ready, students can use two different borduns in a song to provide harmony for the melody. For the song "Shady Grove," E and B can be used as a simple bordun pattern that can be played on resonator bells, Orff instruments, or the piano. See **Visual H10**.

VISUAL H10

SHADY GROVE

American Folk Song

Cheeks as red as the bloom-ing rose, Eyes of the deep-est brown. You

Bass Xylophone

are the dar - ling of my— heart, Stay til the sun goes down.

BX

"Shady Grove" is a Southern mountain tune suitable for a "play party" dance or frolic. It's a song sung and played to express the happiness of good times with friends and neighbors.

FOCUS

Chordal Accompaniment

Learning   A *chord* is the simultaneous sounding of three or more different pitches, as distinguished from a *harmonic interval*, in which two pitches are sounded together.

Strategies **NS 1, 2, 5** (Singing with accompaniment. Reading music.)

Place on the board a C major chord consisting of the pitches C, E, and G. Give a resonator bell with these pitches to each of three students. A *resonator bell* is a barred instrument that plays only one pitch and can be held comfortably in the hand. Have students practice playing their pitches simultaneously, to produce a chord. When they are ready, have them play the C chord on the downbeat of each measure of "Row, Row, Row Your Boat" as the class sings the song. When they are physically mature enough to handle three mallets in two hands, students can play all three notes by themselves on Orff instruments. See **Visual H11.**

VISUAL H11

ROW, ROW, ROW YOUR BOAT

American Round

Row, row, row your boat, gent-ly down the stream.

C Major Chord:

Mer-ri-ly, mer-ri-ly, mer-ri-ly, mer-ri-ly, life is but a dream.

Students should practice playing a simple chord to a number of one-chord songs, such as "Candles of Hanukkah," which can be accompanied with the D minor chord. Place a D minor chord on the chalkboard:

While singing "Candles of Hanukkah," have students play the D minor chord on the downbeat of each measure. Then ask students to sing the song again in the key of E minor, and accompany it using only the E minor chord. See **Visual H12**.

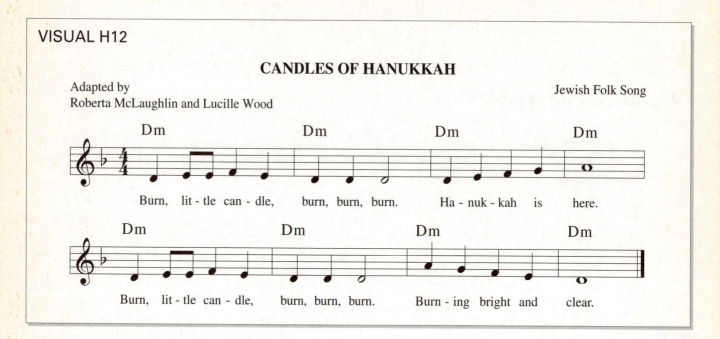

VISUAL H12

CANDLES OF HANUKKAH

Adapted by
Roberta McLaughlin and Lucille Wood

Jewish Folk Song

Burn, lit-tle can-dle, burn, burn, burn. Ha-nuk-kah is here.

Burn, lit-tle can-dle, burn, burn, burn. Burn-ing bright and clear.

Learning   A chord containing three notes, including a root, a third, and a fifth, is called a *triad*.

Strategies **NS 5** (Reading and writing chords.)

Explain that a chord can be built on any pitch of a scale. Draw a C major scale on the board. Build a three-note chord on each tone of the scale, as in **Visual H13.** Tell students that a chord having three different pitches is called a *triad*. Emphasize that the notes within a triad are placed in a line-line-line or space-space-space position.

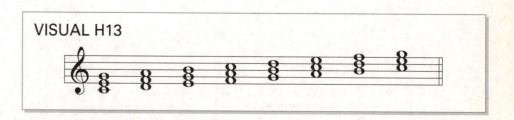

VISUAL H13

Give students practice in building triads by providing them with a beginning tone and having them spell triads aloud. See **Visual H14.**

_____   _____   _____   _____   _____   _____
_____   _____   _____   _____   _____   _____

a. __D__   b. __G__   c. __E__   d. __C__   e. __A__   f. __B__

Identify the bottom tone of a chord as the *root*, the middle tone as the *third*, and the upper tone as the *fifth*, as in **Visual H15.**

VISUAL H15

fifth
third
root

F Chord

Learning

The *primary chords* in any key are the most important chords, because they determine in what key a song is written. In any key, major or minor, the primary chords are those built on the first, fourth, and fifth tones of the scale. These chords are called the *tonic* or I chord, the *subdominant* or IV chord, and the *dominant* or V chord, respectively. All the remaining chords are called *secondary chords*. Secondary chords are used to add color and interest to a song.

Strategies **NS 1, 2** (Sing a song and add a chordal accompaniment.)

When students are able to perform a one-chord song using only the tonic chord, introduce the dominant chord built on the fifth tone of the scale. Place on the board the tonic and dominant chords for "Clementine," as in **Visual H16.** After practicing the chords on resonator bells or Orff instruments, have the students play them as indicated in the song, while singing the words of the song.

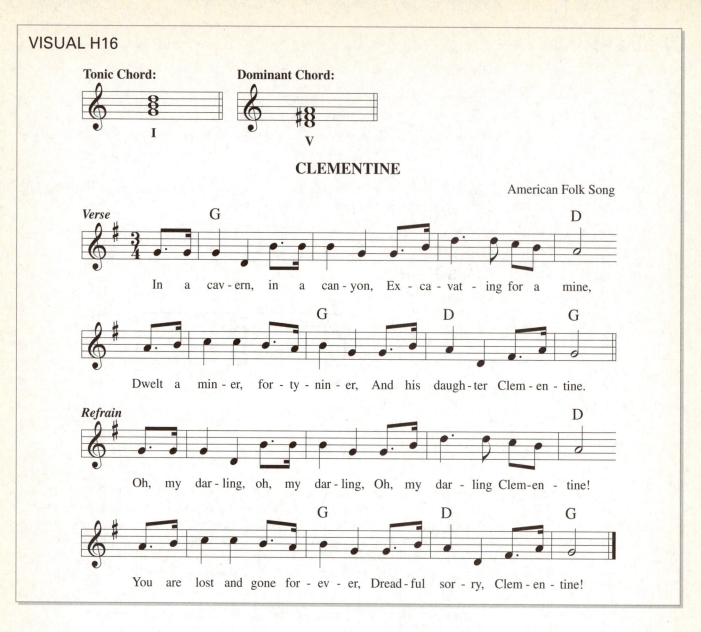

Have students perform additional songs that can be accompanied with the tonic and dominant chords, such as "Mein Hut" and "Juanito."

JUANITO
(LITTLE JOHNNY)

English Words by Alice D. Firgau

Children's Song from Spain

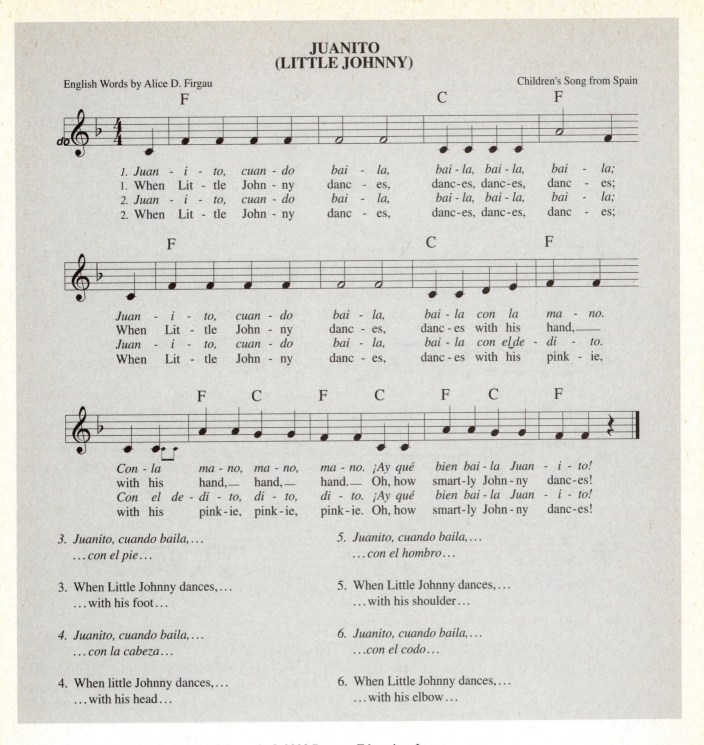

3. *Juanito, cuando baila,...*
   ...con el pie...

3. When Little Johnny dances,...
   ...with his foot...

4. *Juanito, cuando baila,...*
   ...con la cabeza...

4. When little Johnny dances,...
   ...with his head...

5. *Juanito, cuando baila,...*
   ...con el hombro...

5. When Little Johnny dances,...
   ...with his shoulder...

6. *Juanito, cuando baila,...*
   ...con el codo...

6. When Little Johnny dances,...
   ...with his elbow...

After students have had sufficient practice with two-chord songs, introduce the subdominant chord, built on the fourth tone of the scale. Place on the board the primary chords for "Tinga Layo," as in **Visual H17.** After students have practiced these chords, use them to accompany the song while singing its words.

Primary Chords:

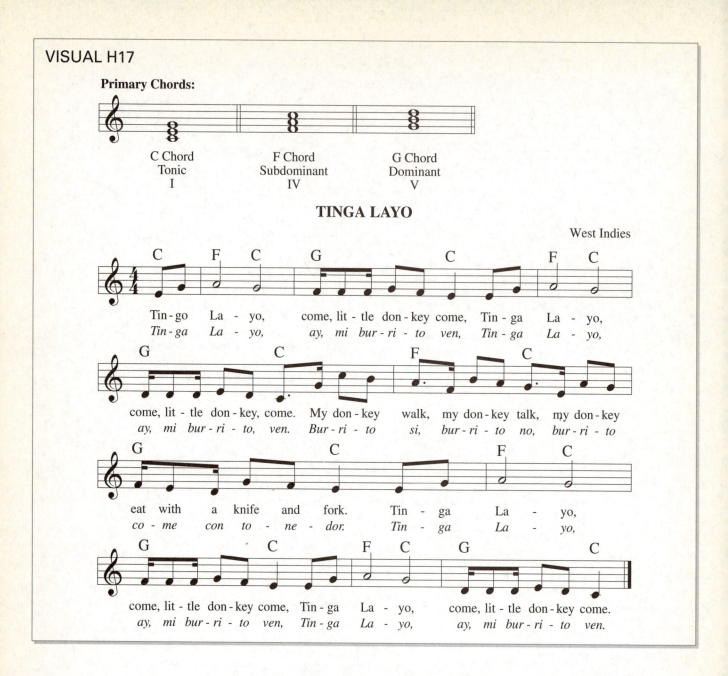

C Chord   F Chord   G Chord
Tonic   Subdominant   Dominant
I   IV   V

TINGA LAYO

West Indies

Tin - go La - yo, come, lit - tle don - key come, Tin - ga La - yo,
Tin - ga La - yo, ay, mi bur - ri - to ven, Tin - ga La - yo,

come, lit - tle don - key, come. My don - key walk, my don - key talk, my don - key
ay, mi bur - ri - to, ven. Bur - ri - to si, bur - ri - to no, bur - ri - to

eat with a knife and fork. Tin - ga La - yo,
co - me con to - ne - dor. Tin - ga La - yo,

come, lit - tle don - key come, Tin - ga La - yo, come, lit - tle don - key come.
ay, mi bur - ri - to ven, Tin - ga La - yo, ay, mi bur - ri - to ven.

Find other songs that use the I, IV, and V chords for accompaniment; have students identify the chords, place them on the board, and play them while singing the song. "Au Clair de la Lune" and "El Florón" can be used to reinforce the playing of primary chords.

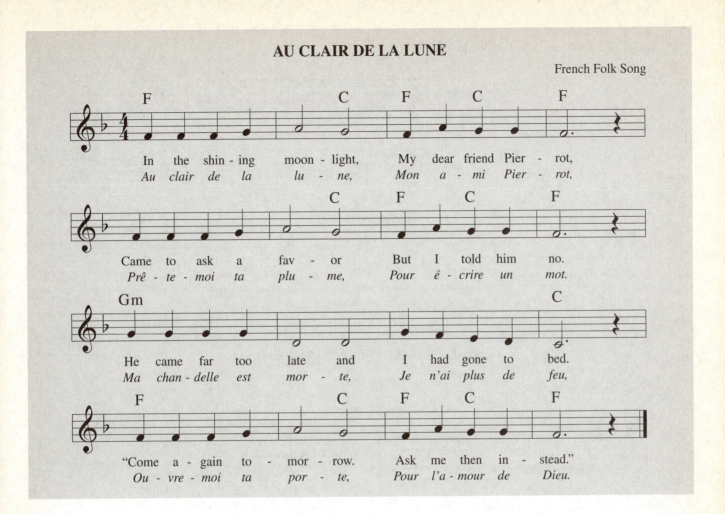

AU CLAIR DE LA LUNE

French Folk Song

In the shin - ing moon - light, My dear friend Pier - rot,
Au clair de la lu - ne, Mon a - mi Pier - rot,

Came to ask a fav - or But I told him no.
Prê - te - moi ta plu - me, Pour é - crire un mot.

He came far too late and I had gone to bed.
Ma chan - delle est mor - te, Je n'ai plus de feu,

"Come a - gain to - mor - row. Ask me then in - stead."
Ou - vre - moi ta por - te, Pour l'a - mour de Dieu.

To ensure the understanding of primary chords, have students spell the tonic, the subdominant, and the dominant chords in various major keys. Using **Visual H18,** the following steps can be applied to facilitate this exercise:

Step 1: Draw a D major (or any major) scale; designate the tones on which the I, IV, and V chords will be built.

Step 2: Build a triad on each of these three scale degrees.

Step 3: Place accidentals where they belong, as indicated by the key signature.

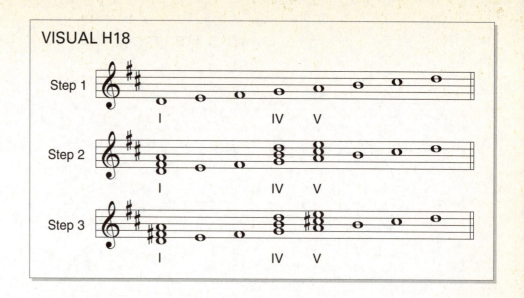

EL FLORÓN (THE FLOWER)

English Words by Verne Muñoz

Singing Game from Puerto Rico

El flo - rón pas - ó por a - quí,
Pass the flow - er round and a - round.

Yo no lo vi, Yo no lo vi.
Will it be found? Will it be found?

¿Que pa - se, que pa - se,
Where is it? Where is it?

Que pa - se el flo - rón?
Where can the flow - er be?

Source: El Florón (The Flower) English words © 1988 Silver Burdett Ginn.

Building the dominant chord in a minor key is a bit more difficult than building it in a major key because it involves the use of an accidental; that is, the seventh tone of the scale must be raised. The seventh tone of the scale is the same as the third of the dominant chord, as can be seen in **Visual H19.**

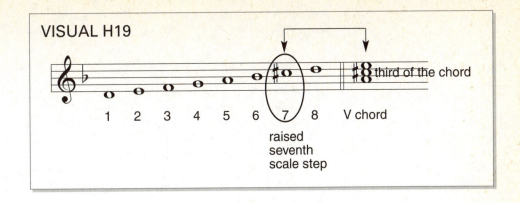

VISUAL H19

1 2 3 4 5 6 7 8   V chord

raised
seventh
scale step

third of the chord

To accompany a song in a minor key, always remember to raise the third of the V chord. Practice doing this when accompanying "Joshua Fought the Battle of Jericho."

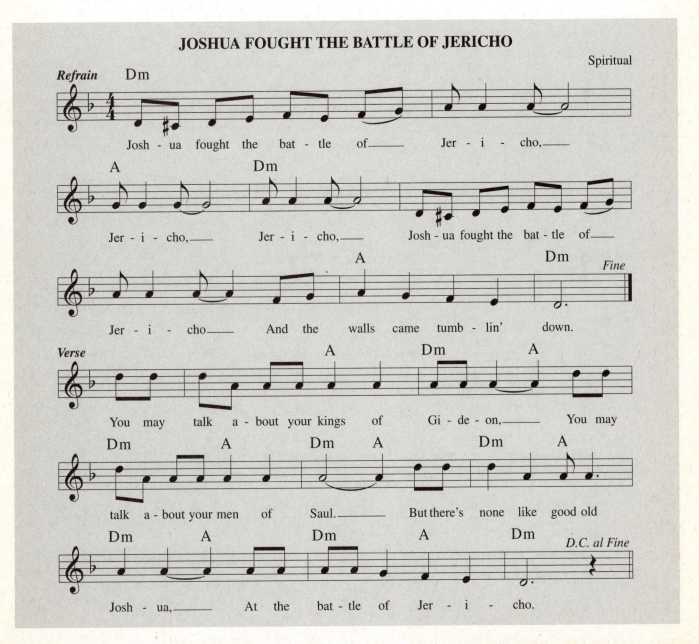

JOSHUA FOUGHT THE BATTLE OF JERICHO

Spiritual

Strategies **NS 1, 2, 5**

Place on the board a seventh chord built on G; play the chord. Identify this as a seventh chord because it has four different pitches, each an interval of a third apart. Tell students that this chord is called "seventh" because the top pitch (F) is a distance of seven tones from the bottom pitch (G). Explain that a seventh chord may occur on any pitch of the scale. One of the most important seventh chords, however, is the one that occurs on the dominant chord (V). A dominant seventh chord is indicated by the symbol V^7. See **Visual H20**.

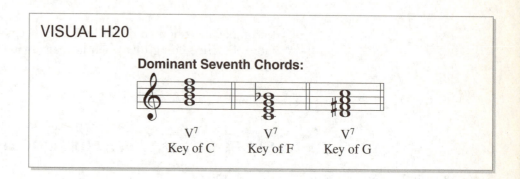

Practice playing a number of songs containing dominant seventh chords (V^7), such as "Tinga Layo."

Learning Each triad contains two intervals consisting of a third each. These thirds may be either major or minor.

A *major third* consists of four half steps:

A *minor third* consists of three half steps:

FOCUS

Blues

Learning The 12-bar blues form represents 12 bars or measures of music in 4/4 time that is set to a specific harmonic pattern. (See below.) Once the pattern is completed, it begins again until 36 beats of music have been completed. It is one of the most popular forms of music that can be heard in styles such as rhythm and blues, gospel, rock, and jazz.

The melody, which is played or sung over a 12-bar harmonic pattern, is based on a special scale that is called the "blues" scale. The "blues scale" is different from either the major or minor scale because it contains altered notes that are labeled "blue notes." The most commonly used "blue notes" are the flattened third, fifth, and seventh of the major scale. These "blue notes" allow for a unique kind of expression that belongs to the blues style. Expressions of tension, yearning, hurt, and passion can easily be felt when using these "blue notes." A major scale beginning on "F" would look like this.

F Major Scale

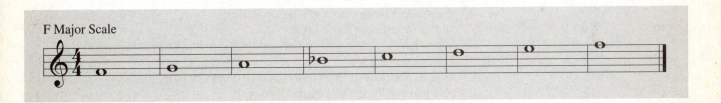

A blues scale that begins on "F" would look like this:

Blues Scale

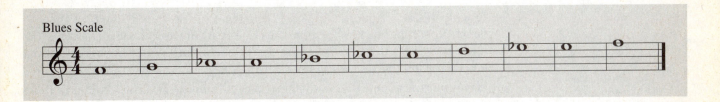

A 12-bar chord progression in 4/4 time that is commonly found in blues is made up of I, IV, and V chords. (Remember that Roman numerals are always used to tell the chord name. For example, the I chord in F Major is called the tonic chord and is spelled F-A-C; the IV chord is called the subdominant chord and is spelled Bb-D-F; and finally, the V chord is the dominant chord. In the key of F major, the dominant chord is spelled C-E-G.)

Each of the chords below represents the harmonic structure of an entire measure of a "blues" progression in 4/4 or common time.

I	I	I	I	IV	IV	I	I	V	IV	I	I

When students perform the first four blocks or measures represented in the above example, they will play the following chords in the key of F.

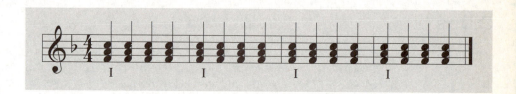

Strategies **NS 1, 6** (Listen to, sing, play, create and analyze the 12-bar blues.)

Have students use the Internet to find and listen to recordings from the following Favorite Children's Blues List. All of these favorites use a 12-bar blues progression.

Favorite Children's Blues List

1. "Good Morning Blues" by Leadbelly
2. "Joe Turner Blues" by Leadbelly
3. "You Ain't Nothing But A Hound Dog" (Recorded by Elvis Presley)
4. "Blue Suede Shoes" (Recorded by Elvis Presley)*
5. "Rock Around the Clock" (Recorded by Bill Haley)*
6. "Everyday I Have the Blues" by B.B. King
7. "In the Mood" by Glenn Miller
8. Any blues selection from Volume 44, "Blues in all Keys" recorded by Jamie Aebersold.
9. "Shake, Rattle and Roll" (Bill Haley and the Comets)
10. " Now is the Time" by Charlie Parker
11. "Backwater Blues" by Dinah Washington
12. "Johnny B. Goode" by Chuck Berry
13. "12-Bar Original" by the Beatles (Released in Anthology 2 Disc, 1996)

*These pieces have short introductions that lead into the 12-bar blues form.

Provide a beat chart or map of a 12-bar blues progression for each of the students. Note that one symbol represents one beat. In the following chart, the triangle represents the I or tonic chord; the circle the IV or subdominant chord and the square the V or dominant chord.

Have students choose one of the blues pieces from the Favorite Children's Blues List and tap along on their beat map with their pencil. Students will notice that as the symbols change, the harmony changes, thus outlining the entire 12-bar blues progression.

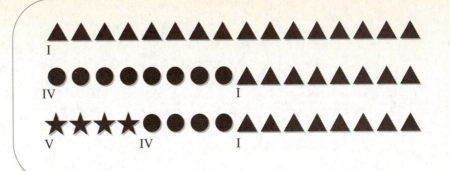

Use this beat map, or a similar chart, to listen and follow along with other blues selections from the list above.

Learning   The lyrics of the blues are usually very sad, but they also reflect the possibility of hope for a better tomorrow. Blues lyrics also have a special form.

The first line of lyrics is sung and then repeated exactly the same. This "AA" pattern is followed by a "B" line of lyrics, whose last word rhymes with the last text words in the "A" section. "The St. Louis Blues," written by W. C. Handy, was one of the first blues songs that used this AAB form. The lyrics are as follows:

A   I hate to see the evening sun go **down,**
A   I hate to see the evening sun go **down,**
B   'Cause it make me think, I'm on my last **ground.**

Strategies   **NS 2, 6** (Listen to, play and analyze 12-bar blues.)

Have students listen to the AAB song form of the blues in the pieces listed above. Give them lots of practice telling which words rhyme in the AAB pattern.

Then, students create and write their own "blues" lyrics. Jamey Aebersold's Volume 44, "Blues In All Keys," is highly recommended for this assignment. It will provide students with the opportunity they need to choose just the right blues key and tempo for them. This product can be ordered from: P.P. Box 1244C; New Albany, IN 47151-1244; 1-800-456-1388.

Practice playing the 12-bar blues progression on Orff-barred instruments, the guitar, or piano, and then add lyrics.

While in small groups, have students perform their blues piece in front of an audience of their peers.

Sing "City Blues." Create another verse about another city. Share with the class.

CITY BLUES

American Folk Song

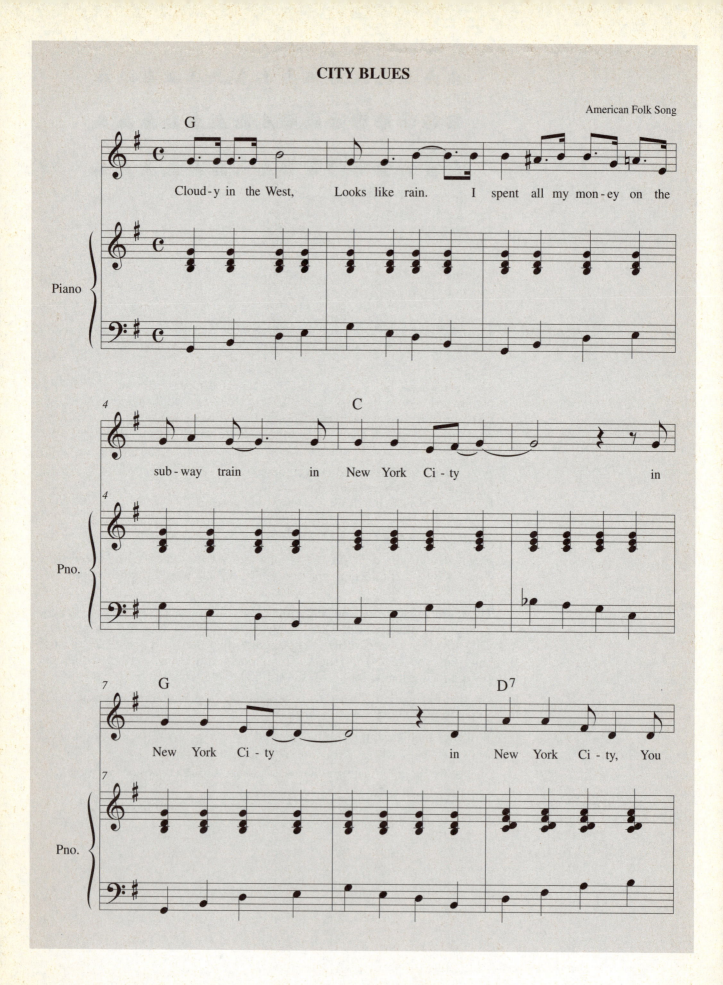

I went to visit the President in Washington D.C.
I showed up at the White House, they just looked at me,
In our capitol city, In our capitol city,
In our Capitol city, You really got to know your way.

I stopped in Philly, Oh what a town!
I hoped to hear the Freedom Bell, but it made no sound,
In Philadelphia, In Philadelphia
In Philadelphia, you really got to know your way.

Found the Queen City on the Ohio,
Folks were making music, I just loved it so!
In Cincinnati, In Cincinnati,
In Cincinnati, you really got to know your way.

Went to Detroit, it was fine,
I watched the cars movin' off the assembly line,
In Detroit City, in Detroit City,
In Detroit city, you really got to know your way.

I looped the loop, I rocked and reeled
I saw the Cubs play ball in Wrigley Field
In the Windy City, In the Windy City,
In the Windy city, you really got to know your way.

INTRODUCING THE STRUCTURAL COMPONENTS OF HARMONY

Suggested Sequencing by Grade Level

Kindergarten

1. Harmony preparation
   a. Aural awareness
   b. Doing two things at once: recite a rhyme or sing while moving

Grade One

1. Simple rhythmic ostinati
2. One-note drone
3. Spoken round

Grade Two

1. Simple melodic ostinati
2. Borduns
3. Sung round

Grade Three

1. Countermelody
2. Singing in thirds or sixths
3. Partner songs

Grade Four

1. Descant
2. Simple two-part singing

Grades Five and Six

1. Harmonic intervals
2. Chords: I, IV, V
3. Two- and three-part singing
4. Seventh chords: V^7

The Singing Voice NS 1, 5, 6

Singing is one of the most important of all musical experiences. In fact, it could be considered the heartbeat of the music program in the primary years. The human voice is an instrument that most individuals possess, making singing the one musical skill that many elementary teachers can afford to develop. Unless there is a physical defect in the vocal mechanism, almost every child can learn to sing. Many of the basic musical learnings presented throughout this book can be realized through singing experiences.

Content Standard 1, as outlined in the National Standards for Arts Education, emphasizes students' ability to "sing, alone and with others, a varied repertoire of music." It is highly recommended that students:

a. sing independently, on pitch and in rhythm, with appropriate timbre, diction, and posture, and maintain a steady tempo
b. sing expressively, with appropriate dynamics, phrasing, and interpretation
c. sing from memory a varied repertoire of songs representing genres and styles from diverse cultures
d. sing ostinati, partner songs, and rounds
e. sing in groups, blending vocal timbres, matching dynamic levels, and responding to the cues of a conductor

It is important, therefore, for classroom teachers to become vocally competent, so that they can guide their students in experiencing the joy, excitement, and understanding that comes from singing.

Many beginning teachers feel insecure and uncomfortable when using their singing voice. Nevertheless, if a teacher possesses an open mind and willingness to try, it is possible to develop the vocal mechanism to a respectable level of performance.

ADULT VOICE

In the typical music methods course for classroom teachers, there are many levels of vocal competency from one student to the next. For example, there are adults who:

1. have much difficulty in matching pitch
2. match pitch, but have difficulty in sustaining correct pitches throughout a song
3. have been influenced by poor advisors and role models in their environment and, as a result, misuse the entire vocal mechanism
4. sing acceptably with good tone quality and have varying degrees of music reading experience

Regardless of how competent or incompetent a singer may be, all prospective teachers can develop their vocal abilities. A brief explanation of the singer's vocal mechanism is helpful in understanding how musical sounds are produced.

VOCAL MECHANISM

The entire body, as well as an individual's psychological state, contributes to the production of good tone. There are several stages involved in this process:

1. The brain begins the activity. It is the brain that sets into motion the concepts that will be formulated and gives the signal, through the central nervous system, to the participating muscles, organs, and limbs, to begin tone production.

2. The breathing system goes into action, relying heavily on the strength and support of major muscles used in singing. The diaphragm is the most important of these muscles. The *diaphragm* is a large muscle that lies across the body under the lungs. Its up-and-down motion provides the impetus that becomes the foundation of the entire breathing system. The sides, ribs, and lower back muscles of the body work with the diaphragm to control intake and outflow of air in the lungs.

3. The production of sound follows. The process of *phonation*, or making sound with the voice, takes place when vocal bands in the larynx vibrate. The vibration is a direct result of breath pressure supported by the diaphragm.

4. The resonating chambers of the chest and the head (mouth and nasal cavities) work to amplify, shape, and project the tone produced. The art of placement allows the performer to sing a sequence of correctly shaped sounds, resulting in a continuous, well-pitched vocal line.

5. The tongue, palate, lips, teeth, and jaw work to articulate vowels and consonants.

The following diagram points out the different parts of the vocal mechanism used to produce a musical sound.

Vocal Mechanism

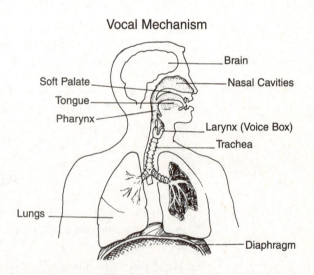

ADULT VOICE CLASSIFICATIONS

Male and female voices are usually classified according to the timbre or quality of tone produced by the voice, as well as its range. There are four basic classifications of voices: soprano, alto, tenor, and bass. The female *soprano* usually sings the highest pitches represented on the treble staff, while the female *alto* sings the lowest pitches on the treble staff. The *tenor* is the highest male classification, and the *bass* voice is the lowest classification for male singers. Each of these four categories can be subdivided into more specialized categories. For example, a soprano who is incapable of performing the extreme high pitches of the treble staff and possesses a fuller or richer quality of tone may be classified as a *mezzo-soprano* or medium soprano. A female voice capable of singing extremely low pitches and possessing a much deeper tone quality than the average alto is classified as *contralto*. Likewise, the tenor voice may be divided into a *first* (extremely high) and *second* (medium-voiced) tenor. Many male voices fall comfortably into a range that lies between that of a bass and a second tenor. These voices are usually classified as *baritones*. The following diagram provides ranges for each of these major classifications.

Adult Voice Classifications

Note: Tenor voices are written one octave higher than they sound.

VOCAL REGISTERS

When singing, the human voice moves through different positions of the vocal range, known as *registers*. At the top and bottom of the vocal register, differences in vibration rate occur. There is a faster vibration rate the higher one sings, and a slower vibration rate the lower one sings. The changes in vibration rates make it necessary for a person's voice to adjust or change to a different position, similar to a car having to change gears to accelerate in speed. Since registers are an integral part of the voice, prospective singers must be able to recognize them aurally and use them effectively.

There are many theories regarding the number of vocal registers within the human voice. One of the most commonly accepted is that the human voice has two registers, the head and the chest. The *head register*, or lighter vocal register, is governed by a set of throat muscles that control the vocal mechanism for upper register singing. Head cavities are used, for the most part, to resonate the tone. The *chest register*, or heavier vocal register, is governed by a different set of throat muscles that control lower register singing. When sounds are produced in the chest register, the chest cavities act as the primary resonators. Tones produced in the chest register are usually thick and heavy and possess great power and depth. Tones produced in the head register are generally lighter and thinner in texture. Lower pitches are often sung using the chest register, and higher pitches are more easily performed in the head register.

Professional singers practice for years to "bridge" the two registers so that the "break" between them is not noticeable to listeners. The beginning adult singer may find it helpful to identify the break that occurs in the voice where the high and low registers overlap. Analyze what happens at this break point: How does the voice change? Is there any straining or tenseness occurring? Does a breathy quality appear in the voice? Does the change of register affect the projection capabilities of the voice?

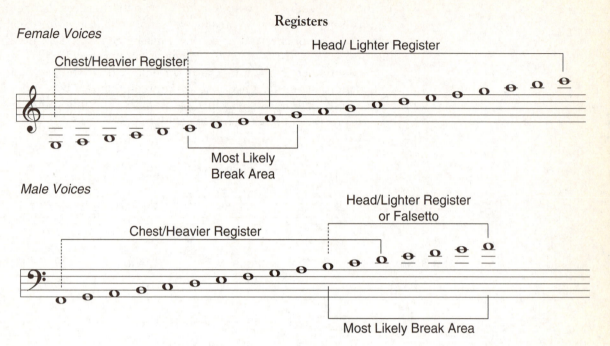

Women generally sing in the head register, and men's voices lie, for the most part, in the chest register. All voices, however, use both registers, and the best adult singing draws from the benefits of both the head and the chest registers.

Adult students can practice simple exercises in preparation for teaching children to sing correctly. The following exercises have been sequenced according to skill level. These exercises should be performed over the complete vocal range; repeat each exercise a number of times, each time beginning a half step higher or lower. Care should be taken not to strain the voice by forcing it to sing too high, too low, or too loudly. The exercises should be repeated often, so that the adult student learns to control the singing voice. Special attention should be given to the production of good tone quality. Students should strive for clear, resonant, and well-supported tones without strain or tenseness. Exercises should be played and sung one octave lower for male voices.

CHARACTERISTICS OF THE CHILD'S VOICE AT THE PRIMARY LEVEL

The quality, range, volume, and flexibility of children's singing voices differ from those of adult voices. A child's singing voice is light and clear in tone. The volume of correctly produced tones is usually soft, not exceeding mezzo-forte in its dynamic volume. In fact, it is almost impossible for children to perform songs at a fortissimo level or louder without straining and possibly damaging the vocal mechanism. The most comfortable singing range, or *tessitura*, of children's voices during primary years is usually limited to an interval of a sixth. Because of the high, flute-like quality of the child's voice, the use of the head register or head voice is desired.

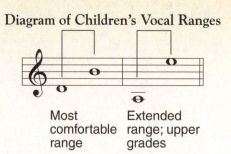

Diagram of Children's Vocal Ranges

Most comfortable range

Extended range; upper grades

CHARACTERISTICS OF THE CHILD'S VOICE AT THE UPPER ELEMENTARY LEVEL

Although the soprano-like tone color of girls' and boys' singing voices is similar during the primary years, some boys' voices begin to develop a deeper, more resonant sound starting as early as fourth or fifth grade. Gradually, the boy's changing voice drops into the alto register and often has a very limited, unstable range for a few months.

Boys need to know what to expect when their voices start to change. Their voices may "crack" or change register suddenly when they are speaking or singing. Temporarily, their voices may not be as flexible or manageable. Boys may have trouble matching pitches until they have become accustomed to the sound of their new voices. These are all natural signs of physical growth and maturation.

Many girls' voices continue to retain their light and clear texture throughout the elementary years, while a few girls will develop a heavier tone quality. During adolescence, however, both groups of female voices may take on a breathy quality. With proper vocal guidance and physical maturity, this breathiness will usually disappear.

SOLVING VOCAL PROBLEMS IN THE OLDER STUDENT

Teachers should strive to help their students understand the physical and psychological phenomena that affect their singing voices. Skilled teachers who explain the problems that their singers may be encountering and treat these problems in a positive way will have a great impact on their students' future attitudes toward singing.

Teachers can take immediate steps to help remedy many of the problems that arise among singers whose voices are beginning to change. The following suggestions might solve some of these problems:

1. Lower the key of the song being sung. Often, songs are pitched too high, and students become self-conscious in their singing.
2. Select song literature that appeals to the fifth- and sixth-grade singer. It is important to win the confidence and spark the enthusiasm of singers by selecting songs from a variety of styles and cultures. Contemporary melodies and harmonies, both popular and classical, should be included in students' repertoire.
3. Avoid songs that have words that, though acceptable at the time the song was written, contain double meanings that would be embarrassing for a young adult to sing today.
4. Write out special parts for boys' changing voices. Range and technical passages must be appropriate to the limitations of these voices. "Rock-a My Soul" is an example of a song designed for the changing voice. Note that there are three independent parts. All parts should be taught separately and eventually sung simultaneously.

ROCK-A MY SOUL

Spiritual
Arr.: Boyer

Part I

Rock - a my soul in the bos - om of A - bra - ham,

Rock - a my soul in the bos - om of A - bra-ham, Rock - a my soul in the

bos - om of A - bra-ham, Oh, Rock - a my soul.

Part II

Rock - a my soul,_____ Oh yes, Rock - a my

soul, Oh, Lord - y Rock - a my soul_____ in the

bos - om of A - bra - ham, Hal - le - lu - jah, Oh, a

Part III

Rock, Rock, Rock - a my soul in the

bos - bos - bos - om of A - bra-ham, Rock, Rock, Rock -

a my soul in the bos - om of A - bra-ham.

PHYSICAL CHARACTERISTICS
OF GOOD SINGING

Posture. One of the first and most basic requirements for good tone production is correct posture. Just as athletes ready themselves physically and mentally before engaging in a physical activity, so must singers prepare themselves to produce good tone. As early as first grade, students are presented with series books that contain colorful pictures, music, and diagrams. When concentrating on producing good tone, however, students should give full attention to the teacher. Having books in their hands may distract them.

Because oversized and undersized chairs continue to present a physical problem for children at the elementary level, it is sometimes best to have young students sit as erectly as possible on the floor with their feet crossed and tucked close to the body. This does not take precedence, however, over properly sized chairs or stools that allow students to establish good posture, thus making it possible for the vocal instrument to function as it should. When seated, students should come forward in their chairs as though they are about to stand. They should sit tall with their shoulders relaxed and down. Students should automatically return to this "singing" position when requested to do so by the teacher. If children must sit on the floor, the teacher should make sure that students alternate between this position and standing. This will help to avoid unnecessary slumping, cramping, and restlessness that result from children being in the same position too long. When standing, children should stand up straight and tall with their feet firmly grounded on the floor, one foot slightly in front of the other. Correct posture will allow the vocal mechanism to do its job without being hampered in any way.

Breathing. After the procedures involved in acquiring good posture have been set in place, teachers should focus on correct breathing techniques. Children should work on being able to produce a steady stream of air with the proper amount of support from the diaphragm. They should understand that proper breath control and support are crucial to the development of good vocal tone, just as a bow is important to a violin's sound. If the bow stops, the violin will no longer speak. If the air pressure stops, vocal tone can no longer be projected. As the air pressure disappears, the lack of support will cause the tone to flatten in pitch. Therefore, the ability to control the flow of air is especially important in maintaining a smooth, legato-like style of singing.

The following two exercises should help students grasp the concept of diaphragmatic breathing:

1. Have students place one hand on their chests and the other on the abdomen, below the waist. Next, have students pretend to put an imaginary drinking straw to their lips and slowly "sip" a glass of juice to the count of 3. Exhale on s-s-s to the count of 5. Students should feel their abdominal muscles expand but should not feel movement of the hand on the chest. If this procedure is followed, students should be breathing correctly. Repeat this process, but this time have students "sip" to the count of 4 and exhale to the count of 6.
2. Have students place their hands on their abdomens and pretend that they are a locomotive chugging to pull a heavy load. They should feel the abdominal muscles at work as they make the sounds ch, ch, ch, ch.

Articulation. Children often forget to sing the texts of songs so that they can be understood by a listener. Not only is the pronunciation of words not recognizable at times but also the enunciation of vowels and consonants needs serious attention. Teachers should have students exaggerate by overenunciating if positive results are to occur. This will force children to open their mouths and produce clearly articulated tones.

HELPING CHILDREN FIND THEIR SINGING VOICE

Introduction. For years, teachers have experienced problems in helping first graders learn to sing. Some first graders still do not know that there is a difference between the speaking and the singing voice and that in singing, speech is sustained and lengthened to produce a tune. These students attempt to sing on what can be described as a *speech drone:* They sing only on one pitch, much lower than the rest of the class. Teachers can begin work to correct this problem in young singers by helping them focus on differences between speech and singing.

By having students echo melodic fragments as well as spoken fragments, teachers can help children differentiate aurally and vocally between the two. For example, a teacher might ask students to echo the following:

"Little Bunny Foo Foo" provides an example of a child's play song designed to assist children in distinguishing between speaking and singing voices. Appropriate physical actions can be used throughout the song to enhance children's interest. For example, students can make a bunny with their fist and two fingers (for ears). "The rabbit" should hop from one side of the body to the other to demonstrate how a rabbit would hop through a forest. The entire hand should move in a scooping position, followed by a gentle tap on the top of the head. Students will enjoy creating their own movements for the play song that follows.

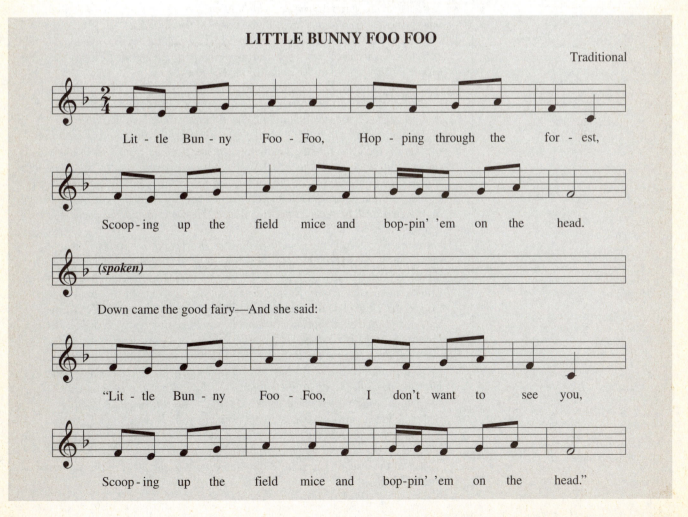

(spoken)

1. "I'll give you three chances, And if you don't behave
2. "I'll give you two more chances, And if you don't behave
3. "I'll give you one more chance, And if you don't behave
4. "I gave you three chances and you didn't behave.

Go back to the beginning.

(spoken)

1. "I'll turn you into a goon!" The next day:
2. "I'll turn you into a goon!" The next day:
3. "I'll turn you into a goon!" The next day:
4. Now you're a goon! POOF!"

And the moral of the story is: "Hare today; goon tomorrow."

Children can use a variety of means to explore their vocal range, such as children's stories, singing games, and vocal improvisations. "Between the Valleys" is an example of one story that is designed to help children experiment with the upper and lower range of the voice. Each time the teacher comes to "up the hill and down the hill" in the story, children should join in. At this point the voice should travel up and down with the words. In this way children who normally use a speech drone will be encouraged to experiment with other parts of their vocal range.

BETWEEN THE VALLEYS

This is Roscoe the Rabbit. (Form a fist with the right hand and raise fingers 1 and 2 for rabbit ears.) Roscoe is a very happy fellow who lives at the top of a grassy hill. Roscoe has many friends who live with him in the Valley of the Twin Oaks and others who live even farther away in the Valley of the Big Rocks.

This is Guppy the Goose, Roscoe's best friend. (Have all the fingers on the left hand stick together while they move in contrary motion to the thumb.) Guppy the Goose lives in a pond in the Valley of the Big Rocks.

One day Roscoe the Rabbit decided to pay Guppy the Goose a visit in the Valley of the Big Rocks. So he opened his door, stepped outside, closed the door, and proceeded down the hill and up the hill and down the hill and up the hill and down the hill to Guppy's pond. (Encourage children to join in with the teacher on the last sentence, allowing their voices to go from high to low as they go "up and down" the hills.) When Roscoe arrived, Guppy the goose was nowhere in sight, so Roscoe the Rabbit had to turn around and go back home. Up the hill and down the hill and up the hill and down the hill and up the hill he traveled until he reached his own house. He went inside and decided to call it a day.

The next morning, Guppy the Goose wanted to visit Roscoe the Rabbit. So he opened his door, stepped outside, closed the door, and went up the hill and down the hill and up the hill and down the hill and up the hill to Roscoe's house. When Guppy the Goose arrived, Roscoe the Rabbit was nowhere to be found, so poor Guppy the Goose had to return home. Down the hill and up the hill and down the hill and up the hill and down the hill he waddled until he reached his pond in the Valley of the Big Rocks.

On the third day, Roscoe the Rabbit decided to try it again, and Guppy the Goose made a similar decision. So they began their journey. One went down the hill, and the other went up the hill until ... they met at the very top. Roscoe the Rabbit said in a very high voice, "How do you do, Guppy?" Guppy responded in a very low voice, "And how are you, Roscoe?" They talked. Finally, when the sun began to set, each returned home again, going down the hill and up the hill and down the hill and up the hill—Roscoe the Rabbit to the Valley of the Twin Oaks and Guppy the Goose to the pond in the Valley of the Big Rocks.

Other activities that can help students discover and explore their vocal ranges include the imitation of sirens and other environmental sounds. Students can produce siren sounds that move up or down the whole range of their imaginary "vocal paths." Teachers can help students become even more comfortable with their vocal range by having them move their hands up and down with the rise and fall of the melody they are singing. Students can also draw the contour of a melodic line in the air while singing.

Many vocal problems that are encountered by primary students often stem from poor exposure to music at home, at church, in preschool programs, and in their everyday environment. Children have a strong tendency to imitate what they hear around them. Unfortunately, what they hear is often not appropriate for imitation. For example, they hear pop and rock singers perform in keys that are totally unrealistic for children to even attempt; yet, the child tries to duplicate the songs of these popular artists as loudly and forcefully as possible. Sadly, the beginnings of vocal abuse are rampant at a very early stage in the child's vocal development. Much of this abuse can be attributed to the fact that children just don't know any better. They have never been informed about the physical dangers—such as the development of vocal nodes—that they may encounter if improper use of the voice continues. It becomes the teacher's job not only to inform students of such dangers, but also to help restore their damaged voices, if possible.

These suggestions can serve as guides to help students find and adjust to their appropriate vocal registers:

1. Insist that children sing softly.
2. Explain that everyone has two voices within his or her body: a "lighter" voice or head voice and a "heavier" voice or chest voice. Each of these voices should be explored. Students should talk about and attempt to describe "how it feels to sing using a lighter and then a heavier voice." Talk about which is more comfortable. Create a dialogue that involves the use of both these registers. Practice to develop the lighter and the heavier registers by having students:
   a. Stretch and yawn: then sigh on a high-to-lower pitch, beginning on fourth line D. Using the vowel *oh*, sustain the first pitch; then make a *glissando* (rapidly sliding up or down with the voice) to a lower pitch.
   b. Remind students that they need to breathe deeply to support the tone and to sing the pitches that are low in their range and close to their speaking voices. Ask students to imagine they have an inner tube around their waists. Place their hands at the waist. Blow out the "old" air and deeply inhale the "new" air as the teacher counts to 3. Their hands should feel their waists expanding. As students let air escape, they should "sizzle" or make a "hissing" sound and move their hands to their sides. This activity should be repeated, inhaling to the count of 4 and exhaling to the count of 6.
   c. Have students hum the letter *n* on fourth line D, with lips and teeth slightly apart and the tip of the tongue resting lightly against the bottom teeth. Lower the jaw and change to an *oo* sound. Do this exercise by half steps down to G. Continued practice of this exercise will increase the vocal range and bridge the two singing registers.
3. Become knowledgeable about the background of the song. Try to be as culturally authentic as possible when performing and teaching the song. Many folk songs, depending on where they come from, are more accurately sung using the heavier register of the voice and not the lighter register. Help students understand this and encourage them to make necessary adjustments.
4. Choose songs that have a narrow range, comfortably located within the range of the child's voice.
5. If a student is not accurately matching pitch, toss a beanbag to him or her and make, in the lighter register, an *oo* sound that follows the arc of the bag's path. Have the student toss the bag back to the teacher or to another classmate and encourage him or her to use the head voice in imitating the rise and fall of the beanbag's arc.

6. Place uncertain singers between stronger and more confident singers. Suggest that the students adjust their volume so that they are always able to hear both singers on either side of them.

7. Before students begin singing, make sure they are together on the same starting pitch. Have them hum and sustain the beginning pitch of the song until everyone has it.

8. Provide assistance on a daily basis, if possible. It only takes a few minutes to involve each student in musical conversations similar to those below. Exercises of this type will be helpful in developing the child's listening and vocal performance skills.

OBJECTIVES AND GUIDELINES FOR SINGING AT THE ELEMENTARY LEVEL

The following objectives will give direction to the development and use of the singing voice at the primary level. Young students should be able to:

1. hear and repeat a short melody accurately and expressively.
2. develop some control in the quality of sound used when singing.
3. sing a wide variety of songs, in many styles.
4. demonstrate knowledge of rhythm, melody, form, harmony, dynamics, tempo, and tone color through singing.
5. demonstrate the ability to sing accurately a variety of melodic intervals, using their accompanying hand signs (see p. 247 for hand signs).
6. sight read the notation of simple songs.

As students mature in their abilities to use their voices, more difficult vocal challenges can be presented. The older student should be able to:

1. hear and reproduce from memory more complex melodic patterns both in singing songs and in echo singing.
2. sing more difficult literature with better tone quality, pitch accuracy, and expressiveness.
3. recognize and respond to more difficult interval relationships with syllables, hand signs, and number and/or letter names.
4. read and perform more difficult pieces of music.
5. demonstrate greater vocal independence. They should feel comfortable in performing echo songs, descants, rounds, and melodic ostinati.
6. improvise, using the singing voice.
7. harmonize by "ear."
8. use concepts previously learned to help facilitate learning new songs.

TEACHING A SONG BY ROTE

Introduction. In the initial stages of musical development, children learn songs best through an imitative process called *rote learning*. Rote learning takes place when a teacher speaks, sings, or moves and students imitate. The process is repeated until the song is learned well. Learning a song by rote allows children to focus their attention on the beauty of the sound being imitated, the production of correct interval relationships, the expressive interpretation of the music, and the clear enunciation of vowels and consonants. The most common approaches used to teach songs by rote are the part or phrase method and the whole song method. The teacher's choice of method is determined by the length and difficulty of the song material, the children's previous musical background and experience, basic mental and musical aptitudes, and the motivation and interest children possess in regard to the song.

The Whole Song. The **whole song method** can be applied to the learning of a song in two different ways. The **first approach** is used to teach songs that can usually be imitated by students after one or two hearings. Songs that are short and have much repetition in text and melody are usually taught using the whole song approach. The following steps can assist the teacher in using this approach:

1. Motivate interest in the song through the use of appropriate pictures, stories, or questions.
2. Ask children to listen for something specific in the song before its actual presentation.
3. Present the whole song to the class.
4. Ask questions about the children's understanding or enjoyment of the song.
5. Sing the song one or more additional times, depending on the children's readiness to participate.
6. Have the class join in.

"I'm Gonna Sing" is an example of a song that can be taught to children by rote, using the whole song approach. The song is short and very repetitive. It also allows room for creative movement and playing activities. The song needs little discussion to attract students' attention. The tempo and bouncing rhythms throughout the song provide adequate attention getters. After learning the song, children can be invited to create movements other than those suggested by the song. Students might substitute actions such as: "I'm gonna walk, skip, slide, or turn when the spirit says_____." Students can also replace the movement actions with the sounds of different rhythmic instruments, which can be performed in various ways. "I'm gonna hit, rub, shake, or scrape when the spirit says_____," are some examples. Discussion should follow regarding the overall meaning and style of the song.

The **second approach** to using the whole song method is useful with songs containing many verses, with each verse having areas of repetition. This type of song is more challenging for children to learn because it is difficult for them to remember the order of the verses. "Ida Red," found in Chapter 10, has several verses, each one ending differently:

… Ida Red, Ida *Blue*, I got stuck on Ida too.
… Ida Red, Ida *Gold*, She is something to behold, etc.

To facilitate the learning of this song, the teacher can make a set of flash cards, each one containing a little girl dressed in a different color—in blue, in gold, and in the other colors found in subsequent verses. The teacher should sing through the entire song, holding up the appropriate card for each verse. The second time through the song, the teacher should invite the students to join in wherever possible. By the completion of the third singing, the children will know the song quite well, if they can refer to the flash cards to help them sing the verses in the correct order.

I'M GONNA SING

Spiritual

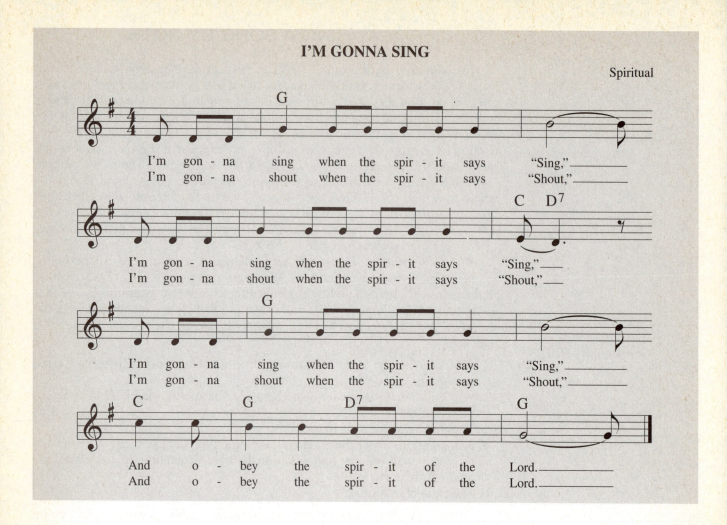

The Part or Phrase Method. The *part* or *phrase method* is used to teach a song that is longer and more complex, and that cannot be easily learned after just one or two hearings. This method also has two different approaches. The steps used in teaching a song using the phrase method are similar to steps 1 through 4 of the whole song approach. The change occurs when children are ready to join in, at step 5. When using the **first approach** to the phrase method, the following steps can be used:

5. The teacher sings phrase 1 and the children repeat it.
6. The teacher sings phrase 2 and the children repeat it.
7. The teacher sings phrases 1 and 2 and the children repeat them.
8. The teacher continues throughout the song in a like manner.
9. When the song is completed, the teacher returns to the beginning and sings through the song again, two phrases at a time, and the children repeat. Any step in the above process can be repeated if children need additional hearing or singing of a phrase.
10. When all phrases have been sung, the teacher invites the children to sing the song through from beginning to end. If there are still a few problems, the teacher addresses them at this time.

"The Magic Penny" is a more complex song that can be taught best by using the first approach to the phrase method. Because of the overall length of the piece and lack of constant repetition, it is more practical for students to learn one phrase at a time.

THE MAGIC PENNY

Malvina Reynolds

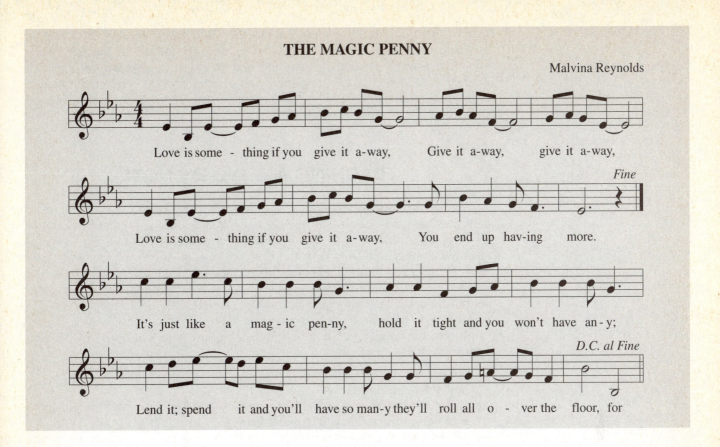

Love is some - thing if you give it a - way, Give it a - way, give it a - way,

Fine

Love is some - thing if you give it a - way, You end up hav - ing more.

It's just like a mag - ic pen - ny, hold it tight and you won't have an - y;

D.C. al Fine

Lend it; spend it and you'll have so man - y they'll roll all o - ver the floor, for

The **second approach** to the phrase method of learning a new song consists of the teacher singing the first part of a phrase and the children completing it. A song such as "Bow Wow Wow," found in Chapter 6, lends itself well to this approach:

Beat:	1	2	3	4
	Bow	wow	wow	
	Whose	dog art	thou	
	Lit-tle	Tom-my	Tuck-er's	dog
	Bow	wow	wow	

Once again, the teacher can begin the lesson using steps 1 through 4 of the whole song method. Then the following steps can continue:

5. The teacher asks the children to listen very carefully as the song is sung a second time.

6. Children are invited to sing the "mystery words" whenever the teacher stops singing. Using the following order:
   a. the teacher sings the first three beats of each phrase, and the children sing only the last beat—in this song, beat 4 in phrase 3;
   b. the teacher sings the first two beats of each phrase; the children complete the last two beats;
   c. the teacher sings the first beat of every phrase; the children sing the last three beats;
   d. the children sing the song through from beginning to end. Any of the steps may be repeated along the way if there is a problem.

The teacher should always sing or play a recording of the entire song first, so that children become acquainted with it before it is presented in shorter segments. Sometimes a discussion of the text is needed if it contains unfamiliar words or words used in any unusual manner.

When teaching songs, remember to give students the starting pitch of the song or of each phrase. A piano, pitch pipe, resonator bell, or soprano recorder may be used. The teacher should sound the pitch and then sing the pitch on a syllable such as "loo." When needed, students can imitate the teacher's pitch and then transfer it to the beginning text of the song. Regardless of which method is used to teach a new song, the teacher must be an active listener, isolating rhythmic and melodic problems and clarifying their correct production throughout the learning process.

TEACHING A SONG BY NOTE

Although teaching songs by rote during the early years has its advantages, continued dependence on this type of teaching and learning process will eventually become a hindrance to the musical development of the student. Teachers must also provide students with the basic knowledge and skills needed to read music by note, so that students can learn a musical work independently of the teacher. Learning music *by note* implies that students have a working knowledge of staff notation and interval relationships, which will enable them to sing or play a melody without anyone's assistance.

It is recommended in Content Standard 5 of the National Standards for Arts Education that all students:

a. read whole, half, dotted half, quarter, and eighth notes and rests in 2/4, 3/4, and 4/4 meter signatures

b. use a system (that is, syllables, numbers, or letters) to read simple pitch notation in the treble clef in major keys

c. identify symbols and traditional terms referring to dynamics, tempo, and articulation and interpret them correctly when performing

d. use standard symbols to notate meter, rhythm, pitch, and dynamics in simple patterns presented by the teacher

Zoltán Kodály. It was the Hungarian composer and music educator, Zoltán Kodály, who developed a philosophy based on the belief that young children should learn to read and write music just as they learn to read and write the language of their mother tongue. He strongly believed that the development and use of the singing voice should be at the core of a school's approach to music literacy for every child.

Kodály emphasized the use of solmization and the movable "do" system as major vehicles through which musical literacy could be achieved. *Solmization* is a technique that involves assigning syllables to pitches to facilitate the hearing and reproduction of melodic intervals. *Solfège syllables*—do (doh), re (ray), mi (me), fa (fah), so (soh), la (lah), ti (te)—represent each of the tones of the diatonic scale. *Hand signs* can be used as tools to reinforce the inner hearing of the intervals; they provide a visualization in space of the tonal relationships being sung. Hand signs usually accompany the singing of solfège syllables. They were developed in England around 1870 by John Cürwen. Since then, the signs have been revised and are presented here in their revised form.

Kodály observed that, during childhood, children in Hungary naturally express themselves through singing games and other singing experiences. Many of these singing experiences consist of tonal patterns that are particularly easy for children to sing and read. The interval of the descending minor third, so-mi, or the "call" as it is often named, appeared to be one of the most common intervals used among young children. Further research affirmed that an extension of the minor third, so-mi-la, was heard in children's natural and undirected play all over the world. This pattern has since become known as the "chant." The process of music literacy that was proposed by Kodály suggested that if teachers include song literature that contains these easy-to-sing-and-read tonal patterns, they should be able to accelerate the vocal progress of children.

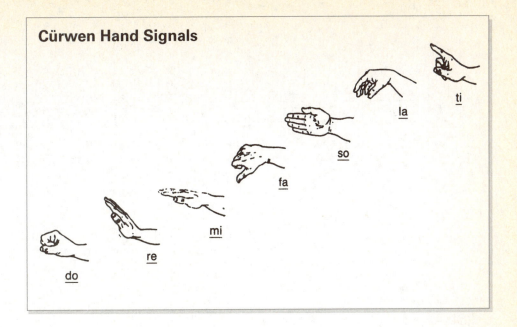

Cürwen Hand Signals

Pentatonic Scales. Kodály found the pentatonic scale to be most valuable in teaching musical literacy because it does not contain half steps, which are difficult to sing in tune, and the scale has only five different sounds. This more limited range of tones can be easily manipulated by children with limited ability, as well as by those with more advanced skills. The choice of pitches used in composing melodies is much freer, because the more dissonant half step is not used.

During the elementary years, sequencing the teaching of musical structures and skills must be organized to correspond with the developmental level of children. This means that children should begin with the simplest two- and three-note melodies as well as the simplest rhythms and gradually progress to more complex structures.

The following songs and strategies demonstrate a step-by-step procedure that can be used not only to help children develop in their abilities to hear and produce good tone, but also to serve as guidelines that will assist them on the road toward reading music by note.

Solmization. Begin students' introduction to solmization by singing songs containing the interval most often chanted by small children at play: so-mi. The following songs can be used to teach this interval.

STAR LIGHT

American Folk Song

Star light, star bright, First star I see to-night,

Wish I may, wish I might, Have the wish I wish to-night.

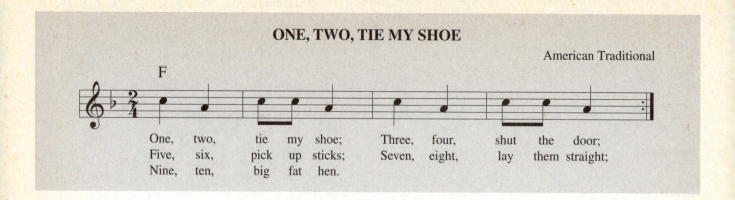

ONE, TWO, TIE MY SHOE

American Traditional

One, two, tie my shoe; Three, four, shut the door;
Five, six, pick up sticks; Seven, eight, lay them straight;
Nine, ten, big fat hen.

Once children are familiar with the songs, the names of the corresponding solmization syllables can be sung. **Visual S1** shows the solmization syllables for "Star Light."

VISUAL S1

so   mi   so   mi   so   mi mi   so so mi

Hand signs are often used to reinforce the inner hearing of melodic or harmonic intervals; they accompany the singing of solmization syllables. **Visual S2** shows the hand signs for "Star Light." Students should sing the song and use the appropriate hand signs.

VISUAL S2

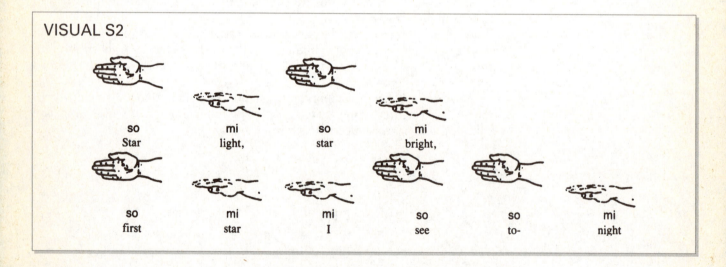

so   mi   so   mi
Star   light,   star   bright,

so   mi   mi   so   so   mi
first   star   I   see   to-   night

The so-mi, mi-so interval should be placed on the staff so that children understand that there is always a line or space between the two tones of the interval, as in **Visual S3.**

VISUAL S3

so - mi *or* so - mi *or* so - mi

To further reinforce the minor third interval, place either mi or so on the staff and have the children complete the interval as in **Visual S4.**

VISUAL S4

so - mi   so - mi   so - mi

When students are comfortable with the minor third and can sing it on pitch in a variety of songs, a new solmization syllable can be introduced. A suggested sequence for introducing the syllables is given in **Visual S5.** Remember to reverse the order of each interval presented, besides singing it in its original form. For example, the interval do-so should also be sung as so-do.

VISUAL S5

Suggested Sequence for Introducing Intervals

so-mi:	so-mi (**reverse** = mi-so)					
la:	la-so	la-mi				
do:	do-so	do-mi	do-la			
re:	re-so	re-mi	re-la	re-do		
la,:	la,-so	la,-mi	la,-la	la,-re		
so,:	so,-so	so,-mi	so,-la	so,-do	so,-re	so,-la,
do':	do'-so	do'-mi	do'-la	do'-do	do'-re	do'-la,	do'-so,
fa and ti	all combinations					

Notice the way pitches are symbolized when written below and above the primary scale being sung: below = la,; above = do'.

la, ti, do re mi fa so la ti do' re'

primary scale

The following songs can be used to reinforce the singing of intervals through solmization:

LUCY LOCKET

mi-so-la
do: C

American Game Song

Luc - y Lock - et lost her pock - et, Kit - ty Fish - er found it,
Not a pen - ny was there in it, on - ly rib - bon round it.

RING AROUND THE ROSY

do-mi-so-la
do: C

American Game Song

Ring a - round the ros - y, Pock - et full of pos - y,

Ash - es, ash - es, All fall down.

BUTTON

do-re-mi-so-la
do: F

American Game Song

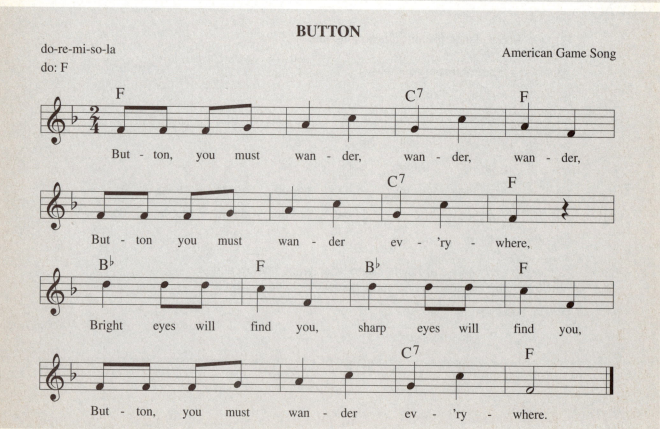

But - ton, you must wan - der, wan - der, wan - der,

But - ton you must wan - der ev - 'ry - where,

Bright eyes will find you, sharp eyes will find you,

But - ton, you must wan - der ev - 'ry - where.

LAND OF THE SILVER BIRCH

la,-do-re-mi-so-la

do: F

la: D

Canadian Folk Song

Land of the sil - ver birch, home of the bea - ver,

Where still the might - y moose wan - ders at will,

Blue lake and rock - y shore, I will re - turn once more,

Boom de de boom boom, boom de de boom boom boom.

NOW LET ME FLY

so,-la,-do-re-mi-so-la

do: G

Spiritual

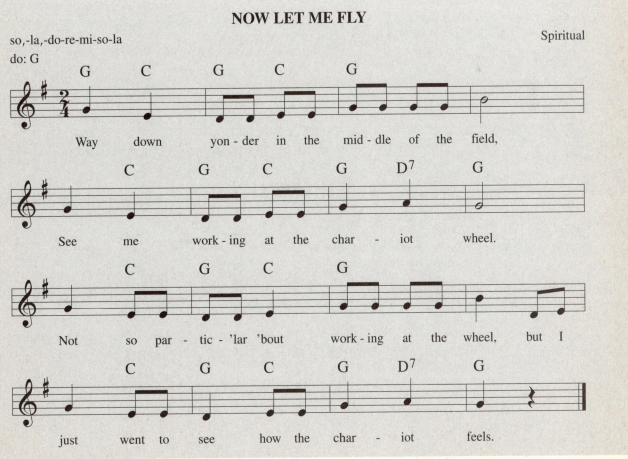

Way down yon - der in the mid - dle of the field,

See me work - ing at the char - iot wheel.

Not so par - tic - 'lar 'bout work - ing at the wheel, but I

just went to see how the char - iot feels.

WHEN THE TRAIN COMES ALONG

do-re-mi-so-la-do'
do: C

American Folk Song

When the train comes a-long—— when the train comes a-long——
I'll meet you at the sta-tion when the train comes a-long.
It may be ear-ly, it may be late,
But I'll meet you at the sta-tion when the train comes a-long.

ORANGES AND LEMONS

do-re-mi-fa-so
do: C

English Folk Song

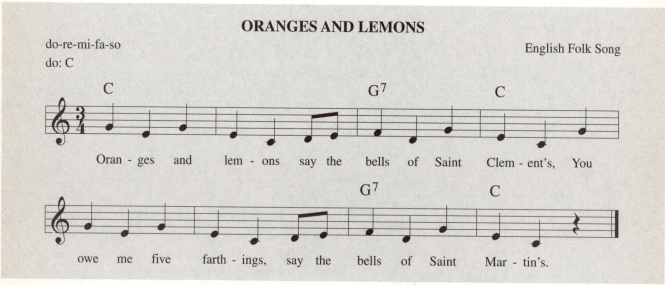

Oran-ges and lem-ons say the bells of Saint Clem-ent's, You
owe me five farth-ings, say the bells of Saint Mar-tin's.

LAUGHING SONG

Sweden

so-la-ti-do'
do: C

Ha ha ha! Hee hee hee! An - der - son and Pe - ter - son and

Jen - son and me. Ha ha ha! Hee hee hee!

Sing - ing all to - geth - er, sing - ing mer - ri - ly.

Once children are familiar with the syllable do, the movable *do clef* (𝄐) can be placed on the staff. Intervals can then be related to the position of do. For example, when do is on a line, so and mi are on lines. When do is in a space, so and mi are in spaces, as in **Visual S6.**

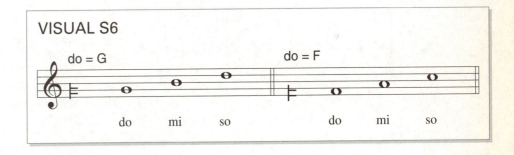

VISUAL S6

do = G   do = F

do   mi   so   do   mi   so

Notice that in "Mi cuerpo hace música," do = C. Have students analyze this song and then outline all pitches included in the scale of C Major. Place these pitches in their correct order on the staff following the song.

MI CUERPO HACE MÚSICA
(THERE'S MUSIC IN ME)

English Words by David Eddleman

Folk Song from Puerto Rico

Source: "Mi cuerpo hace música" (There's Music Inside Me) English words © 2002 Pearson Education, Inc.

WRITTEN AND PERFORMANCE-RELATED ASSESSMENTS THROUGH COOPERATIVE LEARNING ACTIVITIES: SINGING VOICE

1. Assign to each group the same recording of a song performed by a children's choir. Ask students to listen to the recording and list all the things they liked about the way the song was performed. Then ask them to list what they would change if they were to perform the song as a group.
2. Give each group a different, known folk song compatible with the class's level of music skill development. The starting solfège syllable should be indicated on each song. Ask each group to mark the solfège first and work out the hand signs. Then the group should practice singing and signing the song until the students can perform it smoothly for the class.
3. Give a simple, unknown song and a resonator bell to each group. Have students clap the rhythms of the song and speak the rhythm syllables first. Then have them mark the solfège syllables and work out the hand signs. After sounding the resonator bell for their starting pitch, students should practice the song using the solfège syllables and hand signs. When the song is learned well, they should sing it with words. When they are ready, students should be able to sing and sign the song individually for the teacher.

Playing Musical Instruments
NS 2, 3, 5

PLAYING CLASSROOM INSTRUMENTS

From an early age, children seek creative ways to produce sound by shaking, striking, or scraping whatever can be found in their environment. It is natural, therefore, for children to want to continue their exploration of sound by experimenting with a variety of musical instruments found in the classroom. In addition, the playing of musical instruments contributes to the development of children's kinesthetic abilities, which are vital to their total musical growth. Simple classroom instruments can also be important pedagogical tools for teaching and reinforcing the elements of music and their structural components.

Content Standard 2, outlined in the National Standards for Arts Education, states that children must "perform on instruments, alone and with others, a varied repertoire of music." To achieve this standard, teachers should have students:

a. play instruments on pitch, in rhythm, with appropriate dynamics and timbre, and maintain a steady tempo;

b. perform easy rhythmic, melodic, and chordal patterns accurately and independently on rhythmic, melodic, and harmonic classroom instruments;

c. perform expressively a varied repertoire of music representing diverse genres and styles;

d. echo short rhythms and melodic patterns;

e. perform in groups, blending instrumental timbres, matching dynamic levels, and responding to the cues of a conductor;

f. perform independent instrumental parts while other students sing or play contrasting parts.

Classroom instruments can be divided into two groups: rhythm instruments and melody instruments.

Rhythm Instruments

An assortment of rhythm instruments is available for classroom use. The following are among the most useful and interesting.

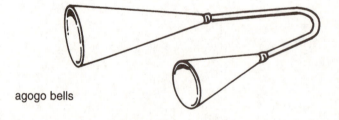

agogo bells

Agogo bells are two conical metal bells, each having a different pitch. They may be struck with a small metal rod to produce a ringing sound.

bongo drums

These two small, connected drums are usually played by placing them between the knees with the larger drum to the right. *Bongos* may be hit with the palm of the hand or with the first two fingers to produce a two-pitched percussive sound.

cabasa

The *cabasa* consists of metal beads encircling a large wooden spool. The handle attached to the spool can be turned or shaken, producing an unusual raspy sound.

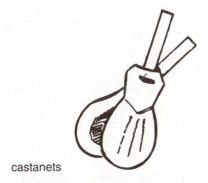
castanets

Castanets are two semihollow disks of wood attached to a stick by a cord. When shaken or hit against the palm of the hand, castanets produce a strong, staccato, tapping sound.

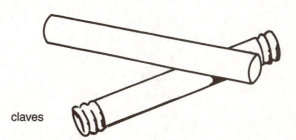
claves

Claves are two wooden cylinders containing hollowed spaces that provide resonating chambers. One cylinder is cupped in one hand while the other cylinder is used to strike it with the opposite hand.

conga drum

The *conga drum* is a long cylindrical drum that is open at the bottom. It may be played by striking the head with the palms of the hands, the fists, or the fingers.

cowbell/mallet

The *cowbell* is a metal instrument that is struck with a mallet or a metal bar. It produces a ringing timbre.

cymbals

Cymbals are metal disks. One is held in each hand. To produce a sound, they are struck together using a vertical movement. One disk continues upward, the other, downward, after being struck. Pairs of cymbals come in various sizes.

finger cymbals

Finger cymbals are small, two-inch metal plates that are attached to the thumb and a finger of one hand. When struck together, they produce a very high-pitched, delicate sound.

gong

The *gong*, a disk-shaped metal instrument, is struck with a soft-head mallet. Its sound may be sustained for a long period of time, depending on the gong's size.

guiro

The *guiro* is a hollow gourd with horizontal grooves cut across its surface. It is scraped or hit with a small wooden stick. This instrument is often referred to as "the fish" because of its fishlike shape.

hand drum

A *hand drum* is a cylindrical drum head. The drum is held by the rim while being struck with the opposite hand. Various timbres are produced, depending on where the drum head is struck and the amount of power used to hit it. Hand drums come in various sizes.

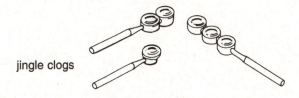

jingle clogs

Jingle clogs or *jingle taps* are instruments that have one or more pairs of metal disks loosely attached to a handle. When shaken or hit against the palm of the hand, they produce a jingling sound.

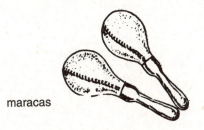

maracas

Maracas are gourds that contain dried seeds. The gourds produce a rattling sound when shaken. Maracas are usually played in pairs, with one in each hand.

ratchet

The *ratchet* is a miniature machine-like instrument that produces an extremely raspy, grinding sound. A handle, which is turned in a circular manner, allows the player to determine the duration of the ratchet's sound.

rhythm sticks

Rhythm sticks are long, narrow, cylindrical pieces of wood that are hit together to produce sound. Their surfaces are either smooth or ridged. Ridged rhythm sticks can be scraped together like a guiro.

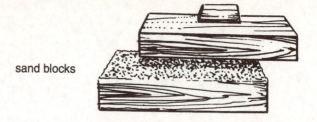

sand blocks

Sand blocks are blocks of wood covered with sandpaper, ranging from fine to coarse texture. A small handle on each block allows the player to hold the instruments while rubbing one against the other.

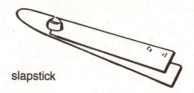

slapstick

The slapstick is a paddle-like instrument made of two pieces of wood hinged together to make one piece flexible. When controlled by a quick, short wrist movement, one side of the instrument slaps against the other, making a sound similar to that produced by a whip.

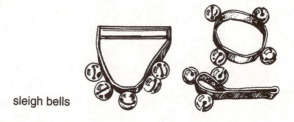

sleigh bells

Sleigh bells are bells that are attached to a handle or a piece of material. When shaken, they produce a jingling sound. Sleigh bells may be held in the hand or worn around the wrist or the ankle.

tambourine

The tambourine is a round rim of wood with several pairs of metal disks attached to it. It can be shaken or hit against the body.

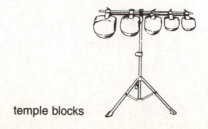

temple blocks

Temple blocks are hollowed gourds of varying sizes that are attached to a frame. Gourds of different sizes produce different pitches. Temple blocks are struck with a mallet.

triangle

The *triangle* is a triangular piece of metal suspended from a cord. It is struck by a metal stick to produce a high-pitched, ringing sound.

vibra-slap

The *vibra-slap* is an instrument that vibrates when slapped by the hand or hit against the body. Its ability to vibrate for a long period of time and its unusual timbre make the vibra-slap a popular instrument for producing sound effects.

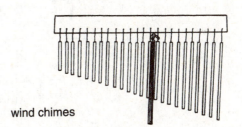

wind chimes

Tubular pieces of metal of different lengths are attached to a bar to produce *wind chimes*. When gently swept with the hand, this instrument produces a gentle, ethereal sound.

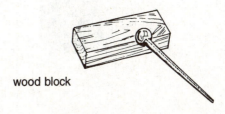

wood block

The *wood block* is a semihollow, rectangular-shaped piece of wood. It is either cupped in the hand or suspended from a cord to allow for its full resonating potential. It is struck with a wooden mallet.

Other instruments commonly seen in today's classrooms include:

Djembe*		Djundjun*	
	A west African drum that dates back to the Mandinka people in the 12th century. Originally made from the hollowed piece of tree log with a piece of goat skin as its head, it is played with both hands.		This single drum rests on its side and is played with a special stick or mallet. Often a bell is attached on one end which allows the drum to create different timbres of sounds
Bell tree*		Cajon	
	This vertical nesting of metal discs on a metal rod, can often be heard in Asian music.		The cajon is an Afro-Peruvian box-shaped percussion instrument usually made of plywood. It is played by slapping the box with the hand or a mallet.
		© istockphoto	
Talking drum*		Slit drum*	
	This west African drum whose pitch can be regulated to actually serve as a communication device.		The slit drum was originally carved out of a log. It usually has three slits which helps it to resonate.
		Gankoqui*	
			The gankoqui is a double bell with its origins in Africa.

*Courtesy of Peripole-Bergerault, Inc.

Several examples for incorporating rhythm instruments into the music class follow. Other suggestions have been included in Chapters 2 and 4.

The song "Hey, Betty Martin" can be used with rhythm instruments to explore their sounds. The original words of the song are:

Hey, Betty Martin, Tiptoe, tiptoe,
     Hey, Betty Martin, Tiptoe fine;
Hey, Betty Martin, Tiptoe, tiptoe,
     Hey, Betty Martin, Tiptoe fine.

The words in the second measure of each phrase can be replaced to designate a specific instrument to be played, as shown here.

Numerous songs and speech activities can be performed in a more interesting way by simply adding a rhythm accompaniment. In "Chumbara, Chumbara," for example, instruments are played on specific beats—beats 1 and 3. If repeated throughout, a simple ostinato accompaniment is created. More difficult ostinati patterns can be used with songs such as "Mary Ann." Sing "Chumbara, Chumbara" and accompany it with the following pattern:

Ostinato pattern:

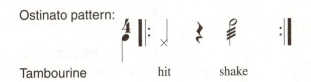

Tambourine   hit   shake

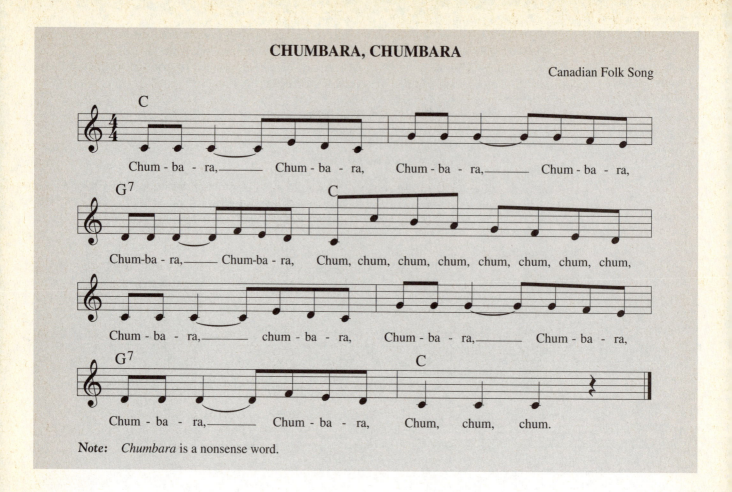

CHUMBARA, CHUMBARA

Canadian Folk Song

Chum - ba - ra,_____ Chum - ba - ra, Chum - ba - ra,_____ Chum - ba - ra,

Chum-ba - ra,_____ Chum-ba - ra, Chum, chum, chum, chum, chum, chum, chum, chum,

Chum - ba - ra,_____ chum - ba - ra, Chum - ba - ra,_____ Chum - ba - ra,

Chum - ba - ra,_____ Chum - ba - ra, Chum, chum, chum.

Note: *Chumbara* is a nonsense word.

Sing "Mary Ann" and provide the percussion parts notated here:

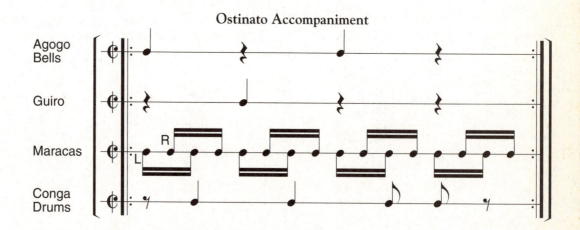

Ostinato Accompaniment

Agogo Bells

Guiro

Maracas

Conga Drums

Classroom percussion instruments can also be added to recordings of popular music, especially those with a strong, regular pulse.

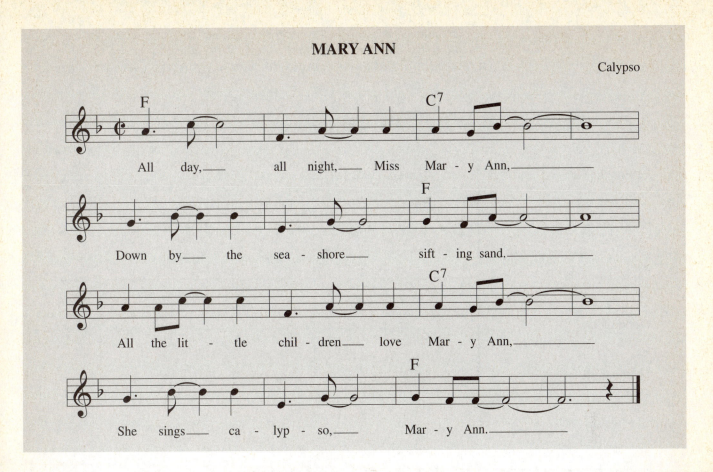

MARY ANN

Calypso

All day,— all night,— Miss Mar - y Ann,—

Down by— the sea - shore— sift - ing sand.—

All the lit – tle chil - dren— love Mar - y Ann,—

She sings— ca - lyp - so,— Mar - y Ann.—

Students can create their own rhythmic compositions. The rondo below is an example that incorporates both predetermined rhythms and improvisation performed on rhythm instruments. Each student should choose a different rhythm instrument to play the B and the C themes.

RONDO

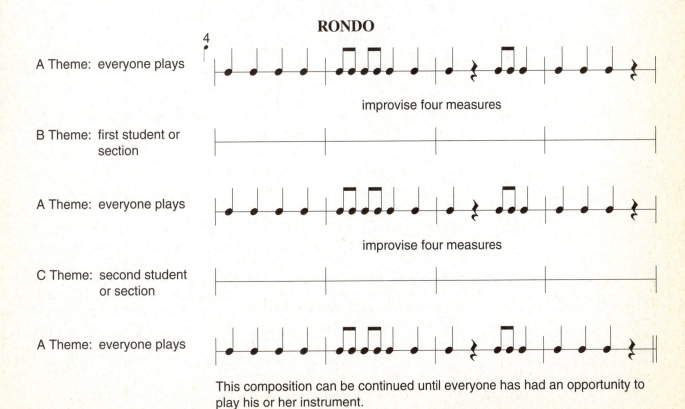

A Theme: everyone plays

improvise four measures

B Theme: first student or section

A Theme: everyone plays

improvise four measures

C Theme: second student or section

A Theme: everyone plays

This composition can be continued until everyone has had an opportunity to play his or her instrument.

"Stanpipes" is a thirteenth-century instrumental piece. The class can be divided into five groups to perform this work. When the class knows the piece well, it can be performed with one or two students to a part, as an added challenge.

STANPIPES

13th Century

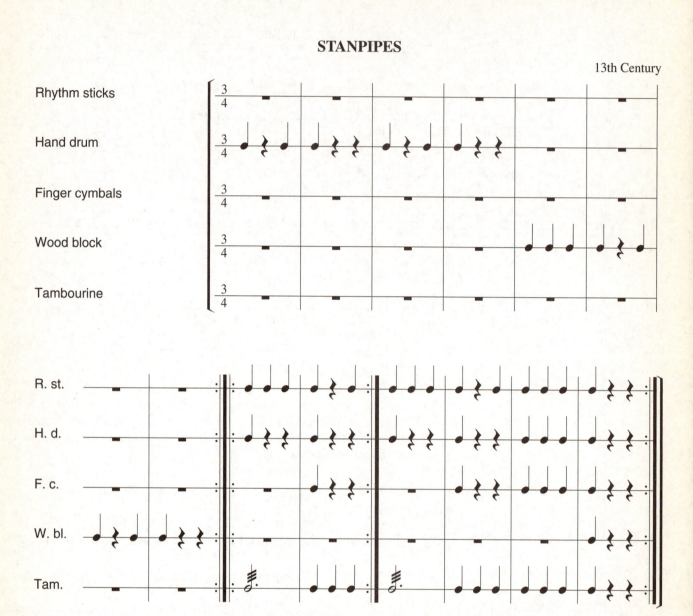

Melody Instruments

Resonator bells are individual metal bars tuned to each tone of the chromatic scale. Each bar is mounted on a block of wood containing a resonator. A set of resonator bells usually includes one to two octaves of bars. Small rubber mallets are provided for each bar. Resonator bells are easily manipulated; therefore, they can be used to teach such structural components as high and low pitch, intervals, scales, and chords. Because they can be easily distributed and used by more than one child at a time, resonator bells have earned a permanent place in music instruction at the elementary level.

resonator bells

One or more resonator bells can be added to a song to reinforce the melody or to create harmony. For example, in "St. Paul's Steeple," students can reinforce the C major scale by playing a resonator bell on each scale tone as they sing the melody.

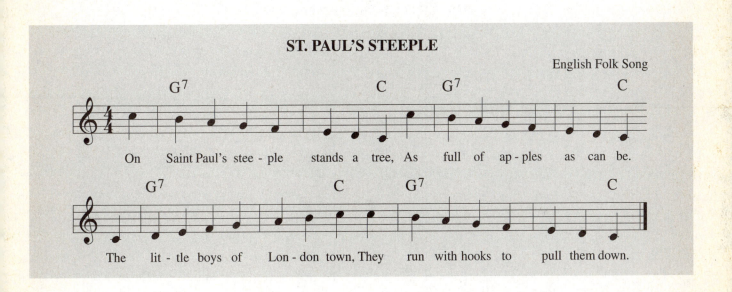

ST. PAUL'S STEEPLE

English Folk Song

On Saint Paul's stee-ple stands a tree, As full of ap-ples as can be.

The lit-tle boys of Lon-don town, They run with hooks to pull them down.

Clusters of chords can be created with resonator bells to provide a harmonic accompaniment. The song "St. Paul's Steeple" contains two chords: I (C) and V_7 (G7). Resonator bells having the tones of the tonic chord (C, E, G) can be given to three students. Likewise, resonator bells can be distributed for the dominant seventh chord. Students should play their resonator bell when it corresponds to the chord indicated in the song.

Carl Orff. Carl Orff (1895–1982) was a German educator and composer. Orff believed that speech, music, and movement were inseparable. His understanding of elemental music included the belief that children must relive the early stages of historical development in music if they are to develop musically; early involvement with music must center around active participation that is untrained, unsophisticated, and inseparable from speech and movement. Orff teachers provide experiences for children to develop their creative potential, which manifests itself in a child's ability to improvise. Opportunities for improvisation are continually provided as children are encouraged to explore space, sound, and form. Special instruments are a distinctive feature of Orff's approach to teaching. Under the guidance of Orff, these instruments were developed in

1928 by Karl Maendler. The instruments, called the *instrumentarium*, include barred instruments—xylophones, metallophones, and glockenspiels; recorders, drums, and woods, such as claves and maracas; metals, including cymbals and cowbells; and strings, such as guitars and cellos. In fact, since the Orff approach to teaching involves a creative process, nothing is excluded. Rocks and stones, pots and pans, and even shoes clicking together are acceptable if the student musician hears that these sounds are valuable to the musical work being created.

Primary among the melody instruments devised by Carl Orff as part of his instrumentarium are glockenspiels, metallophones and xylophones—known collectively as *Orff* or *barred instruments*. Each of the barred instruments is composed of a series of tones that is specifically designed to help in developing a child's improvisatory skills. Each barred instrument can be played with two or more mallets. They also possess both B-flat bars as well as F-sharp bars. However, the other sharps and flats, called *chromatics*, are also available should a teacher want to purchase them. The most attractive characteristic of the Orff barred instruments is that each of the bars on the instruments is removable, making it very easy for children to successfully improvise in several different keys.

Though costly, these instruments can add enormously to students' ability to create and perform their own music.

In addition to the basic melody instruments, which are often called barred instruments, contra-bass bars are also available. These huge bars act as bass pedals to the entire instrumentarium.

ORFF INSTRUMENTS

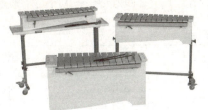

Soprano Glockenspiel

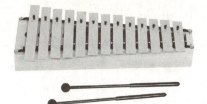

Alto Glockenspiel

Soprano Metallophone

Bass Metallophone

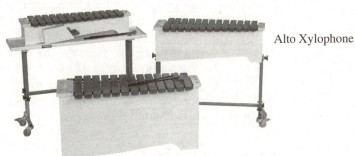

Soprano Xylophone

Alto Xylophone

Bass Xylophone

Contra-bass

Range	Glockenspiel	Metallophone	Xylophone
Soprano	Sounds two octaves higher than written	Sounds one octave higher than written	Sounds one octave higher than written
Alto	Sounds one octave higher than written	Sounds as written	Sounds as written
Bass		Sounds one octave lower than written	Sounds one octave lower than written

PLAYING THE ORFF BARRED INSTRUMENTS

Although special tables or legs can be purchased for the barred instruments, many children are directed to simply sit on the floor to play these child-sized instruments.

Barred instruments are played with two or more mallets or beaters. However, beginning players are limited to just two. A pair of beaters or mallets that is appropriate for the instrument will be included with the purchase of that instrument. Teachers should be careful not to allow students to play the metal barred instruments with metal or wooden mallets. A yarn- or felt-covered mallet should be used instead. Correct mallet selection will ensure against ear damage and damage to the instrument.

Holding the Mallet or Beater

Each student should have two mallets, one for each hand. Students should be told to hold their arms in the same position as they would if they were riding a tricycle, bike, or big wheel—elbows should be out with index fingers curved inward toward the palm of the hand. (Children tend to rest their index finger on top of the mallet. This prevents the light bounce of the mallet off the bar and results in a deadened tone.) They should then be directed to grip the mallets. The back of the hands should be in an upward position. The mallets should be held with the thumb and index and middle fingers. The fourth and fifth fingers should be curved around the end of the stick.

Pre-Mallet Practice

Children should be carefully guided in the use of the mallets. Guidelines should include:

• **Put the beat on the knees or thighs.** This is called *patschen*. First practice patting the thighs together at the same time and then try alternating, using different rhythms. Once a child can successfully mirror the movement of the teacher or another student's rhythmic movements, he/she is able to then transfer the movement directly to a barred instrument.

When alternating hands, teachers should always demonstrate a pattern of rhythm in reverse, if standing in front of the children. Your left hand is their right hand.

• **Aim for the center of the bar.** The tone hole is directly underneath, and if the head of the mallet is aimed properly, not only will the instrument vibrate and sound its best, but the students will produce the best tone.

• **Bounce off the bar.** When practicing *patschen*, encourage children to allow their hands to lightly bounce off their thighs or knees using a quick wrist action. This is important. Once children are allowed to play the barred instruments, they should realize the importance of having the head of the mallet bounce off the bar. Some children allow their mallets to stick to the bar, like bubble gum. When this happens, the bar does not vibrate and as a result does not produce an appropriate sound.

- **Alternate hands.** Encourage children to alternate the use of their hands when patching or playing the barred instrument. It is important to develop strength and control in both hands.
- **Cross over.** This is also a technique that will be used extensively when playing the barred instruments. This is a fun technique that will allow students to play and improvise using the entire instrument.

Tell students that they must not place mallets in or near the mouth, throw the mallets, bend the mallet, or unravel the mallets.

Preparing the Instrument

Preparing the instrument for practice is the first step in playing successfully.

A teacher or the students themselves will want to remove specific bars from the instrument to allow for instant success when playing and improvising. The teacher should direct students to place hands at the ends of a bar and lift directly up in order to remove a bar from an instrument. This prevents the pins that hold the bars in place to be pulled out of the instrument. This preventive measure will also help teachers avoid costly damage to the instruments.

The pentatonic scale (see page 247 for more information on this scale) allows each child to improvise without difficulty. The removal of half steps, 4th and 7th degrees, from the major scale will result in a pentatonic scale. A pentatonic scale based on C will include the following pitches:

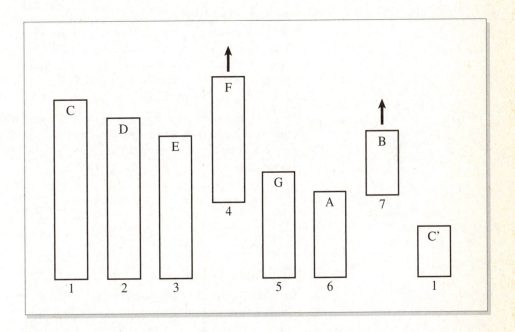

You will notice that the 4th degree of the C Major scale, note F, and the 7th degree of the C Major scale, note B, have been removed.

Once the pentatonic scale is in place, have students repeat the words of a favorite rhyme or poem. They should be able to say the rhyme, clap or pat the beat on their thighs while saying the rhyme, and then ultimately clap the rhythm of the words. This preparation is helpful in providing a secure knowledge of a specific rhythm that can be transferred directly to a barred instrument. Two examples of rhymes are below.

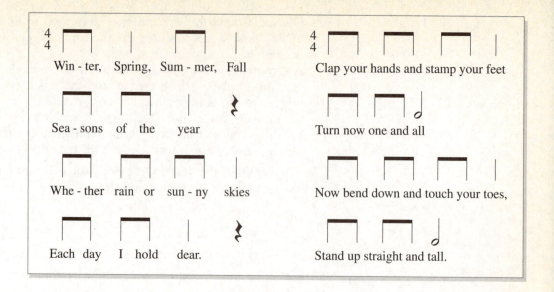

Have students pat the basic beat as they say the rhythm of the above poem(s). Transfer the basic beat to a drone or bordun pattern on the bass xylophone.

Bass Xylophone

Now that the bordun or drone is set, the student composer may wish to create a simple melody to go with the text of the rhyme. In the beginning, two pitches are quite sufficient. Pitches that are usually recommended for use by beginning composers are sol and mi or G and C because these pitches are at the core of the pentatonic scale. After students have created their melodies, add the C-G drone to accompany the melody.

This marks a first, but major step in guiding a child in his creative journey in the music classroom. It is a carefully sequenced process that, if followed, will encourage children to want to create and express themselves through music for years to come.

PITO, PITO

ORFF LESSON 1

Behavioral Objectives

Students will become familiar with a Spanish game song entitled, "Pito, Pito." Students will perform an ostinato accompaniment using rhythmic instruments.

Materials

A copy of the words to the folk song, "Pito, Pito" (see page 274)
Rhythm instruments: agogo bell, guiro, vibra-slap, small drum

Procedure

1. Have students speak the words to "Pito, Pito" while playing the basic beat on their laps.
2. Speak the rhyme again and clap the rhythm of the words.
3. Divide the class into two groups. Direct group 1 to clap the rhythm of the words while group 2 pats the beat. Switch parts.

4. Ask the children to look and listen to the last line as the teacher recites it.

Ping,   Pong,   fue-ra!

5. Ask students to suggest ways in which the rhythms in the last line can be played on different parts of the body. One suggestion might be:

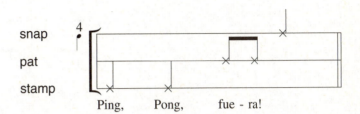

snap

pat

stamp

Ping,   Pong,   fue - ra!

Practice this with the students until they are comfortable with the pattern and its corresponding movement.

6. Tell the class that the pattern they just learned can be used as a *rhythmic ostinato*. A rhythmic ostinato consists of a rhythmic pattern that is repeated again and again and used as an accompaniment.

7. Divide the class again into two groups. Have group 1 say the speech and group 2 perform the ostinato. Switch parts.

8. Ask students to suggest an instrument that can play the rhythm that is in the feet. Suggest another that can play the rhythm on the thighs and another that can take the place of the finger snap. A final transfer from the body to instruments may look like this.

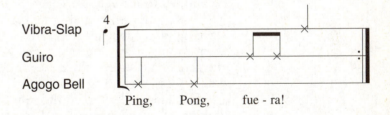

Vibra-Slap

Guiro

Agogo Bell

Ping,   Pong,   fue - ra!

9. Assign students to each of the accompanying instruments and have them play while the rest of the class performs the speech activity.

Summary/Evaluation

The teacher could ask the students the following:

a. What do we call the steady, continuous pattern that we played on our laps? (beat/pulse)

b. What do we call the varied lengths of sounds and silences as demonstrated through the speech or the words of "Pito, Pito"? (rhythm)

c. What do we call a pattern that repeats and is used as an accompaniment? (ostinato)

d. Name the instruments we used in the ostinato pattern. (agogo bell, guiro, vibra-slap)

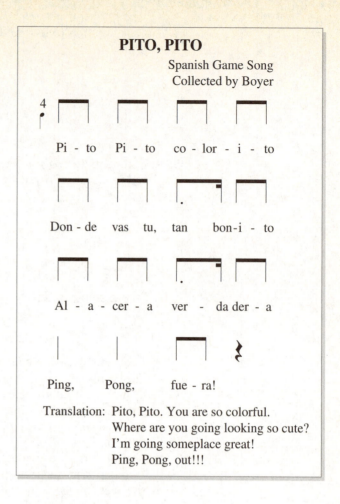

PITO, PITO

Spanish Game Song
Collected by Boyer

Pi - to   Pi - to   co - lor - i - to

Don - de   vas   tu,   tan   bon-i - to

Al - a - cer - a   ver - da der - a

Ping,   Pong,   fue - ra!

Translation: Pito, Pito. You are so colorful.
Where are you going looking so cute?
I'm going someplace great!
Ping, Pong, out!!!

Singing and Playing Activities

Orff-Schulwerk is a creative process. Therefore, it is recommended that children be allowed to actively participate in the creation of their first musical pieces. The use of the pentatonic scale as a beginning stepping stone to tonal understanding is recommended because, as discussed in Chapter 9, this scale enables them to sing, play, or create a melody without anyone's assistance. Central to the pentatonic scale is the minor third interval (so-mi), which is known as the "call" by Orff specialists.

The addition of "la" to the so-mi creates a universal "chant" sung by most children. The chant tones are then extended by adding mi, re, do, thus creating the pentatonic scale or five-tone scale—the beginning of the tonal sequence in the Orff-Schulwerk process.

ORFF LESSON 2

Behavioral Objectives

Students will set "Pito, Pito" to a pentatonic melody.
Students will better understand the meaning of "tonal center."

Materials

Melody instruments; staff paper, pencil, chalkboard

Procedure

1. Have students take their places behind the Orff barred instruments.
2. Have students properly remove all Bs and Fs (burgers and fries) by placing their fingers on the top and the bottom of a bar and lifting it directly off. Tell the students that they are now set up to play in C pentatonic and that C is the tonal center.

3. Give students about three minutes to compose a tune to "Pito, Pito." Let them know that they must begin their tune on "so" and end the piece on "do" or "C." Also inform them that changing the rhythm in this activity is not allowed.
4. Have students who wish to do so perform their tunes for the class.
5. As a group, choose one of them.
6. Write out the tune together on the board, using a five-lined staff. The tune may look like the following:

Do C   Pi - to   Pi - to   co - lor - i - to   Don - de   vas   tu,   tan   bon - i - to

Al - a - cer - a   ver - da der - a   Ping,   Pong,   fue - ra!

7. Play the tune on the barred instruments.

Summary/Evaluation

Ask the students to describe the process they went through to compose a piece of music.

ORFF LESSON 3

Behavioral Objectives

Students will learn the function of a drone or bordun.
Students will create a variety of drone patterns that can accompany "Pito, Pito."
Students will layer three drones on top of one another to create a more complex harmonic structure.

Materials

Orff barred instruments

Procedure

1. Tell the students, "Every good melody deserves harmony." Orff introduces us to various drone or bordun patterns, which allow students to accompany themselves using pentatonic melodies in a nonthreatening way.
2. Tell students that drones or borduns are made up of the first and fifth degrees of the scale. See **Visual P2** for Barred Patterns for Simple Accompaniments.
3. Have students demonstrate how many combinations of notes C and G they can create. Encourage them to play the pitches together and apart.
4. The teacher should ask each student to mirror herself or himself as she or he pats a variety of drone patterns on her or his lap. This technique is called patching. *Patsching* is a German word that means hitting the knees or thighs. Usually this procedure is used to physically prepare the student to play a specific pattern on the barred instruments.
5. Have students create a simple bordun accompaniment on the bass xylophone to the song "Pito, Pito."
6. Have students then create a simple bordun that can be played on a metallophone. Metallophones have a more sustained tone, and therefore students should play longer notes on them.
7. Play the melody on a glockenspiel.

8. Starting with the lowest instrument, the bass xylophone, layer in all the parts to create an interesting accompaniment of which all the children can be proud.

9. Sing the song "Pito, Pito" while playing an accompaniment.

Summary/Evaluation

The children's ability to successfully put all this together should be praised. They are now ready to do it again.

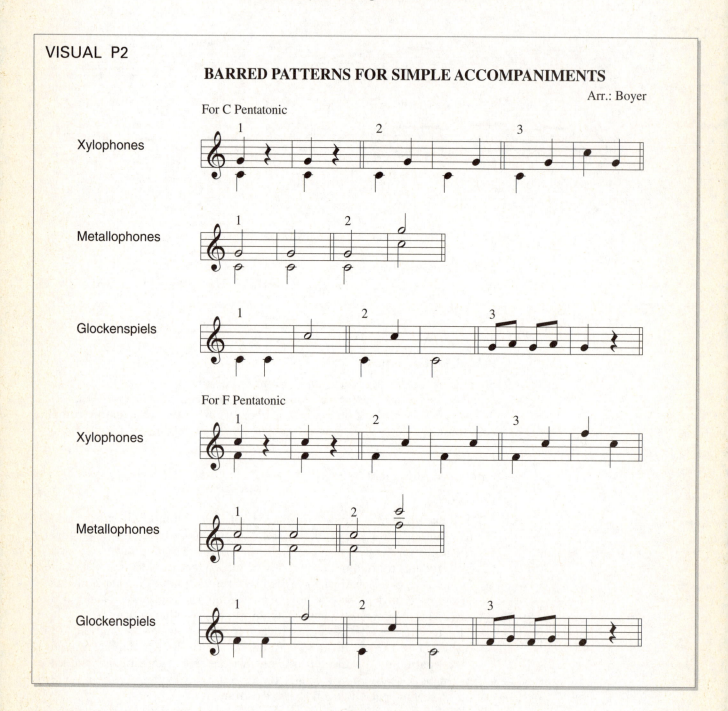

VISUAL P2

BARRED PATTERNS FOR SIMPLE ACCOMPANIMENTS

Arr.: Boyer

For C Pentatonic

Xylophones

Metallophones

Glockenspiels

For F Pentatonic

Xylophones

Metallophones

Glockenspiels

Rhythm and melody instruments can be combined to add to the interest of a musical composition. "Ida Red" provides opportunities for combining rhythmic and melodic timbres in a creative way.

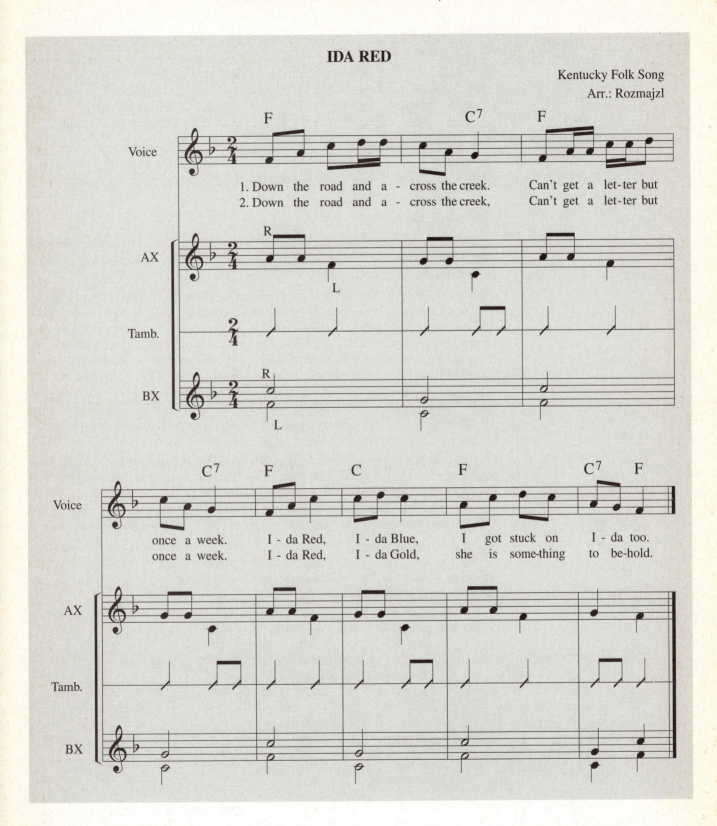

IDA RED

Kentucky Folk Song
Arr.: Rozmajzl

Drum Circle

Learning Drum circles provide opportunities for students to come together to explore music through playing a variety of non-pitched percussion instruments. The drum circle focuses primarily on a student's ability to keep a beat, accurately play patterns of rhythms on a percussion instrument, maintain a specific rhythm pattern without deviation, follow a "leader" and, improvise on an instrument within the context of the whole group as designated by the "leader."

Finally, a drum circle affords all students in the classroom an opportunity to experience a variety of timbres and texture. It also helps students learn about different cultures as they take an active playing role in a performing ensemble.

Strategies NS 2, 7, 9

(Performing on percussion instruments with others. Listening and evaluating the performance. Understanding and becoming sensitive to drumming as it has evolved from other countries.)

Make available a variety of unpitched instruments. If these instruments are not readily available in the school, the teacher should offer a unit of study that focuses on making percussion instruments. For example, a simple cardboard box can make a great drum. Dowel rods from a local hardware store are relatively inexpensive and can serve as rhythm sticks, and shakers can be made from empty plastic bottles. Simply put beans, peas, or rice inside the bottle, screw on the top and shake. Metal objects that can add "color" to a drum circle are easy to find as well. Tire irons are quite popular, as is a pot or pan top. Scrub boards can serve as scrapers or rasps as can the grooved sides of many detergent containers. In short, anything can work.

Assign students to seats in a circle, depending on the instruments they will be playing. We recommend placing students in sections depending on the make-up and sound of their instruments. As previously mentioned in this chapter, percussion instruments fall into the categories of being either skin, rattle, metal, or wood. This is a good place to start the classification of instruments within the drum circle.

After seating has been determined, a "leader" should be selected to direct the group. In the beginning, it is usually the teacher who serves as leader until students within the ensemble develop sufficient understanding and proficiency to guide such an ensemble.

Use "Jingo Ba," a traditional folk piece for drumming from Nigeria, as a starting point. Using "call and response," teach "Jingo Ba."

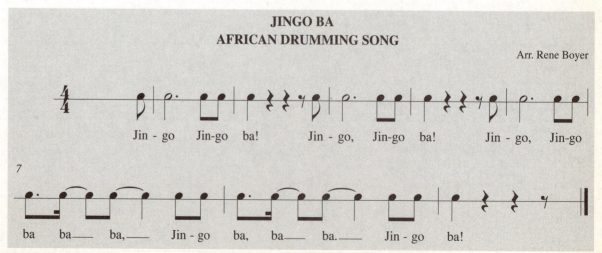

JINGO BA
AFRICAN DRUMMING SONG

Arr. Rene Boyer

Jin - go   Jin-go   ba!   Jin - go,   Jin-go   ba!   Jin - go,   Jin-go

7

ba   ba— ba,   Jin - go   ba,   ba— ba.—   Jin - go   ba!

After students are comfortable with expressively singing "Jingo-Ba," the "leader" can begin to layer rhythmic ostinati patterns, similar to those in **Visual P1** to accompany the song.

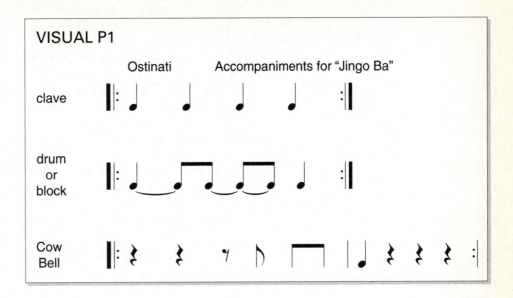

VISUAL P1

Ostinati   Accompaniments for "Jingo Ba"

clave

drum
or
block

Cow
Bell

The first step for the "leader" is to establish the beat or pulse of the piece that is to be accompanied.

The "leader" can accomplish this by gently patting the beat on his or her chest with one hand. This gives a clear indication to all players that it is time to begin playing the beat or pulse. It also establishes the fact that in order to be a successful participant in the ensemble, it is necessary for players to listen and follow the leader in silence, while feeling the power of the ensemble as it grows and develops into a vibrant musical art form. A good rule to remember is that the main objective of a drum circle is to make music. Talking and giving verbal direction is not necessary.

Once the beat has been established, it is now the "leader" who must create other rhythm patterns or ostinati to be layered on top of the beat. The leader can also invite, with nonverbal gestures, an individual player or small groups of players to improvise on their instrument(s). The role of the leader grows in importance when directing and manipulating the various rhythms within the ensemble. It soon becomes clear to the leader that assuring equal opportunity among participants is an important factor in a successful drum circle.

The drum is the favorite instrument to be included in the drum circle. The most popular of these drums is the djembe, which has its roots in Africa.

Learning   There are three major tones that children should be encouraged to practice on the djembe, even though there are many others. For each of these sounds, the player should remember to let his or her hand rebound as soon as it has made its sound.

   a. **Bass:** This is the lowest and most resonant of the djembe sounds. To make a bass tone, drop your hand down near the center or middle of the drumhead (called the bass) with the flat palm of the hand. Hold your hand firm, but relaxed. Avoid curving the hand. The thumb should be tucked in, almost parallel to the fingers. Let your hand rebound like it's coming off a trampoline.

b. Tone: Back your hands away from the center of the drum and tilt your wrist in. The open tone is played with the underside of your four fingers. The joint where the fingers join the hand should be cupped around the rim of the drum. The thumbs should be away from the edge of the drum. If the thumbs are too close and accidentally hit the edge, nerve injuries may occur. For the open tone, bend your wrists a bit more. As you strike the drum (away from the center is the tom), you will notice that the tone produced is more hollow.

c. Slap: This is one of the more difficult tones to produce because it involves two major parts of the hand on two different parts of the drum head—the rim and the area closest to the rim (the tom). The hand position is almost identical to the tone position. Again, you must be careful not to injure your hands. Spread your fingers out and use them, along with most of the "padded" part of the hand (just below the wrist) where your fingers join your hand, to hit the rim of the drum. The very edge of the padded part of your hand just below (toward your wrist) where your fingers join your hand should hit the rim of the drum.

Parts of the djembe drum

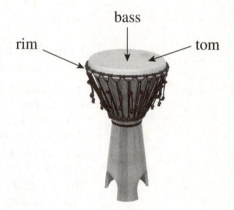

Strategy **NS 2** (Playing the djembe)

With practice, students can successfully play at least two of these three major techniques. These two techniques will allow for contrasting and exciting patterns that can be played on the drum.

The following drumming piece consists of four different parts that use two of the major drumming techniques, the bass and the tone. Students should play the following ostinati patterns when directed to do so by the teacher or the "leader."

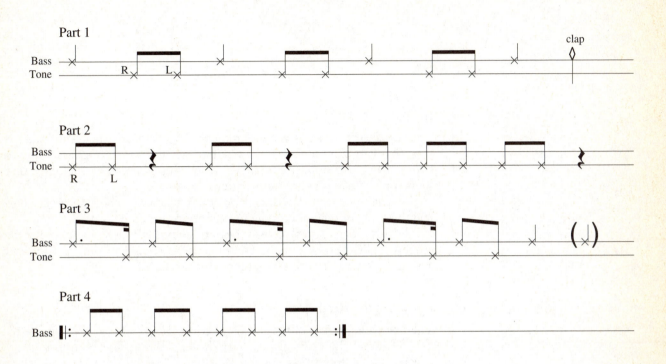

 Repeat the above ostinati patterns. Feel free to add variations of the above patterns. The key is to have fun while improvising. Make up a dance that can accompany the drum circle rhythms.

PLAYING THE SOPRANO RECORDER

The twentieth century witnessed a revival of interest in recorder playing. The recorder emerged as a melody instrument in the fifteenth century and was popular until the eighteenth century, when it was replaced by the modern flute. It is usually made in six sizes: sopranino, soprano, alto, tenor, bass, and contrabass. The recorder can assist a student in learning to read music, in improvising, and in developing performance skills. The soprano recorder continues to be an integral part of elementary music education because it is inexpensive and easy to play, and it closely parallels the tone quality of the child's voice. In addition, it provides an opportunity for students to perform literature written by some of the greatest composers in our history. The study of the soprano recorder usually begins in third or fourth grade.

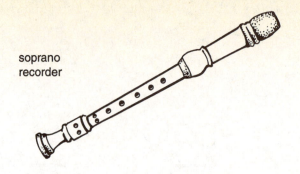

soprano
recorder

Introducing the Recorder

The soprano recorder is a C instrument, which means that the lowest possible tone that can be produced is C. The range of the soprano recorder encompasses two octaves; therefore, it is capable of playing almost any melody. All pitches sound one octave higher than written.

The holes on the top and back of the recorder, when covered, change the length of the air column, producing variations in pitch.

Two standard types of recorders are commonly used in schools today: Baroque (English) and German. The fingerings are slightly different for each. The activities presented in this chapter are for the Baroque recorder.

Fingering the Recorder

The first three fingers of the left hand cover the top three holes on the recorder. The left-hand thumb is placed over the back hole. The bottom four holes are covered by the four fingers of the right hand, leaving the right-hand thumb free to support the instrument.

Care must be taken to ensure that the holes being used are completely covered. Escaping air will cause the instrument to squeak. To avoid this, the player should cover the holes with the fleshy pads of the fingers.

When playing the recorder, hold it with the bell slanted toward the floor, not straight out from the body.

Blowing into the Recorder

The mouthpiece of the recorder should be held firmly by the lips, not between the teeth. Blow gently and evenly into the recorder while articulating the syllables "doo" or "too" against the roof of the mouth, near the upper teeth. It is important to continue the airflow while articulating the syllables. This technique is called *tonguing*. Tonguing is used to sound each pitch unless otherwise indicated in the music.

When playing the recorder, be careful not to overblow. Squeaks will also result if too much air is forced into the pipe.

Because of the moisture buildup that occurs inside the recorder while playing, it is important to place the index finger over the tone hole and blow forcefully to clear the moisture from the tube when it becomes excessive.

Playing Music

Covering the holes for the thumb and the first finger on the left hand, improvise a variety of rhythmic patterns until you are comfortable blowing into the instrument. This pitch is B and will always correspond to the staff notation and the recorder fingering diagrams shown here.

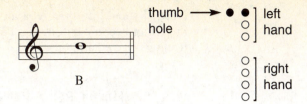

Practice playing the following exercises:

By simply adding the second finger of the left hand to the fingering for the pitch B, the new pitch A is produced.

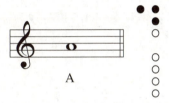

Practice the following exercises:

Note G is fingered by adding the covered third hole to the A fingering.

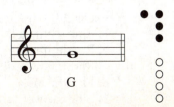

Note G should be practiced alone and with notes B and A until the students' fingerings become automatic. Playing the following songs will help reinforce the reading of B, A, and G.

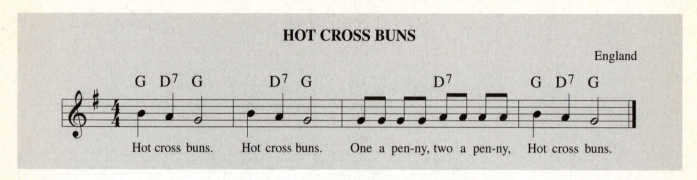

HOT CROSS BUNS

England

Hot cross buns. Hot cross buns. One a pen-ny, two a pen-ny, Hot cross buns.

GOOD NEWS

Spiritual

Good news! Char-iot's com-ing! Good news! Char-iot's com-ing!

Good news! Char-iot's com - ing! Don't leave me be - hind.

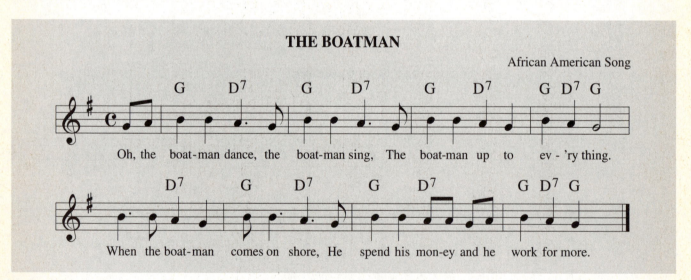

THE BOATMAN

African American Song

Oh, the boat-man dance, the boat-man sing, The boat-man up to ev - 'ry thing.

When the boat-man comes on shore, He spend his mon-ey and he work for more.

As the student continues to learn new notes on the recorder, it may be helpful to use the following procedures:

a. Clap the rhythm of the song first.
b. Sing the melody using the letter name of each note.
c. Repeat item "b" and finger the notes on the recorder.
Rest the recorder comfortably on the chin while doing this exercise.
d. Play the music on the recorder.
e. Sing the words to the song.

Practicing the Recorder

Notes learned: G-A-B
New Note: D′

D′

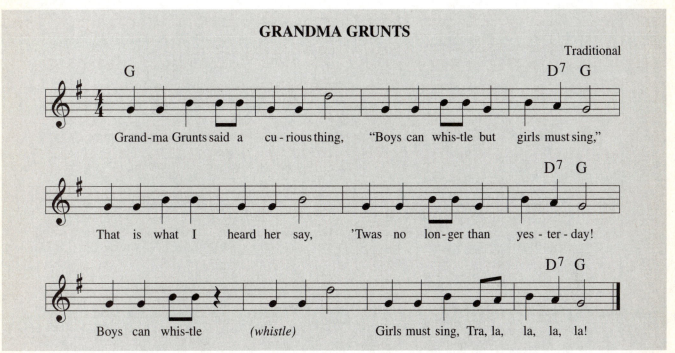

GRANDMA GRUNTS

Traditional

G ... **D⁷ G**

Grand-ma Grunts said a cu-rious thing, "Boys can whis-tle but girls must sing,"

D⁷ G

That is what I heard her say, 'Twas no lon-ger than yes-ter-day!

D⁷ G

Boys can whis-tle (whistle) Girls must sing, Tra, la, la, la, la!

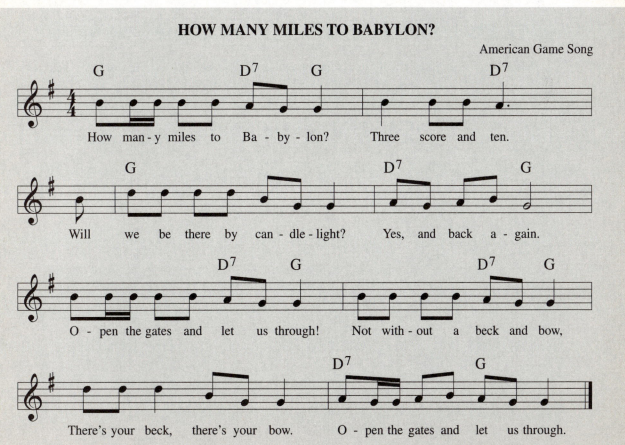

HOW MANY MILES TO BABYLON?

American Game Song

G **D⁷ G** **D⁷**

How man-y miles to Ba-by-lon? Three score and ten.

G **D⁷ G**

Will we be there by can-dle-light? Yes, and back a-gain.

D⁷ G **D⁷ G**

O-pen the gates and let us through! Not with-out a beck and bow,

D⁷ G

There's your beck, there's your bow. O-pen the gates and let us through.

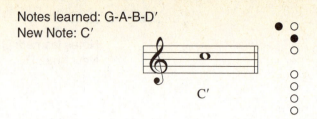

C'

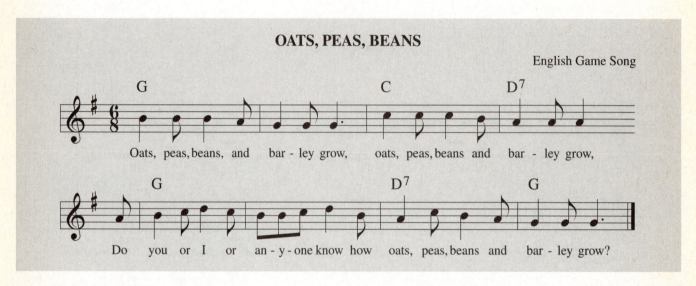

OATS, PEAS, BEANS

English Game Song

G   C   D⁷

Oats, peas, beans, and bar - ley grow, oats, peas, beans and bar - ley grow,

G   D⁷   G

Do you or I or an - y - one know how oats, peas, beans and bar - ley grow?

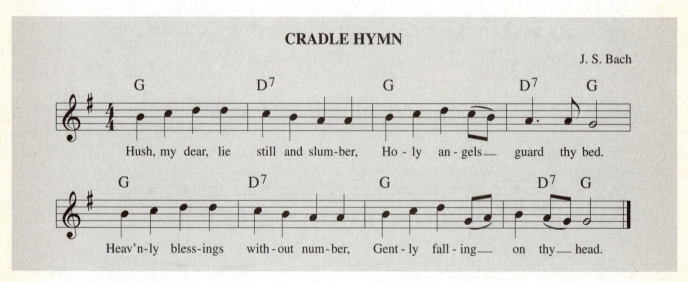

CRADLE HYMN

J. S. Bach

G   D⁷   G   D⁷   G

Hush, my dear, lie still and slum - ber, Ho - ly an - gels — guard thy bed.

G   D⁷   G   D⁷   G

Heav'n-ly bless - ings with - out num - ber, Gent - ly fall - ing — on thy — head.

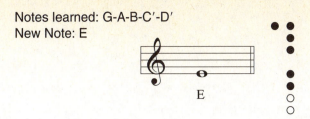

E

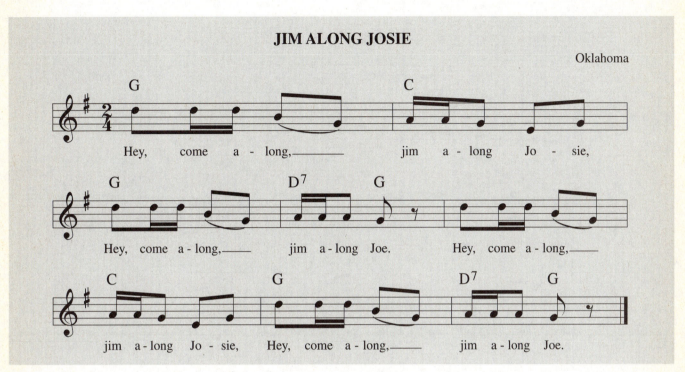

JIM ALONG JOSIE

Oklahoma

Hey, come a - long,_____ jim a - long Jo - sie,

Hey, come a - long,_____ jim a - long Joe. Hey, come a - long,_____

jim a - long Jo - sie, Hey, come a - long,_____ jim a - long Joe.

POOR LITTLE KITTY CAT

American Folk Song

Poor lit - tle kit - ty cat, Poor lit - tle fel - ler.

Poor lit - tle kit - ty cat, Lost in the cel - lar.

AMAZING GRACE

Ionian mode
Traditional

A - maz - ing— Grace how sweet the sound that saved a lost lamb like me,———— I once— was— lost but now— am— found was blind but— now I see.————

OH, WON'T YOU SIT DOWN?

Freely Refrain

African American Spiritual

Oh, won't you sit down?— Lord, I can't sit down.—

Oh, won't you sit down?— Lord, I can't sit down.—

Oh, won't you sit down?— Lord, I can't sit down.—

'Cause I just got to Heav-en, gon-na look a - round.—

End (Fine)

ODE TO JOY

English words by
Henry van Dyke

Ludwig van Beethoven
(Germany, 1770–1827)

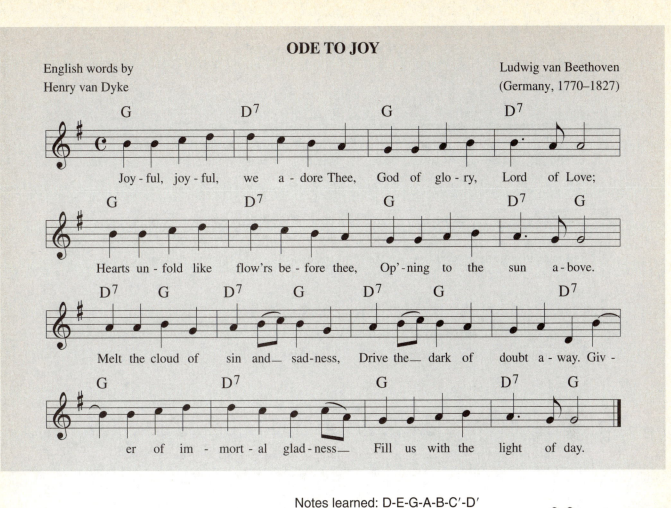

Notes learned: D-E-G-A-B-C′-D′
New Note: C

POURQUOI

American Folk Song

RIDING IN THE BUGGY

Play-Party Song

Rid-ing in the bug-gy Miss Mar-y Jane, Miss Mar-y Jane, Miss Mar-y Jane,

Rid-ing in the bug-gy Miss Mar-y Jane, I'm a long way from home.

Who mourns for me, Who mourns for me,

Who mourns for me, my dar-ling, Who mourns for me?

Notes learned: C-D-E-G-A-B-C'-D'
New Note: F

F

STARS SHININ'

Texas

By'n bye, by'n bye. Stars shin-ing num-ber, num-ber one, Num-ber

two, num-ber three, Good lawd, by'n bye by'n bye, Good lawd, by'n bye.

THE LITTLE DAPPLED COW

Traditional

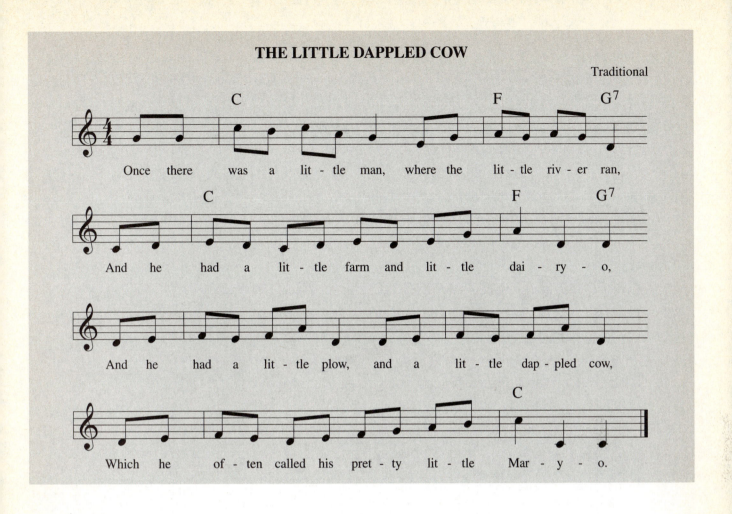

Once there was a lit-tle man, where the lit-tle riv-er ran,

And he had a lit-tle farm and lit-tle dai-ry-o,

And he had a lit-tle plow, and a lit-tle dap-pled cow,

Which he of-ten called his pret-ty lit-tle Mar-y-o.

Notes learned: C-D-E-F-G-A-B-C'-D'
New Note: F-sharp

F♯

VIVA LA MUSICA

Michael Praetorius

Vi - va, vi - va la mu - si - ca! Vi - va, vi - va la

mu - si - ca! Vi - va la mu - si - ca!

SIMPLE GIFTS

Shaker Tune

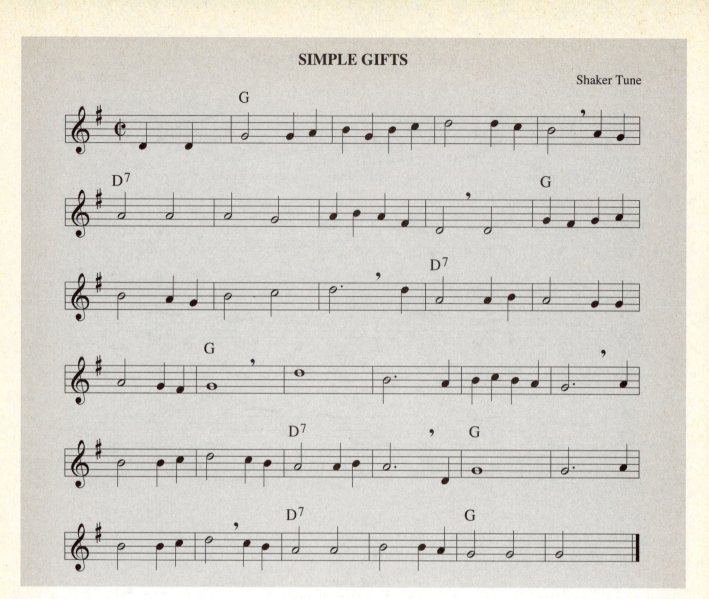

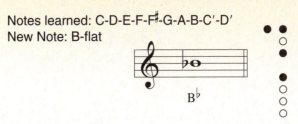

Notes learned: C-D-E-F-F#-G-A-B-C'-D'
New Note: B-flat

B♭

SCARBOROUGH FAIR

England

F   C⁷   F   C⁷   F   C⁷   F   C⁷

F   C⁷   F   C⁷   F

MANGO WALK

Jamaican Calypso

F

My moth-er deed-a tell me that you go man-go walk, you

C⁷   F

go man-go walk, you go man-go walk.

My moth-er deed-a tell me that you go man-go walk, and

D⁷   F

eat all the num-ber 'lev-en.

Unusual meanings:
    deed-a = did
    go mango walk = walk in the mango orchard
    eat all the number 'lev-en = eat the best mangos in the orchard

Playing Duets

In a duet, two different lines of music are played at the same time. Divide the class into two parts. Have half play the top line and the other half play the bottom line.

OVER MY HEAD
(A Duet for Two Recorders)

Spiritual
Arr.: Boyer

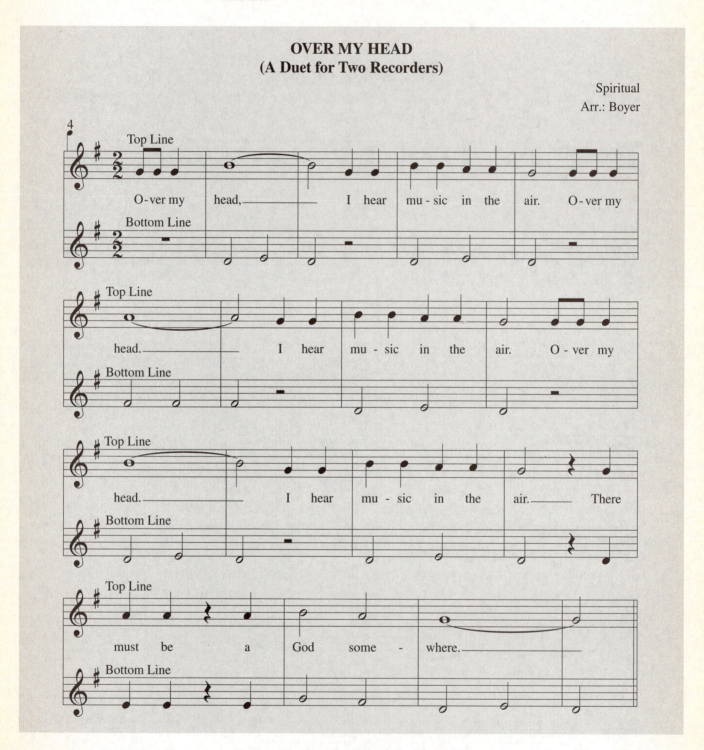

LA PIÑATA
(A Duet for Two Recorders)

Latin American Folk Song
Arr.: Boyer

Translation: This evening's piñata   Hit it, hit it, hit it,
           Looks just like a star   Don't lose your good aim.
           Hurry over for a taste   Measure out the distance,
           Let's have fun with it tonight   From here to there.

Playing Trios

In a trio, three lines of music are played at the same time in harmony. Some play the top line, some the middle line, and some the bottom line.

Divide the class into three sections. Assign each section a line and play "Chop Sticks."

CHOP STICKS

American Folk Tune

Arr.: Boyer

SIMPLE GIFTS FOR THREE RECORDERS
SHAKER HYMN

Arranger
Rene Boyer

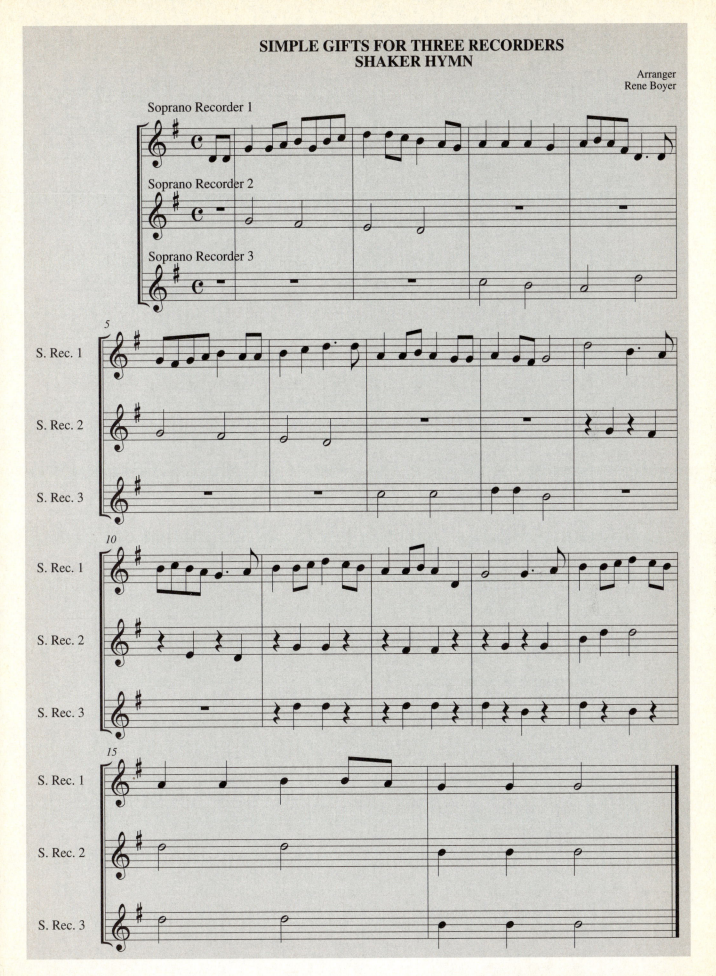

JOYFUL, JOYFUL

Beethoven
Arranged by R.B

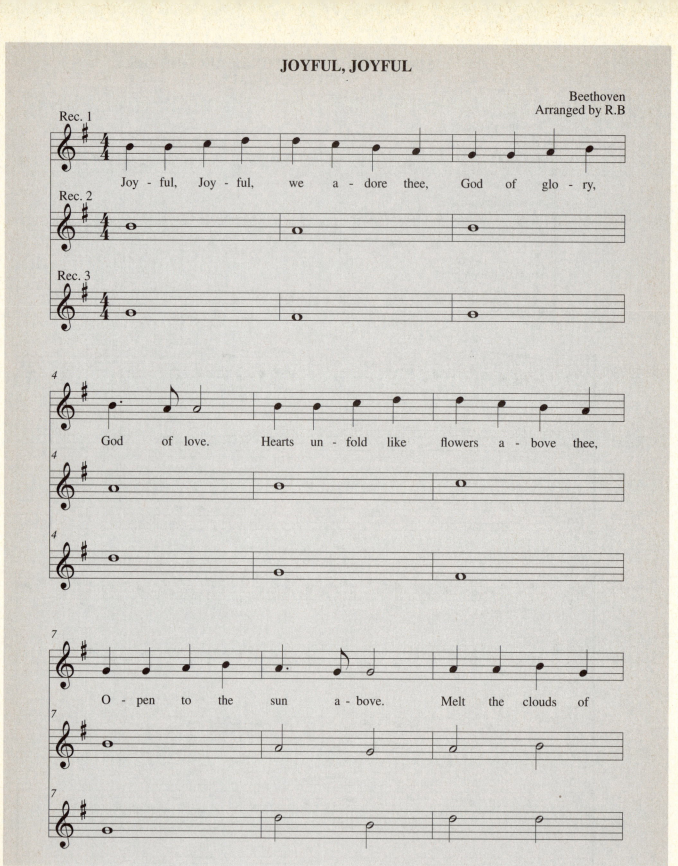

JOYFUL, JOYFUL

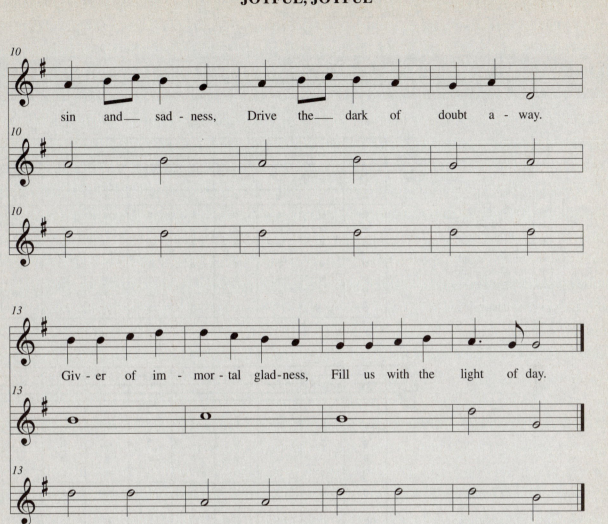

sin and sad-ness, Drive the dark of doubt a - way.

Giv - er of im - mor-tal glad-ness, Fill us with the light of day.

The tones above high D can be produced by adjusting the thumb so that a portion of the thumb hole is left uncovered. These fingerings are included in the fingering chart shown here.

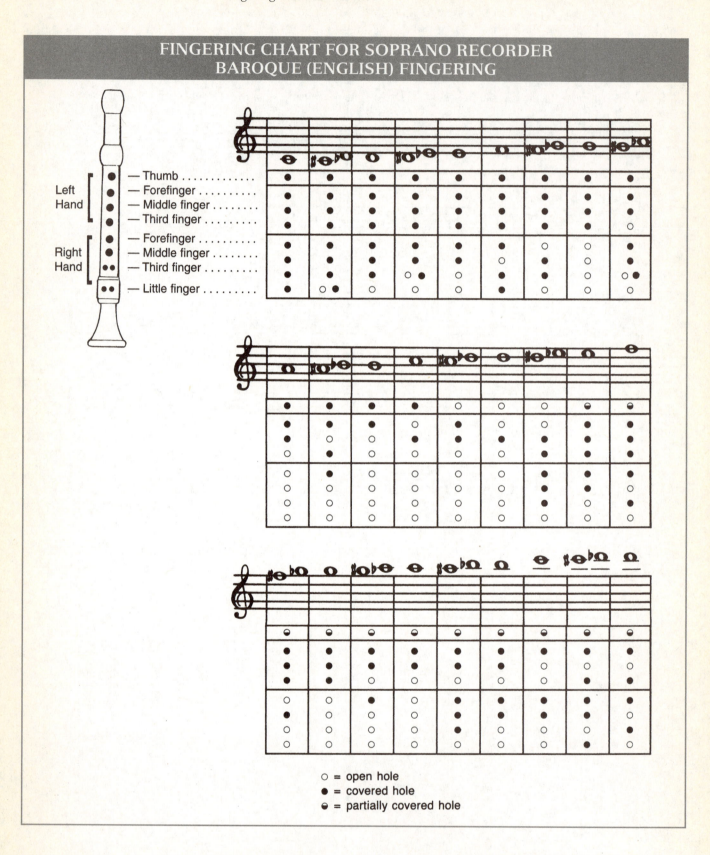

FINGERING CHART FOR SOPRANO RECORDER
BAROQUE (ENGLISH) FINGERING

Left Hand
— Thumb . . . .
— Forefinger . . . .
— Middle finger . . . .
— Third finger . . . .

Right Hand
— Forefinger . . . .
— Middle finger . . . .
— Third finger . . . .
— Little finger . . . .

○ = open hole
● = covered hole
◐ = partially covered hole

300　Playing Musical Instruments

PLAYING THE GUITAR

Because of its wide acceptance by folk artists and popular musicians, the guitar has become a widely used instrument in elementary music education. However, young children are limited in their abilities to play this instrument because their hands are so small. Children in upper elementary grades will have greater success in playing the guitar.

There are many types of guitars. The guitar most commonly used in the classroom is the acoustic, classical guitar with nylon strings. Although the guitar can be used to play melodies, its function in the elementary classroom is to provide accompaniments to songs and other musical compositions. The most important parts of the guitar are shown here:

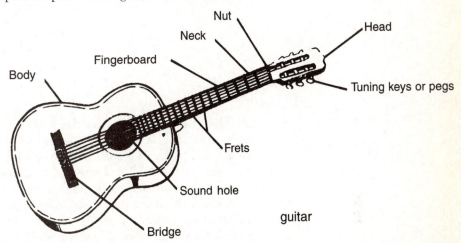

guitar

The acoustic, classical guitar usually has six strings of differing thicknesses and tensions. The common tuning of the strings is E, A, D, G, B, and E'. Although there are several ways to tune the guitar, the easiest and most accurate for beginning players is to tune the strings to the piano. A pitch can be raised or lowered by turning the tuning pegs.

The diagram shows the relationship of each of the six guitar strings to its corresponding pitch on the staff and on the piano keyboard. (Guitar music is notated an octave higher than it sounds.)

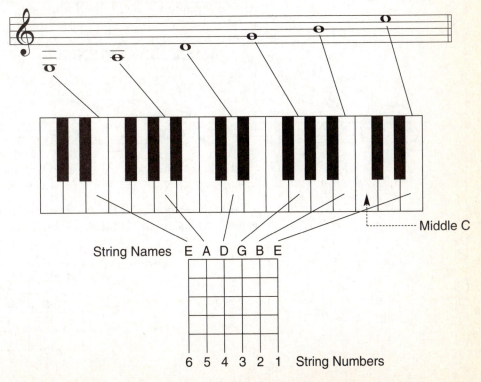

When playing the guitar in a seated position, rest it comfortably on the right thigh with the neck of the guitar slanted upward. The left-hand thumb should rest on the back of the guitar neck close to the nut. Curve the left hand around the guitar neck and arch the fingers over the strings. The fingers of the left hand are numbered from 1 to 4; the index finger is number 1. The right hand can either strum or finger pick the strings over the sound hole.

To learn fingerings for a chord, guitar players refer to fingering charts. The charts correspond to the guitar strings on the fretted fingerboard. Look at the finger chart for the D major chord:

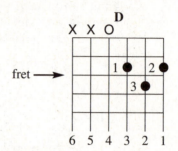

The chart indicates that the first finger of the left hand is placed on the second fret of the third string; finger 3 is placed on the third fret of string 2; and the second finger is placed on the second fret of string 1. String 4 is open, as indicated by the "O," and must be strummed with the first three strings. When playing this chord, strings 5 and 6 are not played, as indicated by the "X."

One of the most important aspects of learning to play the guitar is acquiring strumming techniques. A variety of strums can be learned. The most basic, however, are the sweep strum and the brush strum. The sweep strum involves a downward movement of the right-hand thumb across the strings. For the brush strum, the backs of the fingernails brush downward across the strings. The two strums are often used in combination; the sweep strum is used on accented beats, but either the sweep or the brush strum can be used on unaccented beats. Practice strumming the D major chord with the sweep strum:

Continue strumming the D chord while singing "Make New Friends."

Learn the fingering for the A⁷ chord and practice strumming it. Then combine it with the D major chord and play "Tom Dooley" and "Merrily We Roll Along."

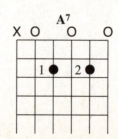

TOM DOOLEY

American Ballad

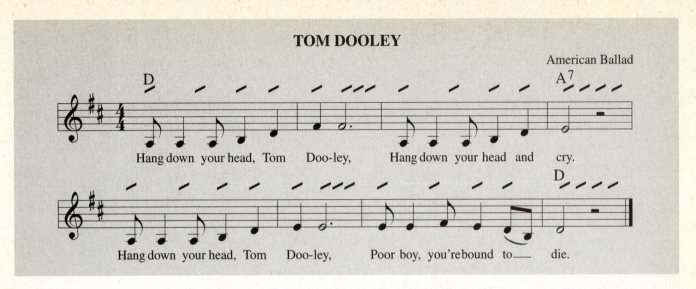

Hang down your head, Tom Doo-ley, Hang down your head and cry.

Hang down your head, Tom Doo-ley, Poor boy, you're bound to— die.

MERRILY WE ROLL ALONG

Traditional

Mer-ri-ly we roll a-long, Roll a-long, Roll a-long.

Mer-ri-ly we roll a-long, o'er the deep blue sea.

After learning the G chord, the player will be able to strum a variety of songs in the key of D. The player should practice "On Top of Old Smoky" and "Hawaiian Rainbows" until he or she can move smoothly from one chord to the next. Students should experiment with both the sweep and the brush strums.

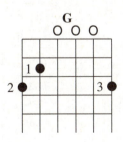

ON TOP OF OLD SMOKEY

American Folk Song

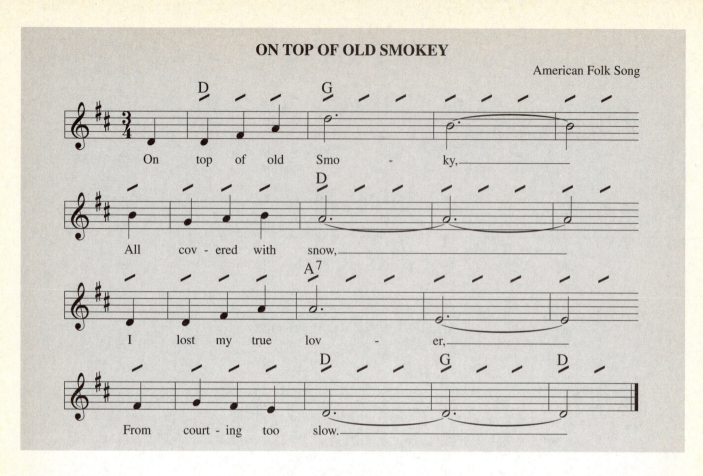

HAWAIIAN RAINBOWS

Hawaiian Folk Song

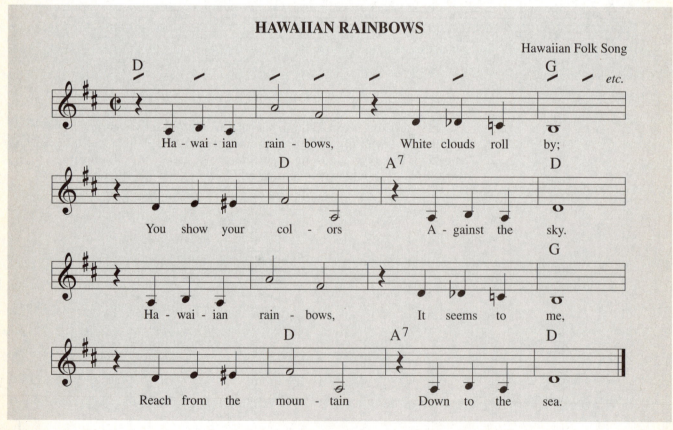

Other songs in the key of D, found in this book, include:

In the key of C, the three primary chords are C (I), F (IV), and G^7 (V^7). Practice these chords. Now play "My Home's in Montana" until the chord changes are smooth. Follow this piece with another folksong favorite.

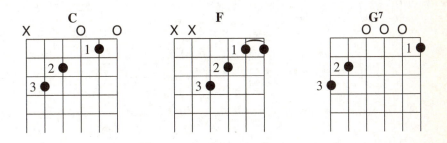

MY HOME'S IN MONTANA

Cowboy Song

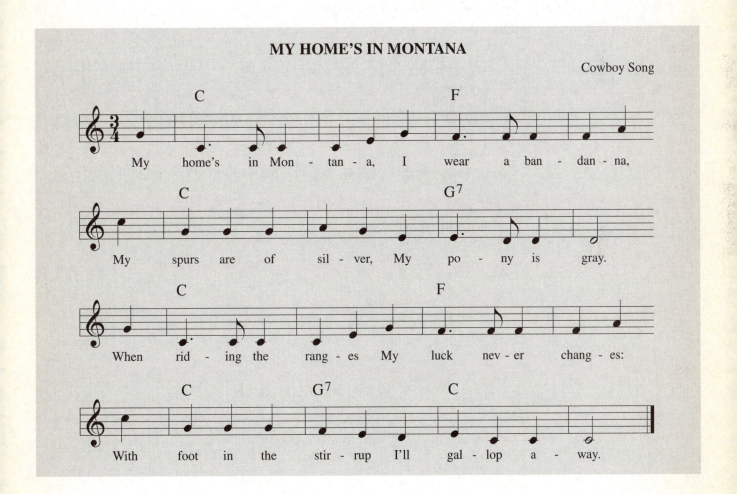

My home's in Mon - tan - a, I wear a ban - dan - na,

My spurs are of sil - ver, My po - ny is gray.

When rid - ing the rang - es My luck nev - er chang - es:

With foot in the stir - rup I'll gal - lop a - way.

SWEET BETSY FROM PIKE

American Folk Song

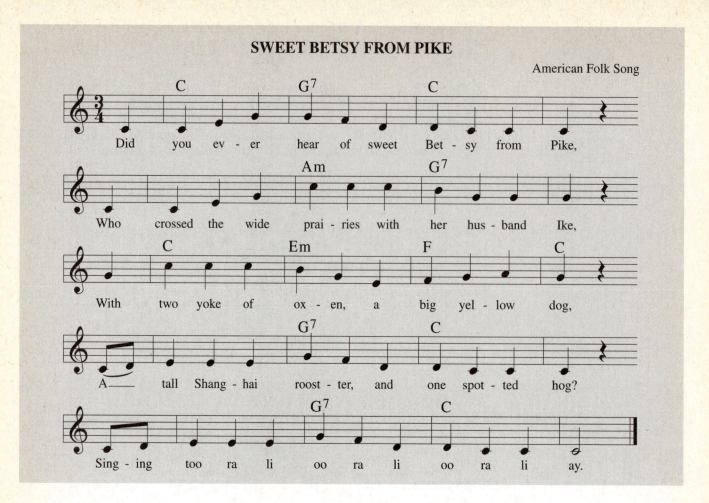

Other songs in the key of C, found in this book, are:

Song	Chapter
New River Train	3
America the Beautiful	6
Over the River and Through the Woods	3

By referring to the following fingering charts, additional chords can be learned to accompany a variety of songs.

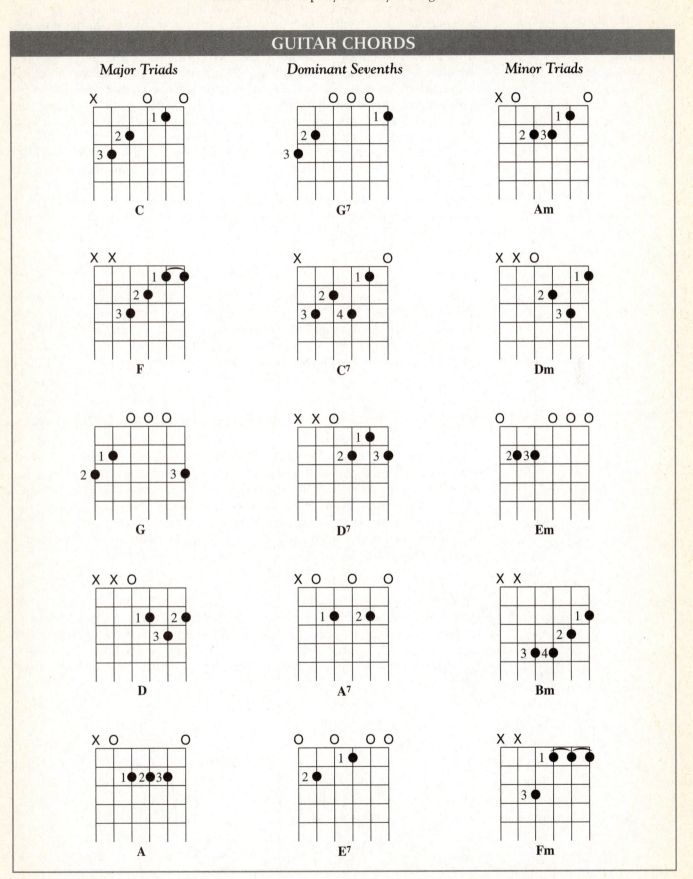

PLAYING KEYBOARD INSTRUMENTS

Keyboard instruments can be useful tools in providing children with enjoyable, creative experiences for melodic and harmonic growth. Primary among keyboard instruments is the piano, whose keyboard includes 88 keys, ranging from a low A to a high C. The piano has been the most popular professional and domestic keyboard instrument in Europe, Asia, and the United States since the late eighteenth century. It was originally called both *forte-piano* and *pianoforte* because of its greater capability in producing dynamic variations of soft and loud tones than was possible on its predecessors, the harpsichord and the clavichord. The terms *piano* and *forte* are Italian for *soft* and *loud*.

The piano was invented around 1709 by Bartolomeo Cristofori (1655–1730), an Italian from Florence. Its form has progressed through a number of sizes and shapes, but the most common forms today are the studio upright (46 inches high), the console (40 inches high), the spinet (36 inches high), and the grand, normally ranging from the nine-foot-long concert grand to the five-foot, two-inch baby grand.

Posture

Students should be seated in front of the middle of the keyboard, usually where the manufacturer's label is located. Attention should be given to a person's posture: (a) the back should be straight but not rigid; (b) the arms should be straight from the elbow to the hand, as the hand rests on the keyboard; and (c) the fingers should be close to the keys and curved slightly.

Keyboard

Notice that the black keys on the keyboard are grouped in twos and threes. The white keys are named for the musical alphabet, from A to G. Middle C is located to the left of the group of two black keys near the center of the keyboard. Play middle C; then find and play other Cs on the keyboard. Find and play the remaining keys of the musical alphabet in the following order: D, B, A, E, F, and G. Notice their placement in relation to the black keys. The black keys are also named for the alphabet letters from A to G; however, because they are a half step higher or lower than the white key bearing the same name, they have a sharp or a flat placed to the right of their name, such as C♯ or B♭.

Fingering

Numbers corresponding to the fingers on the hand are often placed above or below the notes on the staff, indicating which fingers to use when playing those notes. Number 1 designates the thumb on each hand; index fingers are marked 2; 3 refers to the middle fingers; 4 indicates the ring fingers; and the little fingers are 5.

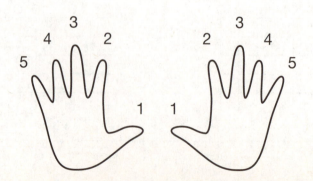

Playing Easy Melodies

The right hand usually plays notes written in the treble clef; the left hand plays bass clef notes. Practice the following melodies with the right hand until they become easy to play:

Repeat the melodic patterns above with the thumb placed on F (remember that the key of F has a B♭) and then on G. When finished, students will have played all the above melodies in the keys of C, F, and G. Experiment with placing the thumb on some of the remaining keys of the musical alphabet, but be sure to play the sharps and flats needed for those keys.

Now, practice these left-hand melodies:

Repeat these left-hand melodies with the fifth finger placed first on F and then on G. When students can play these melodies well in the keys of D, F, and G, let them experiment with playing them in some of the other keys.

Practice playing some of the songs in this book, first with the right hand and then with the left. Some good beginning songs are:

Song	Chapter	Key
Rocky Mountain*	6	C
Hot Cross Buns	10	G
Good News	10	G
The Boatman	10	G
Grandma Grunts	10	G
How Many Miles to Babylon?	10	G
Oats, Peas, Beans	10	G
Cradle Hymn	10	G
Poor Little Kitty Cat*	10	G
Hop Old Squirrel	6	F
Marching	6	F
Candles of Hanukkah	8	F
Merrily We Roll Along	10	D
Jim Along Josie	3	B♭
Skin and Bones	3	Em

Playing Chordal Accompaniments

Teachers can accompany the children's singing by playing the melody of the song with the right hand and appropriate chords with the left hand. Although there are a number of ways to play chord tones, the following are among the easiest:

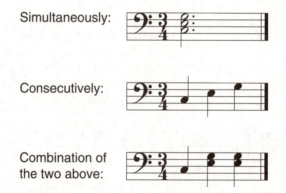

As discussed in Chapter 8, a chord can be built on any tone of the scale, but the most important are the primary chords, built on the first, fourth, and fifth scale tones. Use the left hand to practice the following chord progressions in the bass clef:

*These songs extend slightly beyond the five-finger position. Students will need to decide on an appropriate fingering before practicing them.

Now apply the chords for the key of C, practiced above, to the playing of "Oranges and Lemons." Notice that appropriate chords (C and G^7) are indicated on the musical score. Begin by playing the indicated chord on the first beat of each measure. Repeat the same chord in each measure until a new chord is designated.

ORANGES AND LEMONS

The preceding song, when placed on the grand staff with blocked chords notated, would be written in this manner:

Practice "Oranges and Lemons" until you can play it and sing the words simultaneously. Then practice some of the other songs in the list on page 310, using chords to accompany the melody.

WRITTEN AND PERFORMANCE-RELATED ASSESSMENTS THROUGH COOPERATIVE LEARNING ACTIVITIES: INSTRUMENTS

1. Assign to each group a different, known song. Each group's task is to write ostinati accompaniments for two to six rhythm instruments (depending on skill), similar to those that accompany the song "Mary Ann" in Chapter 10. The rhythmic ostinati should be notated with specific instruments designated. Groups should practice singing their songs and playing the ostinati until they are ready to perform for the class.

2. Give a different song to each group. Groups should create melodic ostinati to accompany their songs. If possible, they should try to notate their ostinato patterns. Patterns should be practiced until groups can perform their songs for the class.

3. Have each group choose a song that it can play on the recorder. Create one rhythmic and one melodic ostinato to accompany the song. Group members should decide on what instruments they will play the ostinati. Practice the song with recorders and ostinati until each group is ready to perform it for the class.

4. Give each group a song that has the chords marked. Group members should practice the song using guitar, autoharp, recorders, and/or barred instruments until they are ready to perform the melody with chordal accompaniment.

5. Assign to each group a song that does not have the chords marked. Group members should study their song and decide what chords they can use to accompany it. Chords should be tested on an autoharp, guitar, or piano. When the group is satisfied with its chord choices, it can practice singing the melody while playing the chords.

CHAPTER 11

Listening Activities and Materials NS 6

Listening to music is an integral part of everyone's life. No matter where we go, we are exposed to music—in the car, at the supermarket, at a baseball game, in a restaurant, at home, in church, and even while jogging. Listening occupies a large portion of our day; therefore, developing and refining listening skills are important activities in the elementary music program. Because of its importance, "Listening to, analyzing, and describing music" is listed as the sixth Content Standard proposed by National Standards for Arts Education.

In the music class, children are continually involved in listening activities. They listen as they sing so that they produce a pleasant tone that is well pitched; they listen as they interpret music through creative movement; they listen while they improvise accompaniment patterns for a musical work. As children's listening skills develop, they progress from concentration on one or two simple concepts to the perception of a more complex musical structure.

GOALS FOR LISTENING ACTIVITIES

Well-designed listening experiences should provide the following outcomes:

1. help the child in developing an aural sensitivity to the works of many composers
2. assist the child in formulating specific music concepts
3. introduce the child to a variety of musical styles
4. acquaint the child with the music of many cultures, in addition to that of his or her own culture
5. help the child experience the satisfaction and joy that come from actively listening to music

GUIDELINES FOR LISTENING

As teachers begin planning the listening lesson, it is helpful to keep the following guidelines in mind:

1. During listening activities, it is important for students to be listening for something. To play a recording and ask the children simply to listen without any guidance usually invites boredom, inattention, and even discipline problems. If students are invited to listen for structural components that are already part of their conscious learning, the listening activity will prove to be a challenging learning tool rather than a frustrating activity.
2. The listening lesson is a portion of the daily music class and does not usually occupy the entire music period.
3. Musical selections used in listening activities should be short. It is not always necessary to play an entire composition; a short excerpt is often just as valuable.
4. It may be necessary to repeat a recording more than once during a lesson if the objectives for the listening activity are to be achieved.
5. If the teacher needs to guide students' attention through the listening process, then the visuals containing guides for listening should be at the front of the class.
6. When students become more independent in listening, individual call charts can be used. A *call chart* presents, in sequence, a visual representation of what is happening in the music. The sequence is usually numbered 1, 2, 3,

and so forth. The teacher calls out or points to each number or item as the musical event occurs. This limits verbal interruptions while the listening activity is taking place.

7. Printing and pictures used on visuals should be large enough to be seen by the entire class.
8. Visuals should be colorful so that they invite the students to look at them.

ORGANIZING LISTENING ACTIVITIES

Among the different kinds of call charts that can be used, three of the most popular types are: those using pictures, those using abstract representations, and those using words. Examples of these three types are presented here along with strategies for their use.

Call Charts Using Pictures

Music: "Frightening" from *Scenes from Childhood Op. 15*, by Robert Schumann

Focus: Rondo Form (ABACABA)

Objective: By the end of the listening activity, students will be able to identify when the first section of "Frightening" reoccurs and when it is followed by a contrasting section.

The visuals presented below represent the form of this piece:

| Swan | Penguin | Swan | Seal | Swan | Penguin | Swan |

Have students listen to "Frightening" as the teacher posts each visual in the front of the room. Each visual should be displayed only when its corresponding section of music is heard. For example, the swan represents the A section of the rondo each time it occurs. Likewise, the B section of the rondo is represented by the penguin. The seal represents section C.

After all visuals have been posted, the teacher should discuss with the students what was happening in the music. Questions might include:

1. Did any part of our music happen over again?
2. Which parts repeated?
3. How could you tell?

After discussing the music, the teacher should be sure that students understand that some parts of the music are the same and some parts are different. This learning can be reinforced through movement. Play the music again and ask the children to improvise movement to each section of "Frightening." One group might move to the smooth, legato melody of section A by pretending to be swans. Another group would portray the short, brisk, stiff melodic line of section B much as a penguin might move. The playful, staccato melody of section C lends itself to the movements of a seal who is preparing to balance a ball on his nose and finally succeeds in doing it.

On another day, show students how sections that are the same can be given a letter name to represent them. Parts that are the same can be labeled with an "A"; contrasting sections are labeled with other letters in sequence, as needed. The form of "Frightening," then, would be ABACABA. This should be identified as rondo form.

Older students will find it a challenge to match the three themes found in "Frightening" with the music as it is heard. The themes presented below could be reproduced for each student to hold up as they occur in the music.

Theme A

Theme B

Theme C

An orchestral version of "Frightening" is available on the recording *The Small Listener*, part of The Small Musician Series published by Bowmar.

Music: "Baroque and Blue" from *Suite for Flute and Jazz Piano*, by Claude Bolling—opening measures only, ABAB

Focus: Baroque and blues styles

Objective: By the end of the listening activity, students will be able to identify simple differences between music in Baroque style and music in blues style.

Students should be asked to listen to an excerpt of "Baroque and Blue" while the teacher displays four visuals corresponding to the music: two visuals contain both a butterfly and a bird, and the other two visuals depict a "cool cat." The flute heard in the music is represented by the butterfly; the piano represents the bird; and the blues combo is characterized by the "cool cat."

A   B   A   B

Have students discuss what they heard in the four ABAB sections. Leading questions might include:

1. How many different parts to this music did you hear?
2. Which part did you prefer?
3. How would you describe the part that you liked best?

After students have discussed the two intertwining melodies performed by the flute and the piano, the teacher should identify this style as Baroque. The blues style should be named after students have discussed the strong syncopated rhythm performed by the small combo of instruments.

Follow-up activities for a different day might include dividing the class into two groups. Have part of the first group move to the flute sounds while the other part moves to the sounds of the piano. The interaction of these two parts in group 1 represents the polyphonic texture of the Baroque period. Group 2 should be alley cats responding in a rhythmic manner to the syncopated rhythms of the blues style.

Music:	Opening theme from *Also sprach Zarathustra* by Richard Strauss—theme used for the film *2001: A Space Odyssey*
Focus:	Contrasts in timbre
Objective:	By the end of the class, students will be able to identify the changing timbres heard in the music: double bass, trumpet, timpani, trombone, organ, and full orchestra

Have students listen to the opening theme of *Also sprach Zarathustra*. Identify the instruments heard in the excerpt.

Distribute a copy of the call chart, shown here, to each student in the class. Replay the opening theme. Call the appropriate numbers on the chart as each instrument or the full orchestra is heard on the recording.

Discuss how the contrasting timbres work together to produce the overall effect of the piece.

Also sprach Zarathustra

1.

2.

3. Orchestra

4.

5.
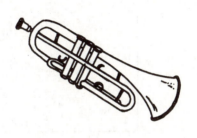

6. Orchestra

7.

8.

9. Orchestra

10.
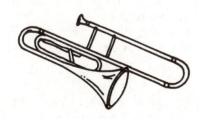

11. Orchestra

12.

Call Charts Using Abstract Representations

Music: *Carmina Burana*, Part Five: "Ecce gratum," by Carl Orff
Focus: Staccato and legato articulation; repetition
Objectives: By the end of the listening activity, students will be able to (a) recognize and move to staccato and legato passages in the excerpt and (b) respond through movement to the repetitions occurring in the music.

Because of the nature of the piece of music being heard, both the aural experience and the visual experience should occur simultaneously. The teacher should prepare abstract visuals, similar to those presented below, that correspond to the music being heard. The teacher should hold the charts in his or her lap so that proper sequencing takes place.

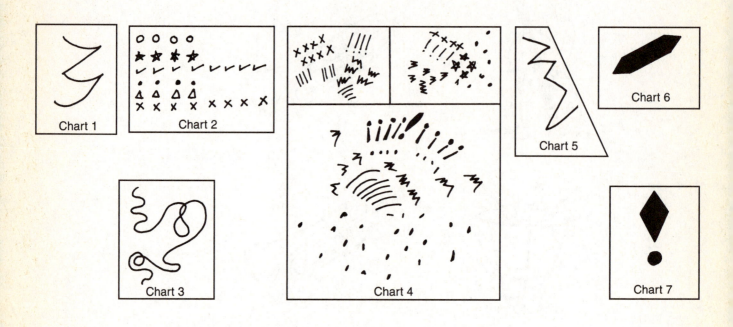

Play the excerpt of *Carmina Burana* while showing the charts in sequence. Help students to verbalize what they heard by asking questions such as:

1. What adjectives might you use to best describe what was heard?
2. Did you notice any repetitions?
3. How many times did the music repeat itself?
4. How might the body express what was heard in the music?

Divide the class into seven groups. Have each group represent one of the seven charts. Give each group time to decide how it will interpret the music represented by its abstract. Play the music while each group, in turn, recreates the music through body movements. Because the music is heard three times in succession, students should be instructed to "freeze" after they have performed their part until it is time for them to perform again.

As a culminating activity, review with the students the lessons that were being reinforced during their listening activity: staccato and legato articulation and repetition.

Music: *Fanfare for the Common Man* by Aaron Copland
Focus: Composers are often inspired to create a piece of music based on their deep passion toward something or someone. In this example, Copland was inspired by the deep love he had for the United States and the many people who live here.
Objective: By the end of class, students will be able to identify musical components that contribute to the expressiveness of a composition.

Ask students to listen to this composition without identifying its name. Have them be especially attentive to instrumentation, the melodic line, rhythm, and other elements that contribute to expressiveness in a composition.

When the composition is finished, ask students what their overall feeling was as they listened. Many will comment on the composition's stateliness or grandeur. Elicit from students the expressive elements that give this music its sense of grandeur. A partial list might include:

- Brass instruments
- Loud dynamics
- Sustained tones and slow tempo markings
- Rising melodies
- Pauses

Play the composition again, this time using the call chart, so students can check their responses.

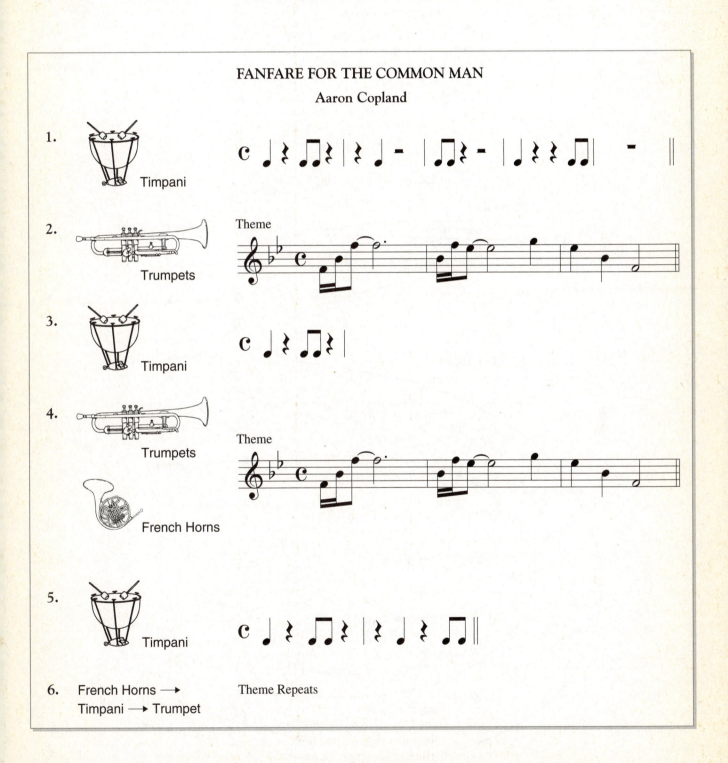

FANFARE FOR THE COMMON MAN
Aaron Copland

1. Timpani

2. Trumpets — Theme

3. Timpani

4. Trumpets — French Horns — Theme

5. Timpani

6. French Horns → Timpani → Trumpet — Theme Repeats

Music: "The Little Train of the Caipira," from *Bachianas Brasileiras No. 2* by Hector Villa-Lobos

Focus: Crescendo and decrescendo; accelerando and ritardando

Objective: By the end of the listening activity, students will be able to recognize when music begins getting louder or softer, faster or slower.

Prepare a large call chart similar to the one below. This chart combines words with abstract representations. Play the recording and call out each number as it occurs in the music; point to the representations as they occur in the music. After the first hearing, have students express what was happening in each part of the music. The following questions may be helpful in eliciting from them an analysis of this composition.

1. Did the music make you think about a train as you listened?

2. What did you hear in no. 1 that sounded like the train might be far away?

3. How did the composer imply in no. 2 that the train was moving along peacefully and steadily?

Similar questions can be asked through no. 8.

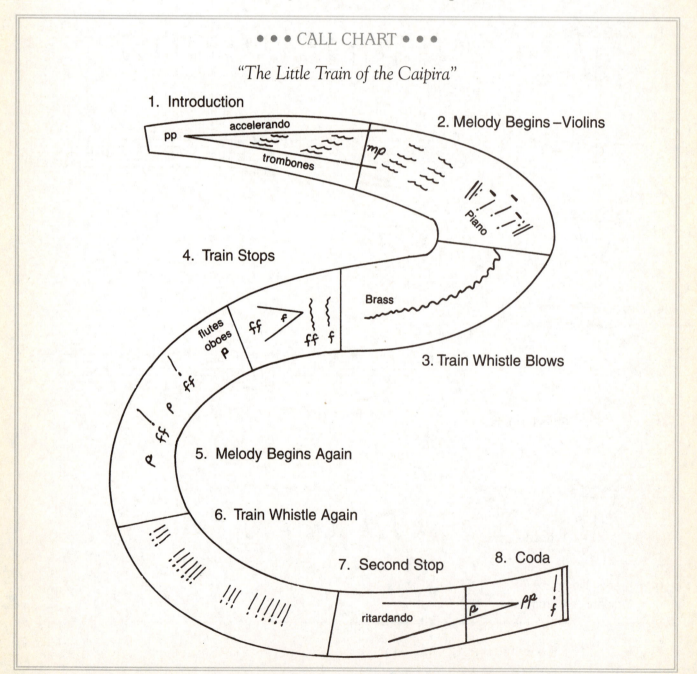

● ● ● CALL CHART ● ● ●

"The Little Train of the Caipira"

1. Introduction
2. Melody Begins—Violins
3. Train Whistle Blows
4. Train Stops
5. Melody Begins Again
6. Train Whistle Again
7. Second Stop
8. Coda

Replay the recording so that students have an opportunity to hear what they may have missed during the first hearing.

On another day, give wooden rhythm instruments to students and practice a simple sixteenth-note ostinato: ♪♪♪♪. Play the recording while students perform the ostinato, beginning slowly and softly. As the music progresses, let the students increase the tempo and dynamic level of their ostinato to match the changes in the score. Repeat several times until the students feel secure in performing the accelerando and crescendo at the beginning of the piece and the ritardando and decrescendo at the end of the piece.

Call Charts Using Words

> **Music:** "In the Hall of the Mountain King," from *Peer Gynt Suite No. 1* by Edvard Grieg
>
> **Focus:** In a musical composition, some elements may remain constant, providing unity through repetition; other elements often change, providing variety in the composition.
>
> **Objective:** By the end of the listening activity, students will be aware of elements that repeat—theme—and those that change—tempo, timbre, dynamics, range—in the Grieg composition.

Discuss with the students the many ways in which a composer can create both unity and variety within a musical work. Demonstrate these principles through the use of a simple tune. Have students decide how to vary the tune to provide variety as the tune is performed over and over. For example, as the tune is repeated (unity), the class may choose to change its tempo, dynamics, range, key, or instrumentation (variety). Have the class perform its composition.

Give each student a copy of the handout for "In the Hall of the Mountain King." Ask students to circle the correct responses as the composition progresses. Notice that, for this particular handout, it isn't necessary for the teacher to "call" any numbers. The students may need to hear the recording several times before completing the handout.

Discuss the responses on the handout. Have students verbalize how Grieg incorporated both unity and variety into his composition.

• • • CALL CHART • • •

"In the Hall of the Mountain King"

Directions: Circle the correct responses.

Introduction: yes   no

Melody/theme: keeps changing   always the same
one theme keeps returning after a different theme is played

Tempo: always fast   always slow   increasingly faster
usually fast with some slower parts

Timbre: progression from a few to many instruments   always full orchestra
different solo instruments keep alternating

Dynamics: increases from soft to loud   always soft   always loud

Melody/range of the theme: progresses from low to high   mostly low   mostly high

Coda: yes   no

Music: *Toccata for Percussion*, Movement 3, by Carlos Chávez

Focus: Every musical instrument has its own distinctive quality or color by which it can be identified. This quality of sound is called *timbre*.

Objective: By the end of the listening activity, students will be able to characterize, through the use of adjectives, the distinctive quality of each instrument heard on the Chávez recording.

Before music class, record the voices of several students. During music class, play the recording and ask students to identify each person speaking. Have students explain how they knew who was speaking on the tape by describing the "color" or "quality" of each voice heard. Identify the color or quality of a sound as *timbre*.

Review the four families of orchestral instruments: strings, brass, woodwinds, and percussion. Explain that each family has its own distinctive quality or color, and that within each family, the individual instruments can also be distinguished one from another because each has its own distinctive quality or timbre.

Ask students to close their eyes. Compare instrumental timbres by playing a variety of percussion instruments—drum, claves, maracas, triangle—and asking students to identify each by the quality of its sound.

Give each student a call chart for *Toccata for Percussion*. Play the recording and call each number as its contents occur in the music. Provide pictures of any unknown instruments heard on the recording. Elicit adjectives from the students that will characterize the quality of each instrument heard. Play the recording again.

On another day, students can study the overall form of the composition, comparing the beginning and ending (nos. 1–6 and 12–16) and describing the middle section.

• • • CALL CHART • • •

Toccata for Percussion, Mvt. 3

1. Timpani alone

2. Snare drum added to timpani

3. Tom-toms enter

4. Claves added

5. Claves and timpani together

6. Timpani alone

7. Snare drum added with tom-toms and chimes

8. Maracas lead, with timpani and snare drum; timpani drops out

9. Chimes, with maracas, timpani, and snare drum

10. Timpani leads, with tom-toms, snare drum, and claves

11. Timpani, with cymbals, tom-toms, and snare drum

12. Timpani alone

13. Snare drum added to timpani

14. Tom-toms enter

15. Claves added

16. Timpani alone to end

Music: "Danse Macabre" by Camille Saint-Saëns

Focus: Sometimes the composer will provide a story or "program" to use in interpreting his music. When this occurs, the composition is called *program music.*

Objective: By the end of the listening activity, students will be able to follow the call chart and hear each event occurring in "Danse Macabre" as the composer portrays it in his "program."

Provide an explanation of program music as a creation of nineteenth-century composers. Prepare for the hearing of "Danse Macabre" by discussing the images associated with Halloween, such as skeletons dancing and tombstones in graveyards. Have students decide what instruments might be used to play themes associated with "death" and "skeletons dancing."

Distribute a copy of the "Danse Macabre" call chart shown on page 324 to each student. Play the themes and have students sing them in a neutral tone until they become familiar with them. Play the recording and ask students to follow each event as the teacher calls the numbers on the chart.

When the recording is finished, talk about what was heard in relation to the discussion preceding the use of the call chart. Were students' choices of instruments realized in the composition? Replay the recording and follow the call chart a second time.

On another day, ask students to listen to "Danse Macabre" without following the program. Discuss the possibility of the music being heard "for itself," apart from any program added to it.

Other examples of program music that can be incorporated into listening activities include:

Program Music	Composer
1. "Sorcerer's Apprentice"	Dukas
2. "Till Eulenspiegel"	Richard Strauss
3. "Don Juan"	Richard Strauss
4. "Peter and the Wolf"	Prokofiev
5. "Billy the Kid"	Copland
6. "Peer Gynt suites"	Grieg
7. "An American in Paris"	Gershwin
8. "The Moldau"	Smetana
9. "Les Préludes"	Liszt
10. "Arlésienne suites"	Bizet
11. "Pelléas et Mélisande"	Debussy
12. "Symphonie Fantastique"	Berlioz

In addition to the use of call charts, teachers can involve students in other activities to enhance their listening skills. These activities include (a) charting a composition using abstract symbols, (b) dramatizing program music using shadow boxes, and (c) identifying a composition's musical characteristics from choices listed on a check sheet. Active involvement should characterize each activity.

Charting with Abstract Symbols

Music: "Ballet of the Unhatched Chicks" from *Pictures at an Exhibition* by Modest Mussorgsky

Focus: Duration, musical line, tempo, and dynamics can be indicated using means other than standard notation.

Objective: By the end of the activity, each student will have charted a musical composition using abstract symbols.

"Danse Macabre"

1. Harp begins the composition by striking the "bewitching" hour of midnight.

2. Death tunes his fiddle.

3. Skeletons begin to dance.

4. Their dance theme is played first by the flute,

Theme 1:

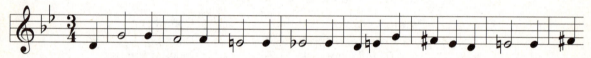

5. Then by the violins.

6. Solo violin (DEATH!) plays a lyrical theme as more skeleton dancers join in the midnight revel.

Theme 2:

7. Dancing becomes wilder as these two themes are thrown about in the orchestra.

8. Building to a loud peak, the sound suddenly softens as the woodwinds and harp play the "Dies Irae," a Latin hymn for the dead. The rhythm of this hymn has been changed by the insertion of quarter rests and the shifting of the accent from where it originally occurred in the hymn.

Theme 3:

9. The third theme is played again by the trumpet and pizzicato violins.

10. A new setting of the second theme is played by solo violin and harp.

11. Rapid chromatic scale passages in the strings represent the wind blowing through the trees.

12. Different themes, including the three above, intertwine in an increasingly agitated manner, building to a climax that is suddenly interrupted by the crowing of the cock, heard in the oboe.

13. The revel comes to an end with the dawn of a new day.

14. Death plays his final notes, and the spirits evaporate into the atmosphere.

Review the processes used to chart the Orff or Villa-Lobos compositions. Discuss different, abstract ways to represent musical line, duration, and increases or decreases in tempi and dynamics. Play "Ballet of the Unhatched Chicks" and have students listen for the form of the piece (Introduction AABA). Once the form is identified, give students the handout shown below on which to place their abstract representations. Except for the short introduction, every line on the chart represents eight measures in 2/4 meter.

● ● ● SYMBOL CHART ● ● ●

"Ballet of the Unhatched Chicks"

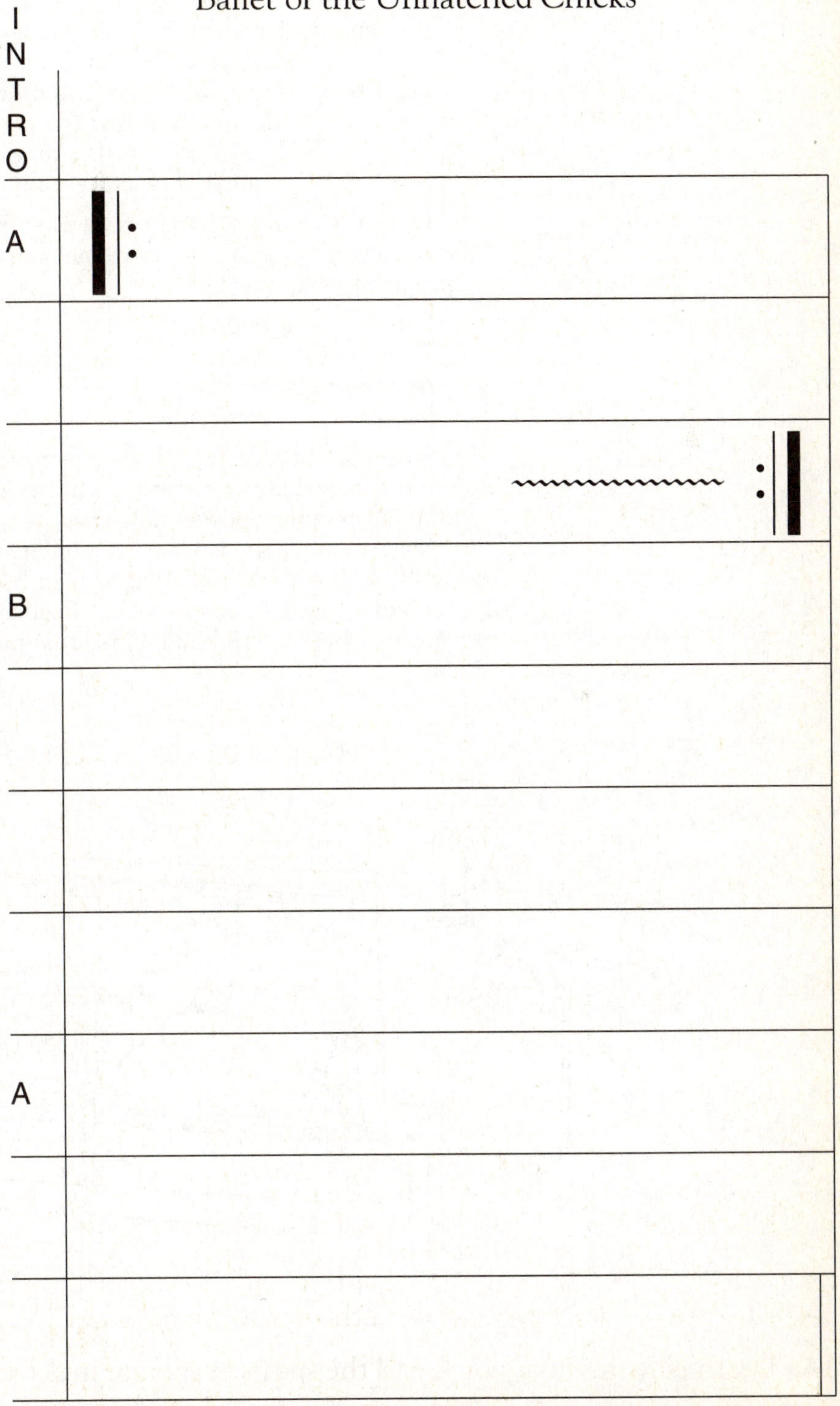

When students have finished charting the composition, they can review their charts with the teacher, choose the best one, or combine parts from different charts. The final choices of abstract representations should be drawn on a long piece of paper (rolls of brown packaging paper work well). The teacher can then attach the paper to the wall, at eye level for a small child, and use the chart with children in the lower grades. Kindergarten and first-grade children can watch the chart as they listen to the composition and simultaneously create movements to represent what is happening in the music.

Shadow Box Dramatizations

Music: *Peter and the Wolf* by Sergei Prokofiev
Focus: Different instruments playing designated melodies can represent a specific animal or person.
Objectives: By the end of the listening activity, students will be able to identify the sound of a flute, oboe, bass clarinet, bassoon, French horn, kettledrums, bass drum, and strings within the context of program music.

Prepare students for their first listening of *Peter and the Wolf* by showing them a picture of each solo instrument in the music and identifying whom the instrument represents:

flute:	bird	French horn:	wolf
oboe:	duck	kettledrums:	hunters
bass clarinet:	cat	bass drum:	
bassoon:	grandfather	violins:	Peter

Give each of several students a puppet on a stick, representing each character in the story. Play the recording, and as each character appears, have the child with the appropriate puppet hold it up.

Make a simple shadow box. A taut bed sheet on a frame or fabric attached to a cardboard box works well. Place a light behind the sheet.

Scenery can be placed on the sheet if desired. Play the recording; as each character is heard, the child holding that puppet parades it behind the sheet.

SHADOW BOXES AND PUPPETS

Peter and the Wolf

WRITTEN AND PERFORMANCE-RELATED ASSESSMENTS THROUGH COOPERATIVE LEARNING ACTIVITIES: LISTENING

1. Give students an opportunity to develop a call chart of their own. Have them bring to school a piece that they consider to be good popular music, with enough variety that it will lend itself to a call chart. After reviewing the possibilities, the teacher can choose one song for charting. Play the song so that the students become familiar with it. Divide the class into small groups. Have each group develop its own call chart, including items in specific categories, such as melody, rhythm, form, and dynamics.
2. Rather than have each student create an abstract symbol chart for a composition such as "Ballet of the Unhatched Chicks," let the members of the groups work on the chart together.
3. Play a piece of program music, such as "The Sorcerer's Apprentice," until students are familiar with it. Have each group work on a narrative for the music. The teacher can provide the puppets, or students can make their own in art class. When narrations are completed and refined, assign each group to a particular grade; that is, Mrs. Brown's first grade, Mr. Sanchez's first grade, and so on. Each group performs its narration and puppet play for its assigned grade.

To children, movement can be one of the most natural vessels for musical expression. Children are born into this world as kinesthetic and tactile learners. They begin to discover their environment through touch and movement. While at play, they climb, hop, toss balls, chase one another, and take part in organized singing games that involve rhythmically complex hand clapping and movement of the entire body.

With carefully designed movement activities in the classroom, children can become more aware of how they can use their bodies to express a variety of musical concepts and feelings. In addition, they will find that their musical heritage includes a wide variety of music in which movement plays an integral part.

Emile Jaques-Dalcroze (1865–1950), a Swiss music theory instructor, was a pioneer in using movement to attain musical goals. Jaques-Dalcroze is credited with encouraging musicians and teachers to include movement as an integral part of the development of musicianship in students. His approach contributes to self-understanding by helping students become aware of and develop the expressive possibilities of their bodies. As part of his approach, a vast range of feeling is recognized and cultivated through the use of creatively designed movement activities.

Dalcroze realized that people interpret what they hear in different ways; as a result, the movements of each student express individual interpretations. In this chapter, a focus on internalizing the basic music concepts of rhythm, melody, harmony, dynamics, and form is brought to fruition through movement improvisation, singing games, and folk dance, using elements of Jaques-Dalcroze's eurhythmics as a basic foundation.

PREPARING FOR MOVEMENT ACTIVITIES

The Movement Environment

Movement activities should take place in an area that is free of obstacles that might cause harm or inhibit children's freedom. If possible, desks and chairs should be pushed to the side or against the walls of the classroom so that an open space is available. A clean floor should be free of splinters or rough areas that might be damaging to children's feet, hands, arms, and other body parts. If available, a carpeted room should be used.

Dressing for Movement

Because of the many and varied experiences that children encounter during the school day, some administrators and classroom teachers recommend that children dress casually, in loose-fitting sweatsuits or jeans and sneakers. This style of dress works well when doing movement activities. Teachers may want to inform parents ahead of time that their children will be engaging in movement activities on a regular basis.

Individual Spaces

Each child should be assigned a personal space for movement activities. Classroom rules must be established and enforced by the teacher to avoid bumping, hitting, or other bodily contact that could cause problems.

BEGINNING MOVEMENT ACTIVITIES

Initial experiences in movement should be approached in a relaxed and spontaneous manner. Children should be encouraged and guided by a creative and uninhibited teacher. It is important that the teacher clearly establish defined goals and objectives, such as those listed below, so that some direction and continuity take place in the movement program. Through movement children can:

1. develop and stimulate their imagination and creative gifts
2. discover and understand musical learnings involving melody, rhythm, form, harmony, texture, tempo, and dynamics
3. realize that different styles of music call forth different physical responses
4. realize a common vocabulary that can be transferred from one style of dance to another, regardless of the culture or time period in which the dance originated
5. demonstrate an understanding of improvisation as a major musical tool for expressive response
6. create interpretive accompaniments for listening activities
7. discover how the various parts of the body can be used to create images, feelings, and moods
8. strengthen coordination of gross and fine motor skills
9. come to a greater understanding and awareness of balance, spatial relationships, and their own self-image

Children at different age levels and in different environments perceive environmental phenomena in different ways. Teachers should take into consideration the environment as reflected through the eyes, the sensitivities, the perceptions, and the understandings of the children involved. For example, younger children will truly imagine they are in a bakery as they say and move their fingers to "Five Brown Buns."

• • • "FIVE BROWN BUNS" • • •

Chant:

Five Brown Buns in a Bakery Shop	(Hold up 5 fingers.)
Five Brown Buns with Sugar on the Top	(With other hand "shake" sugar onto buns.)
Along Came a Man with a Penny in His Hand,	(Pointer finger comes from behind back, looks at "buns.")
Took One Bun and away he ran.	(Pointer finger "runs" back to back.)
Four Brown Buns	Repeat same actions
Three Brown Buns	" " "
Two Brown Buns	
One Brown Bun	
***With real emotion and crying!	
No Brown Buns	

Note: Say the last verse slowly as you boo-hoo; then, when it says "and away he ran," speed up.

Children continue to be intrigued with the movement of animals, of clouds, of trees blowing in the breeze. They show interest in the flying of birds and the hopping of grasshoppers and rabbits. In developing creative movement activities for their class, teachers should begin with these interests so that their students' initial movement experiences are natural and enjoyable. The following list provides simple, beginning images to which children can easily relate and, with guidance, transfer to movement.

Images of Childhood

a bird flying through the sky
a child skating on ice
a soldier marching
wind blowing
horses galloping
frogs hopping
a train engine running along the track
throwing a ball
walking like an elephant
rocking a baby
jumping over a puddle of water
a flower growing
batting a ball
blowing up a balloon
stirring food
chopping wood
walking on hot coals
directing a symphony
digging a hole
saying good-bye and hello
sawing wood
hammering nails
knocking on a door

After students have demonstrated their abilities to comfortably reflect on and reenact some of the above childhood images, the teacher can have them string responses of images together into patterns to create stories that are communicated through movement. "The Circus" provides an example of how images can be joined to tell a story. These images are italicized to highlight places where creative movement might occur.

THE CIRCUS

The children were *sound asleep*. One by one *they awoke*. They *stretched their arms and their legs* in preparation for a very active school day. As they *dressed themselves*, making sure to *wash their face, brush their teeth, and comb their hair*, they *shook in excitement*, because this was the day they were to go on a field trip to the circus. After *quickly eating a big bowl of cereal* with bananas and *drinking a glass of cold milk*, they *slipped off to school*. The stairs that led to the second floor classroom *were climbed with ease* this morning; promptness in getting to class was essential.

As the children *sat in their seats*, the teacher called each of their names. This was a signal for them *to line up at the door*. *Down the two flights of stairs* they went and *onto a big yellow school bus*, which waited to take them to the circus. Soon the bus was on its way. How bumpy the road was! It *shook the children forward*. It *shook them backward*. It *shook them up*, and it *shook them back down again*. Finally, they arrived at the circus.

Excitement was everywhere as the *ringmaster appeared on a podium* to announce the day's events. *Roller skaters* from the Land of Derby led the list of events. They were followed by the *leap frogs* from the Land of the Toads. An *elephant* from the jungle *stepped slowly* on stage as a group of mice from the Land of Cheese *scampered nervously* through the crowds. *How exciting* it all was! When the last event was finished, the children knew it was time to leave. What a wonderful day it had been.

Children should be asked to form images or pretend to be only those things that they have experienced previously. Because of limited knowledge or exposure, it is difficult for many students to mimic successfully the movement of some animals or images. Consequently, the teacher should include live presentations, discussions, pictures, or creative descriptions of unfamiliar images that will be recreated through movement. For example, before a teacher directs a group of students to move like unfamiliar zoo animals, it would be advisable for students to watch a video of zoo animals or to visit a zoo and observe the movements of these selected animals. The field experience should be followed by an in-class discussion of what was seen, such as:

1. Name an animal that you saw at the zoo.
2. Describe the animal. What color was it?
3. Was it large or small?
4. Was the animal heavy or light in weight?
5. Did the animal have four legs, two legs, wings?
6. Did the animal move fast or slowly?
7. Can you move like the animal moved?

In brief, the teacher should present to children a logical sequence of questions and experiences that will help them become comfortable with the task of creating through movement. After children have had ample opportunities to imitate the movements of phenomena contained within a familiar environment, the teacher can begin to help them understand basic musical elements through movement activities. Skills and vocabulary unique to the area of movement can also be developed.

CATEGORIES OF MOVEMENT

Many different movements can easily be observed by simply watching children at play. Walking, jumping, running, walking on tiptoe, hopping, galloping, bending, sliding, twirling, creeping, and crawling are examples of movements that children engage in while at play. All of these movements can be put into one of two categories: locomotor movements and nonlocomotor movements.

Locomotor Movements

Locomotor movements occur when children move from one place to another. Examples of locomotor movements include walking, jumping, running, jogging, hopping, and leaping.

Galloping and skipping are examples of combinations of two locomotor movements. Galloping, for example, combines the movements of walking and leaping. Skipping is based on a combination of walking and hopping.

Nonlocomotor Movements

Nonlocomotor movements include movements performed from a stationary position of the body. Twisting, bending, stretching, and curling are examples.

Students should be guided by the teacher to explore both locomotor and nonlocomotor movements. Activities such as the "apple orchard experience" can be used to reinforce children's knowledge of these categories. Have children pretend they are in an apple orchard. They should be directed to:

1. reach as high as possible to pick an apple from the tree
2. bend over to pick up several apples that have fallen to the ground

3. twist their body around to pick up apples that have fallen on the ground around them

4. turn around and toss an apple to a friend

5. walk, run, or skip back home

MOVEMENT AND SPACE

Space surrounds the body on all sides. Every movement in which a child engages takes place in that space. Opportunities to explore and experience the surrounding space help children grow in perceptual understanding and self-awareness. Children should participate in movement activities that require them to (a) place themselves in specific locations, (b) become familiar with the size and availability of the space around them, and (c) understand the possibilities for moving in that space. Several options are available when determining the directions in which children may move in space. They may move forward, backward, up or down, side to side, and diagonally. They may turn, move inward or outward, or move over or under. An activity that reinforces movement in different directions might involve the following:

Have students walk to the steady beat of the drum. During the activity, the teacher could scratch or rub the drum to signal to the children that they are to change direction. If students were walking forward, a change in sound produced by scratching the rim of the drum would be a signal for them to walk backward or sideways. Thus, listening and following directions become an integral part of the movement activity.

In addition to choosing a variety of directions, children should also choose body levels. There are three basic levels to explore: high, medium, and low. Guide students through the Melodic Direction Exercise as a beginning activity for understanding the direction of their own body parts.

• • • MELODIC DIRECTION EXERCISE • • •

8	Where my hair grows	8	On my head is
7	On my head	7	Freddie Flea
6	Past my nose	6	Now he's climbing
5	Past my tummy	5	Down on me
4	Up on me	4	Past my tummy
3	Now he's climbing	3	Past my knee
2	Freddie Flea	2	On the ground
1	On the ground is	1	"Take that you flea!"

Other activities that will reinforce a student's awareness of body levels include having the children bend their knees completely, causing the entire body to lower itself. This is an example of a low body activity.

Crawling is also a good low-level activity. Moving while lying flat on the floor is, of course, the lowest level possible. A middle-level activity can be achieved by moving in a relatively upright position with the arms no higher than shoulder level. A high-level activity involves the extension of the limbs as far as they can reach into the space above the mover. Standing on tiptoe and pretending to reach for the stars is an example of a higher-level activity. The game "statues" can be used to reinforce awareness of body levels. The teacher directs the children to walk, run, skip, or gallop to a rhyme or song they are chanting or singing. Recordings can also be used to accompany the movement activity. When a signal is given, or when the music stops, the children should "freeze" in place.* Children should be encouraged to vary the levels at which they freeze. The rhyme can be chanted while children are playing the statue game:

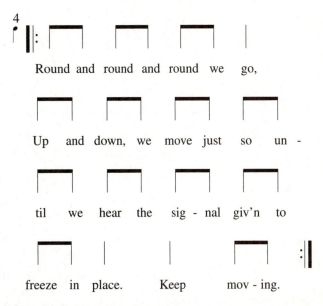

Round and round and round we go,

Up and down, we move just so un -

til we hear the sig - nal giv'n to

freeze in place. Keep mov - ing.

*The freeze signal can be given at any time during the chanting of the rhyme.

Once children have explored the major movement directions and the levels that might accompany those directions, the teacher should direct them in the different ways they can travel from one point to another using straight or curved pathways. Examples of these pathways are represented in the diagram.

Straight Pathways of Movement   **Curved Pathways of Movement**

Straight lines and angles are the two movement possibilities when following straight paths. When following curved paths, the use of semicircles, full circles, and other twisted configurations can assist in the development of creative designs or patterns that ultimately become a larger form or whole. Ask children to form groups and create different designs or shapes, such as those suggested here.

Straight Lines	Curved Lines	Combinations
square	#8	ice cream cone
rectangle	flower top	#2
triangle	#6	#5
#7	#3	pie
#1	rainbow	umbrella
#4	mushroom cap	

MOVEMENT AND IMPROVISATION

Children should be challenged to create movements that are void of metered pulse. This type of natural improvisation is recommended for initial experiences in movement. The poem "Me" provides an opportunity for students to improvise through movement. After students are comfortable with the sequence of movements, rhythm instruments or other sound effects can be added to enhance the overall effect of the dramatization.

Me
by René Boyer

I'm such a tiny little guy
Who loves to sing and dance.
I whirl around into the air
Like horses, I can prance.

Although my hands are tiny
They can do so many things
Like color in my favorite book
And pick the flowers in spring.

I love to spin in circles
Get dizzy and fall down
My arms, my feet, my legs and hands
Lay twisted all around.

I love to kick and jump up high
It makes me feel so free.
Although I'm small, my voice and all,
I am so glad I'm me.

Source: *Walking in the Light of Freedom*, Vol. 3
Author: René Boyer
Published by Hal Leonard ISBN 0-634-04650-0

MOVEMENT AND DYNAMICS

Many different levels of intensity are involved in every movement. Levels of intensity depend on three major factors: weight, muscular tension, and the inner intensity of movement. Combinations of these three factors can result in the expression of a wide spectrum of dynamic levels. Soft, hard, delicate, strong, light, heavy, angry, silent, and loud are a few examples of adjectives that can, with the use of appropriate weight, muscular tension, and inner intensity, be communicated through movement. Children should be given opportunities to develop a body sensitive to dynamic changes. To accomplish this, ask children to demonstrate, through movement, their responses to such questions as:

1. If you were a feather floating down from the sky, how would you move?
2. If you were an angry giant, how would you react?
3. Can you shout without making a sound?
4. Can you be a dancer on top of a music box?
5. How can you show the silence before a storm?

Provide students with many creative stories that they can act out through silent movement. Direct them to pay special attention to the dynamics of the movements as they reflect the actions in the story.

CIRCLE GAMES

Children's movement experiences should include circle games, which add variety to the movement program at the elementary level. In fact, during the primary years, the circle game serves not only as a setting in which children can express themselves, but also reinforces the development of specific learnings and helps them acquire self-management skills. Circle games, and their counterpart, folk dance, also help students fulfill the ninth Content Standard, "Understanding music in relation to history and culture." Clearly, the introduction of folk dance allows students the opportunity to explore, in a nonthreatening way, diversity in musical lifestyles that exist throughout our global society. The following examples are representative of only a few of the many circle games commonly used at the primary level.

Looby Loo

For the song "Looby Loo," act out movements as specified by the words in the text of the song. During the chorus, the children skip around the circle hand in hand.

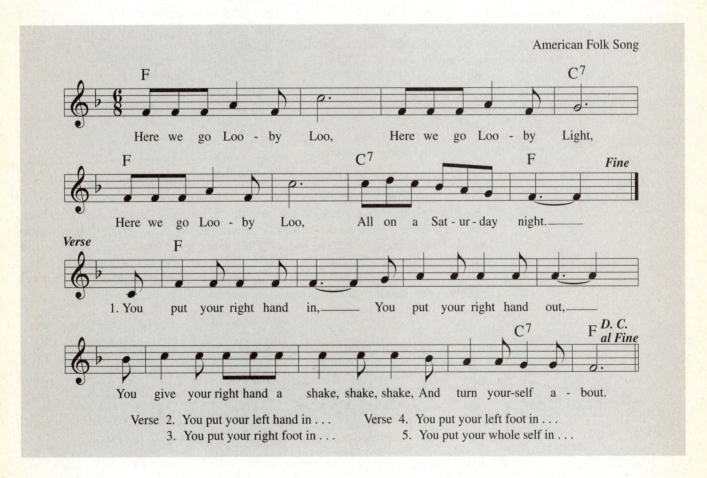

American Folk Song

Here we go Loo - by Loo, Here we go Loo - by Light,
Here we go Loo - by Loo, All on a Sat - ur - day night.

Verse
1. You put your right hand in,___ You put your right hand out,___
You give your right hand a shake, shake, shake, And turn your-self a - bout.

Verse 2. You put your left hand in . . .　　Verse 4. You put your left foot in . . .
3. You put your right foot in . . .　　　　5. You put your whole self in . . .

Mulberry Bush

Children move hand in hand around the circle while singing the chorus of "Mulberry Bush." During each verse, children must stop and demonstrate, through pantomime, the chores designated.

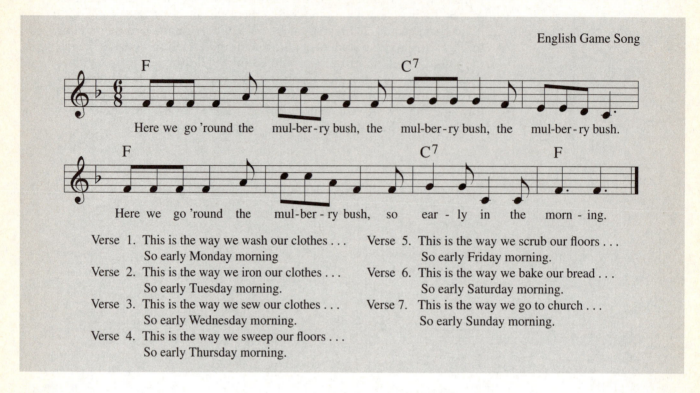

English Game Song

Here we go 'round the mul-ber-ry bush, the mul-ber-ry bush, the mul-ber-ry bush.

Here we go 'round the mul-ber-ry bush, so ear-ly in the morn-ing.

Verse 1. This is the way we wash our clothes . . .
So early Monday morning

Verse 2. This is the way we iron our clothes . . .
So early Tuesday morning.

Verse 3. This is the way we sew our clothes . . .
So early Wednesday morning.

Verse 4. This is the way we sweep our floors . . .
So early Thursday morning.

Verse 5. This is the way we scrub our floors . . .
So early Friday morning.

Verse 6. This is the way we bake our bread . . .
So early Saturday morning.

Verse 7. This is the way we go to church . . .
So early Sunday morning.

Circle 'Round the Zero

During the game "Circle 'Round the Zero," children stand still in a circle while one child walks or skips around the outside of the circle, stopping back to back behind a second child at the words, "Find your lovin' zero." Beginning with the words, "Back, back, zero," the two children bump backs and then turn sideways and bump hips. Next, they face one another and pat hands together on the words, "Front, front, zero." Finally, they tap each other's shoulders. The second child now proceeds to seek out a new partner and the game continues.

American Street Song

Cir-cle 'round the ze-ro, Find your lov-in' ze-ro, Back, back, ze-ro,

Side, side, ze-ro, Front, front, ze-ro, Tap your lov-in' ze-ro.

Circle games can also be used with older children. Stone-passing games such as "Al Citron" are common among the music of many nationalities. "Draw Me a Bucket of Water" has a number of variations; the version used here was collected by Bessie Smith Jones.

Al Citron

All children are seated in a circle on the floor. Each child has a rock or some other object (sponge, shoe, block) to pass to the person on the right.

Latin American Stone-Passing Game

Al - ci - tron de un fan - dan - go, san - go, san - go, sa - ba - ré. Sa - ba - ré de la ron - de - la con su tri - ki, tri - ki trón.

Note: Most of the words are nonsense Spanish words.

Movement

1. All sing the song "Al Citron."
2. Repeat the song and pat lap to the steady beat.
3. First, practice the movement without the rock. Beginning in front of your own body, pretend you are picking up a rock and passing it to the person on your right. If all goes well, there should be another rock in front of you, passed there by the person on your left. Pick up the rock and pass it to your right. Rocks should be picked up on the last beat and passed on the first beat of each measure.
4. When the children are successfully picking up and passing the rocks together on each beat, they can repeat the movements using a real rock.
5. On the measure with "triki, triki, trón," the movements change. The rock is tapped to the right but not released; then it is tapped to the left and back to the right where it is released on "trón":

triki	triki	trón
right	left	right and release

6. To heighten the enjoyment, the song can be sung faster and faster for each repetition.

Draw Me a Bucket of Water

Begin by having children stand in groups of four in a square, each holding hands with their opposite partner. Players 1 and 2 (opposite partners) should hold hands under those of players 3 and 4.

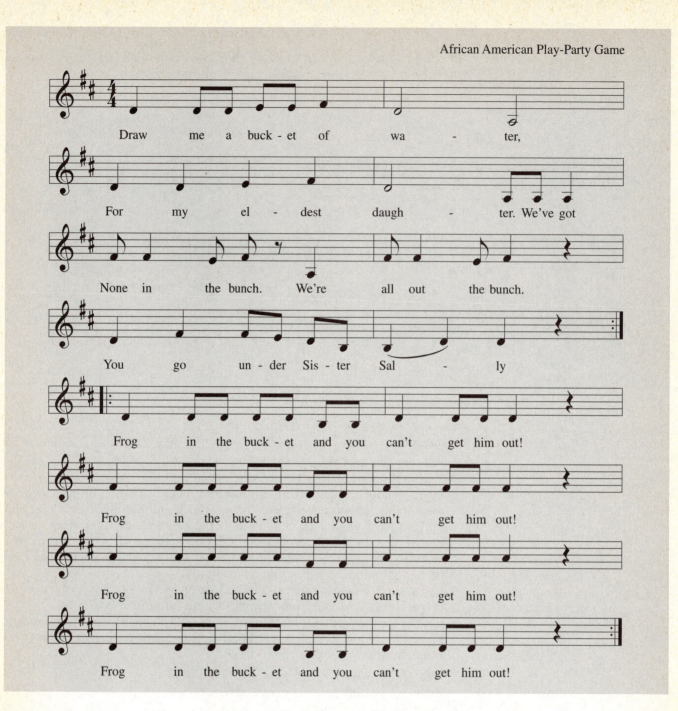

Draw me a bucket of wa - ter,
For my el - dest daugh - ter. We've got
None in the bunch. We're all out the bunch.
You go un - der Sis - ter Sal - ly
Frog in the buck - et and you can't get him out!
Frog in the buck - et and you can't get him out!
Frog in the buck - et and you can't get him out!
Frog in the buck - et and you can't get him out!

Movement

1. Phrases 1 through 3: with hands joined, partners "pull the rope" back and forth, like a seesaw, to the beat.
2. Phrase 4: On the words "You go under Sister Sally," child no. 1 goes under the arms of players nos. 3 and 4, toward the center of the circle. (Be sure that the children do not let go of hands during this activity.) Repeat three more times until children nos. 2, 3, and 4 are also in the center, all hands still joined.
3. Phrase 5 to the end: Children, as a group, jump up and down on the beat, still holding hands. For further joy and excitement, children can spin clockwise during the singing of these phrases.

Little Johnny Brown

"Little Johnny Brown" (Boys) "Little Nellie Brown" (Girls)

In preparing for this game song, boys and girls should form a ring. One person assumes the role of Johnny or Nellie Brown and takes his or her place in the center of the ring. The center player should hold a small comforter, child's blanket, or a large handkerchief and follow the directions of the song.

LITTLE JOHNNY BROWN

Game Song

Lit-tle John-ny Brown lay your com-fort down. Lit-tle John-ny Brown

lay your com-fort down. Fold one cor-ner John-ny Brown, Fold-

a-noth-er cor-ner John-ny Brown Fold a-noth-er cor-ner John-ny Brown Fold

a-noth-er corn-er John-ny Brown. Take it to a-noth-er John-ny Brown Take

it to a-noth-er John-ny Brown. Show them your stuff now John-ny Brown Show

them your stuff now John-ny Brown. Take it to a-noth-er John-ny Brown Take

Take it to a-noth-er John-ny Brown

a. Little Johnny Brown, lay your comfort down. (Lay comfort down.)
b. Little Johnny Brown, lay your comfort down. (Make sure it is straight and organized.)
c. Fold one corner, Johnny Brown. (Fold one corner of the comforter.)
d. Fold another corner, Johnny Brown. (Fold a second corner.)
e. Fold another corner, Johnny Brown. (Fold a third corner.)
f. Fold another corner, Johnny Brown. (Fold a fourth corner.)
g. Take it to another, Johnny Brown. (Pick it up and choose someone to take it to, but do not give it to him or her. Take your time with it. Play around with it and be creative.)
h. Take it to another, Johnny Brown. (Continue to be creative in front of the chosen one.)
i. Show them your stuff now, Johnny Brown. (Show a creative step or movement.)
j. Show them your stuff now, Johnny Brown. (Continue to show your stuff.)
k. Take it to another, Johnny Brown. (Give the comforter to the person you have selected.)
l. Take it to another, Johnny Brown. (The person you have chosen becomes the new center person.)
m. (Chosen one moves to the center and the game repeats.)

FOLK DANCES

Folk dances present special challenges for students in upper elementary grades. As children acquire more physical dexterity and intellectual ability, they are able to perform basic traditional dance steps present in much folk dance in the United States and elsewhere. During their upper elementary years, most children are able to understand the basic elements of movement, realize basic movement vocabulary, and physically implement sequences of well-designed movement patterns. Their skills in coordination, timing, sequencing of movements, and implementing the basic elements of music should be at a level that allows them to participate comfortably in folk dance.

Folk dance involves well-designed sequences of stepping movements. Therefore, before children can begin applying their previously learned skills in movement, they must become acquainted with steps and terminology characteristic of the specific dances they are to experience. For example, among the major types of dances associated with North American folk music are circle, line, and square dances. *Circle dances* can involve dancers in one large circle or in two concentric circles. The *line dance* usually consists of any number of couples who come together in two facing lines, while the *square dance* involves four couples. All three dances often involve a caller who "calls out" the steps and actions that the dancers are to use. To begin a dance, performers are usually in a predetermined position, known as *set formation*. Diagram I represents a typical set formation required for the square dance. Diagram II shows the set formation for line dances.

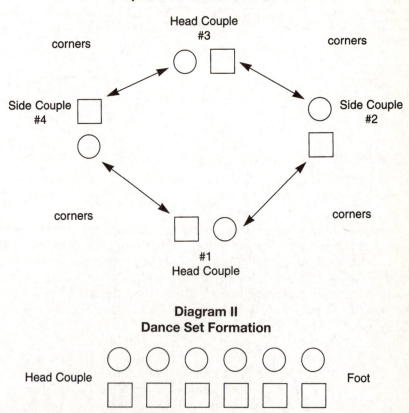

Diagram I
Square Dance Set Formation

Head Couple #3

corners   corners

Side Couple #4   Side Couple #2

corners   corners

#1
Head Couple

Diagram II
Dance Set Formation

Head Couple   Foot

Traditionally, partners in square dances consist of two individuals of opposite sex. However, in the elementary classroom, it is not necessary to pair boys with girls. Teachers can choose, instead, to have students count off in two's and then assign partners on a number basis. Tags of different colors or shapes could be assigned for students to wear to help in the identification of partners.

When introducing folk dance, the teacher should serve as the model. It is the teacher who must describe and demonstrate the designed steps. Although it is essential that the rote process take place in slow motion and be repeated to ensure success for the students, the teacher should be careful not to cause the learner to lose a sense of the "whole."

"Old Brass Wagon" and "Shake Them 'Simmons Down" are examples of **circle dances** that clearly suggest, through their texts, directions for dancers to follow. These dances, which are suitable for use in the second, third, and fourth grades, help provide a transition to the more complex dances performed by children in upper grades. If the children are expected to dance to a song that they have learned in class, it is essential that they know the song well before learning the dance steps.

OLD BRASS WAGON

American Dance Song

1. Cir-cle to the left, Old brass wag-on, Cir-cle to the left, Old brass wag-on,
Cir-cle to the left, Old brass wag-on, You're the one, my dar-ling.

2. Circle to the right . . .
3. Ev'rybody in . . .
4. Ev'rybody out . . .

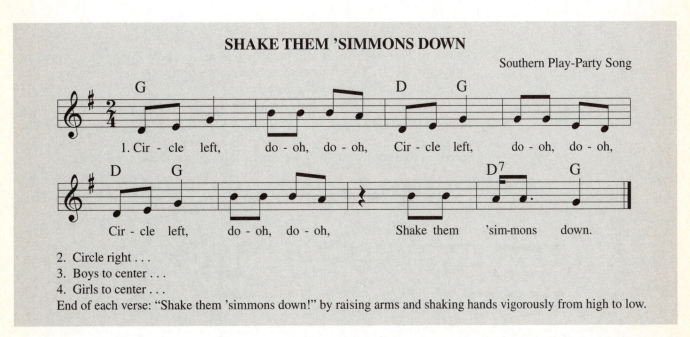

SHAKE THEM 'SIMMONS DOWN

Southern Play-Party Song

1. Cir-cle left, do-oh, do-oh, Cir-cle left, do-oh, do-oh,
Cir-cle left, do-oh, do-oh, Shake them 'sim-mons down.

2. Circle right . . .
3. Boys to center . . .
4. Girls to center . . .

End of each verse: "Shake them 'simmons down!" by raising arms and shaking hands vigorously from high to low.

The texts of "Achshav" and "Round and Round We Go" do not suggest the movements that will be used.

ACHSHAV

Hebrew Folk Dance

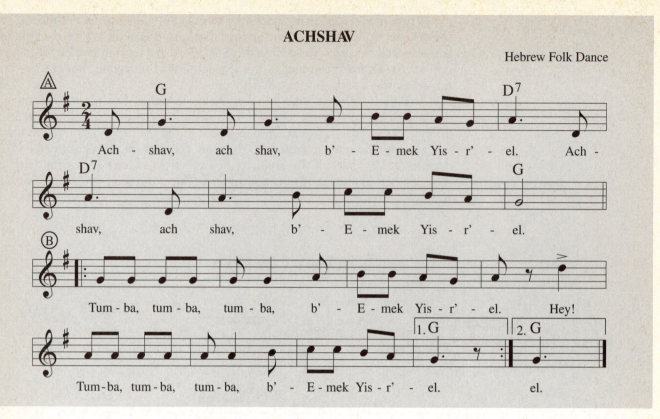

Ach - shav, ach shav, b' - E - mek Yis - r' - el. Ach -

shav, ach shav, b' - E - mek Yis - r' - el.

Tum - ba, tum - ba, tum - ba, b' - E - mek Yis - r' - el. Hey!

Tum - ba, tum - ba, tum - ba, b' - E - mek Yis - r' - el. el.

Movement instructions

Formation; circle (large enough for children to take eight steps to the center)

A section: Hold hands. With weight on the right foot, place the heel of the left foot forward. Hop, changing weight to left foot, with right foot forward. Do this hop-change movement in the following rhythm:

L = Left foot
R = Right foot

B section: Take eight small steps toward the center of the circle, lifting arms for an enthusiastic "Hey!" Lower arms and return to the circle formation by taking eight steps backward. (Repeat the B section.)

The true spirit of moving together can be found in the following folk dance, "Round and Round We Go." Have students form two to three different circles and sing and move to this song. Start the circles at different times in alternate directions to demonstrate how a round can be shown through movement.

ROUND AND ROUND WE GO

Überliedfest

Round and round we go, we hold each oth - er's hands, and

weave our lives in a cir - cle, The day has come, the dance has be - gun.

The following **line dances**, "Oh, Susanna," "A-Hunting We Will Go," and "Alabama Gal" can be used to reinforce beginning folk dance steps at the elementary level. Movements for "A-Hunting We Will Go" and "Alabama Gal" are similar. This allows for a nice variety in music once the directions are learned.

Oh, Susanna

Words	**Movement Directions**
I come from Alabama with my banjo on my knee,	Girls walk forward 4 steps Girls walk backward 4 steps
I'm going to Louisiana my true love for to see.	Boys walk forward 4 steps Boys walk backward 4 steps
It rained all night the day I left The weather it was dry.	Girls walk forward 4 steps Girls walk backward 4 steps
The sun so hot, I froze to death Susanna don't you cry.	Boys walk forward 4 steps Boys walk backward 4 steps

Chorus

Oh, Susanna, Oh, don't you cry for me,	Swing partners to the right 8 counts
I've come from Alabama with my banjo on my knee.	Swing partners to the left 8 counts

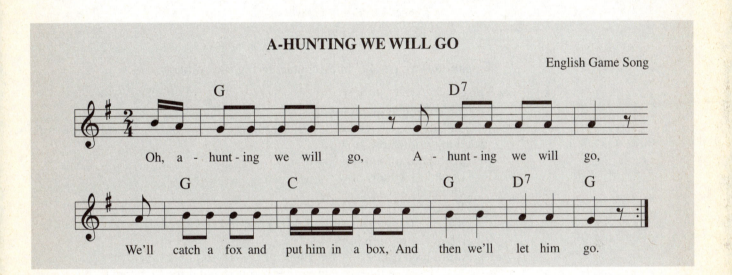

A-HUNTING WE WILL GO

English Game Song

Oh, a-hunt-ing we will go, A-hunt-ing we will go,
We'll catch a fox and put him in a box, And then we'll let him go.

Chorus

Repeat measures 1–8 using the words: Tra, la, la, la, la, la, . . .

Movements to the verse

Measures 1–4   Head couple moves to the front of the set. Head couple joins hands and skips or slides between the lines to the foot of the set.

Measures 5–8   Head couple returns.

Movements to the chorus

Measures 1–8   All face forward and join hands with a partner in skater's position, right hand joined over left. Head couple turns and leads the column to the foot of set. At the foot of set, head couple joins and raises both hands to form an arch. Second couple leads others under the arch, advancing to become the new head couple. Partners should remain on their original side in forming the arch and in passing under the arch.

Repeat the entire dance with each new head couple. The teacher should encourage children to create their own rhymes for line three, such as:

"catch a mouse and put him in a house"
"catch a cat and put him in a hat"
"catch a skunk and put him in a trunk"
"catch a fish and put him in a dish"

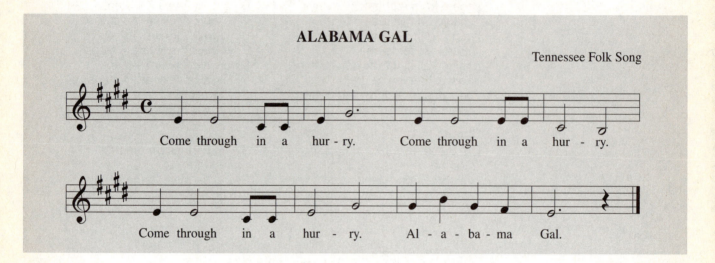

ALABAMA GAL

Tennessee Folk Song

Come through in a hur - ry. Come through in a hur - ry.

Come through in a hur - ry. Al - a - ba - ma Gal.

Formation: Two parallel lines, couples facing each other.

Verses:

1. Come through in a hurry . . .
   First couple sashays down to the bottom of the set and back again to the top.
2. I don't know how, how . . .
   Right hand turn around partner.
   I don't know how, how . . .
   Left hand turn around partner.
3. I'll show you how, how . . .
   First couple casts off and all follow behind. First couple makes a two-hand arch at the bottom of the set.
4. Ain't I rock candy . . . Alabama Gal
   Second couple meets their partner below the arching first couple, takes partner's hand, and goes under the arch and back to their place, becoming the new head couple. All couples follow.
5. Song repeats until all couples have had a turn being the head couple.

A popular **square dance** that children enjoy performing is "Red River Valley." Form a square made up of four couples, the girl on the boy's right in each couple. Specify one couple as the "head" couple. The couple to their right is the second couple; the couple directly across from the head couple is couple number three; the fourth couple is to the left of the head couple.

Verse 1

| Phrases 1–2 | Head couple walks over to the second couple; all join hands and circle four steps to the left, then four steps to the right. |
| Phrases 3–4 | Drop hands, hook elbows and swing opposite partner once around; return to partner and swing once around. |

Verse 2

Repeat actions of verse one, with couple 3.

Verse 3

Repeat actions of verse one with couple 4.

Verse 4

Head couple should be back in original position in the square. On the call "allemande left," the boy faces the girl to his left; they grasp left hands and circle once completely around until all persons are back facing their own partners.

Begin a "grand right and left": extend right hand to partner, pass him or her by and continue to the next person, extending left hand. Continue in this fashion, grasping first right, then left hand, weaving in and out until each person has returned to the original partner. Girls then reverse direction and all promenade back to their original place.

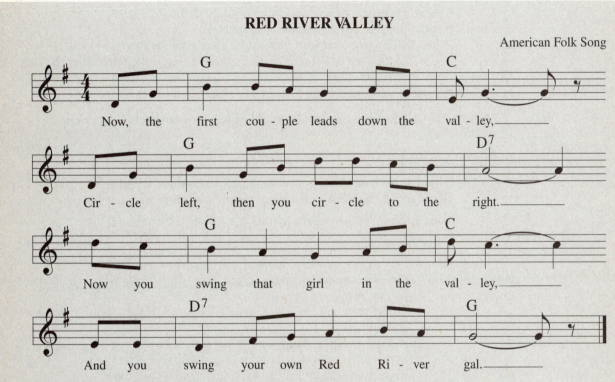

RED RIVER VALLEY

American Folk Song

Now, the first cou-ple leads down the val-ley,_____

Cir-cle left, then you cir-cle to the right._____

Now you swing that girl in the val-ley,_____

And you swing your own Red Ri-ver gal._____

Verse 2. Now you lead right on down the valley, (couple no. 1 dances with couple no. 3).
Circle left, then you circle to the right, etc.

3. Now you lead right on down the valley, (couple no. 1 dances with couple no. 4), etc.

4. Now it's allemande left to your corner,
And a right hand to your own.
And when you meet your partner,
Then you promenade her on home.

Popular Dances

There are a few dances that have become an integral part of the North American culture. Large groups at parties and celebrations, wedding receptions, and other social occasions usually perform them. Not only do children enjoy these family-oriented dances, but adults do also. One of the most famous dances is the *Electric Slide*. Any disco, country, or rhythm and blues recording that has a strong beat that does not move too fast usually accompanies this dance. Samples of music that one can use for this dance are accessible on YouTube. The steps are outlined below.

Electric Slide

Originally danced to a piece called "The Electric Boogie," the Electric Slide is a disco line dance that was created in the 1970s, but achieved even greater popularity in the late 1980s. Choreographer Marcia Griffiths commissioned Ric Silver to create this new dance. This dance is based on a traditional dance step called the *grape vine*, in which the dancer faces forward and walks to the side, crossing one leg over the other to move.

Formation: A group of people positioned side by side in a line, all facing the same direction

Directions:

- Perform three grapevine steps to the right for Steps 1 to 3 and touch the left foot next to the right foot while clapping on Step 4.
- Perform three grapevine steps to the left for Steps 5–7 and touch the right foot next to the left foot while clapping on Step 8.
- Take three steps backwards for Steps 9–12.
- Lift left knee up and lean forward for two beats for steps 13–14.
- On step 15, step backward on the right foot and to the left foot at the right heel for step 16, finishing with a clap.
- Jump to turn your body to the right and start all over again.

One seldom goes on a cruise without learning to do the Macarena.

Macarena

This Latino-based dance accompanied the song, "Los del Rio." The "Bayside Boys Mix" is the most well-known version of this song.

Formation: Lines with people standing side-by-side facing front

Directions:

Beat	Description of Movement
1	Using a swimming motion, put right arm straight out, in front of you, palm down
2	Using a swimming motion, put left arm straight out, in front of you, palm down
3	Right arm straight out, in front of you, turn palm up
4	Left arm straight out, in front of you, turn palm up
5	Right hand grasps inside of the left arm, at the elbow
6	Left hand grasps inside of the right arm, at the elbow
7	Right hand behind right back of neck
8	Left hand behind left back of neck
9	Right hand on left front part of thigh
10	Left hand on right front part of thigh
11	Right hand on right back part of thigh
12	Left hand on left back part of thigh
13	Swivel hips to the left
14	Swivel hips to the right
15	Swivel hips to the left
16	Clap and turn 90 degrees to the right

The Chicken Dance

The Chicken Dance is a tradition in Cincinnati, Ohio, where Oktoberfest is celebrated annually. This German dance song was composed by Werner Thomas in the 1970s, and was originally known as the Vogeltanz, Chicken Dance. The music to the Chicken Dance can be easily accessed on YouTube and can be purchased online.

Directions: Lines, circles, semi-circles

Section A

1. When the music begins, have students hold both hands out in front of their bodies and open and close them like a chicken beak four times during the first four beats of the music.

3. Make chicken wings with their arms by putting their thumbs in their armpits and flapping their wings four times like a chicken.
4. Place their arms and hands like the tail feathers of a chicken and wiggle downward toward the floor for four beats.
5. Clap four times during the next four beats of music while rising back up.
6. Repeat steps 1–5 four times.

Section B: After the fourth time of repeating motions in the A Section, clasp hands of children on either side and everyone moves in a circle.

8. Switch directions.
9. Repeat from the beginning until the end of the music.

WRITTEN AND PERFORMANCE-RELATED ASSESSMENTS THROUGH COOPERATIVE LEARNING ACTIVITIES: MOVEMENT

1. Animal Game: Ask each group to select an animal they have seen in the zoo or on TV. They should discuss among themselves all aspects of the animal's movements: the way the eyes move, the mouth, the nose, the neck, and the body. After a designated time, the first group begins "giving clues" to the other groups to help them guess what animal they are imitating. Group 1 should begin with eye movements, then mouth movements, and continue adding movements until their animal has been named. For every incorrect guess, a group loses 1 point; a group receives 3 points for guessing correctly. When group 1's animal has been identified, group 2 presents its animal, and so on until all groups have had a turn. The group with the highest score wins the game.
2. Distribute to each group a descriptive poem of interest to that age level. Ask students to read the poem carefully several times and then create movements that bring out the imagery in the poem.
3. A different short, descriptive story should be given to each group. Have the groups read through their stories and decide what movement they will use to portray the characters, events, and scenery. After a set time span, each group should present its story for the class's enjoyment.
4. Have small groups of students create a square dance to a song of their own choosing and perform it for the class.
5. Have students perform a popular dance on Friday to reward their progress throughout the school week.

CHAPTER 13 Lesson Planning

Planning musical experiences for children can be an exciting endeavor. A wide assortment of quality resources are available that will contribute to the preparation of interesting and enjoyable musical activities.

Because music is as important as any other subject in the elementary curriculum, it should be included in the daily schedule of every class. The younger the child, the more important it is to provide short lessons daily rather than one long weekly lesson.

While planning musical experiences, the teacher should take several factors into consideration:

1. the characteristics of the group
2. the learnings and skills that should be taught
3. how to teach these learnings and skills
4. how the teacher will know the lesson content was learned
5. the materials that will be needed to teach the content well

CHARACTERISTICS OF THE GROUP

Music materials and activities should center around the interests of the group; interests change from grade to grade and from school to school. Knowing how students relate to one another is important; the way a teacher prepares the class for partner activities may determine their success or failure. An awareness of students who don't work well together for small-group activities is also necessary. In addition, a teacher needs to be particularly sensitive to children who have special needs; with a little forethought and planning, for example, the teacher can provide satisfying activities that will make a child in a wheelchair feel he or she is a part of the group during locomotor activities. Perhaps the most prominent situation that needs the teacher's attention, however, is the problem of differences in levels of musical achievement within a group. The teacher must find ways to meet the needs of those who are behind in music learning while maintaining the interest and growth of those who are ready to progress to the next level.

WHAT SHALL I TEACH?

Goals and Objectives

By formulating goals and objectives, the classroom teacher will be able to provide learning activities that will contribute to musical growth for every child.

Goals. Goals are broad and concise statements indicating desired terminal outcomes. They are few in number and apply to all children in all grades. Usually, the goals of the music program for a school are predetermined for the teacher; they are expressed in the state music curriculum guide and in a school's philosophy. The music content standards of the National Standards, presented in Chapter 1, are the goals currently supported by most music education organizations.

General Objectives. General objectives are more specific than goals in designating desired musical growth over a year's time or month by month. They provide a clear sense of direction for the teacher and are usually expressed in behavioral terms; that is, in terms of what the student will be able to do. General objectives for the school year for grade one might read:

Students will improve their ability to:

a. sing, in tune, short songs with a range of a fourth from mi (3) to la (6).
b. perform accurately (sing, play, move) the steady beat of a song.
c. identify and perform ♩, ♫, and 𝄽 and combinations of these rhythms.
d. organize music into groups of two by correctly stepping or clapping the accented beat.
e. play and improvise simple rhythmic and melodic patterns on classroom instruments.
f. perform music in an expressive manner through the use of loud and soft, fast and slow, and legato and staccato.
g. identify and respond to repetition and contrast in simple music.

It is often helpful to divide lessons, skills, and song materials into monthly blocks so that a teacher can see at a glance the pace needed to present the required material. Generally, the first and last two weeks of school are review times when no new lessons are introduced. The following outline is one way to organize lessons month by month for grade one:

September

By the end of the month, children will improve their ability to:

Singing: sing phrases to match tones sung by the teacher
sing review songs from kindergarten:

Star Light, Star Bright	Rain, Rain
One Two, Tie My Shoe	Little Sally Walker
Quaker, Quaker	Where Is Thumbkin
Lucy Locket	Hop Old Squirrel

Moving: take part in activities related to games, finger plays, and other movements associated with their review songs

clap, patsch, step, and move in other ways to the beat of familiar songs and recordings

Playing: play simple rhythmic and melodic ostinati to familiar songs

Listening: identify extremes of loud and soft, fast and slow, high and low, and smooth and disconnected on recorded music or in songs sung by the teacher. These structural components can be reinforced through singing, moving, playing, and creating.

Creating: improvise, through expressive, interpretive movement, the sounds heard on recorded music

October

By the end of the month, children will improve their ability to:

Singing: sing greetings for matching pitches:

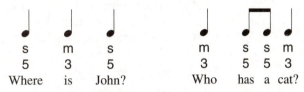

sing songs and phrases containing the minor 3rd as found in:
Star Light, Star Bright   Quaker, Quaker
One Two, Tie My Shoe   Rain, Rain

sing review songs:
Ring Around the Rosy
Other Songs

sing new songs:
Wee Willie Winkle   Mill Wheel
The Clock   Bounce High

Reading: identify the quarter note in various contexts
identify the minor third in various contexts

Writing: notate quarter notes on a felt board; practice drawing quarter notes on the board and with crayons on paper
notate so (5) and mi (3) on the felt board

Playing: keep steady quarter-note beat using rhythm instruments
perform so–mi on barred instruments
play simple rhythmic and melodic ostinati to familiar songs and to recorded music

Moving: move to quarter-note rhythm heard in songs and recordings
clap quarter notes as notated on visuals
perform actions and games to songs from kindergarten

Listening: identify extremes of loud and soft, fast and slow, high and low, and smooth and disconnected

Creating: same as in September

Specific Objectives. Specific objectives are precise, clear, and behavioral in nature. They are usually present in day-to-day lesson plans and provide the basis for evaluation of both the teaching and the learning processes. A few examples of specific behavioral objectives for a first grade lesson would be:

a. match the tones la–so–mi (6–5–3) in a variety of combinations after they are sung by the teacher
b. keep a steady beat while bouncing a ball to "One Two, Tie My Shoe"
c. identify silence occurring in a rhythmic pattern by opening the hands when the appropriate notation (𝄽) occurs
d. sing correctly the intervals of a second and a third (so–la or 5–6; mi–so or 3–5) when they appear in patterns on the board

Notice that the objective specifies the behavior that a teacher is to perceive so that she or he can evaluate both growth in the student and clarity of presentation.

If some children have difficulty in singing the la–so–mi charts, for example, this indicates that either the charts are too difficult and need to be revised (teacher-centered evaluation) or more practice is needed to ensure growth in learning (student-centered evaluation).

Daily Lesson Planning

Preparing daily lesson plans for growth in musical knowledge and skills presupposes that careful long-range planning (preparing goals and general objectives for the entire year) and short-range planning (month-by-month objectives) are already in place. Now the teacher must determine the content and procedures that will best accomplish the desired objectives.

Various formats can be used for planning a lesson. The following format has five important areas that will assist the teacher in preparing a thorough representation of what is to be taught:

1. behavioral objectives,
2. National Standards,
3. elements of music,
4. materials,
5. procedures, and
6. assessment.

(Adaptations for students with learning disabilities; Extensions [for gifted students], and Interdisciplinary Connections and extensions should be considered as optional, yet important parts to any effective plan.)

Lesson # _____		Date _____	Grade _____
Behavioral Objectives	**National Standards**	**Elements**	**Procedures**
Materials / Handouts Links Glossary (optional)			
Interdisciplinary Connections and Extensions			• Adaptations (for students with learning disabilities) • Extensions (for gifted students)
Assessment (Based on objectives)			

Behavioral Objectives. Behavioral objectives tell us exactly what students must do to realize the objective being taught. Examples of behavioral objectives were given above in the section "Specific Objectives."

National Standards. These standards, recommended by the Music Educators National Conference (MENC), encourage consistency in what is being taught in the music curriculum nationwide. When students move or transfer from one school to another, this consistency becomes of major importance to the student.

Elements of Music. In a balanced lesson, the teacher usually teaches content containing several musical elements from the following list:

a. rhythm
b. melody
c. timbre (tone quality)
d. dynamics
e. tempo
f. form
g. texture
h. harmony

The elements being taught should be clearly stated so that a teacher can see at a glance what element(s) needs to be addressed.

Materials. Names of songs to be included in the lesson should be indicated, with their page number and source. All too often, a teacher goes back to a particular lesson a year or so later and can't remember the sources for the songs used. Recordings, charts, flash cards, and other aids should be clearly indicated; this allows the teacher to quickly set up before the lesson begins. Needed equipment that is not part of the classroom's furnishings should also be noted.

Procedures. Step-by-step procedures should be carefully sequenced for maximum enjoyment and learning. They should contain diversified activities that continually call for student participation and should be well paced to maintain interest. Teachers must be able to move from one musical activity to the next and not spend too much or too little time on any one activity.

Skills. Every music lesson should contribute to the development of some degree of psychomotor, cognitive, and affective skills. These skills include the following:

Psychomotor Skills	Cognitive Skills	Affective Skills
moving	recalling	attending
listening	interpreting	responding
singing	applying	valuing
playing	analyzing	
reading	synthesizing	
writing	evaluating	
creating		

Students should be involved in extending their abilities in a variety of skills, but not all skills will be included in every lesson.

Assessment. If a means other than observation is to be used to assess a musical activity, this process should be clearly indicated in the plan. Usually, only student assessment procedures are recorded. It should be understood, however, that assessments are always a dual process; they indicate how well the child is progressing and how clearly the teacher is presenting the lesson.

The 30-minute plan for first grade, printed here, is one example of how all five parts of the daily lesson plan work together for musical growth.

| Lesson # _____ | Date _____ | Grade _____ |

National Standard: #1 (Singing with others)	Elements	Procedures

Behavioral Objectives

By the end of class, students will improve their ability to:

1. match pitches sung by the teacher	melody
2. sing the intervals of a second and a third accurately	melody
3. keep a steady beat when bouncing a ball, using body percussion and playing instruments	rhythm
4. identify changing rhythms through use of body percussion and notation cards	rhythm
5. identify silence occurring in a rhythmic pattern by opening hands and notation	rhythm
6. play a melodic ostinato on bells	harmony
7. identify the sounds of sticks, sleigh bells, and resonator bells	timbre

Materials

1. so-la-mi cards
2. "If You're Happy," p. 8, *Singing With Children*
3. "The Clock," p. 150, *Kodály Method*
4. "Little Sally Water," p. 214, *Kodály Context*
5. "Jig Jog," p. 67, *Music For Fun*
6. ball, rhythm cards, chart, sticks, E and G resonator bells, sleigh bells

Assessment

By observation

Procedures

Stand in a Circle
1. Sing greeting and have students respond:

so	la	so	so	mi
5	6	5	5	3
How	are	you	to-	day

Review la-so-mi (6-5-3) pitches with flash cards

2. Sing review song: "The Clock"
   a. pat and clap the beat while singing
   b. teacher in middle; bounce ball to each student on the beat while singing

Sit
3. Sing "The Clock" again, this time clapping the word rhythms while singing
   a. identify rhythms ♩ ♫ ♪
   b. perform patterns on chart incorporating these rhythms
   c. give individual packets containing cards with these symbols; clap patterns for children to notate using cards

4. Sing review song: "Jig Jog"
   a. give E and G resonator bells for A section
   b. middle section: sleigh bells
   c. rest of children play sticks on beat
   d. identify timbres by name

Stand
5. Begin learning new song: "Little Sally Water"
6. Sing review song: "If You're Happy"
   a. different children in middle of circle to perform new motion

HOW SHALL I TEACH?

Classroom teachers may choose to use an inductive approach to learning, a deductive approach, or a combination of the two. Whichever approach is used, teachers must remember that children learn best through active involvement in the learning process; activities should be child centered.

When using the *inductive approach* to learning, the teacher leads students through a sequence of activities from a part to the whole, from the specific to the general.

The *deductive approach* is just the reverse in process. The teacher begins with the general and leads children to the specific.

COOPERATIVE LEARNING

Cooperative learning is a teaching method that involves students with all levels of performance ability working together in small groups to achieve a common goal. In this setting, the same grade is usually earned by all students in the group. If individual grades are given, students are in competition for those grades. By eliminating grade competition, teachers have discovered that students work more rapidly, produce better results, and interact in a friendlier, more helpful manner than do groups where the highest grade goes to the one who contributes most to the project.

There are a number of different approaches to cooperative learning. One of the easiest to organize and the one favored for the activities in this book involves working in heterogeneous groups of three to five members on some assigned activity having specific objectives.

Assessment depends on the nature of the activity. The following are some possibilities:

1. Some worksheets, creative projects, listening activities: Each group hands in a single completed sheet and members of the group receive the same grade.
2. Performance skills (each student on the same instrument), flash cards, some worksheets: When the group feels that each member is ready, the teacher observes the individual performance of each student and grades each one separately.
3. Performance skills (each student on a different instrument): When the group feels it is ready, the entire group performs first for the teacher and then for the whole class. All members of a group receive the same grade.

Cooperative learning activities must be carefully organized. Students should understand that they are accountable for both their own learning and the learning of members in their group. Students must also realize that their conduct should not prevent any other group from accomplishing its activity objectives. Group leaders can be appointed who are responsible for keeping group members on task. Objectives, time constraints, and directions should be clearly and concisely indicated on each group's handout.

HOW WILL I KNOW THE STUDENT LEARNED IT?

Much assessment of a student's learning, particularly in the primary grades, is achieved through observation. The teacher listens and watches to determine whether a child can match pitches, keep a steady beat, sing so-mi, or move creatively to a recording.

One means of assessing students' musical achievement is the use of a *rubric* or guideline. Rubrics provide the needed characteristics on which a judgment can be made of a student's performance at each grade level. The students being assessed, in turn, have an understanding of how well they have performed the skill required or assimilated the information being taught. The following rubrics are general examples of how guidelines can be written for musical assessment. The numbers denote the level achieved.

Rubric for Assessing Written and Performance-Based Activities Related to Rhythm

3 Student adequately reads and notates rhythms in a variety of both old and new songs and speech pieces.

2 Student usually responds to rhythmic notation, but is unable to transfer this skill to new musical literature or activities.

1 Student reads and notates rhythms after multiple repeats of the same material.

0 Student does not read or notate rhythms.

Rubric for Assessing Written and Performance-Based Activities Related to Melody

3 Student adequately reads and then sings a variety of songs alone and with others.

2 Student recognizes melodic symbols, but is unable to transfer reading knowledge to new songs.

1 Student sings songs after many repetitions, with little knowledge of reading.

0 Student does not participate in singing.

Rubric for Assessing Written and Performance-Based Activities Related to Form

3 Student is able to adequately examine, analyze, and describe the form of a piece of music.

2 Student recognizes and is able to analyze the form of familiar musical literature, but is not able to analyze unfamiliar musical literature.

1 Student recognizes form in music, but is unable to analyze what it is.

0 Student cannot recognize or analyze form.

Rubric for Assessing Written and Performance-Based Activities Related to Harmony

3 Student sings in harmony.

2 Student sings in harmony as long as there is some support from others.

1 Student sings in harmony after much practice and support from others.

0 Student cannot sing in harmony.

Rubric for Assessing Written and Performance-Based Activities Related to Timbre

3　Student is able to identify names of classroom instruments and demonstrate how to play them.

2　Student recognizes some of the classroom instruments, but has difficulty in playing some of them.

1　Student is severely limited in recognizing classroom instruments and in ability to play them.

0　Student cannot recognize or play the classroom instruments.

Rubric for Assessing Written and Performance-Based Activities Related to Texture

3　Student is able to look at a score and listen to a musical piece and then describe its texture.

2　Student is able to look at a score and listen to a musical piece, but is not always able to analyze or describe its texture.

1　Student has difficulty in describing the musical texture of a piece.

0　Student is not able to recognize or describe the texture of a piece.

Rubric for Assessing Written and Performance-Based Activities Related to Expressive Elements

3　Student adequately responds to the elements of musical expression and is able to respond to expressive symbols while reading and performing.

2　Student shows recognition of many of the expressive elements when reading and performing familiar music, but does not always respond to them when reading and performing new music.

1　Student's recognition of expressive elements is inconsistent when reading and performing musical literature.

0　Student does not respond to expressive elements on a musical score or when performing.

Growth in learning can also be determined by the type of verbal explanations a student offers, by the accuracy of board activities, by the results of improvised and other creative endeavors, by the quality of outcomes from cooperative learning activities, and by responses given on computer or written assignments.

The following written assignments can be used to assess growth in the understanding of rhythmic, melodic, harmonic, and formal concepts. Create a number of different worksheets for each idea, using different songs or patterns.

Rhythm

1. On a worksheet, place a series of known rhythm patterns. As the teacher claps one of the patterns, each child draws an arrow to the pattern heard. Example:

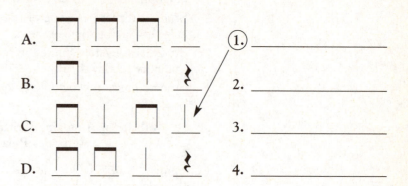

2. On another day, clap one of the patterns in item 1 above. Each child recopies that example on the line beside the number 1. Continue the clapping and writing until all patterns have been performed and written.

3. Give children a handout containing the rhythms of a known song. Omit the rhythms on some of the beat lines. Children fill in the missing rhythms. Example: "Bow Wow Wow"

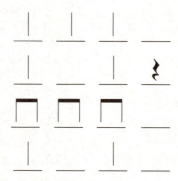

4. Ask the children to write out all the rhythms for a known song. Their handout should contain the beat lines for the song, one phrase per line. Example: "Bow Wow Wow"

5. Have children place accents, bar lines, and the meter sign on a handout containing the rhythms of a known song.

6. On another day, children can mark the counting for the song in item 5.

7. Place on a handout the rhythms of a known song. Children fill in the missing measures. Example: "Paw Paw Patch"

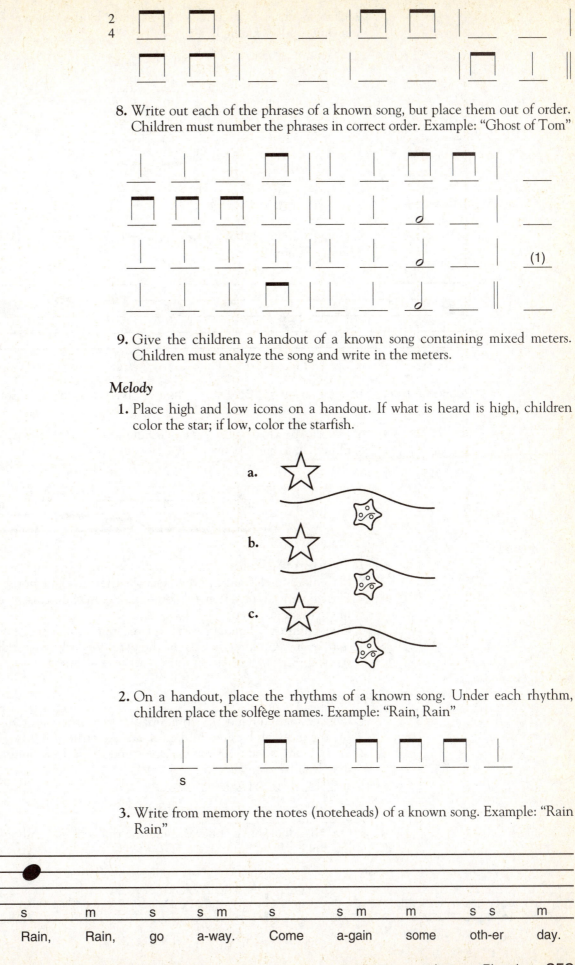

8. Write out each of the phrases of a known song, but place them out of order. Children must number the phrases in correct order. Example: "Ghost of Tom"

(1)

9. Give the children a handout of a known song containing mixed meters. Children must analyze the song and write in the meters.

Melody

1. Place high and low icons on a handout. If what is heard is high, children color the star; if low, color the starfish.

a.

b.

c.

2. On a handout, place the rhythms of a known song. Under each rhythm, children place the solfège names. Example: "Rain, Rain"

s

3. Write from memory the notes (noteheads) of a known song. Example: "Rain Rain"

s	m	s	s m	s	s m	m	s s	m
Rain,	Rain,	go	a-way.	Come	a-gain	some	oth-er	day.

4. Draw an arrow to each melody performed by the teacher. Teacher sings the melody on loo. Example:

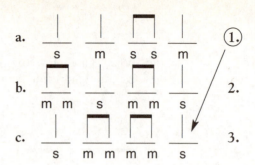

5. On a handout, children write in the solfège names for "Bounce High, Bounce Low." Example:

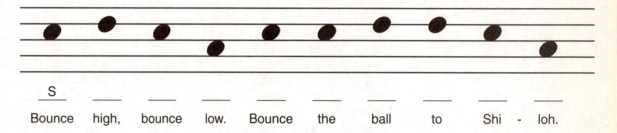

6. Place a known song on a staff. Children must circle one wrong note in each phrase. Example: "Bounce High, Bounce Low"

7. Place part of a known song on a staff. Children write in the missing notes.
8. Place notes on a staff. Children identify their absolute note names.
9. Place noteheads on a staff. Children must draw the stems, up or down, according to the rules given.
10. Give children a handout with a blank staff. Under the staff, place absolute note names. Children must draw the notes for each letter indicated and place stems correctly.

Harmony

1. Give children a handout containing different intervals. Children must identify the intervals by size: third, fifth, and so forth.
2. Play a series of I and V₇ chords. On a handout, children indicate which chords were heard. Example:
   1. <u>(I)</u> <u>(I)</u> <u>(V₇)</u> ____ ____
   2. ____ ____ ____ ____
   3. ____ ____ ____ ____
3. On a handout, have children build the triads (or seventh chords) indicated. Example:

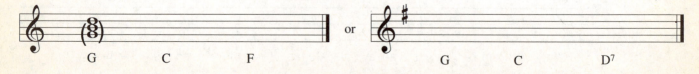

Form

1. Write out the rhythms to a known song, one phrase per line. Have children identify the phrases using letters of the alphabet. Example: "Ring Around the Rosy"

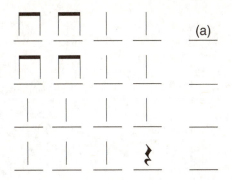

2. Give children a copy of a song notated on a staff. Children must bracket each phrase first, then identify each phrase by a letter name. Example: "Ring Around the Rosy"

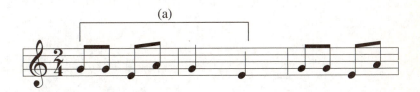

3. Give each child a copy of the song "Cradle Hymn." Children must indicate the first and second endings and cross out unneeded measures.

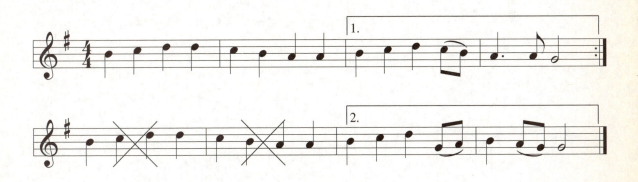

Many creative activities can be developed as aids for written assessment. Response charts can be provided to measure growth in musical knowledge. The response charts on the next pages give ideas that can be used both before and after children can read.

Example 1: Grade 1

Directions given verbally. Listen to the music; then, if the music goes fast, circle the leopard; if it goes slowly, circle the snail. (Repeat directions for each example played.)

Example 2: Grade 3

Directions. Listen to the pattern I am going to play. Then, in number 1, circle the pattern heard. (Repeat the directions for each pattern played.)

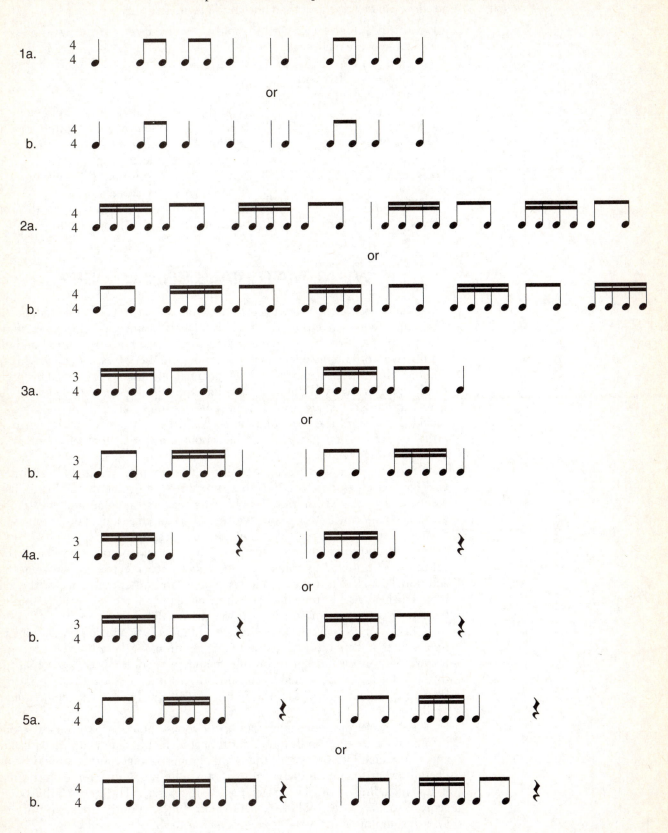

Example 3: Grade 5

Directions. Listen to the recording of "Anitra's Dance" from *Peer Gynt Suite #1* by Grieg. Circle the correct response. I will play the selection three times. Listen for the form during the second and third playings.

1. Music begins and ends with   chord   scale   few notes
2. Section of the orchestra
   most prominent: strings   brass   woodwinds
3. Percussion instrument
   heard in background
   now and then: cymbals   triangle   xylophone
4. Melody is   legato   staccato   alternates both
5. Dynamics are   continually increasing   continually decreasing   neither
6. Tempo   continually slows down   continually speeds up   neither
7. The form is   two parts with some repetition: ABA   three parts with some repetition: AB

WHAT MATERIALS SHALL I USE?

Usually each elementary classroom contains a set of books for students' use. These may come in either the traditional book format or electronic student editions. These series books have teachers' manuals, both traditional and electronic, that contain excellent materials and a number of sequenced lessons that reinforce the National Standards. These manuals are also accompanied by interactive lesson planners and calendars that have proven to be extremely useful when preparing units of study and daily lessons. Teacher resource masters are also included as part of the curriculum package. These masters allow the teacher to print out worksheets, quizzes, and other resource materials that will reinforce the concepts being taught.

Recordings for every song and listening example are included with the packaged series, as well as DVDs that show actual movement, playing of instruments, and animated listening lessons. The teacher's manual and the teacher's own imagination will provide many other ideas for charts, puppets, pictures, and teaching aids that can be used during the music lessons.

If the school has a music room, teachers should become familiar with its contents. The music specialist is also a good resource person who may have additional songbooks, games, audiovisual aids, and other materials for the classroom teacher's use. Often educational media offers sequenced music lessons that teachers may want to work into their weekly schedule.

Check public, school, and university libraries and media centers for other resources that can be used to motivate children for learning. Utilize online resources to review current recordings, materials, performances, and other ideas that will further assist in making lessons interesting for students. Keep in mind, however, that not all songs and recordings are of equal value; use the best quality available.

Use a variety of song materials. Folk songs should be a primary resource because they are the expression of our thoughts, feelings, and culture. Folk songs and games characteristic of all the ethnic groups in our country should be used liberally when planning daily music classes. Use recordings representing many styles, including music by contemporary composers. The best of the popular genres should also be included, such as jazz, blues, country, rock, and hip-hop. They are an important part of our cultural heritage.

CHAPTER 14 Integrating Music Across the Curriculum NS 1, 3, 6

Every child should have frequent opportunities to respond to music by singing, listening, moving, creating, reading, writing, and playing musical instruments. Simultaneously, however, music can also be experienced in its relationship to other subjects. Classroom teachers have many opportunities to use music at different times throughout the school day, when teaching the other basic disciplines. Whether it is story time or time for art, history, or English, teachers can incorporate music into many aspects of the daily lesson plan.

LANGUAGE ARTS

Story Time

Students can become aware of tempo, dynamics, and voice register when retelling favorite stories. For example, using high, medium, and low registers for the voices of baby bear, mama bear, and papa bear can develop flexibility in the child's voice and an awareness of high versus low registers. Saying baby bear's lines quickly and softly and papa bear's more slowly and loudly contribute to an understanding of tempo and dynamics. Other favorite stories can be used to reinforce these learnings.

Musical instruments are effective tools for emphasizing the actions of characters in children's stories. Children enjoy using drums, triangles, guiros, maracas, and other rhythm instruments to imitate story characters running, walking, climbing, and falling. Melody instruments can also give an added touch, by sounding one or more tones or playing a glissando at important moments in the story.

Short, improvised musical phrases can be created and sung at different moments in children's favorite stories. *The Ghost-Eye Tree* by Bill Martin, Jr. and John Archambault is a favorite story of second and third graders. This story tells about the fear of a young boy every time he has to walk by a large, scary tree at night. The story can be given to three readers: a narrator, the sister, and the brother; or, all the girls could read the sister's part and all the boys, the brother's part. At significant moments in the story, a short refrain could be sung to heighten the suspense, such as the following:

GHOST-EYE TREE CHANT

Rozmajzl

The half - way tree, the Ghost - eye tree

I'm not scared Ohhhh no! NOT ME!

The world of fantasy has been captured by Walt Disney in many charming movies, such as *Winnie the Pooh, Sleeping Beauty, Peter Pan, Alice in Wonderland,* and *The Lion King.* The teacher can pause periodically during the reading of one of these stories to play one of the songs whenever it fits into the scene being read.

Other recordings available that address the world of fantasy are:

Compositions	Composer
Three Bears	Coates
Cinderella Suite	Prokofiev
Mother Goose Suite	Ravel
Sleeping Beauty Waltz	Tchaikovsky
The Sorcerer's Apprentice	Dukas
Peter and the Wolf	Prokofiev
Till Eulenspiegel's Merry Pranks	R. Strauss

The words to a number of children's folk songs have been illustrated in children's books. Often, the folk song music is included at the end of the book. Some of children's favorites include:

"Cat Goes Fiddle-I-Fee"
"Mary Wore Her Red Dress"
"Oh, A-Hunting We Will Go"
"There's a Hole in the Bucket"
"There Was an Old Woman Who Swallowed a Fly"
"This Old Man"
"The Wheels on the Bus"

Drama

Children love to act in plays and skits. Many playlets are available for children to dramatize. These are often interspersed with simple songs and easy instrumental accompaniments. Many children's stories also lend themselves to dramatization. *Little Red Ridinghood*, a folk tale set to music by Ruth Boshkoff, is one example of how a story can be dramatized with both spoken and sung parts. Simple instrumental accompaniment is also included in this book. *Expressions of Freedom*, a three volume set by René Boyer, includes numerous playlets to celebrate African American history.

The following lesson plan shows how a teacher can approach the dramatizing of a folk tale. Based on the Irish folk tale, "A Small Fish Story," which can be found on page 367, this folk tale involves children in rhythmic and speech activity, movement, and playing instruments.

Elements: Melody, Rhythm, Timbre

National Standard: Composing and arranging music with specified guidelines.

Behavioral Objectives: Students will be able to identify various actions within a folk tale and bring these actions alive musically.

Anticipatory Set: Tell students that any story can be brought alive with careful planning. Music, especially melodies, rhythms, and various percussion sounds can serve as a major indicator of what is happening in a story or folk tale. Discuss how music can tell a story, represent characters, and spark one's creative imagination.

Procedure: Choose a folk tale such as "A Small Fish Story—An Irish Folk Tale." Have students:

- Listen to the story, and then discuss what happened.
- Make suggestions for sounds and create simple improvised tunes that can best represent the characters and actions in the folk tale.

Ideas might include the following:

a. A simple improvised 8-measure pentatonic melody on an Orff instrument can serve as an opening to this folk tale. A simple drone accompaniment to the melody can make it even more interesting.
b. The "Man's movement" might consist of three pitches on an Orff metallophone or xylophone or other keyboard instrument.
c. One Fish   (a melody bell or triangle sounding once)
d. Two Fish   (a melody bell or triangle sounding twice)
e. Three Fish   (a melody bell or triangle sounding three times)
f. The Widow   (a pentatonic scale in minor—for contrast)

Extension: A continuation of the activity could be creating a full production with a narrator telling the story, musicians playing instruments, and performers acting out the scene, with costumes, masks, and background sets.

Extension: Students transfer some of their original artwork onto a PowerPoint presentation that can serve as a background for the set.

Assessment: Have students:

- keep a record of their creative contributions to this project in a journal.
- Show their understanding of the factual information contained within the folk tale.

A SMALL FISH STORY—AN IRISH FOLK TALE (RETOLD BY RENÉ BOYER)

Narration A: Once upon a time there was a man who was always generous to others. This man was once a beggar himself who traveled over the country with only the clothes on his back, his staff, and an old wooden pail.

Narration B: One day he came to a little town by the sea where almost no one was willing to help him. All day he stood on the street, asking for alms. But by the time evening fell, only three people had taken pity on him: a fisherman, a woman, and a priest. Strangely enough, each of them had given him the same thing—not a coin, but a small fish.

Narration C: He put all three fish into his pail filled with water and walked on until he came to a house where a very poor widow lived with her children.

Old Man: "Begging your pardon Madam, but might a person stay here overnight?"

Widow: "Of course," the widow answered, "but we only have water, soup and a crust of bread for supper."

Old Man: "Supper won't be a problem! Look here! I have three fish. You can fry them and we and the children will eat them together."

Narration D: The widow looked doubtfully into the beggar's pail. She had no way of knowing the three little fish had been growing in there. By the time she saw them, they had become quite large.

Widow: "What a joy!" the woman cried. "I haven't seen such big fish for a long time, not even at the market!"

ONE FISH, TWO FISH, THREE FISH DO I SEE! PLENTY FOR MY CHILDREN AND ENOUGH FOR ME!

Narration D: She happily lit the fire and began to cook the fish over the glowing coals. While she was about her work, the Old Man asked,

Old Man: "Do you have a pail?"

Widow: "Yes, indeed I do."

Old Man: "I'll thank you to fill it with water and bring it to me."

Narration A: The woman did as he asked. Soon the fish were ready to eat. And how delicious they were! The widow and the children were so hungry they left nothing but the bones.

Old Man: "Don't throw those bones away. Give them to me."

Narration B: The children and their mother looked at one another in surprise.

Children: "What is he up to?"

Narration C: But they were so grateful for a good meal at last that they didn't question the Old Man.

Narration D: After they had eaten, the family lay the bones of all three fish on a plate. The Old Man picked up the bones by the tail and threw them into the widow's pail. Again, everyone was surprised.

Children: "Why is he doing that?"

Narration A: Then as the Widow was about to carry the pail outside to empty it, she noticed three live fish swimming in the water!

Widow: "What? How could that be?"

ONE FISH, TWO FISH, THREE FISH DO I SEE, PLENTY FOR MY CHILDREN AND ENOUGH FOR ME!

Narration B: Who knew where the fish came from except the Old Man, and by that time he was sound asleep.

Narration C: The next morning, the Old Man said,

Old Man: "Please fix these fish for breakfast."

Narration D: The Old Woman gladly did so, and once again everyone had enough to eat.

Narration A: When they all finished, again the Old Man said,

Old Man: "Bring me the pail and give me the bones."

Narration B: Then he threw them into the water and continued.

Old Man: "You must always do this. That way, you will always have fish and you and your children won't be hungry any more."

Narration C: Then the Old Man swung his wooden pail over the end of his staff, said goodbye, and walked off down the road.

Narration D: The widow and her children never saw the Old Man again, but they lived well for a long time. Until one day . . . the mother left a single child alone at the home while she and the others went to visit relatives. The child at home got hungry, so he tiptoed over to the widow's pail and looked in:

Child: **One fish, two fish, three fish do I see,**
Enough for the others and plenty for me!

Narration A: With that, he scooped out one of the fish and fried it for himself. Afraid that his mother would find out and scold him, he threw the bones away.

Narration B: When the Widow returned, the first thing she did was to go to the pail for dinner.

Widow: "One fish, two fish, thr—"

Narration C: But now there were not three fish swimming in the water. There were only two. And from then on, that had to be plenty for all of them!

Poetry

As a component of language arts, children are often invited to write their own poems using simple forms, such as the Japanese haiku. The haiku is usually cast in a five-seven-five syllable form:

Cascading water,
    Glistening in the sunlight—
        Nature's pot of gold.

Children can set their haiku and other original poems to music that the whole class can then perform. Simple accompaniments can be added.

Poems can also be presented as choral readings to develop an awareness of register, tempo, dynamics, and thick versus thin textures:

ONE STORMY NIGHT

Two little kittens	All
One stormy night,	
Began to quarrel,	
And then to fight.	
One had a mouse,	Girls
The other had none;	Boys
And that's the way	All
The quarrel begun.	
"*I'll* have that mouse,"	First boy
Said the bigger cat.	Three boys
"*You'll* have that mouse?	First girl
We'll see about that!"	
"I *will* have that mouse,"	First boy
Said the eldest son;	Three boys
"You *sha'nt* have the mouse,"	First girl
Said the little one.	Three girls
The old woman seized	Girls
Her sweeping broom,	
And swept both kittens	Boys
Right out of the room.	
The ground was covered	All
With frost and snow:	
And the two little kittens	
Had nowhere to go.	
They lay and shivered	Second boy
On a mat at the door	

While the old woman Was sweeping the floor.	Second girl
And then they crept in, As quiet as mice,	All girls
All wet with the snow, And as cold as ice,	All boys

And found it much better,
  That stormy night,
To lie by the fire
  Than to quarrel and fight.
	All

SOCIAL STUDIES

In social studies, students learn about the United States and other countries: their history, people, and customs. Many songs and instrumental works are available to highlight these areas and to add to students' understanding of important events in a country's history. The suggestions given below show the richness of musical selections available:

U.S. and World History

People

"Abraham, Martin, and John"
  (commemoration of the assassinations
  of Lincoln, King, and Kennedy)
	Holler

A Lincoln Portrait	Copland
An American in Paris	Gershwin
Appalachian Spring (pioneer couple in Appalachian Mountains)	Copland

American Indian

"Breezes Are Blowing"	Luiseno
"Duck Dance"	Seminole
"Grinding Corn"	Hopi
"Ho, Ho, Watanay"	Iroquois
"Indian Lullaby"	Quinault
"Open Plain"	Arapahoe
"Stick Game Song"	Paiute
"Sun-Dance Song"	Sioux
"Sunrise Song"	Zuni

American Cowboy

Billy the Kid	Copland
"Chisholm Trail"	
"Cowboy's Lament"	
"Git Along Little Dogies"	
"Goodbye Old Paint"	
"Home on the Range"	
"I Ride an Old Paint"	
"My Home's in Montana"	
Rodeo	Copland

Places

"American Salute"	Gould
"America the Beautiful"	Ward/Bates
Grand Canyon Suite	Grofé
Mississippi Suite (people and events associated with the Mississippi River)	Grofé
"Three Places in New England"	Ives
Variations on "America"	Ives

Events
Revolutionary War
"Chester" from New England Triptych (hymn   W. Schuman
    adopted as a Revolutionary War marching song)
"Midnight Ride of Paul Revere" from selections   Phillips
    from McGuffey's Reader

Civil War
"Battle Hymn of the Republic"   Howe/Steffe
    (written to inspire Union soldiers)
"I Wish I Was In Dixie Land"   Emmett
"When Johnny Comes Marching Home"   Lambert

World Wars
"I Left My Heart at the Stage Door Canteen"   Berlin
"Over There"   Cohan
"Threnody for the Victims of Hiroshima"   Penderecki
"War Requiem"   Britten
"We Did It Before and We Can Do It Again"   Friend and Tobias

Railroads
"Casey Jones"
"500 Miles"   West
"John Henry"
"This Train"
"The Train Is A-Coming, Oh Yes"
"The Wabash Cannon Ball"

1960s
"A Hard Rain's A'Gonna Fall"   Dylan
    (social evils: war, prejudice, poverty, oppression)
"Ghetto" (poverty)   Baez
"Last Train to Nuremberg"   Seeger
"Like a Rolling Stone" (social conventions,   Dylan
    authority)
"Turn, Turn, Turn"   Seeger
"Where Have All the Flowers Gone"   Seeger
"We Shall Overcome" (adaptation of an old hymn   American Freedom Song
    used during Civil Rights movement)

Children can be aided in understanding other cultures by singing songs and performing the dances of many countries. Classroom teachers have many opportunities to incorporate multicultural music into units highlighting specific countries. These ethnic songs are among the most popular and accessible for children:

Africa
"Banuwa"   Liberia
"Everybody Loves Saturday Night"   Ghana
"Kum Bah Yah"   South Africa
"Nana Bread"
"Nigerian Boat Song"   Nigeria
"Obwisana"   Ghana
"Tina Singu"
"Tue Tue"   Ghana

Canada
"Going Over the Sea"
"Huron Carol"
"Land of the Silver Birch"
"Lots o' Fish in Bonavist' Harbor"

China
"Crescent Moon"
"Jasmine Flower"
"Trot, Pony, Trot"
"Song of the Dragon"

Czech Republic and Slovakia
"Above the Plain"
"Ifca's Castle"
"Let Us Sing Together"
"Waters Ripple and Flow"

England
"Bell Horses"
"Greensleeves"
"Gypsy Rover"
"Hey, Ho! Anybody Home?"
"Hot Cross Buns"
"London Bridge"
"Muffin Man"
"There Was a Jolly Miller"

France
"Frère Jacques"
"The Happy River"
"In the Moonlight (Au clair de la lune)"
"Pat-A-Pan"
"A Rat and the Cat"

Germany
"All Things Bright and Beautiful"
"Little Cabin in the Wood"
"Music Alone Shall Live"
"My Hat"
"O Christmas Tree"
"Silent Night"

Israel (Hebrew)
"Artsa Alinu"
"Hanukkah"
"Hava Nagila"
"Zum Gali Gali"

Mexico
"Counting Song"
"De Colores"
"Don Gato"
"El Rorro"
"La Bamba"

Japan
"Bento-Uri"
"Japanese Rain Song"
"Sakura"
"Teru Teru Bozu"

Russia
"Birch Tree"
"Minka"
"The Peddler"
"Russian Slumber Song"

Scotland
"Aiken Drum"
"Charlie Is My Darling"
"Did You Ever See a Lassie?"
"Skye Boat Song"

Spain
"A la Puerta del Cielo"
"Fum, Fum, Fum, (Catalonia)"
"Niño Querido"
"Zumba, Zumba"

MATHEMATICS

For centuries children have played counting games at home, at school, and on the playground. Through singing, hand-clapping games, skipping, and jump-rope activities, children have always used counting in rhyme as a major means for keeping the beat and feeling rhythm. Fortunately, these kinds of games that often involve counting, adding, subtraction, and multiplication have served to assist children in developing vocabulary that leads to an understanding of mathematical concepts. The suggested activities here demonstrate only a few of the numerous children's rhymes and games that reinforce the development of math skills.

NINE LITTLE BEARS (ADDITION) CHILDREN'S FINGER PLAY

One little bear
Wondering what to do
Along came another
Then there were two!

Two little bears
Climbing up a tree
Along came another
Then there were three!

Three little bears
Ate an apple core
Along came another
Then there were four!

Four little bears
Ate honey from a hive
Along came another
Then there were five!

Five little bears
Were caught in lots of sticks
Along came another
Then there were six.

Six little bears
Laid down to look at Heaven
Along came another
Then there were seven.

Seven little bears
Went inside the gate
Along came another
Then there were eight!

Eight little bears
Ate salmon off a line
Along came another
Then there were nine.

Nine little bears
Waded 'round the bend
Along came another
Then there were ten.

SIX LITTLE TEDDY BEARS CHILDREN'S GAME (SUBTRACTION)

Six little teddy bears—sleeping in the bed
Five at the foot—and one at the head.
One teddy said, "This bed is too full!"
So he grabbed at the blanket
And started to pull.
He pulled and he pulled and he pulled some more,
Two little teddies went
BOOM! On the floor.

Four little teddy bears—sleeping in the bed.
Three at the foot and one at the head.
One teddy said, "This bed is too full!"
So he grabbed at the blanket and started to pull.
He pulled and he pulled and he pulled some more,

Two little teddies went
BOOM! On the floor.

Two little teddy bears sleeping in the bed,
One at the foot and one at the head.
One Teddy Bear said, "Two is just right!"
Then the two little Teddy Bears said,
"Good Night!"

The following songs are loved by most children. Children should be encouraged to act out the songs and, where appropriate, create a hand-clapping game that can be used while singing the song.

THE ANTS GO MARCHING

Children's Counting Song

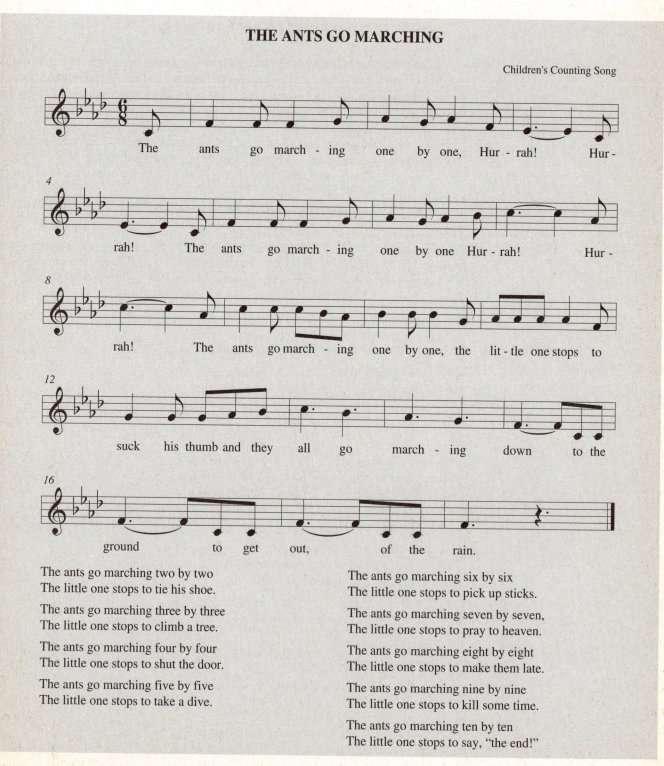

The ants go marching two by two
The little one stops to tie his shoe.

The ants go marching three by three
The little one stops to climb a tree.

The ants go marching four by four
The little one stops to shut the door.

The ants go marching five by five
The little one stops to take a dive.

The ants go marching six by six
The little one stops to pick up sticks.

The ants go marching seven by seven,
The little one stops to pray to heaven.

The ants go marching eight by eight
The little one stops to make them late.

The ants go marching nine by nine
The little one stops to kill some time.

The ants go marching ten by ten
The little one stops to say, "the end!"

BILLY

Children's Clapping Game

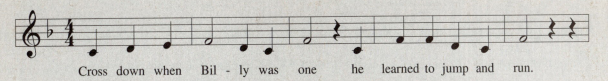

Cross down when Bil - ly was one he learned to jump and run.

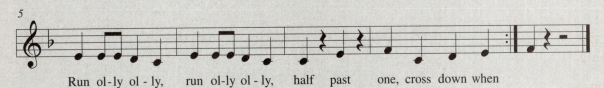

Run ol-ly ol - ly, run ol-ly ol - ly, half past one, cross down when

2. Billy was two, he learned to tie his shoes.
3. Billy was three, he learned to climb a tree.
4. Billy was four, he learned to shut the door.
5. Billy was five, he learned to swim and dive.
6. Billy was six, he learned to pick up sticks.
7. When Billy was seven, he learned to look to heaven.
8. When Billy was eight, he learned to roller skate.
9. When Billy was nine, he learned to sing so fine.
10. When Billy was ten, he learned to start again.
11. When Billy was eleven, he learned to count to seven.
12. When Billy was twelve, he learned to ring the bell.

COUNTING SONG

Mexican Folk Song

U - no, dos, y tres, Cua - tro, cin - co seis; Sie - te, o - cho, nue - ve,

I can count to diez. La la la la la, La la la la la, La la la la la la;

La la la la la, La la la la la, La la la la la la

COUNTING BY 4S

Boyer

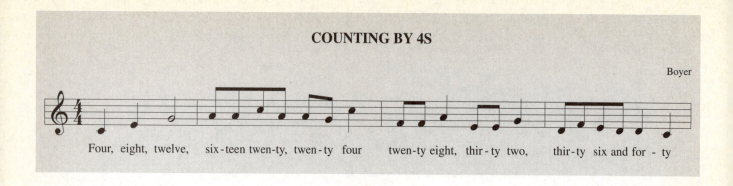

Four, eight, twelve, six-teen twen-ty, twen-ty four   twen-ty eight, thir-ty two,   thir-ty six and for-ty

All Hid–Counting by Fives

Hide and Seek Chant

Last night, night be-fore,   Twen-ty four rob-bers at my door,   I got up,   to let them in,

Hit 'em in the head with a rol-li' pin.   All hid!____   All hid____   All hid____

All hid.____   Five, ten fif-teen twen-ty   All hid____   twen-ty five thir-ty,   thir-ty five for-ty,

for-ty five fif-ty   fif-ty five six-ty   All hid____   Six-ty five seventy,   seventy five eight-y

eight-y five nine-ty   nine-ty five, a hun-dred!   All hid____

Some children's recordings contain songs dealing with mathematics, such as the Hap Palmer recordings: *Learning Basic Skills Through Music*. These include "The Number March" and "Triangle, Circle, Square." Other Palmer recordings containing aids to learning math are *Math Readiness—Vocabulary and Concepts*, *Math Readiness—Addition and Subtraction*, and *Singing Multiplication Tables*. See the outline below of other Hap Palmer materials that focus on the integration of math and music.

There are certain math concepts that can be difficult to grasp, especially if the student is young. Learning the multiplication table is perhaps one of the most challenging math facts children have to conquer. Fortunately, there is a new CD called *Multiplication Mountain* that can help kids master this concept faster.

In this CD, multiplication facts are presented in a logical sequence, starting off with the easiest and slowly moving on to more challenging facts. Children learn multiplying by 2s, 10s, 5s and 11s on the first level. On the second level, they learn multiplying by 3s, 9s, and 4s, followed by 6s and 8s on the third level. As they reach the top of the multiplication mountain, kids tackle multiplying by 7s before finally reaching the sun where the number 12 is located.

Each fact in "Multiplication Mountain" has a corresponding song that makes learning how to multiply less tedious and more fun. All the songs are well written and catchy; it also incorporates different styles of music like waltz, classical, and rock and roll. Each song is repeated twice; the first one with the complete lyrics and the second one minus the answers to the multiplication fact being learned.

Note: Hap Palmer materials can be ordered online at www.happalmer.com.

SCIENCE

Music can be an added dimension in the world of science. Whether studying birds, animals, weather, or sound, a variety of recordings can be used to enhance the science lesson. Some appropriate recordings include:

Carnival of the Animals	Saint-Saëns
Clouds	Debussy
Dance of the Mosquito	Liadov
Flight of the Bumble Bee	Rimsky-Korsakov
Four Seasons	Vivaldi
From the Diary of a Fly	Bartok
Happy Farmer	Schumann
Lightning	Glass
Little Windmills	Couperin
The Planets	Holst
Sea Piece with Birds	Thomson
To the Rising Sun	Torjussen
Wild Horseman	Schumann

Recordings that can be used with a lesson on sound and how it is produced might include:

Ancient Voices of Children	Crumb
Composition for Synthesizer	Babbit
Dripsody	Le Caine
Electronic Study No. 1	Davidovsky
Ionization	Varèse
Piece for Tape Recorder	Ussachevsky
Poème Electronique	Varèse
Variations for Flute and Electronic Sound	Carlos

PHYSICAL EDUCATION

A variety of music materials are available for use with physical fitness activities. Developing coordination and muscle strength is easier when activities are set to music. Some useful recordings are:

Clap, Snap, and Tap	Brazelton
Fitness Fun for Everyone	Jervey
Multicultural Rhythm Stick Fun	Stewart
Musical Ball Skills	Greiger and Popper
Perceptual-Motor Rhythm Games	Capon, Hallum, and Glass
Rhythm Stick Activities	Glass and Hallum
Synchronized Lummi Sticks	Hughes
Tinikling	Kazan

RELATED ARTS

Relating the arts through the use of common principles is an effective way to help children develop an understanding of artistic concepts. The use of such principles as repetition-contrast, simplicity-complexity, tension-relaxation, balance, and motion can provide variety to music class presentations while highlighting important aspects of music, art, and literature.

One way to approach the study of repetition and contrast in related arts is to ask children to close their eyes and imagine a "nose," any nose—on a friend, an elephant, a pig. We all know what a nose is, even though they may come in different shapes and sizes, depending on who's "wearing" it. The arts have things in common also, even though what is common may take on different aspects in a painting than in a poem or a song. Have children experiment with different aspects of repetition and contrast. Provide a variety of shapes (▷ ○ □) of different sizes and colors. Ask students to create art by arranging the shapes on paper with very little contrast present. Students may choose one color and shape in varying sizes:

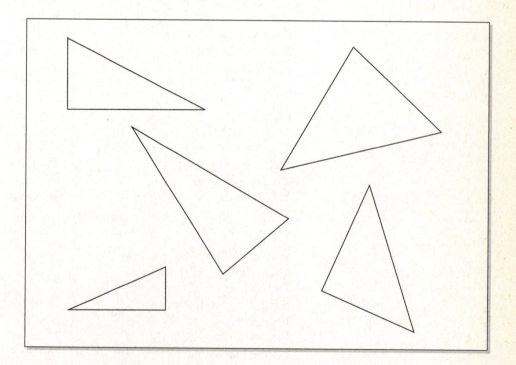

Then have students experiment with maintaining some repetition, but increasing the amount of contrast.

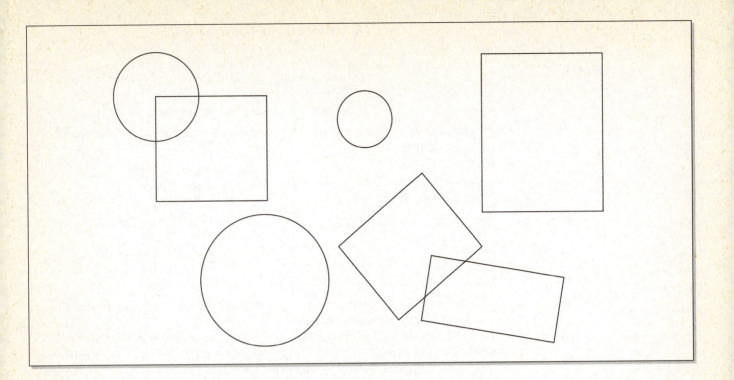

Students can look for repetition and contrast in objects in their environment and in the design of their clothing. Provide examples of repetition and contrast in a variety of folk art, such as beaded moccasins, quilts, and ceremonial masks. Paintings are also rich sources of good examples of repetition and contrast, such as:

Three Musicians	Picasso
Coca Cola	Warhol
Composition with Red, Blue, Yellow	Mondrian
Broadway Boogie Woogie	Mondrian
Casiopée	Vasarely
Homage to the Square	Albers
The Piano Lesson	Bearden

Students can apply the principles of repetition and contrast to poetry by studying a variety of poems and identifying where examples of these principles occur. Read the poem "The Wind" by Robert Louis Stevenson. Ask students where repetition occurs. How would the poem change if we removed the repetition? Is there a balance between repetition and contrast in this poem?

THE WIND

I saw you toss the kites on high
And blow the birds about the sky;
And all around I heard you pass,
Like ladies' skirts across the grass—
   O wind, a-blowing all day long,
   O wind, that sings so loud a song!

I saw the different things you did,
But always you yourself you hid.
I felt you push, I heard you call,
I could not see yourself at all—
   O wind, a-blowing all day long,
   O wind, that sings so loud a song!

O you that are so strong and cold,
O blower, are you young or old?
Are you beast of field and tree,
Or just a stronger child than me?
O wind, a-blowing all day long,
O wind, that sings so loud a song!

Provide other good poems that contain clear examples of repetition and contrast, such as:

"Poem"	Langston Hughes
"African Dance"	Langston Hughes
"House on the Hill"	E. A. Robinson
"Lazy Jane"	Shel Silverstein
"The Clam"	Shel Silverstein
"Serenade"	H. W. Longfellow
"The Tide Rises, the Tide Falls"	H. W. Longfellow
"Swift Things Are Beautiful"	E. J. Coatsworth

Children will enjoy creating poems that demonstrate their understanding of the use of repetition and contrast.

Students should be invited to sing a song containing a clear example of repetition and contrast. A good beginning song might be the Czechoslovakian folk song "Above the Plain." After they have learned the song, students should identify how phrases 1 and 2 are contrasting, with one melody line rising and the other falling. Phrases 3 and 4 are exactly the same. Show the repetition and contrast in this song by using letters of the alphabet: abcc.

ABOVE THE PLAIN

Czech Folk Song

Other songs having clear examples of repetition and contrast are:

"Sarasponda"
"Twinkle, Twinkle, Little Star"
"Twelve Days of Christmas"
"Some Folks"   Foster
"On the Road Again"   Nelson
"To a Wild Rose"   MacDowell

INTEGRATION OF THE ARTS

Music, visual art, and poetry can be integrated into a variety of lessons in the general classroom:

1. When studying units in social science, students can perform the songs and dances of a country, view a video demonstrating the country's music, study the country's visual art (paintings, sculpture, architecture), read poems or stories about the country, or write their own poems and short stories about some interesting characteristic of the country.

2. Students can make individual collages about themselves and the country (or one of the countries) of their ancestry. They can perform a song from each of the countries represented in the class and read poems or stories about those countries. Some students may even have traditional dress or other traditional objects that they can show to the class.

3. Instead of making collages, as in number 2, students can be organized into groups representing the country of their origin. Each group is responsible for completing a mural portraying characteristics of its country. White or brown butcher or wrapping paper works well for the murals.

4. When studying a topic in the natural sciences (weather, animals, plant life, insects), students can sing songs whose words address the topic, read or write poems about the topic, and use the topic in an art activity.

WRITTEN AND PERFORMANCE-RELATED ASSESSMENTS THROUGH COOPERATIVE LEARNING ACTIVITIES: SPECIALIZED AREAS

1. Give each group a short story. The group should read through the story and decide what kind of sound effects (body sounds, instruments) would enhance it. The story should be practiced and then performed for the class. (Language Arts)

2. After studying a particular country in Social Studies, each group should prepare a short drama incorporating information about such things as the history, geography, customs, arts, and food of the country. Each drama can be presented to the class. (Language Arts/Social Studies)

3. The murals suggested under the title "Integration of the Arts" can be organized as a cooperative learning activity. Each mural should include some aspect of the country's musical life. (Social Studies)

4. Give each group a folk dance characteristic of a particular country or countries being studied. Group members must work out the movements and be ready to perform the dance for the class. (Social Studies)

5. Give each group a different set of materials, each set containing a picture of an art work, a poem, and a known song. Students must study each art form to discover in what ways repetition and contrast (or balance, motion, or tension-relaxation) are present. When finished, they can present their conclusions to the class. (Related Arts)

Glossary

absolute pitch names names of the musical alphabet: ABCDEFG

accent a symbol placed above or beneath a note head to emphasize the sound of that note: >

accidentals symbols that are used to alter a pitch in some way: ♯, ♭, ♮

adagio tempo marking indicating that the music should proceed slowly

afuche *See* cabasa.

agogo bells two conical, metal bells, each having a different pitch and struck with a small rod to produce a ringing sound

alla breve cut time or 2/2

allegro fast, but cheerful pace

alto female voice range lower than mezzosoprano

anacrusis an incomplete measure of one or more notes found at the beginning of a composition; also known as pick-up notes

andante walking, moderate pace

augmented triad a triad containing two major thirds

baritone a male voice classification that lies between the bass and tenor ranges

bar line a vertical line used to separate accented groups of rhythms and/or pitches

bass the lowest of male voice classifications

bass or F clef a symbol used for notating relatively low pitches

beat the underlying, unchanging, repeating pulse found in most music

beat note the note designated by the time signature to receive one full beat within the measure

behavioral objective a statement that contains the specific understanding or skill that is desired of a learner as well as the process through which a learner will be led to achieve the understanding or skill

bell tree a vertical nesting of metal discs on a metal rod that is played with a metal stick

binary a composition that is divided into two sections, the second being different from the first; written as AB or binary form

blues form 12-bars or measures of music in 4/4 time that is set to a specific harmonic pattern

blues scale a major scale whose third, fifth and seventh are altered

bongo two small, connected drums usually played by placing them between the knees and hitting them with various parts of the hand

brass family a family of instruments whose basic instruments include the trumpet, trombone, French horn, and tuba

brush strum a downward movement of the right hand across the strings of the guitar, using the backs of the fingernails

cabasa a rhythm instrument consisting of metal beads encircling around a large wooden spool

canon a device whereby the melody of one part is strictly imitated from beginning to end in a second voice or even a third or fourth voice

capo a device that can be attached to the guitar neck to raise the pitch of the strings, making transposition to a key easier to achieve

castanets two semihollow disks of wood attached to a stick by a cord

chant a single, unaccompanied, melodic line; monophonic music

chest register that part of the vocal range governed by a set of throat muscles that control lower-register singing

chord the simultaneous sounding of three or more pitches

chordal *See* homophonic.

chord inversion a triad or seventh chord whose root is not at the bottom of the chord

circle dances dances involving one large circle or two concentric circles

claves two wooden cylinders containing hollow spaces that resonate when struck together

clef sign a symbol indicating the relative highness or lowness of the pitches notated

coda a passage added to the last major section of a form

common time another name for the 4/4 time signature: ᴄ

compound interval an interval that is larger than an octave

compound meter a time signature whose upper number is a multiple of three and whose beat note can be divided into three equal parts, creating a ratio of 3:1

conducting patterns hand and arm patterns, used by music directors, that represent the time signature

conga drum a long, cylindrical drum that is open at the bottom and played by striking the head with the palms of the hand

contour the direction or shape of a melody

contralto the lowest range of the alto voice

countersubject a second theme, found in some fugues, that follows the statement of the first theme

cowbell a metal instrument that is struck with a mallet or metal bar

crescendo a gradual increase in volume

cut time another name for the 2/2 time signature: ¢

cymbals two metal disks struck together using a vertical movement

Da capo al fine a common symbol (D.C. al fine) used to direct the performer to repeat a piece of music from the beginning to the term *fine*, where the piece ends

decrescendo a gradual decrease in volume

deductive approach an approach to learning that leads students through a sequence of activities from the general to the specific

descant a countermelody or second melody that is sung higher than the original melody

diaphragm a large muscle that lies across the body under the lungs; with an in-and-out motion, it supplies the impetus that becomes the foundation of the entire breathing system

diatonic stepwise

diatonic sequence a succession of pitches moving in an ascending or descending stepwise manner: ABCDEFG

diminished triad a triad consisting of two minor thirds

diminuendo a gradual decrease in volume

djembe a west African drum dating back to the 12th century

djunjun a drum that rests on its side and is played with a stick

dominant seventh a four-toned chord built on the fifth degree of the scale; the added seventh above the root gives it its name

dot a sign following a note or rest which adds to that note or rest one-half of its value; a dot on top of or beneath a note will cause the note to be shortened in duration

double bar line two bar lines that designate the end of either a musical section or the complete work

downbeat the first beat in a measure

drone the playing of a constant pitch or pitches

duple meter a time signature having a top number divisible by two: 2/4, 2/8, 2/2

duration the length of sound or silence of a designated note or rest

duration syllables nicknames used to designate different rhythmic structures

dynamics the degree of volume in a musical composition, ranging from very soft to very loud

elements the musical dimensions that undergird all music: rhythm, melody, harmony, texture, form, timbre, dynamics, and tempo

enharmonic terms used to designate two pitches having the same sound but different letter names

fermata a musical sign indicating that the note should be held longer than its normal duration: ⌢

fifth the top tone of a triad

finger cymbals two metal disks, held by the fingers, that are struck together using a vertical movement

flat a symbol used to lower the pitch of a note one-half step: ♭

followers voices that follow the lead voice in a canon

form the structure or design of a piece of music

fugue a polyphonic composition based on a theme, called the subject, which is stated unaccompanied at the beginning of the piece and then is taken up imitatively in other voices, called the answers, in close succession

gankoqui a double bell with its origins in Africa

general objectives statements that are usually expressed in behavioral terms indicating what the student will be able to do over a year's time or month-to-month

glissando rapidly sliding up or down with the voice or on an instrument

glockenspiel a small, metal, barred instrument belonging to the Orff Instrumentarium

goals broad and concise statements indicating desired terminal outcomes

gong a disk-shaped, metal instrument struck with a soft mallet

grand staff the combination of treble and bass clefs

grave tempo marking meaning as slowly as possible

guiro a hollow gourd with horizontal grooves cut across its surface that is scraped or hit with a small wooden stick

half step the smallest interval used in most of the music of Western civilization

hand drum a cylindrical drum head that is held by its rim

hand signs designated hand signals that are used to reinforce the inner hearing of intervals

harmonic interval an interval consisting of two pitches that are sounded simultaneously

harmony the simultaneous interaction between pitches in a melody and sounds in an accompaniment

head register that part of the vocal range governed by a set of throat muscles that affect upper register singing

homophonic texture a texture consisting of a succession of chords that support a melody

icon pictorial representation used to designate something other than itself, depending on its context

improvisation a musical extemporization for voice or other instruments, performed without much preparation

inductive approach an approach to learning that leads students through a sequence of activities from the specific to the general

interlude a passage added to the interior of a composition that connects one section to another more smoothly than would occur if it were absent

introduction a passage that occurs at the beginning of a musical work, before its major sections

jingle clogs an instrument possessing one or more pairs of metal disks loosely attached to a handle

key note starting note of a scale or home tone of a key

key signature a sign placed at the beginning of a song, immediately following the clef sign, that tells the performer the names of the sharps or flats that occur in the music

koto 13-string zither, native to Japan

largo very slow pace

leader the beginning voice in a canon

leap two notes that are more than a skip apart melodically

ledger lines extra lines that are added above and beneath the staff to accommodate additional pitches

legato a smooth, corrected progression from note to note

line dance a dance consisting of any number of couples who come together in two facing lines

locomotor movement moving from one place to another

major scale a sequence of tones consisting of the following whole- and half-step relationships: WWHWWWH

major third an interval consisting of four half steps

major triad a triad that consists of the intervals of a major third on the bottom and a minor third on the top

maracas gourds that contain dried seeds that produce a rattling sound when shaken

measure the space between two bar lines

melodic interval the distance in pitch between two notes sounded consecutively

melody a linear succession of sounds and silences ordered in time

metallophone a barred instrument made of metal that belongs to the Orff Instrumentarium; its tone possesses a high, resonating quality

meter signature *See* time signature

mezzo soprano a soprano with a medium-high voice range

Middle C a name given to the C located in the middle of the grand staff or the C located approximately in the middle of the piano keyboard

minor scale a scale built on the sixth tone of the major scale

minor third an interval consisting of three half steps

minor triad a triad consisting of the intervals of a minor third on the bottom and a major third on the top

mode an arrangement of the eight tones of the octave according to a fixed pattern, such as the major or the minor mode

moderato a tempo marking designating a medium speed

monophonic texture a single, unaccompanied melodic line

musical alphabet the first seven letters of the alphabet, ABCDEFG, used to name musical pitches

natural a symbol used to cancel a previous sharp or flat: ♮

natural minor scale a minor scale consisting of the following whole- and half-step sequence: WHWWHWW

neumatic notation a style of writing music, common to the Middle Ages, that uses neumes instead of standard notation

nonlocomotor movements originating from a stationary position of the body

notes musical symbols representing sounds or pitches that are usually placed on a staff

ostinato a rhythmic, melodic, or harmonic pattern that repeats; used primarily as an accompaniment

ottava Latin term for *octave*

part method *See* phrase method

partner songs two or more songs that share an identical harmonic structure and can be performed simultaneously

patsching the hitting or patting of the knees or thighs with the hands; used as a readiness activity for mallet techniques

pentatonic a scale consisting of a sequence of five tones within the octave

percussion family the largest family in the symphony orchestra; includes instruments of both definite and indefinite pitch

phonation the process of producing sound

phrase a musical line that contains a coherent grouping of pitches, similar to a sentence in language which contains a coherent grouping of words

phrase method an imitative process used in teaching songs that are longer, more complex, and not easily learned after one or two hearings; part method

pick-up the incomplete measure of one or more notes found at the beginning of a composition; also called an *anacrusis*

pitch the relative highness or lowness of a musical sound

polyphonic texture two or more independent melodic lines sounding simultaneously, causing harmony to result between the horizontal lines

portamento a sliding technique used when playing the trombone

prestissimo a tempo marking designating a pace that is as fast as possible

presto very fast pace

primary chords the tonic, subdominant, and dominant chords

program music music intended to suggest images, incidents, or people

quadruple meter a time signature having a top number divisible by four: 4/4, 4/8, 4/2

ragtime a musical form or style that is characterized by a syncopated melody over a regular, march-like bass line

range the span of the highest to the lowest pitch in a melody, or that which defines the capacity of a voice or instrument

ratchet a miniature, machine-like instrument that produces a raspy, grinding sound

refrain the same melody and words sung after each verse of a song

registers the different portions of the vocal range, which are marked by differences in vibration rate

relative keys a name given to a major and a minor key using the same key signature

repetition restating the same note or notes on the staff

resonator bells individual metal bars tuned to each tone of the chromatic scale; each bar is mounted on a block of wood and resonates when struck by a mallet

rests music symbols used to represent silence

rhythm varied lengths of sound or silence over an underlying beat

rhythmic ostinato short, repeated rhythm patterns used to accompany speech, songs, other rhythms, instrument playing, or movement

rhythm sticks long, narrow, cylindrical pieces of wood that are hit together to produce sound

rondo a form consisting of an original theme which always returns after each digression or contrasting theme; usually symbolized by ABACA or ABACABA

root the tone upon which a chord is built in thirds; bottom tone of a triad

rote learning an imitative process through which children learn to speak, sing, or move

round a canon in which each performer returns to the beginning of the song after its conclusion

rubric guideline for assessment

sand blocks blocks of wood, covered with sand paper, that are rubbed against one another to produce sound

scale an orderly ascending or descending arrangement of pitches within the limits of an octave

secondary chords chords built on the second, third, sixth, and seventh scale degrees

section the result of musical phrases being combined into a larger unit

set formation a predetermined position in line, circle, and square dances

seventh chord a chord containing four pitches

sforzando a musical symbol requiring a sudden, strong accent on the note above it: *sf*

sharp a symbol that raises the pitch of a note one-half step: ♯

simple meter a time signature in which the upper number is a 2, 3, or 4 and the beat note is divisible into two equal parts, creating a ratio of 2:1

skip a distance larger than an interval of a second between two consecutive pitches

slapstick a paddle-like instrument made of two pieces of wood hinged together; when slapped together, the sound of a whip results

sleigh bells bells attached to a handle or a piece of material; when shaken, they produce a jingling sound

slit drum a drum carved out of a log. It usually has three slits

slur a curved line connecting two or more notes having different pitch names

solfège syllables syllables that represent scale tones: do, re, mi, fa, so, la, ti

solmization a technique that involves assigning solfège syllables to scale tones

soprano the highest female voice classification

specific objective precise and clear objectives usually present in day-to-day lesson planning and providing the basis for evaluation of both the teaching and the learning processes

speech drone a low, single-pitch tone produced by children who have difficulty in matching pitches

square dance a dance, involving four couples, whose set formation is a square

staccato a reduction in the value of notes that have a dot placed over or under the note head

staff five parallel lines and four spaces upon which musical notation is written

step the movement of a pitch on the staff from a line to the next space directly above or below or from a space to the next line directly above or below

stick notation a shorthand form of rhythmic notation

string family a family of instruments whose basic instruments include the violin, viola, cello, string bass, and harp

strophic a form consisting of any number of A sections, depending on the number of stanzas in the text being used

structural components subsets of musical elements

surdo a large drum used in Brazilian music

sweep strum a downward movement of the right-hand thumb across the strings of the guitar

symphony orchestra a grouping together of the four major families of instruments—brass, woodwinds, strings, and percussion—the dominant family being the string family

syncopation a rhythm resulting from a change in placement of the normal metrical accent

talking drum a west African drum whose pitch can be regulated to serve as a communication device

tambourine a round rim of wood with several pairs of metal disks attached to it that is shaken or hit against the body or hand

temple blocks hollowed gourds of varying sizes that are attached to a frame; each gourd produces a different pitch when struck with a mallet

tempo the speed of the basic, underlying beat of a composition, ranging from very slow to very fast

tenor one of the highest male voice classifications

ternary a three-sectional composition in which the second section is different from the first, but the third section is the same as or similar to the first section; symbolized as ABA

tessitura the most comfortable singing range of the voice

texture horizontal and vertical elements that come together to add depth or substance to a musical composition

theme and variations a composition in which the theme is repeated again and again but is altered in different ways for each succeeding repetition

third the middle tone in a triad; an interval of three or four half steps

tie a curved line that joins two duration symbols of the same pitch; the first note is held for its own duration as well as the duration of the note to which it is tied

timbre distinctive qualities of sound distinguishing one sound source from another; tone color

time signature two numbers, found at the beginning of a musical work, that represent how many beats are in a measure and what note or rest receives the beat

tone color distinctive qualities of sound distinguishing one sound source from another; timbre

tonguing a technique used in producing pitches on wind instruments

transposing the technique of rewriting a song in a key different from that in which it was originally written

treble or G clef a symbol used for notating relatively high pitches

triad a chord containing three notes, including a root, a third, and a fifth

triangle a triangular piece of metal suspended from a cord that is struck by a metal stick to produce a high-pitched, ringing sound

triple meter a time signature having a top number divisible by three: 3/4, 3/8, 3/2

triplet a note value that is divided into three equal parts

upbeat the last beat in a measure

verse different words and sometimes a different melody sung between repetitions of the refrain of a song

vibra-slap an instrument that vibrates when slapped by the hand or hit against the body

whole-song method an imitative process used to teach songs that can be sung in their entirety by students after one or two hearings

whole step a combination of two half steps

woodblock a semihollow, rectangular piece of wood that, when hit with a wooden mallet, produces a resonated knocking sound

woodwind family a family of instruments in which the basic instruments are divided into three major groups: double, single, and no reed; major instruments include piccolo, flute; clarinet, oboe, English horn, bassoon, and contrabassoon

xylophone a barred instrument, made of wood, that belongs to the Orff Instrumentarium

List of Songs and Rhymes

SONGS AND RHYMES METER	COMPOSER/ TYPE COUNTRY	CHAPTER	PAGE	KEY/ TONAL CENTER	MAJOR/ MINOR	METER
A-Hunting We Will Go	English Folk Song	12	343	G	Major	2/4
*A Ram Sam Sam	Moroccan Folk Song	2	54			
Above the Plain	Czechoslovakian Folk Song	14	380	F	Major	2/4
*Achshav	Israeli Folk Song	12	342	G	Major	2/4
Alabama Gal	American Folk Song	12	344	E	Major	2/4
Al Citron	Latin American	12	337	G	Major	2/4
All Through the Night	Welsh Folk Song	5	144	G	Major	4/4
Amazing Grace	Traditional	10	288	G	Major	3/4
America	Smith/Carey	3	104	G	Major	3/4
*America the Beautiful	Bates/Ward	3/6	104, 181	C	Major	3/4
*Arirang	Korean Folk Song	8	207	G	Pentatonic	3/4
Au Clair de la Lune	French Folk Song	8	221	F	Major	4/4
Bate Bate	Mexican Game Song	2	25			
Battle Hymn of the Republic	Howe/Steffe	3	105	B-flat	Major	4/4
Bear Hunt	American Traditional	2	14			
Bell Horses	Mother Goose	2	22			
Bingo	Scottish Folk Song	3	89	E	Major	2/4
Bluebird	Game Song	3, 6	99, 186	D/C	Pentatonic	4/4, 2/4
Boatman, The	African American Song	10	284	G	Pentatonic	4/4
Bounce High	Traditional	3, 8	81, 207	D/F	Pentatonic	2/4
Bow Wow Wow	Game Song	6, 8	166, 208	F	Pentatonic	4/4
Button You Must Wander	American Game Song	3, 9	100, 250	F	Pentatonic	2/4
C-Saw	Boyer	3	85	C	Major	3/4
Candles of Hanukkah	Jewish Folk Song	8	216	D	Minor	4/4
Cherry Bloom (Sakura)	Japanese Folk Song	5	155	B	Pentatonic	2/2
Chumbara, Chumbara	Canadian Folk Song	10	264	C	Major	4/4
Church Bells	Boyer	3	77	C	Major	6/8
Circle Round the Zero	American Street Song	12	336	D	Pentatonic	2/4
City Blues	American Blues Song	8	228	G	Major	4/4
*Clementine	American Folk Song	8	218	G	Major	3/4
Cradle Hymn	J.S. Bach	10	286	G	Major	4/4
Dancing Leaves	Rozmajzl	3	77	C	Major	2/4
Dippity Doo	Boyer	2	48			
*Dona Dobis Pacem	Latin Hymn/Round	3, 7	111, 196	G, F	Major	3/4
*Down by the Station	Southern Folk Song	8	206	F	Major	4/4
Down the River	American River Chantey	5	145	F	Major	6/8

*Songs preceded by an asterisk are included on the CD accompanying the text.

SONGS AND RHYMES METER	COMPOSER/ TYPE COUNTRY	CHAPTER	PAGE	KEY/ TONAL CENTER	MAJOR/ MINOR	METER
Draw Me A Bucket of Water	African American Folk Game	12	338	D	Major	4/4
*El Florón	Puerto Rican Singing Game	8	222	C	Major	6/8
Estrellita (Twinkle Twinkle)	Traditional	3	79	C	Major	4/4
Engine, Engine Number Nine	American Traditional Game	2	21			
For Health and Strength	Old English Round	3	110	F	Major	4/4
February Celebrations	Boyer	2	55			
*Free At Last	African American Spiritual	3	118	E-Flat	Major	2/2
Frère Jacques (Are You Sleeping?)	French Round	7	194	G	Major	4/4
Fudge, Fudge	African American Game	2	16			
Ghost Eye Tree Chant	Rozmajzl	14	366	D	Minor	4/4
Good News	African American Spiritual	10	284	G	Pentatonic	4/4
Go To Sleep	Canadian Lullaby	3	74	D	Pentatonic	4/4
Grandma Grunts	Traditional	10	285	G	Pentatonic	4/4
Hansel and Gretel Dance	Wette/Humperdinck	6	187	D	Major	2/4
*Hawaiian Rainbows	Hawaiian Folk Song	10	304	D	Major	2/2
Hello, Hello Everyone	Boyer	2	18			
Hey, Ho! Nobody Home	English Round	7	196	E	Minor	4/4
Hey, Betty Martin	American Folk Song	10	263	G	Major	4/4
Hickory, Dickory Dock	Mother Goose/Elliot	5	158	C	Major	6/8
Hoo, Hoo!	Crowninshield	5	151	G	Major	4/4
Hop Old Squirrel	African American	6	188	F	Pentatonic	2/4
Hot Cross Buns	England	10	284	G	Pentatonic	4/4
How Many Miles to Babylon?	American Game Song	10	285	G	Pentatonic	4/4
Hush Little Baby	American Folk Song	5	149	G	Major	4/4
Icka, Backa Boo!	American Game	2	15			
*Ida Red	Kentucky Folk Song	10	277	F	Pentatonic	2/4
If You're Happy and You Know It	Traditional Children Song	5	150	F	Major	4/4
I Got A Letter	South Carolina Folk Song	5	146	e	Pentatonic	4/4
*I Love The Mountains	Traditional Folk	8	209			
I'm Gonna Sing	African American Spiritual	9	244	G	Major	4/4
I Move Along	Boyer	2	53			
Jazz Rondo	Boyer	6	173			4/4
Jingle Bells	James Lord Pierpont (1822–1893)	5	148	B-FLAT	Major	4/4
Jim Along Josie	American Folk Song	10	287	G	Pentatonic	2/4
Jingo-Ba	Nigerian Drumming Song	10	278			

SONGS AND RHYMES METER	COMPOSER/ TYPE COUNTRY	CHAPTER	PAGE	KEY/ TONAL CENTER	MAJOR/ MINOR	METER
Johnny Has Gone For A Soldier	Revolutionary War Song	3	96	a	Minor	4/4
Jolly Miller, The	New England Song	6	167	G	Pentatonic	2/2
Jolly Old St. Nicholas	Traditional Carol	7	200	G	Major	2/4
*Joshua Fought the Battle of Jericho	African American Spiritual	8	223	d	Minor	4/4
Joyful, Joyful (For 3 Recorders)	Beethoven/Boyer	10	298	G	Major	4/4
*Juanito	Children's Song from Spain	8	219	F	Major	4/4
Just Gimme The Beat	Boyer	2	56			
Kum Ba Yah	Traditional	5	154	C	Major	3/4
Land of the Silver Birch	Canadian Folk Song	9	251	D	Pentatonic	2/4
La Pinata	Mexican Folk Song	3, 10	88, 295	B-flat, C	Major	2/4
Laughing Song	Sweden	9	253	C	Major	4/4
Lavender's Blue	England	8	212	D	Major	6/8
*Lift Every Voice and Sing	J. Rosamond Johnson	3	107			
Little Bunny Foo Foo	Traditional	9	239	F	Major	2/4
Little Dappled Cow, The	Traditional	10	291	C	Major	4/4
Little Johnny Brown	African American Play Party	12	339	C F	Major Major	4/4 6/8
'Liza Jane	American Folk Song	3	98	C	Pentatonic	2/4
Loch Lomond	Scotland	5	160	G	Major	4/4
Look At Me	Boyer	3	117	C	Major	4/4
London Bridge	England	6	185	F	Major	2/4
Looby Loo	American Folk Song	12	335	F	Major	6/8
Lucy Locket	American Game Song	9	250	C	Pentatonic	2/4
Magic Penny, The	Reynolds	9	245	E-flat	Major	4/4
Make New Friends	Round	7, 10	195, 302	E-flat/D	Major	4/4
Mango Walk	Jamaican Calypso	10	293	F	Major	2/2
Marching	Hungary	6	165	F	Pentatonic	2/4
*Mary Ann	Calypso	10	265	D	Pentatonic	4/4
Mein Hut (My Hat)	German Folk Song	8	218	C	Major	3/4
Merrily We Roll Along	Traditional	10	303	D	Pentatonic	4/4
*Mi Cuerpo	Puerto Rico Folk Song	9	254	C	Major	4/4
Mister Rabbit	African-American Folk Song	5	159	G	Pentatonic	2/4
Moon Shine	Boyer	3	77	C	Major	3/4
Mulberry Bush	English Game Song	7, 12	197, 336	F	Major	6/8
*Music Alone Shall Live	German Round	7	198	F	Major	3/4
My Grandfather's Clock	Henry Clay Work (1876)	5	157	G	Major	4/4
My Home's In Montana	Cowboy Song	10	305	C	Major	3/4
New River Train	American Folk Song	3	89	C	Major	3/4
*Nobody Knows The Trouble I've Seen	African American Spiritual	6	176	G	Major	4/4

SONGS AND RHYMES METER	COMPOSER/ TYPE COUNTRY	CHAPTER	PAGE	KEY/ TONAL CENTER	MAJOR/ MINOR	METER
Now Let Me Fly	African American Spiritual	9	251	G	Pentatonic	2/4
Oats, Peas, Beans	English Game Song	10	286	G	Major	6/8
Ode To Joy	Beethoven	10	289	G	Major	4/4
*O Hanukkah	Jewish Traditional	3	114	d	Minor	4/4
Oh, Rocka My Soul	Hairston/Spiritual	7	202	F	Major	4/4
Oh, Won't You Sit Down?	African American Spiritual	10	288	G	Pentatonic	4/4
Oh, Susannah	Foster	6	163	F	Major	2/4
Oh, When the Saints	African American Spiritual	5	150	G	Major	4/4
Old Brass Wagon	American Dance Song	12	341	G	Pentatonic	2/4
One, Two, Tie My Shoe	American Traditional	9	248	F	Pentatonic	2/4
On Top of Old Smokey	American Folk Song	10	304	D	Major	4/4
Oranges and Lemons	English Folk Song	9, 10	252, 311	C	Major	3/4
Over My Head	African American Spiritual	10	294	G	Major	4/4
Over the River	Traditional	3	110	C	Major	6/8
*Pat Works On the Railway	American Railroad Song	3	102	b	Minor	6/8
Paw Paw Patch	American Singing Game	3	90	D-flat	Major	2/4
*Pin Pon	Latin American Folk Song	3	91	C	Major	4/4
Pito Pito	Mexican Game Song	10	274	C	Major	4/4
Poor Little Kitty Cat	American Folk Song	6, 10	168, 287	G	Pentatonic	4/4
Pourquoi	American Folk Song	10	289	C	Pentatonic	4/4
Red River Valley	American Folk Song	12	345	G	Major	4/4
Riding in the Buggy	Play-Party Song	6, 10	174, 290	C	Pentatonic	2/4
Ring Around the Rosey	American Game Song	9	250	C	Pentatonic	2/4
Rock-a-My Soul	Spiritual/Boyer	9	237	E-flat	Major	2/4
Rock of Ages	Gottlieb/Jewish Traditional	3	115	E-flat	Major	4/4
Rocky Mountain	Southern Folk Song	6	164	C	Pentatonic	2/4
Round and Round We Go	Uberliedfest	12	342	e	Minor	4/4
Row, Row, Row Your Boat	American Round	3/8	93, 214	D/d/C	Major	6/8
*Sakura	Japanese Folk Song	5	155	b	Pentatonic	2/2
San Sereni	Puerto Rico	8	210	D	Major	2/4, 6/8
Scarborough Fair	England	10	293	F	Major	3/4
Scotland's Burning	Traditional	6	184	G	Pentatonic	2/4
Shady Grove	American Folk Song	8	214	e	Pentatonic	2/4
Shake Them 'Simmons Down	Southern Play Party Song	12	341	G	Pentatonic	2/4
Shenandoah	American Chantey	3	92	E-flat	Major	4/4, 3/4
Shoo Fly	Reeves, Campbell	6	172	D	Major	2/4
*Simple Gifts	Shaker Tune	10	292	G	Major	2/2
Simple Gifts for Three Recorders	Shaker Tune Arr. by Boyer	10	297	G	Major	4/4

SONGS AND RHYMES METER	COMPOSER/ TYPE COUNTRY	CHAPTER	PAGE	KEY/ TONAL CENTER	MAJOR/ MINOR	METER
Skin and Bones	Southern Folk Song	3	109	e	Minor	6/8
Skip To My Lou	American Singing Game	7	197	F	Major	4/4
St. Paul's Steeple	English Folk Song	10	267	C	Major	4/4
*Star-Spangled Banner	Key/Smith	3	106	B-flat	Major	3/4
Star Light	American Folk Song	9	247	C	Pentatonic	2/4
Star Shinin'	Texas	10	290	C	Major	4/4
Sweet Betsy From Pike	American Folk Song	10	306	C	Major	3/4
Syncopated Rondo, The	Boyer	2	52			
This Little Light Of Mine	African American Spiritual	6	163	G	Major	2/2
This Old Man	England	7	197	F	Major	2/4
*This Train, Oh When the Saints, Swing Low	African American Spirituals	8	213	G	Major	4/4
Three Rogues	Ohio Folk Song	5	152	G	Major	2/2
Tinga Layo	West Indies	8	220	C	Major	4/4
Tom Dooley	American Ballad	10	303	D	Major	4/4
Touch A Star	Boyer	3	77	C	Major	6/8
Twelve Days of Christmas	English/Traditional	3	112	F	Major	4/4
Two, Four, Six, Eight	Traditional Rhyme	2	15			
Viva La Musica	Praetorius	10	291	G	Major	4/4
Wayfaring Stranger	Traditional	3	96	d	Minor	3/4
We've Got to Change	Boyer	2	57			
When That I Was A Tiny Little Boy	Elizabethan Song	5	159	d	Minor	2/4
When the Train Comes Along	American Folk Song	9	252	C	Pentatonic	4/4
Where Is Thumbkin?	American Folk Song	3	88	F	Major	4/4
Wind the Bobbin	Winding Game	5	156	G	Pentatonic	4/4
Willum	Traditional	3	97	e	Minor	2/4
*Yankee Doodle	Traditional	3	109	G	Major	2/2
Young Man Who Wouldn't Hoe Corn, The	American Frontier Ballad	3	101	e	Pentatonic	2/4

Credits

"Arirang," in *Holt Music Book*, Grade 6. Orlando, FL: Holt, Rinehart and Winston, 1984.

"Au Clair de la Lune," in Dallin, *Heritage Songster*, Dubuque, IA: William C. Brown Company, Publishers, 1980.

J. S. Bach, Chorale, "Ermuntre dich, mein schwacher Geist." In W. Duckworth, *Creative Approach to Music Fundamentals*, Third Edition. Belmont, CA: Wadsworth Publishing Co., 1989.

"Candles of Hanukkah," in J. O'Brien, *Creative Music Fundamentals*. Upper Saddle River, NJ: Prentice Hall, Inc., 1985.

"Draw Me a Bucket of Water." Written and adapted by Bessie Jones. Collected and edited by Alan Lomax. TRO-© Copyright 1972 Ludlow Music, Inc., New York, N.Y. Used by permission.

Judith Eisenstein, "O Hanukkah," in *Getaway to Jewish Music*. Wyncote, PA: Reconstructionist Rabbinical College. Reprinted by permission.

Jester Hairston, "Oh, Rocka My Soul." New York: Bourne Co., 1950. Reprinted by permission.

"Hansel and Gretel Dance." Schott's Sohne, Mayence, 1895.

"Hoo, Hoo!" from *New Songs and Games* by Ethel Crowninshield. Copyright © 1941 (Renewed) by Boston Music Company, a division of Music Sales Corporation. International Copyright Secured. All Rights Reserved. Reprinted by Permission.

Langston Hughes, "Dreams," in *Don't You Turn Back*. Reprinted by permission of Harold Ober Associates Incorporated. Copyright 1932 by Alfred A. Knopf, Inc. Copyright renewed 1960 by Langston Hughes.

"Jig Jog, Jig Jog," in Birkenshaw. *Music for Fun, Music for Learning*, Stainer & Bell Ltd., London, and Galaxy Music Corporation, New York.

"Joey" from *Where the Sidewalk Ends* by Shel Silverstein. Copyright 1974 by Evil Eye Music Inc. Text only reprinted by permission of HarperCollins Publishers, Inc.

"Jolly Miller" from 150 *American Folk Songs*, edited by Peter Erdei. Copyright 1974 by Boosey & Hawkes, Inc. Reprinted by permission.

"The Little Dappled Cow" from 150 *American Folk Songs*, edited by Peter Erdei. Copyright 1974 by Boosey & Hawke, Inc. Reprinted by permission.

"Love Somebody" by Joan Whitney and Alex Kramer, © Copyright 1947, 1948 by Kramer-Whitney, Inc. Copyright Renewed. Worldwide Rights Assigned to Bourne Co. All Rights Reserved. International Copyright Secured. ASCAP.

"Magic Penny." Words and Music by Malvina Reynolds. Copyright 1955, 1958 by Northern Music Co. Rights Administered by MCA

Music Publishing. New York, NY: International Copyright Secured. Made in U.S.A. All rights reserved.

"Marching," in Lois Choksy, *The Kodály Method: Comprehensive Music Education from Infant to Adult*. Upper Saddle River, NJ: Prentice Hall, Inc., 1974.

"Nighttime," in Lois Choksy, *The Kodály Method: Comprehensive Music Education from Infant to Adult*. Upper Saddle River, NJ: Prentice Hall, Inc., 1974.

"Now Let Me Fly," in Lois Choksy, *The Kodály Method: Comprehensive Music Education from Infant to Adult*. Upper Saddle River, NJ: Prentice Hall, Inc., 1974.

"Oh, Rocka My Soul" by Jester Hairston, © Copyright 1950 by Bourne Co. Copyright Renewed. All Rights Reserved. International Copyright Secured. ASCAP.

"Old Mother Twitchett," in B. F. Wright. *The Real Mother Goose*. New York: Checkerboard Press. Macmillan Publishing Co., 1944.

"Oranges and Lemons" reprinted from *Sally Go Round the Sun* by Edith Fowke with permission from The Writers' Union of Canada.

Poem beginning "My stomach growls" from *Only the Moon and Me* by Richard J. Margolis. (J.B. Lippincott) Text copyright 1969 by Richard Margolis. Reprinted by permission of HarperCollins Publishers, Inc.

"Poor Little Kitty Cat," in Lois Choksy, *The Kodály Context: Creating an Environment for Musical Learning*. Upper Saddle River, NJ: Prentice Hall, Inc., copyright 1981. Reprinted by permission.

Sakura, "Cherry Bloom," in *Holt Music Book*, Grade 3. Orlando, FL: Holt, Rinehart and Winston, 1984.

"San Sereni" from *Sail Away*, edited by Eleanor Locke. Copyright 1988 by Boosey & Hawkes, Inc. Reprinted by permission.

"Scarborough Fair," in Burakoff and Lettick, *Sweet Pipes Soprano Recorder Book I*. Levittown, NY: Sweet Pipes, 1980. Reprinted by permission.

"Skin and Bones" © 1952 Jean Ritchie, Geordie Music Publishing. Used by Permission. All Rights Reserved.

Robert Louis Stevenson, "The Wind," in *A Child's Garden of Verse*. Frank Watts, Inc., Oxford University Press, 1966.

"Tinga Layo," in *Musical Growth in the Elementary Classroom*, Fifth Edition. Oyster Bay, NY: M. Baron Company, 1943.

"When That I Was a Tiny Little Boy." In Swanson and Sannerud, *Music Through Folk Song*. Belmont, CA: Wadsworth Publishing Company, 1977.

"The Young Man Who Wouldn't Hoe Corn," in Lois Choksy, *The Kodály Method: Comprehensive Music Education from Infant to Adult*. Upper Saddle River, NJ: Prentice Hall, Inc., 1974.

CD Credits

"A Ram Sam Sam." Folk Song from Morocco. ℗ 1995 Silver Burdett Ginn.

"Achshav" (Awake! Awake!) Folk Song from Israel. English Words by David Eddleman. © 1995 Silver Burdett Ginn. ℗ 1995 Silver Burdett Ginn.

"Awake! Awake!" (Achshav) Folk Song from Israel. English Words by David Eddleman. © 1995 Silver Burdett Ginn. ℗ 1995 Silver Burdett Ginn.

"America, the Beautiful" Music by Samuel A. Ward; Words by Katharine Lee Bates. ℗ 2002 Pearson Education, Inc.

"Dona nobis pacem" (Grant Us Peace) Traditional Canon. Attributed to Joseph Haydn. ℗ 2005 Pearson Education, Inc.

"El florón" (The Flower) Singing Game from Puerto Rico. English Words by Verne Muñoz. © 1988 Silver Burdett Ginn. ℗ 2002 Pearson Education, Inc.

"The Flower" Singing Game from Puerto Rico. English Words by Verne Muñoz. © 1988 Silver Burdett Ginn. ℗ 2002 Pearson Education, Inc.

"Free at Last" African American Spiritual. Arrangement © 1995 Silver Burdett Ginn. ℗ 1995 Silver Burdett Ginn.

"I Love the Mountains" Traditional. ℗ 2002 Pearson Education, Inc.

"Juanito" (Little Johnny) Children's Song from Spain. English words by Alice D. Firgau. © 2002 Pearson Education, Inc. ℗ 2002 Pearson Education, Inc.

"Little Johnny" Children's Song from Spain. English words by Alice D. Firgau. © 2002 Pearson Education, Inc. ℗ 2002 Pearson Education, Inc.

"Lift Every Voice and Sing" Music by J. Rosamond Johnson. Words by James Weldon Johnson. ℗ 1995 Silver Burdett Ginn.

"Mary Ann" Calypso Song from the West Indies "Mary Ann" Arrangement © 2002 Pearson Education, Inc. ℗ 2002 Pearson Education, Inc.

"Mi cuerpo hace música" (There's Music in Me) Folk Song From Puerto Rico. English Words by David Eddleman. © 2002 Pearson Education, Inc. ℗ 2002 Pearson Education, Inc.

"There's Music in Me" Folk Song From Puerto Rico. English Words by David Eddleman. © 2002 Pearson Education, Inc. ℗ 2002 Pearson Education, Inc.

"Pin Pon" (Spanish) Folk Song from Latin America as Sung by Maria de Leon Arcila. English Words by Sue Ellen LaBelle. © 2002 Pearson Education, Inc. ℗ 2002 Pearson Education, Inc.

"Yankee Doodle" Traditional. Words by Dr. Richard Shuckburgh. ℗ 1988 Silver Burdett Ginn.

Index

395